Understanding Abnormalities in Biblical Figures

Studies in the Reception History of the Bible 11

Understanding Abnormalities in Biblical Figures

Edited by Guido Baltes, Lukas Bormann, and Martin Meiser

Network for the Study of the Reception History of the Bible
Åbo Akademi University
2023

Studies in the Reception History of the Bible

Editor in Chief:
Antti Laato (Åbo Akademi University)

Editorial Board:
Lukas Bormann (Philipps-Universität Marburg)
Erkki Koskenniemi (Åbo Akademi University)
Jacques van Ruiten (University of Groningen)
Martin Tamcke (Georg-August Universität Göttingen)

Network for the Study of the Reception History of the Bible
Åbo Akademi University
Distributed by Eisenbrauns, an imprint of Penn State University Press
ISBN: 978-952-12-4243-4
ISSN: 2342-5741

Preface

The editors are especially thankful for the financial support they received from the German Academic Exchange Service and the Academy of Finland in the years 2019–2021. The research group comprising scholars from Åbo Akademi University, Turku, and Philipps-Universität, Marburg, met during these years far less often in person than planned due to the Covid-19 pandemic. The papers of this volume were presented in several workshops and a concluding online conference in October 2020. The authors choose between British and US English. The abbreviations used throughout the volume are based on the SBL Handbook of Style, 2nd edition. The index was compiled in several stages by Lisa Sunnus and in its final form by Lea Trugenberger.

Marburg, September 2022

Table of Contents

Table of Contents

Introduction

Guido Baltes, Lukas Bormann and Martin Meiser

The term "abnormality" refers to a configuration that is based on the distinction between deviance and normality. In the history and culture of humankind, this distinction has been developed again and again and expressed in various representations. In modern times, several scientific disciplines deal with this configuration: philosophy, psychology and sociology. They have developed criteria according to which deviant and normal behavior can be identified, analyzed and critically reflected upon and which form the basis of historical and cultural studies in abnormality.

The following short overview is intended to introduce the different approaches to the topic. In the phase of the basic hermeneutic consensus in the humanities, which is associated with the names of Karl Jaspers, Martin Heidegger and Hans-Georg Gadamer and which dominated until the 1970s, most scholars agreed that normality and deviant behavior were self-evident phenomena. The idea was to have grasped the basic constitution of being human in a way that unquestioningly presupposed the distinction between normal and abnormal. In Heidegger's fundamental-ontological analysis there is the idea of a boundary that is crossed in deviating behavior. However, what was seen beyond the boundary, the abnormal, was not worth mentioning; on the contrary, Heidegger determined humanity from the boundary by stating:

> A boundary is not that at which something stops but, as the Greeks recognized, that from which something begins its presencing.[1]

---

[1] Martin Heidegger, "Bauen, Wohnen, Denken," in *Vorträge und Aufsätze*, 10. Auflage (Stuttgart: Klett-Cotta, 2004), 139–156, 149: "Die Grenze ist nicht das, wobei etwas aufhört,

Introduction

From the boundary, the border between deviance and normality, the human being experiences its being, and defines itself from the border to the area of the excluded, therefore from a hermeneutic point of view needs knowledge about deviance, deviation, and madness to differentiate itself from them and to define normality and clarity. It is no question that this notion affirmatively captures the boundary between deviance and normality as the basic categories of "authentic being" (Germ.: "eigentliches Sein"). The terminology of hermeneutic questioning, which often seems very humane and speaks of encounters and fusion of horizons ("Horizontverschmelzung") in understanding, presupposes this distinction as a condition for the permanent process of existence and the freedom to design oneself. Deviance and normality were considered basic concepts of the hermeneutical process.

At the same time, the hermeneutical approach to the phenomena of being human opened up the understanding that differences in behavior between epochs and cultures are a challenge for understanding. The "foreign" and the "other" became the opposites to develop one's own identity in the process of understanding. This detour of accepting the understanding of the "foreign" and the "other" as a basic problem of hermeneutics also opened up the possibility of accepting the abnormal and deviant in the vicinity as a challenge for understanding and not transferring it to a different epoch or culture.

It was Michel Foucault in his *Histoire de la folie* who identified "the other" as the product of reason and the normal.[2] For Foucault, deviance and abnormality are not fundamental anthropological constants, nor are they necessary distinctions per se for the existence of human societies, as the ethnologist Mary Douglas states, for example, by defining norms, law and taboo as fundamental concepts affecting every social order.[3] Rather, Foucault identifies the other, that which deviates, as a product of the normal. Deviance and abnormality are necessary products of the social

---

sondern, wie die Griechen es erkannten, die Grenze ist jenes, von woher etwas sein Wesen beginnt."

[2] Michel Foucault, *Histoire de la folie, à l'âge classique* (Paris: Gallimard, 1998).

[3] Mary Douglas, *Purity and Danger: An Analysis of the Concepts of Pollution and Taboo* (London et al: Routledge, 1995).

Guido Baltes, Lukas Bormann and Martin Meiser

constitution as a process. The "gouvernementalité", as Foucault describes the whole of this power-based process of socialization and its protection, penetrates the population with the dispositive of security as its essential technical instrument: the prison, the poorhouse, and above all the madhouse. It is in these places that everyone whose behavior does not correspond to the constantly newly produced and manufactured social expectations of society should be kept.[4]

Whether one follows Douglas and understands the configuration of deviance and normality as a basic question for any social order, or whether one follows Foucault and connects the emergence of this configuration with a certain phase in the development of modern society, the historically-oriented sciences today will consider the configuration of deviance and normality in each context it occurs and to which it refers.[5] According to Gordon Blennemann, deviance has to be researched in the "context-related analytical penetration of cultural dynamics and variance of meanings."[6]

From the historical perspective, the forms of representation of the normal and the deviant come into focus. It is also noticeable in historical studies that deviance does not necessarily mean exclusion. Often social exclusion is only a last resort. Rather, deviant behavior can also contain a creative potential with great historical impact. The destabilization of contexts of meaning can be a prerequisite for new consensus-building. The ambivalent process of the emergence and spread of Christianity can be described as a process that emanated from deviant conversion communities, destabilized the basic consensus, and led to the formation of a new consensus. In any case, the relationship between deviation and norm, between deviance and context of meaning, is central to historical considerations, even if the creation of this configuration is understood by Foucault as processual and discursive. According to Blennemann, two questions are central: "1. According to which procedure is deviance classified

---

[4] Michel Foucault, *Geschichte der Gouvernementalität. 1., Sicherheit, Territorium, Bevölkerung : Vorlesung am Collège de France 1977 - 1978* (Frankfurt am Main: Suhrkamp, 2006), 162.
[5] Gordon Blennemann, "Heiligkeit und Devianz in vormodernen Kontexten. Perspektiven einer möglichen Systematisierung," in *Sakralität und Devianz. Konstruktionen—Normen—Praxis*, ed. Klaus Herbers (Stuttgart: Steiner, 2015), 299–306.
[6] Blennemann, "Heiligkeit," 299.

from what is seen as conventional? 2. With what argumentative means is this classification realized?"[7]

One of these procedures is the definition, the demarcation of the discursive field with which deviance and deviation are linguistically recorded. In important publications in recent years by Klaus Herbers and Jörg Rüpke, a definition of deviance is used as a basis, which can be found in the sociology textbook published by Hans Joas and which goes back to Fritz Sack.[8] His definition is the following:

> Deviant is any action that is believed to violate a generally accepted norm of a society or a specific group of that society. Therefore, deviance is not an occurrence that is merely considered atypical or unusual (e.g., kite flying is an unusual but not deviant behaviour). For behaviour to be considered deviant, it must be assessed as violating binding, socially defined standards. And since some such standards are enshrined in law while others are not, deviance includes both criminal behaviour (...) and behaviour that, while not considered illegal, is generally unethical, immoral, idiosyncratic, indecent, or simply seen as "sick."[9]

It is noticeable that Sack, in his rather synthetic or meandering definition, ultimately thinks he has to resort to the metaphor "sick," which is unusual for a sociologist. It seems there is a gap of understanding in the disciplinary approach of sociology, which ultimately can only be captured metaphorically with the emotive words "simply sick." And this brings us to the science that has taken on this task in the present: psychology. Based on empirical studies, psychology has developed internationally recognized and constantly revised manuals that attempt to capture normality and

---

[7] Blennemann, "Heiligkeit," 304: "1. Nach welchen Verfahren wird Abweichung gegenüber dem als Konvention gedachten (...) eingeordnet. 2. Mit welchen argumentativen Mitteln wird diese Einordnung realisiert?"

[8] Fritz Sack, "Abweichung und Kriminalität," in *Lehrbuch der Soziologie*, 4. Auflage, ed. Hans Joas (Frankfurt: Campus, 2020), 275–319; Andreas Nehring, "Ambivalenzen des Heiligen – Religionswissenschaftliche Perspektiven zu Sakralität und Devianz," in Herbers, *Sakralität und Devianz*, 9–18, 14; Jörg Rüpke, *Aberglaube oder Individualität? Religiöse Abweichung im römischen Reich* (Tübingen: Mohr Siebeck, 2011), 5.

[9] Sack, "Abweichung," 276.

deviation.[10] Psychology is the leading science today when it comes to developing and justifying processes that define what is understood as "deviation" and what is to be understood as "mental disorder." The World Health Organization defines mental disorders:

> Mental disorders comprise a broad range of problems, with different symptoms. However, they are generally characterized by some combination of abnormal thoughts, emotions, behaviour and relationships with others. Examples are schizophrenia, depression, intellectual disabilities and disorders due to drug abuse. Most of these disorders can be successfully treated.[11]

The fifth edition of the Diagnostic and Statistical Manual of Mental Disorders (DSM-5) defines "mental disorder" as follows:

> A mental disorder is a syndrome characterized by clinically significant disturbance in an individual's cognition, emotion regulation, or behavior that reflects a dysfunction in the psychological, biological, or developmental processes underlying mental functioning.
>
> Mental disorders are usually associated with significant distress or disability in social, occupational, or other important activities. An expectable or culturally approved response to a common stressor or loss, such as the death of a loved one, is not a mental disorder.
>
> Socially deviant behavior (e. g., political, religious, or sexual) and conflicts that are primarily between the individual and society are not mental disorders unless the deviance or conflict results from a dysfunction in the individual, as described above.[12]

In the Bible and its environment there are frequent references to extraordinary states of mind. This happens from many different perspectives. On the one hand, it is reported that biblical narrative characters are placed in extraordinary states that determine their behavior. The best known is probably the "evil spirit" (*ruach raah*; רוח־רעה)

---

[10] American Psychiatric Association, *Diagnostic and statistical manual of mental disorders. DSM-5*, 5th ed. (Washington, DC [et al]: American Psychiatric Publishing, 2013).

[11] World Health Organization (WHO: https://www.who.int/news-room/fact-sheets/detail/mental-disorders; 07.04.2022).

[12] DSM-5, p. 20.

that entered into King Saul, making him melancholic and causing David to soften that melancholy by playing the harp (1 Sam 16:14–23). The sadness and fear that came over Saul are referred to as an "evil spirit" taking the place of the spirit of YHWH. This statement follows the assumptions of Hebrew-biblical anthropology. The human being is an animate body or inanimate body, living or dead. Life is given by the "spirit" in the sense of the life spirit or breath. In Gen 2:7 a breath of life (*nischmat chajim*; נשמת חיים) is blown into the inanimate body formed out of the earth so that it becomes a living man (Gen 2:7). Finally, in Ezek 37:7–10 it is made clear that this breath of life (*ruach*; רוח) is the Spirit of God that enlivens the inanimate bodies lying on the field of the dead: "I prophesied as he commanded me, and the breath came into them, and they lived and stood on their feet...." (Ezek 37:10).

In the sequence of these texts we also see that the terminology is not uniform, for example on the one hand "breath of life" in Gen 2:7 and "spirit" in Ezek 37. The ideas and their linguistic designations are not static. In further in-depth reflection, a discourse then takes place on the question of how this "breath of life" can be traced back to God and whether the evil spirit of life that comes over the melancholy can also be from God. This discourse, which we already see in these selected texts, is continued in the translation, re-narration and interpretation of these texts. The Greek translation of the Hebrew Bible, the Septuagint, translates the spirit of life in Gen 2:7 with πνοὴ ζωῆς and *ruach* mostly with πνεῦμα. The Septuagint version of 1 Sam 16:14 also calls the "evil spirit from God" (πνεῦμα πονηρὸν παρὰ κυρίου) τὸ πνεῦμα, and again in Ezek 37.

As a preliminary result, one can state that Hebrew anthropology distinguishes the inanimate body from the animate body, but does not separate body and soul. The human being is either an animated body or a corpse. This life spirit is called *ruach* or *pneuma*. But it can also be evil—and then it becomes complicated.

Where does this "evil" spirit come from? In 1 Sam 16 it is traced back to God, who takes away his spirit, the Spirit of God, and lets another spirit, the "evil spirit of God" come upon Saul. This "evil spirit" takes control of Saul. This basic anthropological constellation is found in the Gospels of

Mark and Matthew. Both gospels name this the "unclean spirit" (Mark 1:23.26–27: τὸ πνεῦμα τὸ ἀκάθαρτον; cf. Matt 10:1).

Based on Hebrew anthropology, the texts of Second Temple Judaism and the New Testament reflect the question: How do human beings and the mind relate to one another? Influenced by the anthropology of the great philosophical schools of Platonism, Aristotelianism and the Stoics, the idea that humankind is best understood anthropologically within the framework of a body-soul dichotomy or a body-soul-spirit/mind trichotomy was also gaining a foothold in Judaism.[13] On the other hand, the various in-depth reflections of Greek philosophy on the inner form of the soul, such as its three parts and forces according to Plato, are not included in the transmission of biblical texts. The soul-body dichotomy also forms the framework for the reception of biblical texts on abnormality and deviance in patristic literature. The church fathers are primarily interested in the ethical dimension of deviant behavior performed by biblical figures, which range from the madness of Saul (1 Sam 16) and David (1 Sam 21:14–16) to Noah's drunkenness (Gen 9:21). Since the Church Fathers predominantly assume that the biblical heroes integrated by God into the history of salvation are also models of morality, they are particularly challenged by the texts in which deviant behavior is described. The question thus also opens up an ethical dimension to the history of biblical reception.

The following articles examine the tension between normality and deviance in the Hebrew Bible and the New Testament as well as in their reception in Second Temple Judaism and patristic literature. It becomes clear that the ideas expressed in these texts about deviant behavior are primarily influenced by changes in anthropological and theological assumptions. The authors adapt the tradition to the contemporary understanding of normality and deviance to reach their rhetorical aim to convince the reader about their interpretations of the Biblical figures.

---

[13] Bernd Janowski, *Anthropologie des Alten Testaments* (Tübingen: Mohr Siebeck, 2019), 12.

Part I: Hebrew Bible and its Reception

Taking the designation of Elisha, or one of his disciples, as "madman" (*mᵉšuggaʿ*) in 2 Kgs 9:11 as her starting point, *Lotta Valve* analyses deviant behavior in the Elijah-Elisha cycle. Some aspects of the two prophets' behavior were met with negative reactions already by their contemporaries, which shows that they were perceived to transgress social and cultural boundaries. Other aspects, which remained unchallenged at the time, would be considered deviant from a modern perspective. The Jewish and Christian reception of these problematic character traits differ: while in Christian sources references to deviant behavior are either omitted or exculpated, the Jewish reception appears more nuanced, as Elijah is "whitewashed", but Elisha is criticized for his behavior by some authors. In the New Testament gospels, some verbal parallels to the Elisha narrative suggest that the Elisha figure was used as a type for Jesus not only by Luke, which is commonly accepted, but already early on in the process of gospel transmission. *Kirsi Huoponen* analyses abnormal behavior in the book of Ezekiel, some of which has been diagnosed as symptomatic of mental illness by modern authors. Some formulaic expressions, such as "the hand of YHWH upon him" and "the Spirit of YHWH" have parallels in other biblical accounts of prophetic trance and ecstasy as well as in ancient near eastern descriptions of abnormal behavior. Ezekiel's sign-acts are intended to shock his audience and evoke reactions of rejection. However, Huoponen argues convincingly that neither the ecstatic phenomena nor the sign-acts are beyond the range of what was "normally" expected from prophets. Rather, some extreme expressions of his prophetic activity can be ascribed to his priestly background, while others simply mirror the extreme experiences of destruction and exile Ezekiel shares with his Israelite contemporaries. Ezekiel could, therefore, according to Huoponen, be described as a "normal prophet" and a "normal man," living in abnormal circumstances which provoke extreme behavior.

The contribution of *Antti Laato* focuses on abnormal phenomena in the Samson narrative (Judges 13–16). Arguing from discrepancies in the chronology within the book of Judges, Laato suggests that the narrative reflects two conflicting concepts of the "Nazirite," one originating from an older, pre-deuteronomistic source and the other from later priestly redaction. An older understanding of the Nazirite and a warrior of YHWH could explain why some aspects of Samson's behavior not only transgress social and cultural boundaries of his time but also stand in conflict with regulations of Nazirite law as reflected in Num 6. Later Jewish reception viewed these "deviant" aspects of Samson's behavior critically, but he remained a heroic figure of Israelite history in corporate memory.

In his article on instances of "deep sleep" (תרדמה, Gen 2:21 and 15:12) in the Hebrew Bible and their reception in the book of Jubilees, *Topias Tanskanen* traces different interpretations of the term as reflected in varying translational choices. While in Jubilee's rendition of Gen 2:21, תרדמה is translated with the respective word for "sleep, slumber," underlining the passivity of Adam vis-à-vis God's sovereign action, in Gen 15:12 the same term is rendered with a term signifying a tumultuous state of mind, involving fear and terror, rendering someone unable to act. This suggests at least some kind of conscious participation of Abraham in the act of covenant-making in Jubilees' rendition of the narrative.

Pekka Lindqvist analyses early Jewish and rabbinic strategies to cope with Moses's violent behavior in Exod 2:11–12. While the episode is completely omitted by Josephus, Philo exculpates Moses's deviant behavior by characterizing the Egyptian as particularly cruel. In later midrashic expansions of the story, three further apologetic motives are to be found: in the first, the Egyptian rapes an Israelite woman and attempts to murder her husband, so that Moses's action saves the life of his fellow Israelite; in the second, Moses seeks non-violent solutions but none are to be found; and in the third, Moses does not engage in physical violence but merely invokes the name of YHWH which leads to the Egyptian's death. However, in another rabbinic source, Moses also feels remorse for his violent act and is placed in juxtaposition with a murderer.

In the last contribution within Part I, *Mikael Nouro* focuses on the term *hebel* in the book of Qohelet. While Christian tradition, influenced by the Vulgate's rendition of *vanitas*, has underlined notions of emptiness and lack of value, in Jewish tradition the term has largely been understood as denoting the brevity and temporality of human experience. However, Nouro's article primarily interacts with the modern proposal of Michael Fox to translate *hebel* as "absurd." Arguing for an influence of Hellenistic philosophy, especially the stoic concept of *eudaimonia*, on the book of Qohelet, Nouro suggests reading *hebel* as an expression of "indifference" (*adiaphora*), denoting things that neither contribute to nor distract from the pursuit of *eudaimonia*. Externals of life, like food, sleep, work and pleasure, are devalued; however, they might be enjoyed if they are not considered to be a source of meaning, purpose or happiness. If they are rightly understood as gifts of the creator, their enjoyment can even be a way to enter into dialogue with God. Understood this way, *carpe diem* for Qohelet becomes an equivalent for the fear of God.

Part II: New Testament

In the section New Testament, the first contribution by *Lukas Bormann* reflects upon the development from the anthropological assumption of the unity of body and soul in the Hebrew Bible to the Hellenistic concept of body-soul-dichotomy in Gen 2:21 and 15:12 and its history of reception. Whereas Hebr. *tardemah* designates the state of "deep sleep" based upon the unity of body and soul, the Greek concept of ecstasy is based upon the body-soul dichotomy. Ecstasy allows reflection and closeness to God. The article by *Guido Baltes* takes us from anthropology to social norms. Jesus is famously labelled a "glutton and drunkard" (Luke 7:34). The wording used here is often misinterpreted as a polemical reply to Jesus's festive meal practices. However, as Baltes demonstrates, it is far more plausible that the wording is taken from a sapiential tradition teaching the law of the disobedient "rebellious son" (Deut 21:18–21). The wording is understood as a phrase to stereotype members of the community who demonstrate a behavior seen as deviant from social norms in a broad sense but does not point to violating purity laws or excessive indulgence as often argued.

A complex reflection on space, gender and deviant behavior based on new methodological insights is presented by *Aliyah El Mansy*. Behavior labelled as "possession," "madness," "inspiration" or "disease" is allocated a space suitable to it. Reflecting on several sorts of spaces such as public and domestic, space, and sacred, it can be demonstrated that the same deviant or abnormal behavior is either forbidden, accepted or even expected in distinct spaces. *Bart J. Koet* turns to dreams and visions as a significant representation of abnormality seen in antiquity as acceptable.

According to Acts, Paul receives revelations in the form of dreams and visions or a voice from heaven. In line with ideas about dreams and visions we can find in the Hebrew Bible, Luke uses the quotation from Joel in Acts 2:17–21 to legitimize dreams and visions in Acts as divine revelations. In Romans 10:13, however, a different interpretation far more original and unique is presented but not followed by Luke who underscores the continuity of God's revelations in dreams and visions to his people. *Eva-Maria Kreitschmann* analyses abnormality in Acts. The two leading figures of Acts, Peter and Paul, are both related to the state of mind called ecstasy. Kreitschmann demonstrates the key function of ecstasy in the Cornelius episode with Peter and the re-narration of Paul's Damascus experience (Acts 10:9; 22:17). In both cases, the concept of ecstasy functions to reintegrate the socio-religious innovative insights of both apostles into the sphere of Jewish piety.

Part III: Patristics

Patristic reception of biblical texts is embedded in a hermeneutical framework for which multiple layers are characteristic: 1. Biblical narrative texts are considered an inerrant reproduction of events that occurred. 2. The Holy Scriptures are written "for our instruction"; therefore, every detail is relevant. 3. It is the task of human reason to fill gaps in the narrative and to reconcile supposed contradictions. Human reason, however, has to be oriented to the specifications of faith. 4. Even offensive texts are to be interpreted in such a way that ecclesiastical custom and morality are not called into question but are strengthened.

The majority of the contributions in the patristic section of this volume deal with texts and motifs in which biblical figures are considered deviant from the perspective of non-believers or the perspective of Christian tradition. *Anni Maria Laato* explores the early Christian interpretation of Wisdom of Solomon 5:4 in Cyprian and Jerome. For Cyprian, the "fools" speaking in this sapiental text are not the Christians despised by the non-Christians but non-Christians who do not understand the Christian eagerness for martyrdom and do not realize the coming Day of Judgement. Jerome used Wisdom of Solomon 5:4 to characterize both the non-Christian Roman aristocracy and more moderate Christians in their perplexing incomprehension of why some rich women (and Jerome himself) chose an ascetic life and gave up their status and wealth. *Martin Meiser* deals at first with concepts of ἔκστασις (Gen 2:21; 15:12; prophetic ἔκστασις), signs of prophets reported in the books of Isaiah and Ezekiel, but also with the motif of the prophet's imperfection, exemplified by Saul (1 Sam 19:24–25), before turning to the unwise behavior of the wise man in the patristic reception (Noah's drunkenness, David's madness and his dancing, Jesus as glutton and drunkard) and the reception of the motif "abnormality as punishment" (Dan 4:30). Comments on abnormalities follow the common intention of biblical exegesis to help Christian life in faith and morality and to counterbalance apparent contradictions. *Timo Nisula* underscores the divergences in Augustine's evaluations of outbursts of violence in some biblical narrations. Moses's killing of the Egyptian (Exod 2:11–14) against the Manichean Faustus was justified as a promising prospect of Moses's ability to become the leader of Israel. Phinehas's killing of the two lovers (Num 25:1–13) was justified due to his zeal for Israel's God and his love for his nation. With regard to questions of ecclesial discipline concerning the cure of erring souls, the non-violent type of Jesus Christ should be followed. The suicide of Razi (2 Macc 14:37–46), however, applied by the Donatist bishop Gaudentius to justify his announcement of self-immolation in a situation of imperial violence against the Donatists, is rebuked due to a lack of humility and patience.

Michaela Durst describes how the preacher John Chrysostom shows himself to be a skillful psychagogic therapist in reading Gen 22 as a central text for Christian understanding and guidance of human agency. In his homilies on Genesis, John presents Abraham in his faithfulness to God's command in Gen 22:2 as an example of how to deal with his thinking in exceptional situations. Abraham, as εὐγνώμων, resists the contradiction between the divine command and his paternal love arising from human reasoning; based on an adequate γνώμη, Abraham's προαίρεσις is oriented to the fulfillment of God's will. Chrysostom can also draw on this exegetical feature in other homilies, e.g. in a homily on 2 Corinthians where he refers to a *triplex munus* of all baptized Christians (cf. 2 Cor 1:21). In the case of kingship and priesthood, he again uses the Gen 22 pattern. While kingship refers to the mastery of the λογισμοί, which Abraham achieved even though he was in emotional turmoil, priesthood is linked to the sacrificial scene as mystery, in which Abraham showcases his acting according to the divine voice by simultaneously thrusting with the sword and being prevented from doing so. *Catalin-Stefan Popa* describes how Syriac exegetes, dealing with Noah's drunkenness according to Gen 9:20–27, understood this behavior of an otherwise lauded human being. Syriac exegetes agree that Noah planted the vineyard in the first year after the flood. When he drank from the wine is answered differently. Noah's drunkenness is explained because he was not accustomed to drinking wine. The exegetes ask how Noah, though sleeping, could be aware of Ham's act; they further ask why Noah curses not Ham but Canaan, who was Ham's son. From a moral perspective, the need for moderation in the consumption of wine is urged; Noah's drunkenness is a warning example.

Part I: Hebrew Bible and its Reception

Deviant Behavior in the Elijah–Elisha Cycle and its Reception

Lotta Valve

Introduction

When approaching the topic of our volume, "Abnormalities in Biblical Figures," the Elijah–Elisha cycle seems a very appropriate place to start. This is, namely, one of the few instances in the Hebrew Bible, where a main protagonist is explicitly called a "madman."[1] Therefore, the story cycle offers a fruitful viewpoint into the question of what deviant behavior consists of in the Old Testament framework.

One methodological problem is that all the "miracles," performed by both Elijah and Elisha, could be considered part of their deviant behavior, as these were actions that were not possible for any ordinary human beings to do. Indeed, in certain instances in the stories, the miracle cannot really be separated from other aspects of the prophet's deviant behavior. To overcome this obstacle, I thus mainly concentrate on Elijah and Elisha's actions that, according to the story, received at least partly *negative responses from their audiences*. This is an indication that these particular actions were considered somewhat deviant or abominable in the cultural framework described in the story. I omit the smaller units that belong to the Elijah–Elisha cycle but which are related to other prophetic figures (for

---

[1] *mᵉšuggaʿ*, 2 Kings 9:11: "When Jehu came back to his master's officers, they said to them, 'Is everything all right? Why did that madman come to you?' He answered them, 'You know the sort and how they babble.'" (The translation is according to the NRSV, as in all following quotations from the Bible.) The reference in 2 Kings 9:11 seems to be to a disciple of Elisha but was plausibly in tradition connected to Elisha himself as the disciple's prophetic authority. Concerning the "madness" of prophets in the Hebrew Bible, see Jer 29:26; Hos 9:7, where the term *mᵉšuggaʿ* is also employed. The term is inherently derogatory; compare with the use of it in the story about David's faked insanity, 1 Sam 21:13–15.

example, the story about Micaiah, son of Imlah, in 1 Kings 22, or the unit about another prophet in 1 Kings 20:35–43).

In addition, I discuss a few cases where the response to Elijah or Elisha is not explicit but could be surmised to be negative (for example, judging from tradition), and I also mention a few cases which could be considered as deviant behavior according to modern standards. Another difficulty in my undertaking is that, particularly in the case of Elisha, people's (emotional) reactions towards the prophet's actions are often not reported at all in the biblical narrative. This is quite a remarkable qualitative difference between the Elijah and Elisha cycles, and a major obstacle vis-à-vis the title of this paper. For any observant reader, the Elisha cycle appears as less coherent, less thoroughly redacted and less integrated in the overall Kings narrative than the Elijah cycle. Many of Elisha's reported miracle acts give the impression that they are indepen-dent pieces of tradition.[2] This notion, in turn, may have some bearing on the third part of my paper.

To overcome the difficulty described above, some help from reception history is needed to build up this article. I, thus, shed some light on how the selected deeds of the two prophets were received in both the Jewish and Christian tradition. Among the Christian authors, I have chosen to highlight the commentary on the books of Kings attributed to Ephrem the Syrian, which is practically the only actual patristic commentary on these books. The authenticity of this commentary is, however, disputed, and it may actually originate from a date slightly later than Ephrem.[3] On the other hand, earlier patristic comments on the Elijah and Elisha cycles are

---

[2] For discussion about the integration of the Elijah–Elisha cycles into the composition of the books of Kings in the Deuteronomistic framework, see, for example, Jyrki Keinänen, *Traditions in Collision: A Literary and Redaction-Critical Study on the Elijah Narratives 1 Kings 17–19*, Publications of the Finnish Exegetical Society 80 (Helsinki: Finnish Exegetical Society; Göttingen: Vandenhoeck & Ruprecht, 2001); Gary N. Knoppers, "Theories of the Redaction(s) of Kings," in *The Books of Kings: Sources, Composition, Historiography and Reception*, ed. Baruch Halpern and André Lemaire, VTSup 129 (Leiden: Brill, 2010), 69–88; Winfried Thiel, "Deuteronomistische Redaktionsarbeit in den Elia-Erzählungen," in *Congress Volume Leuven 1989*, ed. John Adney Emerton, VTSup 43 (Leiden: Brill, 1991), 148–71.

[3] For this, see Marco Conti (ed.), *Ancient Christian Commentary on Scripture Old Testament V* (Downers Grove: InterVarsity, 2008), xlvii. In Conti's opinion, the text probably dates from "a period between the end of the fifth century and the sixth century."

4

limited to sporadic notions in the writings of Church Fathers and mostly concentrate on issues that are not central to the focus of this article. I have, nonetheless, selected a few quotes from these other authors.

Later tradition does not tell us anything about the reactions of Elijah and Elisha's original audiences, but does give us insight into the values of the later authors and their times and, thus, adds an interesting dimension into how Elijah and Elisha's deviant behavior was once viewed in Judaism and Christianity. As could be expected, the incidents were often retold showing the two prophets in a better light. For the sake of clarity, I treat the Elijah and Elisha cycles in the Bible separate from one another. Hence, I first discuss the Elijah cycle and its Jewish and Christian reception and then move on to the Elisha cycle and its reception.

Finally, as the third part of this paper, I briefly discuss some aspects of Elisha's deviant behavior that resemble Jesus's conduct as described in the New Testament Gospels. As some New Testament scholars have argued, there is reason to uphold the importance of the Elijah–Elisha narratives for the form and content of the Gospels, especially Luke.[4] I shall, thus, demonstrate this feature by discussing the similarities between the few New Testament reports about Jesus's mental reactions and those of Elisha and ask whether these instances can be seen as purposeful intertextuality and early Christian reception of the Elijah–Elisha cycle.

---

[4] See, especially, Thomas L. Brodie, *Luke the Literary Interpreter: Luke-Acts as a Systematic Rewriting and Updating of the Elijah–Elisha Narrative in 1 and 2 Kings* (Rome: Pontificia Studiorum Universitas a Sancto Thoma Aquinate in Urbe, 1987); idem, *The Crucial Bridge: The Elijah–Elisha Narrative as an Interpretive Synthesis of Genesis-Kings and a Literary Model for the Gospels* (Collegeville, MN: Liturgical, 2000); Craig A. Evans, "Luke's Use of the Elijah/Elisha Narratives and the Ethics of Election," *JBL* 106 (1987): 75–83; cf. also Wolfgang Roth, *Hebrew Gospel: Cracking the Code of Mark* (Oak Park: Meyer-Stone, 1988); D. Gerald Bostock, "Jesus as the New Elisha," *ExpTim* 92 (1980): 39–41; Raymond E. Brown, "Jesus and Elisha," *Perspective* 12 (1971): 85–104; Richard E. Hays, *Echoes of Scripture in the Gospels* (Waco: Baylor University Press, 2016), 237–43; Magnus Zetterholm, "The Books of Kings in the New Testament and the Apostolic Fathers," in Halpern and Lemaire, *The Books of Kings*, 561–84.

Elijah

Elijah's Behavior in 1 Kings
In the Elijah narrative in 1 Kings, one characteristic response to Elijah is that often people were not delighted to see him. Thus, it can be said that Elijah's status as prophet, and his somewhat deviant behavior in, for example, hiding himself or confronting authorities were not met well by many individuals. This pattern can be seen already in Elijah's introduction to the scene in 1 Kings 17 with the—in principle polite, yet reluctant—welcome he receives from the widow in Zarephath (17:12), and later in the same chapter in her distressed words towards him regarding the illness of her son (17:18).[5] The story continues with Obadiah's reluctance to send Ahab a message from Elijah (1 Kings 18:9–14) and also in Ahab's own negative responses to Elijah. In 1 Kings 18:17, Ahab designates Elijah as the "troubler," *'ôkēr*, of Israel[6] and in 21:20, as his personal enemy, *'oyᵉbî*.

It appears that Elijah's "deviant behavior" and the responses to it are connected precisely to his actions as a prophet. Thus, they are comparable to and in continuity with many Old Testament depictions of prophetic actions and negative reactions against prophets who tell "unpleasant truths."[7]

Elijah's Behavior According to Reception History

<u>Jewish Reception</u>
The Jewish reception concerning Elijah is exhaustively vast but mostly unrelated to the topic of this article, so I merely highlight a few details connected with the features above. According to Jewish interpretation, the widow with whom Elijah lodged thought that her virtue was as if nothing

---

[5] 1 Kings 17:18: "What have you against me, O man of God? You have come to me to bring my sin to remembrance and to cause the death of my son!"

[6] An intriguing suggestion is to translate the word *'ôkēr* with the term 'hex' due to the cultic/magic associations of the word; see Simon J. DeVries, *1 Kings*, WBC 12 (Waco: Word Books, 1985), 217.

[7] See, e.g., in the prophetic books: Amos 7:12; Jer 20; 26.

6

compared with that of Elijah, and this is why she utters her desperate words against Elijah in 1 Kings 17:18.[8]

After the incident at Mt. Carmel and the subsequent rainfall, it is related in 1 Kings 18:46 that "the hand of the Lord was on Elijah; he girded up his loins and ran in front of Ahab to the entrance of Jezreel." Here, pointing to the relation between Elijah and Ahab, Jewish tradition emphasizes that Elijah's running in front of Ahab's chariot proves that Elijah did not forget the honor that should be shown to a king.[9] This same interpretation appears in Christian tradition, so dependency on a shared source is probable.[10] In contrast, Josephus seems to emphasize and understand the mention of "the hand of the Lord" at the beginning of the verse in a slightly different way, because he states that "the Prophet was under a divine fury and ran along with the king's chariot."[11] This understanding of "the hand of the Lord" perhaps corresponds more closely to the many descriptions of the effects of "the Lord's spirit" in the Samson cycle[12] and pertains to Elijah's reputation as a zealous prophet. Thus, in Josephus's interpretation, Elijah's deviant mental state is underlined.

Christian Reception

Christian tradition (which of course, additionally, tended to interpret Old Testament figures and narratives typologically) similarly wanted to omit or whitewash the negative reactions towards Elijah that can be discerned in the 1 Kings narrative. Thus, in (Pseudo-)Ephrem's comment on 1 Kings

---

[8] Gen. Rab. 50:11; Pesiq. Rab. 3:3 (Friedman 10a). On the contrary, in Pirqe R. El. 33 the widow's reproach of Elijah is elaborated on at length, beyond the 1 Kings narrative.

[9] Mek. Bo (Pisḥa) 13 on Exod 12:31 (Horovitz/Rabin 45).

[10] Ephrem the Syrian, *On the First Book of Kings* 18.46. All the Patristic texts are quoted according to Conti, *Ancient Christian Commentary*. As an additional detail, Ephrem refers to Ahab's grief in this instance, which indicates his base text of 1 Kings 18:45. In this variant, which is attested in the LXX tradition (and its daughter translations), Ahab "wept" instead of "rode." The LXX variant is probably a confusion between or a conscious interpretation involving the Hebrew *wayyibk* and *wayyirkab*, see Marvin A. Sweeney, *I & II Kings: A Commentary*, Old Testament Library (Louisville: Westminster John Knox, 2007), 220.

[11] *Ant.* 8.13.6.

[12] Judg 13:25; 14:6, 19; 15:14. Compare, however, also the depiction of ecstatic prophetic vision in Ezek 1:3.

17:18, the focus is shifted to the humility of the widow whose son had died (or fallen ill), rather than on her harsh blaming of Elijah:

> Observe carefully the tears of that woman, and see her humility in her grief, because she does not at all blame the judgment of God or rise against the prophet. In the humility of her intellect, she recognizes that that sentence struck her because of her guilt, and she says to the prophet, "You have come to me to bring my sin to remembrance."[13]

As regards Ahab, Ephrem is keen to point out that Elijah's reproaches of him were always legitimate, and also that Ahab's responses were often somehow right too; thus Ephrem is, in effect, making the same point as in the example of the widow above:

> This freedom of speech torments Ahab greatly, but he does not fight back or rebuke Elijah about anything, as is related in the two histories of the kings, so that you may know the authority that the Lord had given Elijah over the spirit of the king and the fear toward his prophet that he had put in Ahab's heart.[14]

Elijah's flight from Jezebel (1 Kings 19:1–8) was somewhat problematic for Christian interpreters, but they explained it in such a way so as to put Elijah in a good light. Thus, for example, Ambrose understands the episode allegorically:

> To be sure, it was not a woman that such a great prophet was fleeing, but it was this world. And it was not death that he feared, for he offered himself to the one that searched for him and said to the Lord: "Take my soul." He endured a weariness of this life, not a desire for it, but he was fleeing worldly enticement and the contagion of filthy conduct and the impious acts of an unholy and sinful generation.[15]

---

[13] *On the First Book of Kings* 17.2.
[14] *On the First Book of Kings* 18.8.
[15] *Flight from the World* 6.34.

Elisha

Elisha's Behavior in 2 Kings

Despite their often-noted similarities, the Elijah and Elisha cycles in Kings show some remarkable differences. One branch in tradition-historical scholarship understands the Elisha traditions as the older and/or more important ones, and the Elijah traditions as a spin-off of these.[16] Therefore, and because of their presumed relative antiquity, the Elisha traditions are of special interest for the topic of deviant behavior of a prophet.

One detail in the Elisha narrative that has often been considered to be problematic or unpleasant by readers is the incident in 2 Kings 2:23–24, where Elisha cursed the boys who mocked him, after which bears mauled them. This is both a "miracle" and deviant, or, rather, undesirable behavior on Elisha's part, and tradition was very uncomfortable with this issue. Another element that tradition disliked was Elisha's cursing of his dishonest servant Gehazi with leprosy in 2 Kings 5:26–27. In both these instances, however, the narrative itself does not provide any comment on or response to Elisha's actions.

An interesting example of abnormal conduct in the Elisha cycle is Elisha's ecstatic prophecy in 2 Kings 3:14–19. Elisha gives a contemptuous answer to King Jehoram but, nonetheless, agrees to deliver a prophecy for King Jehoshaphat's sake. The peak of the action is described in verses 15–17,

> "But get me a musician." And then, while the musician was playing, the power of the Lord came on him. And he said, "Thus says the Lord, 'I will make this wadi full of pools.'"

This is, to my knowledge, the only instance in the Old Testament, where a prophet of YHWH is described as having used some means (the sound of the harp[17]) to get into the prophetic mode.[18]

---

[16] For plausible argumentation in regard of this view, see Kristin Weingart, "'My Father, My Father! Chariot of Israel and Its Horses!' (2 Kings 2:12 // 13:14): Elisha's or Elijah's Title?" *JBL* 137 (2018): 257–70. See also Marsha C. White, *The Elijah Legends and Jehu's Coup* (Atlanta: Scholars Press, 1997), 11–17.

[17] The verb used is *naggên*, 'play a stringed instrument.'

Another remarkable report concerning Elisha's physical and mental reaction towards a prophecy coming to him can be found in 2 Kings 8:11.

> He fixed his gaze and stared at him, until he was ashamed. Then the man of God wept.

The Hebrew text is difficult but is most often taken to mean that Elisha was as if petrified or paralyzed in front of his terrible vision before he burst into tears.[19] This case is of interest to people today too, in that it could be considered as "abnormal" but, nonetheless, understandable behavior by modern standards as well. That a prophet feels uncomfortable at large with his mission is, of course, well attested, for example, in the books of Jeremiah and Jonah as well as in the Elijah–Elisha cycles, too.[20]

In Elisha's death narrative, 2 Kings 13, Elisha undertakes a final unexpected act, which cannot be considered a miracle but is rather to be taken as a prophetic sign. He asks king Joash to shoot an arrow and places his own hands on the king's hands. After Joash struck other arrows to the ground according to Elisha's instructions, Elisha becomes angry because the king had not striked the ground sufficiently many times. Thus, almost the very last glimpse that the reader of 2 Kings has of Elisha is that when on the verge of his death, he was enraged. Joash's reaction to Elisha's approaching death was to cry and lament (2 Kings 13:14), but his reaction to Elisha's final prophecy or Elisha's anger is left unreported.

Elisha's Behavior According to Reception History

Jewish Reception
In Jewish reception, the incident with the mocking boys and the bears which mauled them is connected to the previous story in 2 Kings 2:19–22 about Elisha's healing of the waters of Jericho. It appears that interpreters

---

[18] As Sweeney puts it, the scene "illuminate[s] the dynamics of oracular inquiry." (Sweeney, *I & II Kings*, 283.)

[19] For discussion about the grammatical problems, see, e.g., Mordechai Cogan and Hayim Tadmor, *II Kings: A New Translation with Introduction and Commentary*, AB 11 (New York: Doubleday, 1988), 90; T. Raymond Hobbs, *2 Kings*, WBC 13 (Waco: Word Books, 1985), 95.

[20] Jer 15:10–18; 20:7–18; 1 Kings 19:3–14.

wanted to have a more consistent flow in the story; a phenomenon which was already known from early Jewish expositions of the Torah in the Rewritten Bible genre. Thus, Elisha's reputation is whitewashed with the explanation that the "boys" were merchants of water who had been deprived of their business in Jericho after Elisha had cured the waters there.[21]

Otherwise, the Jewish reception of Elisha is ambivalent and even slightly negative in some places. Elisha is rebuked more than Elijah for his harshness. Gehazi, too, has an ambivalent reputation in Jewish reception history, and there is an opinion that Elisha should not have punished him so severely.[22] The statement regarding Elisha's sickness in 2 Kings 13:14, "Now when Elisha had fallen sick with the illness of which he was to die," was interpreted very literally so that he had endured other illnesses before the fatal one.[23] It was sometimes reasoned that these previous illnesses had been a punishment for his harshness. Likewise, Elisha's ecstatic prophecy in 2 Kings 3:15–19 was interpreted as that the spirit of prophecy left Elisha because of his severity against king Jehoram in verses 13–14, and, subsequently, he had to use man-made means to get it back.[24]

Christian Reception

As could be surmised, Church Fathers explain the violent incident in 2 Kings 2:23–24 in such a way that Elisha remains in a good light. Thus Caesarius of Arles,

> Now according to the letter, dearly beloved, we are to believe, as we men-
> tioned above, that blessed Elisha was aroused with God's zeal to correct the
> people, rather than moved by unwholesome anger, when he permitted the
> Jewish children to be torn to pieces. His purpose was not revenge but their
> amendment, and in this fact, too, the passion of our Lord and Savior was
> plainly prefigured.[25]

---

[21] b. Soṭah 46b–47a.

[22] Mek. Yitro (Amalek) 1 on Exod 18:6 (Horovitz/Rabin 193).

[23] b. B. Meṣ. 87a; b. Soṭah 47a; b. Sanh. 107b; y. Sanh. 10 (29b).

[24] b. Pesaḥ. 66b.

[25] Sermon 127.2.

According to (Pseudo-)Ephrem's interpretation, the children who mocked Elisha had been raised by their wicked parents, and thus actually the punishment was also aimed at them:

> Now, Elisha, even though he was upset by the effrontery of the children, was much more enraged by the craftiness and the iniquities of their parents, and he corrected both by a harsh and terrible sentence: he punished the former, so that they might not add to their iniquity by growing up to adulthood; the latter, so that they might be corrected and cease from their wickedness.[26]

This explanation reflects a rather common way of viewing the family and the role of children in antiquity and deviates interestingly from the rabbinic explanations of this passage.

As regards the second case of Elisha's anger, Gehazi's punishment with leprosy, Ephrem explains that Gehazi had been given a chance to repent by answering Elisha's question truthfully (2 Kings 5:25), but when he forwent this opportunity, he received just punishment.[27]

Ephrem, and no other other Church Father to my knowledge, does not comment on Elisha's mental state in conjunction with the ecstatic prophecy in 2 Kings 3:15–19 or regarding Elisha's emotional reaction in 2 Kings 8:11. In both cases, Ephrem is more interested in the contents of the ensuing prophecy. This is in line with his general way of clarifying Scripture.

Ephrem explains Elisha's deathbed scene at length and also comments on Elisha's becoming angry with King Joash:

> But only Elisha clearly knew the mystery, whereas it was hidden from the king; otherwise, he would have not struck the ground three times but ten. And since he was hesitant and drew back, Elisha blamed him—not because he had committed any fault but because his mistake deprived the children of his people of the victory and great profit that would have derived from the extermination of the Arameans and the overthrowing of their kingdom that Elisha strongly desired. He is sad for being frustrated in his hope by the

---

[26] On the Second Book of Kings, 2.20.
[27] On the Second Book of Kings, 5.27.

king who had stopped and had not multiplied the prescribed strokes. But the real motive which prevented the grace was the apostasy of the king and the people and their rebellious will in the worship of idols. That was again the cause that hindered the gift of the grace that was signified in that sign.[28]

A noteworthy additional detail in the Church Fathers' explanations of the Elisha narratives is that the incident of Elisha's miraculous recovery of the ax head from the water (2 Kings 6:1–7) is very thoroughly elaborated on. It seems to be the most important single element in the whole of the Elijah and Elisha cycles for the Church Fathers, and its typological Christological and soteriological explanation appears to be ancient, as it is known in an essentially similar form to at least Justin Martyr, Tertullian[29], Caesarius of Arles[30], and (Pseudo-)Ephrem. According to this interpretation, the fallen heavy ax head symbolizes "Adam," or fallen humanity, whereas the piece of wood that Elisha threw into water symbolizes the cross. Water refers to baptism and the house, which Elisha's disciples were about to build, symbolizes the Church. In Justin's words:

> Elisha, by throwing a piece of wood into the river Jordan, brought up to the surface the iron head of the ax with which the sons of the prophets had begun to cut wood for the construction of a building in which they proposed to read and study the precepts of God; just as our Christ, by being crucified on the wood of the cross and by sanctifying us by water raised up us who had been immersed in the mire of our mortal sins and made us a house of prayer and worship.[31]

This interpretation and its wide attestation are striking. It may, namely, signify that the earliest Christian interpreters, who according to my view saw many similarities between the Elijah–Elisha narratives and Jesus's life (and wrote some of these similarities into the Gospels, too), were possibly troubled by the narrative in 2 Kings 6. Contrary to, for example, the provision of food for a large crowd of people[32], or the raising of dead

---

[28] On the Second Book of Kings, 13.14–19.
[29] *Against the Jews* 13.
[30] *Sermon 130.1–3.*
[31] *Dialogue with Trypho 86.*
[32] 2 Kings 4:42–44 / Mark 6:30–44 par.

persons[33], or the healing of lepers[34] it did not directly parallel any reported incident in Jesus's life or any of his miracles. Therefore, a typological interpretation of the story probably readily suggested itself early on. Its attestation in Justin's *Dialogue with Trypho*, of course, but also its concrete and understandable typological details, speak for the antiquity of this interpretation. Thus, in these Church Fathers' interpretations, Jesus, in effect, becomes a "new Elisha" (just as in the Gospels)—even though they, of course, present the interpretation the other way round, so that Elisha becomes a typos for Christ.

This aside, even if not directly linked to the main theme of this small study, may thus serve as a bridge to the final topic.

Jesus's Mental Reactions (and Reactions to Jesus's Mentality) Compared to those Related to Elisha

In Gospel research, some attention has been given to the few reports of Jesus's mental reactions that are given in the Gospels.[35] However, not many scholars (often not even those who generally maintain the importance of the Elijah–Elisha narratives for the Gospels) have linked these descriptions to the reactions of (or, to) the two prophets as described in the books of Kings. I shall thus, as a final point in my paper, briefly list four cases that I have noticed. All of these relate to Elisha.

Points of Similarity

Elisha (or His Disciple) is Considered a Madman (2 Kings 9:11) / Jesus is Considered a Madman (Mark 3:21; John 10:20)

The first two sets of example texts do not actually describe either Elisha or Jesus's mental reactions, but rather the reactions to Elisha and Jesus's

---

[33] 2 Kings 4:32–35 / Mark 5:35–42 par.

[34] 2 Kings 5:9–14 / Mark 1:40–42 par.

[35] The mental reactions are mostly noted in commentaries in the appropriate places. There is a shortage of special studies; see, however, Simon Mainwaring, *Mark, Mutuality and Mental Health*, SBL Semeia Studies 79 (Atlanta: SBL Press, 2014), who discusses Mark 3:19b–35 (pp. 109–27). In research on the historical Jesus, certain incidents, such as Jesus's "purifying" the temple have, of course, received exhaustive treatment, but these go beyond the scope of this paper.

personalities that were considered to be somehow abnormal by certain audiences. The texts about the claim that the main protagonist is a madman receive, of course, pride of place.

The English translation for the Hebrew text of 2 Kings 9:11 was given above in footnote 1. The word used in the LXX of 2 Kings 9:11 is ἐπίλημπτος, which can be understood as 'possessed' (by a spirit): ἐπί + λαμβάνω. The same term is used to translate Hebrew *mᵉšuggaʿ* also in 1 Sam 21:14–16 where how David pretended to be mentally ill when trying to preserve his life is reported.

In Mark 3:19b–21, in turn, we are told,

> Then he went home, and the crowd came together again, so that they could not even eat. When his family heard it, they went out to restrain him, for people were saying, "He has gone out of his mind."

In this Markan report of Jesus's early career, Jesus's family thus seeks to take him into custody, thinking that he is insane. The verb used in Mark 3:21 is ἐξίστημι, 'be out of oneself,' but the continuation of the text in Mark 3:22–30 is a discourse about demonic possession, which links it conceptually to the terminology employed in the LXX of 2 Kings 9:11. Matthew and Luke have censored the incident in their versions, but John takes up the issue of Jesus's mental health anew, however using the verb μαίνομαι 'be furious, insane.' The discussion in John 10:19–21 is, again, about demons:

> Again the Jews were divided because of these words. Many of them were saying, "He has a demon and is out of his mind. Why listen to him?" Others were saying, "These are not the words of one who has a demon. Can a demon open the eyes of the blind?"

It perhaps deserves mention that "opening the eyes of the blind" is a deed which could, according to biblical precedent, also be associated with Elisha (2 Kings 6:17, 20).

The Markan passage in its entirety (3:20–35), with its theme about the rejection of family ties, may involve a larger intertextuality with the Elisha cycle in so far as Elisha had left his parents when he became Elijah's disciple (1 Kings 19:20–21). Additionally, one can notice that the 2 Kings

9:13 report of Jehu's declaration as king, in turn, resembles the people's reaction to Jesus's riding into Jerusalem (Mark 11:8; Matt 21:8).[36] These details may serve as a further point of contact between 2 Kings 9 and the Gospel of Mark in general. Some other Markan cases will be given in the following two examples.

<u>Elisha is Called "a Holy Man of God" (2 Kings 4:9) and is Later Accused by the Same Person / Jesus is Called "the Holy (Man) of God" and Accused by a Demon (Mark 1:24)</u>

This second set of example texts also concerns reactions to Elisha and Jesus's character. In 2 Kings 4:9, the wealthy Shunammite woman, the house of whom Elisha visits, tells her husband, "Look, I am sure that this man who regularly passes our way is a holy man of God." In the LXX, the line goes as follows, Ἰδοὺ δὴ ἔγνων ὅτι ἄνθρωπος τοῦ θεοῦ ἅγιος οὗτος διαπορεύεται ἐφ᾽ ἡμᾶς διὰ παντός. In the continuation of the story, the same woman first expresses her doubt to Elisha regarding the possibility of her gravidity (v. 16: "No, my lord, O man of God; do not deceive your servant") and then her grief regarding the death of her son (v. 28: "Did I ask my lord for a son? Did I not say, Do not mislead me?") Thus, in this story, Elisha is both acknowledged as "a holy man of God" and later accused of giving false hopes and causing severe sorrow.

In Jesus's very first miraculous act, according to Mark's report, a man possessed by a demon in the synagogue in Capernaum cries out (Mark 1:24): "What have you to do with us, Jesus of Nazareth? Have you come to destroy us? I know who you are, the Holy One of God." In the Greek text, the end of the verse goes as follows, οἶδά σε τίς εἶ, ὁ ἅγιος τοῦ θεοῦ. In this text, Jesus is thus both acknowledged as the holy (man) of God, in line with biblical pattern, and simultaneously accused of a misdeed (towards the demon/s).

The two verbs used in the introductory sentences, γινώσκω and οἶδα are, in principle, different, yet synonymous. In both cases, the speaker (the

---

[36] This similarity is apparent and has been recognized by several commentators, e.g., Hugh Anderson, *The Gospel of Mark: Based on the Revised Standard Version*, NCBC (Grand Rapids: Eerdmans, 1994), 262; Craig A. Evans, *Mark 8:27–16:20*, WBC 34 B (Nashville: Thomas Nelson, 2001), 143.

Shunammite woman and the demon) express a conviction that Elisha or Jesus is a "holy (man) of God."[37] Later (2 Kings 4:16, 28) or simultaneously (Mark 1:24a), accusations are also delivered against Elisha and Jesus respectively.

Here, it could be added that the blame placed on Elijah by the widow of Zarephath in 1 Kings 17:18 (a verse discussed earlier in section I above), also has conceptual affinity to this case; and the harshness of its wording links it rather closely to Mark 1:24.[38] The introductory words and the continuation with the vocative case are very similar: Τί ἐμοὶ καὶ σοί, ἄνθρωπε τοῦ θεοῦ; (1 Kings 17:18 LXX) / τί ἡμῖν καὶ σοί, Ἰησοῦ Ναζαρηνέ; (Mark 1:24). However, a notable difference vis-à-vis 2 Kings 4:9 is the absence of the word 'holy,' ἅγιος, from 1 Kings 17:18.

Elisha Reproaches a Disciple (2 Kings 4:27) / Jesus Reproaches Disciples (Mark 10:13–14 par.)
When the Shunammite woman then approaches Elisha on account of the death of her son, Gehazi tries to push her away. Similarly, Jesus's disciples seek to prevent people bringing children to him.[39] In the LXX version, Elisha reproaches Gehazi with the words Ἄφες αὐτήν, "Let her be"; whereas Jesus reproaches his disciples with the words Ἄφετε τὰ παιδία ἔρχεσθαι πρός με, "Let the children come to me" (Mark 10:13). The verb ἀφίημι in the imperative is thus used in both instances.

Regarding the relationship between the master and his disciple(s), the 2 Kings 4 narrative may again display larger intertextuality with the Gospel of Mark. Gehazi was not able to revive the boy using Elisha's staff, Elisha's own presence was required; similarly, Jesus's disciples, in another narrative, could not drive away the dumb and deaf spirit from a boy, Jesus's own intervention was needed (Mark 9:14–29 par.).

[37] Joel Marcus, in his commentary *Mark 1–8*, AB 27 (New York: Doubleday, 2000), 188–89, also connects the two texts with one another.
[38] Adela Yarbro Collins notices this similarity briefly in her *Mark: A Commentary*, Hermeneia (Minneapolis: Fortress, 2007), 169 n. 72.
[39] The connection was noted already by Rudolf Bultmann, *The History of the Synoptic Tradition*. Translated by John Marsh from the German original *Die Geschichte der synoptischen Tradition*, 1921 (New York: Harper & Row, 1976), 32: "some sort of prototype in the story of Elisha and Gehazi."

Elisha Weeps (2 Kings 8:11–12) / Jesus Weeps (Luke 19:41–44; John 11:35)

As a last point in this brief list of examples, I move away from the Gospel of Mark and pick up a detail from Luke and an interesting parallel in John.

In my view, the two narrative reports regarding visions of calamities caused by warfare, 2 Kings 8:11–12 and Luke 19:41–44, resemble one another rather significantly. Elisha's reaction to the vision which he sees (Hazael attacking Israel, and the atrocities related to this event) is very similar to Jesus's emotional reaction regarding the coming destruction of Jerusalem.[40] The LXX text of 2 Kings 8:11 goes as follows, obviously in order to translate the difficult Hebrew text as literally as possible: καὶ παρέστη τῷ προσώπῳ αὐτοῦ, καὶ ἔθηκεν ἕως αἰσχύνης· καὶ **ἔκλαυσεν** ὁ ἄνθρωπος τοῦ θεοῦ. Luke 19:41, in turn, tells, Καὶ ὡς ἤγγισεν, ἰδὼν τὴν πόλιν **ἔκλαυσεν** ἐπ' αὐτήν.

In terms of vocabulary, the two texts share only the verb κλαίω 'weep' albeit in the same aorist tense. In content, however, the longer passages (2 Kings 8:11–12; Luke 19:41–44) also have similar traits, especially the mentioning of the fate of the children/inhabitants (**καὶ τὰ νήπια αὐτῶν** ἐνσείσεις, 2 Kings 8:12 / καὶ ἐδαφιοῦσίν σε **καὶ τὰ τέκνα σου**, Luke 19:44). The general setting is also comparable: both Elisha and Jesus see, in a prophetic vision, a catastrophic event concerning Israel/Judah, and this vision moves them to tears.

Jesus's shedding of tears on account of the death of Lazarus (John 11:35) is a slightly different case, yet is very interesting in that Jesus's emotions are described in this text (11:33–44) perhaps more fully than in any other Gospel text. Jesus "was greatly disturbed in spirit and deeply moved" (ἐνεβριμήσατο τῷ πνεύματι καὶ ἐτάραξεν ἑαυτόν, v. 33), "began to weep" (ἐδάκρυσεν, v. 35), and was "again greatly disturbed" (πάλιν ἐμβριμώμενος ἐν ἑαυτῷ, v. 38). The great resuscitation miracle that Jesus performs in this pericope is reminiscent of the resuscitation acts of Elijah

---

[40] This similarity is noted also at least by Hays, *Echoes of Scripture in the Gospels*, 240 and Joseph A. Fitzmyer, *The Gospel according to Luke (X–XXIV)*, AB 28A (New York: Doubleday, 1985), 1258. Roger David Aus, in turn, sees a link to David's weeping in 2 Sam 15:30 and the reception of this event in later Jewish tradition; see Roger David Aus, *My Name is "Legion": Palestinian Judaic Traditions in Mark 5:1–20 and Other Gospel Texts*, Studies in Judaism (Dallas: University Press of America, 2003), 209–52.

and Elisha in 1 Kings 17:19–22 and 2 Kings 4:32–35, especially in that each of them, Elijah, Elisha as well as Jesus, are told to have prayed to the Lord. In Elijah and Jesus's cases, even the words of the prayer are recounted.[41] This detail is noteworthy and distinguishes the story in John 11 from that found in Mark 5:39–42 and Luke 7:11–15.

Conclusion

In this short study, I have tried to review how deviant behavior is described in the Elijah–Elisha cycle of the Hebrew Bible and its Jewish and Christian reception. I concentrated on such actions of the two prophets that have received at least a partly negative treatment in the biblical story and/or its reception.

I found out that the negative reactions towards Elijah's conduct voiced in the biblical account are often completely omitted or whitewashed in both Jewish and Christian tradition. With regard to Elisha, however, people (apart from some hostile kings) do not usually express negative reactions directly to him in the 2 Kings story; but there are occasions where his conduct is treated neutrally in the Bible but which caused trouble for later interpreters. It seems that Elisha was not always excused for his deeds in the Jewish tradition, but the Christian tradition consistently puts him in a good light.

As a final point in my survey, I presented a few cases from the New Testament where Jesus's emotional reactions, or reactions to him, resemble those related to Elisha: three texts from the Gospel of Mark (with one parallel in John), and one text from the Gospel of Luke (also with a parallel in John). I also pondered upon the possibility that the three cases from Mark may involve broader intertextuality between the Elisha cycle and the Gospel of Mark.[42] If this is true, it strengthens the claim made by several scholars that the Elijah–Elisha cycle served as a significant typological model for Gospel authors. Many studies have highlighted the importance of the Gospel of Luke. My brief investigation, however,

---

[41] Raymond E. Brown also refers to Elijah in this instance in his *The Gospel according to John (1–12)*, AB 29 (New York: Doubleday, 1993), 437, but connects Jesus's prayer with Elijah's prayer in 1 Kings 18:37.

[42] Cf. Roth, *Hebrew Gospel.*

indicates the presence of this tendency all the way from the early chapters of the Gospel of Mark onwards, which may indeed point to the centrality of the Elijah–Elisha theme for the composition of the (synoptic) Gospels.[43] In addition, this survey adds a slightly new dimension to the discussion by bringing Jesus's and Elisha's emotional reactions and their behavior to the fore.

---

[43] Similarly especially Brodie, *Crucial Bridge.*

The Prophet Ezekiel: Abnormal Man and Normal Prophet?

Kirsi Huoponen

1 Introduction

Ezekiel is possibly the prophet who, more than any other prophet in the Hebrew Bible, has been looked on as a deviant personality. Therefore, he is a most appropriate figure to be discussed within the framework of abnormalities amongst biblical figures. In the book of Ezekiel, hereafter, Ezek, Ezekiel's unusual behavior manifests itself in different ways. He sees dramatic visions, performs bizarre sign-acts and experiences shifts from one place to another and thus, he often appears to exceed the limits of normal human capacity. Ezekiel's behavioral peculiarities have even raised doubts about his mental health insomuch that some scholars have attempted to make a clinical diagnosis of him having some kind of mental illness.[1] We need to bear in mind, however, that our knowledge of Ezekiel's behavioral characteristics comes from a book which has a long literary history and, moreover, that the textual material, including the narratives of his sign-acts and visions, has been extensively elaborated on by the circles who transmitted the prophetic tradition. We cannot, therefore, know with certainty whether Ezekiel actually experienced and performed everything exactly as described in the book or ascertain whether we are dealing with a form of written prophecy from the outset. Nevertheless, the way Ezekiel is portrayed in the book is relevant to the message of the book.

In this article, I mainly discuss Ezekiel's behavior in the light of the peculiar sign-acts recounted in Ezek 4:1–5:4. My intention is not to

---

[1] David J. Halperin, *Seeking Ezekiel. Text and Psychology* (Pennsylvania: Pennsylvania State University Press, 1993).

present any psychological interpretation of Ezekiel; rather, I seek to show how Ezekiel's priestly identity and the extraordinary circumstances in which he was living contribute to our understanding of his behavior.

2 Ezekiel in the Book of Ezekiel

The book of Ezekiel gives an impression of a coherent and elaborate literary whole, which, as scholars have noted, makes it difficult to establish criteria to identify the prophetic tradition.[2] Even if some of the textual material can be attributed to the historical prophet, it is difficult to identify it in the book, since whatever constituted the literary core has subsequently been expanded and new perspectives have been added. The book displays an overall coherence of style which suggests the existence of a prophetic school which elaborated on and updated the prophecies of Ezekiel and produced the final form of the book.[3] In all probability, many passages in Ezek never had a previous oral existence, for example, the historical reviews in Ezek 16, 20 and 23, and Ezekiel's vision reports.[4] Additionally, there is no indication of any public response to anything that Ezekiel says, nor are there any outsiders' comments concerning his

---

[2] Walter Zimmerli, *Ezekiel 1: A Commentary on the Book of the Prophet Ezekiel, Chapters 1–24*, Hermeneia, transl. Ronald E. Clements (Philadelphia: Fortress, 1979), 71; Reinhard G. Kratz, *The Prophets of Israel*, transl. Anselm C. Hagedorn and Nathan MacDonald (Winona Lake: Eisenbrauns, 2015), 61; Joseph Blenkinsopp, *A History of Prophecy in Israel* (Philadelphia: The Westminster Press, 1983), 195.

[3] Zimmerli, *Ezekiel*, 70–74. Zimmerli points to several texts which appear to belong to this updating process carried out by the prophetic school; I will return to this issue in the course of the study when the relevant texts will be analyzed.

[4] For Ezekiel as a book prophet who expressed himself only in writing, see Menahem Haran, "Observations on Ezekiel as a Book Prophet," in *Seeking Out the Wisdom of the Ancients. Essays Offered in Honor Michael V. Fox on Occasion of His Sixty-Fifth Birthday*, ed. Ronald L. Toxel, Kelvin G. Friebel, and Dennis R. Magary (Winona Lake: Eisenbrauns, 2005), 3–19. Haran refers, for example, to Ezekiel's call vision in 1:1–3:15 and the chapters 40–48. For the latter chapters, see also Menahem Haran, "The Law Code of Ezekiel XL–XLVIII and Its Relation to the Priestly School," *HUCA* 50 (1979): 46–53.

peculiar sign-acts and visions.[5] Ezekiel did, however, communicate with the elders who visited the prophet in his house (Ezek 8:1; 14:1; 20:1).

Affinities with other biblical writings, notably the books of Jeremiah and Hosea, and the so-called Holiness Code in Leviticus 17–26, as well as Deuteronomy and the Deuteronomistic History, are characteristic of Ezek.[6] The relationship between Ezek and these biblical books is thought to be the result of a common religious heritage rather than direct literary interdependence since Ezekiel often deviates from them and re-interprets traditions and religious concepts to reflect the circumstances at the time of the exile.[7]

According to Ezek 1:1–3, Ezekiel was a priest. He was a member of the Judaean elite deported along with King Jehoiachin in 597 BCE, when Nebuchadnezzar captured Jerusalem.[8] It was in these exceptional circumstances that Ezekiel was called to be a prophet. The book asserts that Ezekiel's commissioning took place in the fifth year of the exile of King Jehoiachin when the word of YHWH came to Ezekiel, the priest, the son of Buzi in the land of Babylonians where the hand of YHWH was upon him.

---

[5] In Ezek 33:31–32, YHWH makes an ironic comment about the people who come to listen to Ezekiel's words, pointing to the people's negligence concerning the message of Ezekiel, and accusing the people for regarding Ezekiel as a singer of love songs with a beautiful voice.

[6] For a detailed discussion on the parallels between Ezek and other biblical books, see, e,g. Zimmerli, *Ezekiel 1*, 41–52; see also Risa Levitt Kohn, *A New Heart and a New Soul. Ezekiel, the Exile and the Torah*, JSOTSup 358 (London: Sheffield Academic Press, 2002); see, especially, the index on pages 139–46.

[7] Michael Fishbane, *Biblical Interpretation in Ancient Israel* (Oxford: Clarendon Press, 1985), 410; see also Anja Klein, "Prophecy Continued: Reflections on Innerbiblical Exegesis in the Book of Ezekiel," *VT* 60 (2010): 571–82; Jake Stromberg, "Observations on Inner-Scriptural Scribal Expansion in MT Ezekiel," *VT* 58 (2008): 68–86.

[8] The passage in Ezek 1:1–3 contains a problematic double dating. The first date given in Ezek 1:1 does not specify the year, and its reference to the 30th year is obscure; the year is clarified in Ezek 1:2 as the 5th year of the exile of King Jehoiachin. As to the reference to the 30th year, there are various readings; see Zimmerli, *Ezekiel 1*, 112–15; Henry McKeating, *Ezekiel* (Sheffield: Sheffield Academic Press, 1993), 23; Antti Laato, *Guide to Biblical Chronology* (Sheffield: Sheffield Phoenix Press, 2015), 53–61. For a detailed discussion on the system of dating in Ezekiel, see McKeating, *Ezekiel*, 62–72.

Subsequently, the chronology in the book is largely given according to the number of years after Jehoiachin's deportation.[9]

The book of Ezekiel begins with a textual unit in Ezek 1:1–3:15 which composes the narrative of Ezekiel's call. Margaret Odell has proposed that Ezekiel's call narrative in Ezek 1:1–3:15 and the report of the sign-acts in Ezek 3:16–5:17 have been combined into an extended, coherent composition that focuses on Ezekiel's inaugural experience.[10] Ezekiel's role as a prophet begins only at the beginning of Ezek 6 and, therefore, Odell further suggests that in the preceding chapters Ezekiel undergoes a series of experiences that prepare him to be a prophet.[11] This relates to the issue of Ezekiel's role as a priest and a prophet, and whether he relinquished his role as a priest to become a prophet, or, rather, whether Ezekiel should be viewed as a priestly prophet whose calling is remarkably similar to the ordination of priests.[12]

The function of Ezek 1–3 is to introduce the reader to the figure of Ezekiel and it contains important elements which authenticate Ezekiel as a prophet. These chapters also use particular formulaic expressions and motifs which contribute to our understanding of Ezekiel, especially as they show many similarities between earlier prophets and Ezek.

The coming of word of YHWH. The so-called *Wortereignisformel*, consisting of the combination of דבר יהוה with היה and אל, occurs frequently in Ezek. It affirms that the message which Ezekiel is passing on is the word of YHWH. This formula for the reception of YHWH's word is most frequently found in Ezek and Jer, but also appears at the beginning of Hos. It is a strong expression which emphasizes the coming of YHWH's word as a comprehensive event. As Hans Walter Wolff, in his commentary on

---

[9] Zimmerli reckons with twelve original dates which cover the period from the 5th year of Jehoiachin's exile to the 27th year after the deportation; the dates are now, however, in chronological order in the book which seems to be a disturbance caused by later redaction; see Zimmerli, *Ezekiel 1*, 9–10.

[10] Margaret S. Odell; "You Are What You Eat: Ezekiel and the Scroll," *JBL* 117 (1998): 229–48.

[11] Odell, "You are what you eat," 235.

[12] So Pieter de Vries, "Ezekiel: Prophet of the Name and Glory of YHWH—The Character of His Book and Several of Its Main Themes," *Journal of Biblical and Pneumatological Research* 4 (2012): 94–108, here 100.

Hosea remarks, "the word of YHWH" does not mean individual prophetic utterances but rather refers to the prophet's total experience, which includes not only the words of revelation he is to proclaim, but also the divine commands that ordered and directed his own life.[13] This fits in well with Ezekiel too, who himself was to be a sign for Israel (Ezek 12:6, 11; 24:24, 27). The sign-acts that the prophets performed clearly indicated their deep emotional immersion in their message.

The hand of YHWH was upon him. Another formulaic expression which emerges in Ezek is "the hand of YHWH was upon him." This expression occurs in Ezek seven times and is associated with visions (Ezek 1:3; 3:14, 22; 8:1; 33:22; 37:1; 40:1) and experiencing translocations (Ezek 3:14, 22; 8:1; 33:22; 37:1; 40:1). The hand of YHWH, thus, denotes a force and power that can take control of the prophet. This raises the question whether, at least in some cases, the expression is related to a very specific state of mind which resulted in a behavior that was characteristics of prophets and explains why the prophets were mocked for being "mad" (מְשֻׁגָּע).[14] It is likely that particular behavior characteristics were indeed part of the role of a prophet and, thus, to be expected from him/her, which seems to be the case for prophets in the ancient Near East in general. The standard prophetic designation in Akkadian is derived from the verb *maḫû* which means "to become crazy, to go into a frenzy."[15] This may have referred to the distinctive behavior by which societies were able to recognize and validate intermediaries, even though not exclusively so.[16]

---

[13] Hans Walter Wolff, *Hosea. A Commentary on the Book of the Prophet Hosea*, transl. Gary Stansell, Hermeneia (Philadelphia: Fortress, 1974), 4. Like many other scholars, Wolff regards the formula as an indication of a Deuteronomistic redaction; see also Susanne Rudnig-Zelt, *Hoseastudien. Redaktionskritische Untersuchungen zur Genese des Hoseabuches*, FRLANT 213 (Göttingen: Vandenhoeck & Ruprecht, 2006), 105.

[14] Jer 29:26; 2 Kgs 9:11; Hos 9:7.

[15] Moshe Weinfeld, "Ancient Near Eastern Patterns in Prophetic Literature," *VT* 27 (1977): 178–95, 181; Martti Nissinen, *Ancient Prophecy. Near Eastern, Biblical, and Greek Perspectives* (Oxford: Oxford University Press, 2017), 173–74.

[16] So Robert R. Wilson, *Prophecy and Society in Ancient Israel* (Philadelphia: Fortress Press, 1984), 32. As Wilson remarks, not everyone who manifested these behavioral characteristics was automatically considered to be an intermediary, and most societies recognize multiple causes for ecstatic behavior. Although a characteristic, even if an ecstatic, mental state was

Nevertheless, an altered state of consciousness—trance, ecstasy, and possession—is closely connected with the phenomenon of prophecy all over the ancient Near East; so also in Israel where there was a tradition of ecstatic prophecy and trance (cf. 1 Sam 10:6). Nonetheless, it is not obvious that in the case of Ezekiel we should speak of ecstasy or possession albeit some features in Ezekiel's behavior are indeed peculiar. Rather, the question may be about an "inner excitement," an expression used by Abraham Heschel.[17] Like many prophets, Ezekiel experienced assimilation; as Heschel says,

> Prophetic sympathy is not, like love, attraction to the divine Being, but the assimilation of the prophet's emotional life to the divine, an assimilation of function, not being. The emotional experience of the prophet becomes the focal point for the prophet's understanding of God.[18]

References to the hand of YHWH are common in the Hebrew Bible and are connected to particular acts of YHWH.[19] Walter Zimmerli regards the concept of the hand of YHWH as belonging to the old religious language of Israel, and he suggests that its origin may be in the exodus narratives from where it found its way to the language of prophetic schools.[20] Robert Wilson ascribes the frequent use of the formula to the Ephraimite, i.e. northern Israelite, prophetic tradition in particular.[21] Ezek shares many characteristics with this stream of tradition as the occurrence of the expression "the hand of YHWH" in the stories of Elijah and Elisha, and in Jer, also indicate. The hand of YHWH enabled Elijah to run ahead of Ahab's chariot all the way from Carmel to Jezreel (1 Kgs 18:46), caused Elisha to prophecy (2 Kgs 3:15), but also isolated Jeremiah from his contemporaries (Jer 15:17). These particular examples do not point to supernatural

---

required from a prophet, ecstatic behavior did not absolutely mean that the prophets were true Yahwistic prophets as the narrative of the prophets of Baal in 1 Kings 18 implies.

[17] Abraham Heschel, *The Prophets* (New York: Harper Perennial Modern Classics, 2001), 404.

[18] Heschel, *Prophets*, 31.

[19] See Zimmerli, *Ezekiel 1*, 117–18.

[20] Ibid., 117. Zimmerli points to the possibility that the strong emphasis to the hand and arm of YHWH took its origin in the exodus narratives in which the outstretched arms of YHWH and Moses are so important.

[21] Wilson, *Prophecy and Society*, 17–18, 282–86.

experiences but all recognize the hand of YHWH as a dynamic power. Furthermore, as Keith Carley points out, in the case of Jeremiah, the hand of YHWH signified a prophet's calling, marking him as a man apart "who was to manifest in his own life the imminent isolation and grief of those who had deserted YHWH."[22]

The concept of the hand of a deity is not only confined to biblical writings. More or less similar expressions are found in some ancient sources from Mari as well as in an Amarna and an Ugaritic letter. According to Jimmy J.M. Roberts, in these sources the hand of a deity designated "some disastrous manifestation of the supernatural power," especially as seen in times of sickness or plague, and, as Roberts concludes, the expression "hand of Yahweh" was only secondarily applied to the prophetic phenomenon "precisely because that phenomenon bore a remarkable similarity to the symptoms of human illness normally designated by the expression."[23] Against this background, it is possible to understand Ezekiel's dumbness as being caused by the hand of YHWH and, moreover, how it was only after the hand had departed from Ezekiel that the prophet was able to speak again (Ezek 33:21–22).

The motif of Spirit. Ezek 2:2; 3:12, 14, 24; 8:3; 11:1, 24, and 43:5 refer to the Spirit, רוח, alone, and the "spirit of YHWH," רוח יהוה, is mentioned only in Ezek 37:1. The Spirit is sometimes mentioned together with the hand of YHWH; it allows Ezekiel to hear voices, lifts him up and takes him to other locations. The experiences of translocation suggest that Ezekiel felt himself to be freed from normal physical limitations. There are no reports of the response from Ezekiel's audience to this or how they perceived Ezekiel's behavior, although we do know that the prophet experienced a translocation when the elders were at his house (Ezek 8:3). The Spirit was connected with prophesying, since it is recorded that Ezekiel reported everything he had seen in his vision to his fellow exiles (Ezek 11:25). As regards Ezekiel's audience, the elders seem to have visited Ezekiel every

---

[22] Keith W. Carley, *Ezekiel among the Prophets. A Study of Ezekiel's Place in Prophetic Tradition* (Cambridge: Cambridge University Press, 1974), 19–20.
[23] Jimmy J. M. Roberts, "The Hand of Yahweh," *VT* 21 (1971): 244–51. The quotations are from page 250.

now and then (Ezek 8:1; 14:1; 20:3) with the aim of hearing the message that had come from YHWH (Ezek 30:30). As Walter Zimmerli points out in his commentary the visit by the elders in conjunction with the coming of a vision is a very stereotyped situation and has its counterpart in 2 Kgs 6:32 in the narrative of Elisha.[24] The spirit of YHWH is required for prophesying not only in the book of Ezekiel but also Isaiah 61:1 and Micah 3:8, and thus it offers assurance that the word proclaimed by the prophet is the word of YHWH.

In addition to the aforementioned formulaic expressions, Ezekiel's call narrative is also connected with a vision of YHWH. In the famous chariot vision in Ezek 1–3, the prophet saw the appearance of the likeness of the glory of YHWH, and later, in Ezek 10, the glory of YHWH departs from the Temple. The concept of the divine anger connected with the absence of gods from their temples, an idea which occurs in Neo-Assyrian and Neo-Babylonian documents too, may be the background for this vision..[25] By all appearances, Ezekiel was well-educated; he came from a priestly family and, furthermore, the book contains many allusions and borrowings from Mesopotamian culture, which indicate that the prophet had had access to it, perhaps through cuneiform scribal schooling.[26]

The combination of a call narrative and a vision evokes the calls of Isaiah in Isa 6 and Micaiah ben Imlah in 1 Kgs 22:19-21.[27] Ezekiel's call narrative is, however, distinguishable from other prophets in that there is no dialogue between Ezekiel and YHWH. The encounter of the prophet and YHWH is not personal, and Ezekiel remains passive. He does not object to

---

[24] Zimmerli, *Ezekiel 1*, 43.

[25] See Martti Nissinen, "The Exiled Gods of Babylon in Neo-Assyrian Prophecy," in *The Concept of Exile in Ancient Israel and its Historical Contexts*, ed. Ehud Ben Zvi and Christoph Levin, BZAW 404 (Berlin: de Gruyter, 2010), 27–38, here 35.

[26] Jonathan Stökl, "'A Youth Without Blemish, Handsome, Proficient in all Wisdom, Knowledgeable and Intelligent': Ezekiel's Access to Babylonian Culture," in *Exile and Return: The Babylonian Context*, ed. Jonathan Stökl and Caroline Waerzeggers, BZAW 478 (Berlin: De Gruyter, 2015), 223–52. For Ezekiel's familiarity with the ancient myths, see, for example, Bernard F. Batto, "The Covenant of Peace: A Neglected Ancient Near Eastern Motif," *CBQ* 49 (1987): 187–211; Meir Maul, "Adoption of Foundlings in the Bible and Mesopotamian Documents: A Study of Some Legal Metaphors in Ezekiel 16:1–7," *JSOT* 46 (1990): 97–126.

[27] Norman C. Habel, "The Form and Significance of the Call Narratives," *ZAW* 77 (1965): 297–323, here 309–10. See also Zimmerli, *Ezekiel 1*, 98–100.

his call, unless this is implied in Ezek 2:6 where YHWH encourages Ezekiel not to be afraid, and in Ezek 3:14 where Ezekiel's reluctance may lay behind his bitterness and anger.[28] As many scholars have noted, Ezekiel often appears to be an observer, a tool in YHWH's hand—he is "God's marionette" as Lena-Sofie Tiemeyer aptly puts it.[29] The prophet is not even addressed by his proper name but YHWH calls him בֶן־אָדָם, usually translated as "son of man" or "mortal." The address as בֶן־אָדָם completely fades out Ezekiel as an individual and defines the distinctive relationship between Ezekiel and YHWH.

3 Ezekiel's Sign-Acts

The first sign-act is recounted in Ezek 4:1. The prophet is ordered to mimic the siege of Jerusalem by using a brick model; the word "Jerusalem" may not have been in the earlier text, but has been added as an interpretative gloss.[30] This sign-act is the first in a series of sign-acts which depict the fate of a besieged city as it happens in reality, re-creating the siege and building the necessary equipment. Ezekiel is commanded to separate himself figuratively from the city by placing a metal plate, מַחֲבַת, between himself and the city and to turn his face towards the plate. The word מַחֲבַת in 4:3 denotes a metal plate that was used as a roasting or baking tray; apart from Ezek, the word occurs only in Lev 2:5; 6:14; 7:9, and 1 Chr 23:29. In Leviticus, the word is related to the preparation of grain offerings, while in 1 Chr the word occurs in the list of the duties of the Levites, and thus the plate also had a role in sacrificial food preparation.[31] The optical contact here echoes Num 24:2 where Balaam viewed the encamped Israel, but whereas Balaam sees Israel, Ezekiel sees only the

---

[28] Martin J. Buss, "An Anthropological Perspective upon Prophetic Call Narratives," *Semeia* 21 (1981): 9–30, here 20 n20; Zimmerli, *Ezekiel 1*, 98.

[29] Lena-Sofia Tiemeyer, "Ezekiel: A Compromised Prophet in Reduced Circumstances," in *Constructs of Prophecy in the Former and Latter Prophets and Other Texts*, ed. Lester L. Grabbe and Martti Nissinen, SBL Ancient Near East Monographs 4 (Atlanta: Society of Biblical Literature, 2011), 175–95, here 176.

[30] Zimmerli, *Ezekiel 1*, 148. Cf. Isaiah 7:17, 20.

[31] R. Andrew Compton, "The Sign-Acts of Ezekiel 3:22–5:17. Formative Rituals of Priestly Identity," *Mid-America Journal of Theology* 29 (2018): 47–80, here 66.

sign.[32] What seems to be the point here is that the metal plate is communicating not Ezekiel's but YHWH's disposition towards Jerusalem; this is explained in Ezek 5:11 according to which YHWH looks upon Jerusalem without any pity and without any intention to spare it.[33]

This sign-act demanded no supernatural physical efforts from Ezekiel, but its message was shocking since the siege signaled an attack from which no one could escape. As Kevin Friebel remarks,

> Even though theologically God was considered to be the one actively directing the actions against Jerusalem, the historical outworkings of such were performed by the Babylonians. Thus distinction between the historical role of the enemy and the theological role of God was blurred, allowing Ezekiel to take on simultaneously the role of God and the enemy without a definite dichotomy being made between the two.[34]

The second sign-act appears in Ezek 4:4–8. Ezekiel is commanded to lie on his left side for 390 days in order to bear the punishment of the house of Israel on his side; the number of the days assigned by YHWH equals the number of the years (Num 14:34). After these 390 days, the prophet has to lie on his right side for a further 40 days, in order to atone for the sin of Judah. In Ezek 4:7, Ezekiel is commanded to turn his face towards the besieged Jerusalem and, with his arm bared, prophesy against the city; baring one's arm refers to a gesture of a warrior who thus expressed his readiness for battle. Ezekiel is also bound so that he cannot turn from one side to another.

The figures are difficult to interpret. If Jehoiachin's fifth year of the exile corresponds to Zedekiah's fourth regnal year, it is possible that the figure of 430 years signifies the time from the time of Solomon to Ezekiel's own time; another possibility is that 430 years refers to the existence of the First Temple. [35] It is also possible to see a connection between the 430

---

[32] Zimmerli, *Ezekiel 1*, 30.

[33] Kelvin G. Friebel, *Jeremiah's and Ezekiel's Sign-Acts*, JSOTSup 283 (Sheffield: Sheffield Academic Press, 1999), 208–9.

[34] Friebel, *Jeremiah's and Ezekiel's Sign-Acts*, 204.

[35] For this, see Laato, *Guide to Biblical Chronology*, 45, n18. See also Zimmerli, *Ezekiel 1*, 165–67.

years and the exodus tradition. Zimmerli reasons that the figure of 430 years could signify the length of the period that the Israelites, according to Exod 12:40, spent in Egypt and, thus, a new exodus after the time spent in exile will follow after a period of equal length.[36] This may be the case, since Ezek 20:7–8 refers to a tradition which deviates from the dominant biblical tradition by seeing Egypt as the place where Israel worshipped idols and, thus, the people had to atone for this sin in order that the second exodus could take place. Ezekiel reinterprets the tradition of Israel in Egypt pointing out that disasters result from the people's sins. Therefore, exile can be seen as proof of prior transgressions and, thus, eliminating any cause for questioning YHWH's acts.[37] The concept of atonement also relates to Ezekiel's role as a priest, since, as scholars have pointed out, this particular sign-act echoes the action of the priests on the Day of Atonement.[38]

However, the sign-act in Ezek 4:4–8 does not fit well with other sign-acts recounted in 4:1–5:4. First, the command קח־לך used in other sign-acts is omitted, and, second, unlike this sign-act, other sign-acts appear to be in a clear succession as they depict the actual fate of a besieged city. Therefore, Ezek 4:4–8 may be a later insertion in an earlier textual layer.[39]

In Ezek 4:9–17 the prophet is asked to take wheat and barley, beans and lentils, millet and spelt and make a loaf of bread for himself. The mixing of different kinds of cereal in food indicates using scraps and functions as a sign of a city under siege in which food is scarce as does the rationing of food and drink as well.[40] Ezekiel is first commanded to use human dung as fuel which was impossible in the light of priestly regulations for purity.[41] Ezekiel objects to YHWH's command to use human excrement to bake the bread, and is subsequently allowed to use cow excrement instead (Ezek 4:12–14); in fact, this is the only instance when

---

[36] Zimmerli, *Ezekiel 1*, 167.

[37] Shemaryahu Talmon, *Literary Motifs and Patterns in the Hebrew Bible: Collected Studies* (Winona Lake: Eisenbrauns, 2013), 325. As Talmon further states, the idea that Israel's slavery in Egypt was a punishment may come from Ezekiel.

[38] Compton, "The Sign-Acts of Ezekiel 3:22–5:17," 47–80, here 68.

[39] So Zimmerli, *Ezekiel 1*, 155–56.

[40] Ibid., 169.

[41] Cf. Deut 23:12–14; Zimmerli, *Ezekiel 1*, 170.

Ezekiel enters into a dialogue with YHWH. Although Ezekiel's reluctance to consume impure food plays an important role here, I think that Andrew Compton is correct in emphasizing the importance of how the meagre amount of food and drink also depicts the famine in a besieged city.[42]

The sign-act in 5:1–4 is related to shaving and the subsequent distribution of the shaved-off hair. Ezekiel is commanded to divide the cut-off hair (Ezek 5:1): one third will be burned, one third will be struck with the sword all around the city, and one third will be scattered to the wind (Ezek 5:2). A small number of hairs will be bound in the skirts of Ezekiel's robe (Ezek 5:3). From these, some will be burned because that fire will come on the whole Israel (Ezek 5:4). The sign-act is explained in 5:12: a third of the people in Jerusalem will die of the plague and famine, a third will fall by the sword outside the walls of the city, and a third will be scattered to the winds, i.e. exiled. As Friebel summarizes, the shaving of the head shows the depopulation of the city, and the dividing of the cut-off hair indicates the dividing of the people in judgment, and the scattering of the hair to the wind depicts the exile.[43]

Shaving is a central component in various rites, marking a ritual transition, a change of status of the one who has been shaved.[44] It is also connected with humiliation (2 Sam 10:4; 1 Chron 19:4) and shaving is an expression of mourning (Jer 41:5); Isa 7:10 also speaks of "shaving" as destruction. Therefore, this sign-act fits in well with the last of the events describing the fate of Jerusalem: humiliation, destruction, and exile.

To conclude, Ezekiel's sign-acts are used to depict the fate of Jerusalem, and regardless of whether we read them as predicting the fall of Jerusalem or as *ex eventu* prophecy, the main point is the inevitability of the disaster. It is likely that a complex process of growth underlies the passage in Ezek 4:1–5:4; according to Zimmerli, the original text may have been a narrative of three sign-acts describing successive events related to a siege of a city: the beginning of the siege, the food shortage during the actual siege, and the description of the catastrophe encountered by the inhabitants of a

---

[42] Compton, "The Sign-Acts of Ezekiel 3:22–5:17," 47–80, here 74.
[43] Friebel, *Jeremiah's and Ezekiel's Sign-Acts*, 389.
[44] Saul M. Olyan, "What Do Shaving Rites Accomplish and What Do They Signal in Biblical Ritual Contexts?" *JBL* 117 (1998): 611–22, here 622.

besieged city.[45] This means that the sign-act in Ezek 4:4–8 was added to a pre-existing textual layer; as was the explanation of the sign-acts which begins in 5:5.[46] This implies that the "original" sign-acts did not exceed normal human physical capacity. Nonetheless, I want to emphasize that there is no need to eliminate any textual passages merely because they relate to things which we consider to be supernatural, since the descriptions of Ezekiel's behavior, even if literary accounts, do convey his message.[47]

Ezekiel 3:24 indicates that Ezekiel shuts himself in his house on YHWH's command. The obvious question, thus, concerns whether Ezekiel's isolation applies to the enacting of the sign-acts described in Ezek 4:1–5:4. Another oddity relates to Ezekiel's dumbness, since according to Ezek 3:25–26, YHWH made Ezekiel silent. Only in Ezek 33:21–22 is YHWH said to have opened the prophet's mouth again, shortly before the news of the fall of Jerusalem reached him.

Ezekiel's dumbness is connected with his priestly character, since the priests were supposed to be silent when performing their sacrifices. As Israel Knohl states,

> The theological uniqueness of the Priestly Torah is reflected in the special description of its Tabernacle. The outstanding characteristic of this sanctuary is the holy silence within it. In stark contrast to what was common in the temples of the Near East, and indeed to other temples in Israel, the Temple described in the Priestly Torah is a sanctuary of silence

and, furthermore,

> The Priestly corpus in the books of Exodus and Leviticus—which contains detailed accounts of most of the Temple ritual—does not mention any form

---

[45] So Zimmerli, *Ezekiel 1*, 156.
[46] Ibid., 147–78.
[47] With Wilson, *Prophecy and Society*, 283.

of verbal activity that accompanies the ritual. The priest performs his actions in utter silence.[48]

Given that the silence of Ezekiel was connected with his priestly function relating to atonement, he must have been aware of the priestly tradition of the silent sanctuary and followed it. Therefore, his peculiar behavior was due to his understanding of his role as a priest in circumstances where there was no temple.

Ezekiel could speak again only after the fall of Jerusalem. The role of the prophets in the northern Ephraimite traditions was intercession, and, as Robert Wilson suggests, Ezekiel's dumbness may relate to divine refusal of intercessory functions, thus allowing the judgment to take place.[49] It is, thus, possible to think of Ezekiel's dumbness as a sign of YHWH's firm decision: no human intervention could help the people.

4 Was Ezekiel Abnormal?

In many respects Ezekiel is like his prophetic predecessors and his behavior is comparable to and in continuity with them. Therefore, Ezekiel cannot be regarded as an abnormal prophet. However, Ezekiel differs from other prophets in two aspects: Ezekiel had a distinctively priestly identity and he was in exile, and these two attributes explain his behavior.

The sign-acts which I have discussed in this article relate to the fall of Jerusalem and the destruction of the Temple. As Marvin Sweeney points out, many seeming peculiarities in Ezekiel's behavior, including his sign-acts, are priestly attributes: his silence, bearing the guilt of the people, eating common food rather than portions of the Temple sacrifices, and the shaving—they all also relate to Ezekiel's loss of sanctity as priest.[50] Ezekiel is a sign to his fellow exiles: neither Ezekiel nor the people can expect

---

[48] Israel Knohl, *The Divine Symphony. The Bible's Many Voices* (Philadelphia: The Jewish Publication Company, 2003), 71–72; see also Knohl, "Between Voice and Silence: The Relationship between Prayer and Temple Cult," *JBL* 115 (1996): 17–30.

[49] Wilson, *Prophecy and Society*, 284. Wilson also points out that like Ezekiel, Jeremiah was also forbidden to intercede for the people before the fall of Jerusalem (e.g. Jer 11:14–17; 14:11–12).

[50] Marvin A. Sweeney, *Form and Intertextuality in Prophetic and Apocalyptic Literature*, FAT 45 (Tübingen: Mohr Siebeck, 2005), 113.

restoration without purification, and furthermore, there is no purification without atonement. In Ezekiel's thinking, the inevitability of the destruction of Jerusalem, a disaster beyond understanding, was explained as a result of the defilement of the Temple and, thus, it became justified. The purpose of the sign-acts was both to demonstrate YHWH's firm decision and signal that there was no possibility for intercession—therefore, Ezekiel was silent and restricted. According to Sweeney, Ezekiel's familiarity with the scapegoat ritual in Lev 16 is the basis for understanding Ezekiel. In this ritual, one goat is sacrificed as a sin offering and killed, and the other goat is released into the wilderness in order to purify the nation by carrying its sins. Thus, according to Ezekiel, some people are killed in the destruction of Jerusalem, the rest are sent to exile where they will atone for the defilement of Jerusalem and form the basis by which the restoration of Israel will be restored.[51] Therefore, for Ezekiel, the Jehoiachin exiles in Babylonia were the living remnant of the people of YHWH; they had experienced YHWH's punishment and it would be with them that the covenant would be renewed (Ezek 20:1–38).

Ezekiel's sign-acts also provided those in exile with a possibility to identify themselves with Ezekiel. All previous religious fundaments—the Temple in Jerusalem, the city itself, the Davidic kingship—were gone. As David Carr discusses in *Holy Resilience: The Bible's Traumatic Origins*, self-blame became one of the ways to symbolize the trauma the exiles suffered.[52] Ezekiel did not exclude himself from the people. As Carr further remarks, those who suffer from a severe trauma dissociate themselves from the experience, in other words, they become speechless—therefore, in their inability to depict the trauma, those in exile needed a sign and this sign was Ezekiel.[53] Ezekiel's dumbness was their silence, their experience of a "speechless terror" in being in a foreign land, and "with a history that has no place."[54]

---

[51] Ibid., 152.
[52] David M. Carr, *Holy Resilience. The Bible's Traumatic Origins* (New Haven: Yale University Press, 2014), 78.
[53] Ibid., 79.
[54] Ibid., 75.

To conclude, the priest-prophet Ezekiel, insofar as what we can read about him in the book that bears his name, should be viewed neither as an abnormal man nor an abnormal prophet. He was living in abnormal circumstances to which the priest-prophet Ezekiel had to react. We may ask whether there is any possibility to have a normal reaction in abnormal circumstances and, furthermore, how what is normal could actually be defined when there is nothing to compare with. Ezekiel developed a religious view of his own and built it on his role as a priest and reinterpretation of earlier religious traditions and concepts. It became his mission, and it is possible that he felt as Heschel has said about the prophet's mission:

> The mission he performs is distasteful to him and repugnant to others; no reward is promised him and no reward could temper its bitterness. He is stigmatized as a madman by his contemporaries, and, by some modern scholars, abnormal.[55]

---

[55] Heschel, *The Prophets*, 21.

Abnormal Samson

Antti Laato

Introduction

The aim of this article is to discuss how the story of Samson, Judges 13–16 was transmitted in the book of Judges, interpreted and, moreover, how it was understood in early Jewish reception history. A special focus is laid on the abnormal details in the story and Samson's unusual behavior by considering, in particular, how these abnormalities were treated in early Jewish reception history. I shall focus on four abnormal details in the story:

1. Samson's birth was unusual.
2. Samson is characterized as a Nazirite, but his behavior does not corroborate well with the details pertaining to the Nazirite Law in Num 6.
3. Samson has supernatural powers. His supernatural powers were connected with his having long hair.
4. Samson had several affairs with foreign women—something which is presented as being problematic or a sin in many passages of the Hebrew Bible and especially in early Jewish writings.

The structure of the article is as follows: *First*, I discuss some essential problems in the Samson tradition (linked with his abnormal behavior) in the light of the survey of research. *Second*, I argue that the Samson tradition was part of the pre-exilic Deuteronomistic material and integrated into the pre-Deuteronomistic chronological scheme with its different understanding of the Nazirites as part of the Yahweh war institution. Therefore, Samson's Nazirite status subsequently became a problem in the Jewish reception history when Judges 13–16 was discussed in relation to Num 6. *Finally*, I discuss the four aforementioned abnormal themes by considering how they have been treated in early Jewish interpretive traditions.

Central Research Problems in Samson's Story

There is no room here to present any detailed survey of research.[1] I shall deal only with some important problems which have relevance to my topic: the abnormal behavior of Samson.

An essential question in research has been the literary unity of the story. The aim of the literary- and redaction critical studies has been to solve the problem that in Judges 13–16 Samson is depicted as a Nazirite, a military savior, a charismatic leader, the servant (of God) and a judge.[2] Scholars argue that there are several tensions between these different ways of characterizing Samson. Informative is Witte's article where these problems have been listed (see note 2). Especially scholars have argued

---

[1] A good survey of earlier literature can be found in Jichan Kim, *The Structure of the Samson Cycle* (Kampen: Kok Pharos, 1993), 1–114; David M. Gunn, *Judges* (Malden: Blackwell, 2005), 172–230. Gunn has even regarded ancient Jewish and Christian reception of the story. Concerning rabbinical readings of Samson narrative see Richard G. Marks, "Dangerous Hero: Rabbinic Attitudes Toward Legendary Warriors," *HUCA* 54 (1983): 181–94; Ronit Nikolsky, "Rabbinic Discourse about Samson: Continuity and Change between the Tannaitic Culture to the Amoraic," in *Samson: Hero or Fool? The Many Faces of Samson*, ed. Erik M. M. Eynikel and Tobias Nicklas, Themes in Biblical Narrative 17 (Leiden: Brill, 2014), 101–18. For Rashi's way of interpreting the Samson story see Jonathan Cohen, "On Martyrs and Communal Interests: Rabbinic Readings of the Samson Narrative," *Review of Rabbinic Judaism* 11.1 (2008): 49–72. Concerning Christian interpretations see John R. Franke, *Ancient Christian Commentary on Scripture, Old Testament IV: Joshua, Judges, Ruth, 1-2 Samuel* (Downers Grove: InterVarsity, 2005); Erasmus Gass and Boaz Zissu, "Sel'a 'Etam and Samson Traditions, from the Biblical to the Byzantine Periods," in *Man Near a Roman Arch: Studies presented to Prof. Yoram Tsafrir*, ed. Leah Di Segni, Yizhar Hirshfeld, Joseph Patrich and Rina Talgam (Jerusalem: The Israel Exploration Society, 2009), 25*–46*.

[2] For this see especially Markus Witte, "Wie Simson in den Kanon kam: Redaktions-geschichtliche Beobachtungen zu Jdc 13–16," *ZAW* 112 (2000): 526–49. Witte has also made a good survey of different opinions concerning the outcome of the Samson narrative. See further J. Cheryl Exum, "The Many Faces of Samson," in Erik M.M. Eynikel and Tobias Nicklas, *Samson: Hero or Fool?*, 13–31.

that Samson's behavior does not fit well with the Nazirite law (Num 6).[3] This tension has led many scholars to conclude that the original core of the Samson story is to be found only in Judges 14–15, and opinions have often been presented that the story was integrated in the Deuteronomistic History only at the post-Deuteronomistic stage, after which different redactional layers (detectable mainly in Judges 13 and 16) were edited. One of these redactional layers is the Nazirite layer.[4]

In addition to redaction-critical studies, there is another methodological way to approach Judges 13–16, where the focus is laid on the interpretation of the biblical story in its final form. In these approaches, common themes and patterns in the story are used to argue that different parts are integrated.[5] By approaching the story from this angle, Cheryl Exum, for example, argues that Judg 16 parallels the structure and the content of Judg 14–15.[6] James Crenshaw deals with the whole story as one literary unit and argues that "its purpose is two-fold: to provide entertainment and to offer negative example. The story entertains and teaches."[7] In his analysis, Crenshaw sees that "the Samson saga consists of four episodes, each illustrating a different relationship between Samson and a woman."[8] The first woman in the story is Samson's mother and, therefore, Judg 13 is

---

[3] See these problems more closely in Hermann-Josef Stipp, "Simson der Nasiräer," *VT* 45 (1995): 337–69.

[4] See Witte, "Wie Simson in den Kanon kam," and literature referred within. Very influential in this point has been the article of Hartmut Gese, "Die ältere Simsonüberlieferung (Richter c. 14–15)," *ZThK* 82 (1985): 261–80. Gese's view that the Samson story was added later to the Deuteronomistic History is presented already in Martin Noth, *Überlieferungsgeschichtliche Studien* (Halle: Niemeyer, 1943), 61. See further Thomas Meurer, *Die Simson-Erzählungen: Studien zu Komposition und Entstehung, Erzähltechnik und Theologie von Ri 13–16*, BBB 130 (Berlin: Philo, 2001) where he also concludes that the core of the story can be found in Judges 14–15.

[5] For this question see e.g. Joseph Blenkinsopp, "Structure and Style in Judges 13–16," *JBL* 82 (1963): 65–76.

[6] J. Cheryl Exum, "Aspects of Symmetry and Balance in the Samson Saga," *JSOT* 19 (1981): 3–29. Exum's approach in its main points is followed in Elie Assis, "The Structure and Meaning of the Samson Narratives (Jud. 13–16)," in Erik M.M. Eynikel and Tobias Nicklas, *Samson: Hero or Fool?*, 1–12.

[7] James L. Crenshaw, *Samson: A Secret Betrayed, a Vow Ignored* (Atlanta: John Knox Press, 1978), 64.

[8] Crenshaw, *Samson*, 98.

an integral part of the story, and as Crenshaw sees it: "The story combines tragic and comic elements with tremendous effect. Samson's penchant for foreign women drove him closer and closer to dark death, until at least he led an innocent lad into the same darkness."[9]

In addition to the different literary theoretical approaches, the figure of Samson has also been explained in cross-cultural studies. Samson has been related to different ancient Near Eastern mythological figures and the argument has been proposed that these parallels could explain his abnormal behavior.[10]

I will now argue that the Samson story is a part of an older story complex in the pre-exilic version of the book of Judges. This viewpoint helps us, in my view, to understand certain tensions in the story as well as Samson's abnormal features (e.g. his role as a Nazirite).

The Pre-Deuteronomistic Chronological System and the Samson Story

"In the four hundred and eightieth year after the Israelites came out of Egypt, in the fourth year of Solomon's reign over Israel, in the month of Ziv, the second month, he began to build the temple of Yahweh." So begins the account of the temple building in 1 Kgs 6:1. Scholars usually regard this period of 480 years as belonging to Deuteronomistic or even post-Deuteronomistic redaction.[11] In my book *Guide to Biblical Chronology*, I discussed this dating in 1 Kgs 6:1 and argued that it may, after all, be part of the pre-Deuteronomistic tradition.[12] *Firstly*, the verse refers to an old Canaanite name of the month Ziv, indicating that the Deuteronomist apparently based his dating on an older source. *Secondly* and more importantly, the period of 480 years does not correspond to the chrono-

---

[9] Crenshaw, *Samson*, 150.

[10] See e.g. Pnina Galpaz-Feller, *Samson: The Hero and the Man: The Story of Samson* (Judges 13–16), Bible in History (Bern: Peter Lang, 2006); Gregory Mobley, *Samson and the Liminal Hero in the Ancient Near East*, LHBOTS 453 (London: T & T Clark, 2006). Note also A. Smythe Palmer's earlier study, *The Samson-Saga and Its Place in Comparative Religion* (London: Sir Isac Pitman & Sons, 1913).

[11] For this see e.g. Jeremy Hughes, *Secrets of the Times: Myth and History in Biblical Chronology*, JSOTSup 66 (Sheffield: Sheffield Academic Press 1990), esp. 32–33.

[12] Antti Laato, *Guide to Biblical Chronology* (Sheffield: Sheffield Phoenix Press, 2015), 98–105.

logical framework which the Deuteronomist presents in his historical work.

I argued that the 300-year period mentioned in Judg 11:26 was part of the pre-Deuteronomistic 480-year period and that the actual wandering of the Israelite people in the desert was substantially shorter than 40 years (a figure presented often in the Hebrew Bible, Deut 2:7; Josh 5:6; Ps 95:10; Amos 2:10; 5:25). The alternative tradition of wandering (which in my construction included a shorter stay in the desert, i.e. six years) would correspond to the positive version of the exodus tradition which appears in Hos 2:16–17; Jer 2:2, 6 and Isa 40–55 as well as in the tradition behind Num 21:10–30.[13] In this alternative tradition the wandering in the desert is presented not a punishment but rather Yahweh's act of salvation.

My construction implies that the figures of 480 years in 1 Kgs 6:1 and 300 years in Judg 11:26 are part of pre-Deuteronomistic chronology. These two figures contradict the present form of the Deuteronomistic chronology, but enough material remains to present a hypothesis as to how these figures together provided a framework to present an older more coherent chronological system. This being the case, there is a plausible option that 1 Kgs 6:1 and Judg 11:26 are parts of an ancient chronological scheme used in pre-exilic royal archives to connect the past history of Israel (the exodus and the settlement) to the chronology of the monarchy.[14] These results imply that the Samson story was a part of the pre-exilic version of the Deuteronomistic Historical work which was subsequently reworked during the time of the exile.[15] If this is the case, then the Samson story must be examined from the viewpoint that its pre-

---

[13] Concerning Num 21:10–30, see Antti Laato, "The Book of the Wars of Yahweh," in *From Text to Persuasion: Festschrift in Honour of Professor Lauri Thurén on the Occasion of his 60th Birthday*, ed. Anssi Voitila, Niilo Lahti, Mikael Sundkvist and Lotta Valve, Publications of the Finnish Exegetical Society 123 (Helsinki: The Finnish Exegetical Society, 2021), 21–43.

[14] Historically seen, this 480-year period cannot be related to the absolute chronology. It is a well- known fact that the historical period in Canaan during the 1300s is well-documented by the Amarna Letters which indicate that the Israelites were not yet in the land. It is therefore possible to date the exodus from Egypt only to the 13th century BCE. This fact implies that the biblical chronology in the pre-monarchic time cannot be regarded as historically reliable, and it is impossible to build any historical conclusions on that material.

[15] Baruch Halpern and André Lemaire, "The Composition of Kings," in Halpern and Lemaire, *The Books of Kings*, 123–53.

Deuteronomistic version was edited and updated during the time of the exile.[16]

The chronological system based on 480 years in 1 Kgs 6:1 is not the only indication in the Deuteronomistic History that its writer knew older chronological traditions. In my book *Guide to Biblical Chronology* I argue that the synchronic chronology in the books of Kings originates, in its essential details, from older sources which were based on data of the royal archive. The Deuteronomist knew these sources and mainly followed them, but he could also have made his own versions of them. This phenomenon leads us to the methodological problem of how to interpret Deuteronomistic History which may contain 1) traces of older sources, possibly updated linguistically [= old material], 2) textual material based on older sources but formulated by the Deuteronomist [= paraphrases of older material] and 3) new material written by the Deuteronomist [= theological reflections].[17]

The Samson Story in Its Pre-Deuteronomistic Context

Yairah Amit has proposed that the Samson story is a part of the composition of the book of Judges which aims at arguing that Israel needed a righteous king who could establish law and order in the land.[18] According to her, the core of the Book, i.e. Judg 3–16, can be divided in the following way:[19]

---

[16] For the view that the Samson story has a pre-Deuteronomistic version see especially Yairah Amit, *Judges: Introduction and Commentary* [Hebrew] (Mikar LeYisra'el, Tel Aviv: Am Oved 1999), 3–22, esp. 11–13; eadem, *The Book of Judges: The Art of Editing* (Leiden: Brill 1999); eadem, *History and ideology: An Introduction to Historiography in the Hebrew Bible* (Sheffield: Sheffield Academic Press 1999), 34–41. Note also Gregory T.K. Wong, *Compositional Strategy of the Book of Judges: An Inductive, Rhetorical Study*, VTSup 111 (Leiden: Brill, 2006).

[17] Cf. my similar approach to understanding the Abraham story in Genesis in Antti Laato, "Abraham Story in Genesis and the reigns of David and Solomon," in *Abraham's Family: A Network of Meaning in Judaism, Christianity, and Islam*, ed. Lukas Bormann, WUNT 415 (Tübingen: Mohr Siebeck, 2018), 33–58.

[18] Amit, *Art of Editing*.

[19] Amit, *Art of Editing*, 45.

Judge	Sin	Punishment	Crying out	Salvation	Quiet
Othniel	3:7	3:8	3:9a	3:9b–10	3:11
Ehud	3:12a	3:12b–14	3:15a	3:15b–30a	3:30b
Deborah/Barak	4:1	4:2	4:3	4:5–5:31ab	5:31c
Gideon	6:1	6:2–6a	6:6b–10	6:11–8:28b	8:28c
Tola	8:33–35	9:1–57	***	10:1	10:2–5
Jephthah	10:6	10:7–9	10:10–16	10:17–12:6	12:7–15
Samson	13:1a	13:1b	***	13:2–16:31	***

Amit argues that old traditions of the judges were used in the composition of Judg 3–16 in order to demonstrate that they were disappointing rulers.[20] This concerns the Samson story in particular.[21] The last cycle in the core of the composition of Judg 3–16 breaks the pattern at two points because both the "crying out" and "quiet" motifs are lacking. Therefore, the composition "prepares the ground for the concluding description of anarchy during the period of the judges. Samson is in practice an anarchistic judge who surrenders to his impulses, and the period of his rule is a complementary preparation for the description of anarchy in chapters 17–18."[22]

According to Amit, all central elements of the Deuteronomistic pro-gramme, including, for example, the centralization of the cult, the existence of the law book, the status of the prophet predicting future events, and history as a realization of God's plan, are not even alluded to in the book of Judges. Therefore, "the book of Judges is not part of the Deuteronomistic complex but preceded the composition of this litera-ture."[23] Amit dates the composition of Judg 3–16 with its introduction Judg 1–2[24] and conclusion 17–18 to the period after the collapse of the northern kingdom, i.e. to the reign of Hezekiah.

---

[20] Amit, *Art of Editing*, 85–92.

[21] Amit, *Art of Editing*, 90–92.

[22] Amit, *Art of Editing*, 92. See also Amit's detailed analysis on pp. 266–309.

[23] Amit, *Art of Editing*, 366–67; the quotation is from p. 367.

[24] Amit (*Art of Editing*, 364–67) argues that phraseology reminiscent of the so-called Deuteronomistic literature can be found in Judges 1–2 but that the phraseology is not unique for Deuteronomy and its school. Therefore, the borrowing is not from Deuteronomy to Judges but *vice versa*.

According to Amit, four themes illustrate the ways in which Judg 1–18 was linked to the time of Hezekiah: 1) Judg 1–18 argues that the monarchy was needed. This implies a positive picture of the king—something which suits well in the reign of Hezekiah. Amit refers especially to 2 Kgs 18–20; Isa 9:5–6; Prov 25:1. 2) Judg 1–18 gives no room for prophecy. There is no prophet who could predict the future events. On the other hand, Hos 12:14 indicates that the followers of Moses i.e. the judges have been character-ized as prophets indicating that the judges have been colored by prophetic features. 3) There is no hint in Judges 1–18 that the cult would have been centralized. Instead the texts often refer to the removal of Canaanite elements from the Israelite cult and this fits in well with the reign of Hezekiah. Hezekiah's new religious policy was regarded as divinely inspired and is contrasted with the cult of Dan which received divine punishment as expressed in Judg 18:30. 4) The image of God in Judges 1–18 is less sensitive to the abstract concept of God.[25]

In spite of the fact that Amit puts the Samson story in its literary and editorial context she emphasizes that it contains "numerous tensions between the fashioning of his figure as a lustful, loner hero, and his presentation as a messenger of the Lord intended to save his people. In Amit's view "these tensions help him to construct, at the end of the book, a figure of a judge who, at one and the same time, justifies disappointment in the leadership of the judges and explains the significance of the effect of deliverance."[26]

In my view, Amit's analysis provides a good starting-point to under-stand the Samson story in its literary context as well as the peculiar characters that make it an independent tradition among the Hebrew Bible. It helps us to see that the abnormal features in the story must be approached from a tradition-historical perspective rather than from different hypothetical redactional layers. This means that we must evaluate the Samson tradition from the viewpoint that it contains older pre-exilic traditions which have been updated and commented on theologically in the present form of the Deuteronomistic History. This being the case, the tensions which we find, for example, in Samson's

---

[25] Amit, *Art of Editing*, 375–80.

[26] Amit, *Art of Editing*, 308.

abnormal behavior as a Nazirite, may be rooted in the fact that pre-exilic traditions conflict with later established Nazirite law in the book of Numbers. I shall now turn to the four abnormal topics mentioned at the beginning of the article.[27]

Samson's Abnormal Birth

Samson's birth is announced formally with a typical birth oracle (Judg 13:3,5; cf. Gen 16:11-12; Isa 7:14-17) which, in its fullest form, contains four elements: 1) An announcement of the pregnancy and the birth of the child often begins with *hinnê*. 2) The phrase indicating the name which will be given to the child. 3) The phrase *kî* which explains the meaning of the name. 4) Some details about the child and his/her significance. In the story of Samson, elements 1 and 4 are present. More importantly, the story indicates that the birth of Samson was a miracle because the wife of Manoah was barren (Judg 13:3) and this state of condition is used in the story as an indication that the child himself would become an extraordinary or abnormal man.

Samson's abnormal birth can be compared with other birth stories of unusual men who played an important role in the salvation history of God (e.g. Isaac and the continuity of Abraham's family; Moses and the salvation of Israel). The abnormal birth of Samson is related to his being a Nazirite, a topic which is clearly interpreted in the story of Samson in a way which differs from the legal instructions of Num 6. I shall now turn to this problem.

In later Jewish interpretive tradition Samson's birth has been understood as being a miracle. LAB 42 contains an interesting discussion between Manoah and Eluma, the parents of Samson, who quarreled because they had no offspring.[28] They had different opinions as to who was sterile—a discussion which clearly shows that the blame was not

---

[27] For an important reception historical survey of the Samson story cf. Erik M.M. Eynikel and Tobias Nicklas, *Samson: Hero or Fool?*

[28] Concerning the reconstruction of the Hebrew Vorlage behind *LAB* note the important discussion in Howard Jacobson, *A Commentary on Pseudo-Philo's Liber Antiquitatum Biblicarum: With Latin Text and English Translation*, Volume One and Two, AGJU 31 (Leiden: Brill, 1996).

always put on the woman. Eluma receives a divine message that she is barren, but that God will now give her a son. When the story continues in LAB 43 it is noted that the Lord was with the child, indicating that something abnormal and extraordinary had taken place.[29]

In a similar way, Josephus emphasizes that the birth of Samson was "in accordance with God's providential care" and "a child was to be born who would be handsome and of extraordinary vigor" (*Ant.* 5.277).[30] What is interesting, an additional aspect in Josephus's account is Manoah's (or as Josephus renders his name *Manōkhēs* or *Manōkhos*) jealousy toward his beautiful wife—a detail which is not recounted in the book of Judges.[31] The aim of such an addition in the story was to give a reason for the angel appearing once again, in this case to Manoah informing him of the birth of the child (*Ant.* 5.276–284).

The name of Samson is never explained in the book of Judges. A common theory is that it is a diminutive from the Hebrew word *šemeš*, "sun."[32] If that is the case, the end of the Deborah Song (Judg 5:31) explains the meaning of the name well: "So perish all your enemies, O Lord! But may your friends be like the sun as it rises in its might." The whole Samson

---

[29] It is worth noting that *LAB* 43.8 refers to Samson's burial and, as in Judg 16:31, the reference is made to his brothers indicating that Eluma apparently gave birth to several other sons. Such a motif is typical in the Hebrew Bible (see e.g. the case of Hannah in 1 Sam 1–2). See further Shaul Bar, "The Death of Samson," *OTE* 33/1 (2020): 162–74.

[30] See Josephus's text on Samson in Christopher Begg, ed., *Flavius Josephus, Translation and Commentary: Vol. 4, Judean Antiquities 5–7* (Leiden: Brill, 2005). See further the interpretation of Josephus's version of Samson in Louis H. Feldman, "Josephus' Version of Samson," *JSJ* 19.2 (1988): 171–214; Mark Roncace, "Another Portrait of Josephus' Portrait of Samson," *JSJ* 35.2 (2004): 185–207; Tessel M. Jonquière, "Of Valour and Strength: The Samson Cycle in Josephus' Work: Jewish Antiquities 5.276–317," in Erik M.M. Eynikel and Tobias Nicklas, *Samson: Hero or Fool?*, 119–28.

[31] This detail is also mentioned in Ambrosius's Letter to Vigilius (PL 16:1024–36). Ambrosius knew this tradition from Josephus, and he regarded it as dubious. See its English translation in *Saint Ambrose: Letters, 1–91*, transl. Mary Melchior Beyenka, The Fathers of the Church 26 (Washington: Catholic University of America Press, 1954), 174–89.

[32] For this see especially Erasmus Gass, *Die Ortsnamen des Richterbuchs in historischer und redaktioneller Perspektive*, ADPV 35 (Wiesbaden: Harrassowitz, 2005), 360. Gass mentions two other possibilities to derive the name: 1) postbiblical and Aramaic verb *šmš* means "serve" (cf. *LAB* 42.3); 2) the root *šmm* or *šmn* meaning "be strong" (cf. Josephus, *Ant.* 5.285). For these alternatives, see also Witte, "Wie Simson in den Kanon kam," 539.

story indicates in which ways the hero will "be like the sun as it rises in its might." In later Jewish reception history, Samson's name has been explained in different ways. LAB 42.3 states that the name is related to "holiness": "For this one will be dedicated to your Lord." Feldman regards it as possible that the author of LAB related the name of Samson to the verb "*shimesh*, 'to minister' or 'to serve'" and derived the meaning "holy" or "dedicated" from there.[33] Another possibility is that the "holy" has been taken from a textual tradition reflected in Codex Vaticanus where the Hebrew word for Nazirite in Judg 16:17 corresponds to the Greek expression *hagios theou,* but in Judg 13:5 the transcription *nazir* is used—something which may indicate an early interpretation of the Nazirite status of Samson or a tradition of his "nickname." On the other hand, Josephus explains Samson's name as meaning "strong" (*Ant.* 5.285). The background for this may be a Jewish tradition later reflected also in the rabbinical way where the name Samson is related to Ps 84:12 and his power is compared with that of God. As God is "Sun" and "shield" to Israel so was also Samson (b. Soṭah 10a). The rabbinical explanation is interesting because it still maintains a relationship between the name of Samson and "Sun."

Early Jewish reception history indicates that the birth of Samson was regarded as an abnormal event. The sterile woman became pregnant according to the promise given in the divine vision. The abnormal birth was then followed by the quite abnormal life of Samson.

Samson as an Abnormal Nazirite

In current research scholars have often argued that the older story of Samson has been integrated into the priestly Nazirite law in Num 6.[34] However, it is significant that the most apparent linguistic parallels to Num 6 concern Judg 13:5, 7 but the objections to drink alcohol is not given to the son who will be born but rather to his mother. It is said in Judg 13:4–5: "Now be careful not to drink wine or strong drink, or to eat

---

[33] Feldman, "Josephus' Version of Samson," 180–81, n. 21.
[34] So e.g. Stipp, "Simson, der Nasiräer," 337–69; Witte, "Wie Simson in den Kanon kam," esp. 543–44.

anything unclean, for you shall conceive and bear a son. No razor is to come on his head, for the boy shall be a Nazirite to God from birth. It is he who shall begin to deliver Israel from the hand of the Philistines." And further again in Judg 13:7: "he said to me, 'You shall conceive and bear a son. So then drink no wine or strong drink, and eat nothing unclean, for the boy shall be a Nazirite to God from birth to the day of his death.'" The only rule concerning Samson was that no razor was to come to his head (Judg 13:5; 16:17). Indeed, his long hair is an essential theme in Judges 16 and therefore also an integral part of Judg 13:4–5, 7.

In my view, this explanation model of the late Nazirite redaction where the non-Nazirite Samson has been made into a Nazirite is riddled with problems. Why would a priestly oriented editor want to choose Samson as a good candidate to be a Nazirite? Would not such an editing process be quite strange because the behavior of Samson cannot be related in any meaningful way to the laws which restrict the Nazirite's life as presented in Num 6?[35] *First*, Samson kills the lion and eats the honey from its dead body (contra Lev 11:24–25; Num 6:6–7). *Second*, Samson touches unclean animals (foxes) which makes him unclean (Lev 11:27; Num 6:8). *Third*, Samson's intimate relations with foreign women are also problematic in the light of the Nazirite's promise to be holy for God (Num 6:8). *Fourth*, Samson's way of celebrating at banquets with alcoholic drinks was strictly forbidden for a Nazirite (Num 6:2–4). *Finally*, if the priestly-oriented editor wanted to make Samson a Nazirite, he should have applied the restriction on drinking alcohol to apply to the boy too, not only his mother. I regard such a redactional development of the story as highly improbable. A better alternative is to assume that Samson was already regarded as a Nazirite in an older version of the story. In that case the semantic field of the term "Nazirite" was different to that assumed in Num 6. From this perspective, the traditions of Samson and those of the Nazirite law in Num 6 were developed independently. Only later, when the complete books

---

[35] For this see especially Blenkinsopp, "Structure and Style," 66. Even though Cheryl Exum, "The Theological Dimension of the Samson Saga," *VT* 33 (1983): 30–45, esp. 31–33, criticizes Blenkinsopp's remarks the fact is that Blenkinsopp's remarks should be taken seriously when discussing the Nazirite edition of the Samson story. Why on earth would someone interested in Nazirite theology have wanted to make Samson a Nazirite? The whole story is against such a connection.

were interrelated in the canon, were the problems concerning Samson's Nazirite status discussed, as evidenced by the early reception history.[36]

Some scholars have proposed that the term Nazirite could have been used for the warriors or charismatic leaders who were dedicated in the Yahweh war institution. If this were the case, such an (older) understanding of the Nazirite institution could easily be related to the Samson story. Ernst Zuckschwerdt has shown that both the Samuel and Samson stories contain similarities. It is said that both mothers did not drink alcohol (1 Sam 1:15). In addition, the birth story of Samuel refers to no razor ever touching the boy child (1 Sam 1:11). Also worth noting is the Septuagint version of 1 Sam 1:11 where the wording is more clearly associated with the rules of the Nazirite institution. It is also of note that in the Hebrew version of Sir 46:13 Samuel was called a Nazirite (see also m. Naz 9:5 with reference to 1 Sam 1:11).[37]

The term *nāzîr* is derived from the verb *nāzar*, "dedicate, consecrate," and could suit well in military contexts, too. This becomes clear from Deut 23:10–15 which contains older rules concerning the purity of the military camps. Deut 20 contains other rules and among them are stipulations that all who are discouraged should be sent away. This being the case the idea of purity and a dedication to struggle are essential in warfare. There are not many cases outside Num 6 in the Hebrew Bible where the term *nāzîr* has been used, and even in those cases it is difficult to know whether the word means "noble" or "prince" (i.e. one who has been dedicated, separated). Nevertheless, the term Nazirite has been related to Joseph twice in a context where Joseph is depicted as a great warrior. The first example is Gen 49:26 which contains an expression *ûleqodqōd nĕzîr 'eḥāyw*, "and on the head of the Nazirite of his brothers." The context of Gen 49:26 refers to Joseph as a great soldier (Gen 49:22–26). The same Hebrew expression is also used for Joseph in Deut 33:16, and even in its

---

[36] See e.g. Nikolsky, "Rabbinic Discourse about Samson," 104–05.

[37] Ernst Zuckschwerdt, "Zur literarischen Vorgeschichte des priesterlichen Nazir-Gesetzes (Num 6 1–8)," *ZAW* 88 (1976): 191–205. Concerning the relationship between Samson and Samuel episodes, see also Galpaz-Feller, *Samson: The Hero and the Man*, 46–50. See further the detailed survey of the Nazirite institution in early Jewish and Christian sources in Daniel Schumann, *Gelübde im antiken Judentum und frühesten Christentum*, Ancient Judaism and Early Christianity 111 (Leiden: Brill, 2018), 132–301.

literary context Joseph is depicted as a great warrior who will destroy his enemies (Deut 33:17). Quite enigmatic is Lam 4:7 which describes the fatal fate of the group of Nazirites during the destruction of Jerusalem. Johan Renkema, however, argues that the reference there is made to "nobles" rather than "Nazirites."[38]

The expressions in Gen 49:26; Deut 33:16—assuming they do refer to Nazirites—may indicate that a typical feature of their outlook is concerned with their head because *qodqōd* has the connotation of "hairy head." Therefore, some scholars have proposed that the enigmatic expression *biprōaʿ pĕrāʿôt bĕYisrāʾēl* in Judg 5:2 may refer to the time when the Israelite soldiers had long hair: "When locks sprout out in Israel."[39] Such an interpretation would parallel nicely Samson's looks, whose long hair symbolized his willingness to consecrate himself as a warrior for Yahweh. If we approach the story of Samson from this tradition–historical perspective of the Yahweh war, then the connection between the long hair and Samson's warlike nature is in harmony. Samson became a great soldier with abnormal powers.

The Nazirite status of Samson was, in later reception history, related more clearly to Num 6, and consequently many problems then arose, and these are discussed especially in the rabbinical writings.[40] The tendency to relate Samson's Nazirite status to Num 6 can be detected already in LAB 42.3 and *Ant.* 5.278. Both Pseudo-Philo and Josephus reformulate the abstaining of alcohol and the uncleanness of the mother (Judg 13:4) to affect Samson too—as is clearly ordained in the Nazirite Law of Num 6.[41]

Samson's Abnormal Power

In the biblical story, Samson's unusual power is closely linked with the spirit of Yahweh (Judg 14:6; 15:14). Even the long hair plays a role here, but it is presented as an outer sign of the presence of the spirit of Yahweh (Judg 16:19). In the final and fatal struggle Samson's hair began to grow

---

[38] Johan Renkema, *Lamentations*, HCOT (Leuven: Peeters, 1998), 511–15.

[39] For this possibility see, e.g., Patrick Miller Jr., *The Divine Warrior in Early Israel* (Atlanta: SBL Press, 1973).

[40] For this see Nikolsky, "Rabbinic Discourse about Samson."

[41] For this see Jonquière, "Of Valour and Strength," 119–28.

again (Judg 16:22) but he also needed a prayer addressed to God in order to be able to destroy the Philistines (Judg 16:28; cf. also Judg 15:18–19). The story emphasizes that the outer sign of the long hair became visible on Samson's head and therefore his prayer to Yahweh was effective so that God remembered his servant and fulfilled his desire to be executed together with the Philistines.

The Samson story concentrates on the conflicts between Samson and the Philistines and here the hero's extraordinary power is emphasized. These aspects of the story play an important role in early Jewish reception history. This becomes especially evident in LAB 42–43.[42] An interesting detail is LAB 43.2–4 where Pseudo-Philo tells of a battle where Samson was locked in the city of the Philistines but went out from the gates of the city and used one gate as a weapon killing 25.000 men with it. It seems quite obvious that Judg 16:1–3 lurks behind this episode in LAB but was developed in such a way that Samson used not "a jawbone of a donkey" (as in Judg 15:9–17) but a city gate as a weapon! According to Jacobson, the text of LAB is probably corrupted because it does not match well with Judg 16:1–3.[43] However, it seems to me that this way of retelling Judg 16:1–3 was probably based on a midrashic development of the targum-like interpretation of the blessing of Dan in Gen 49:16–18 as depicted in the Samson mosaic in the synagogue of Huqoq.

Matthew J. Grey has published an informative and well documented article where he argues that pictures about Samson in the mosaics of synagogues (Huqoq and Wadi Hamam in Galilee) illustrate the positive role of Samson in Jewish apocalyptic and messianic hopes.[44] He emphasizes especially the role of Jacob's blessing of Dan in Gen 49:16–18 which in the Targum has been seen as referring to Samson.

---

[42] See Erkki Koskenniemi, *The Old Testament Miracle-Workers in Early Judaism*, WUNT 2/206 (Tübingen: Mohr Siebeck, 2005), 216–18.

[43] Jacobson, *Commentary on Pseudo-Philo's Liber Antiquitatum Biblicum*, 996.

[44] Matthew J. Grey, "'The Redeemer to Arise from the House of Dan': Samson, Apocalypticism, and Messianic Hopes in Late Antique Galilee," *JSJ* 44 (2013): 553–89.

Targum Neofiti Gen 49:16–18[45]

From those of the house of Dan *shall redemption arise, and a judge.* Together, *all* the tribes of *the sons of* Israel *shall obey him.* This shall be *the redeemer who is to arise from the house of* Dan; *he will be strong, exalted above all nations. He will be compared to the* serpent *that lies on* the *ground,* and to a venomous serpent *that lies in wait at the crossroads,* that bites the horses in the heels and *out of fear of it* the rider *turns around and* falls backward. *He is Samson bar Manoah, the dread of whom is upon his enemies and fear of whom is upon those who hate him. He goes out to war against those that hate him and kills kings together with rulers.*

Targum Pseudo-Jonathan Gen 49:16–18[46]

From those of the house of Dan *there shall arise a man who* will judge his people *with true judgments.* As one, the tribes of Israel will *obey him.* There will be *a man who will be chosen and who will arise from those of the house of* Dan. *He will be comparable to* the adder *that lies at the cross*roads and to the *heads of the* serpents that *lie in wait* by the path, biting the horses in the heel, and out of fear of it the rider falls, *turning* backwards. *Thus shall Samson, son of Manoah, kill all the warriors of the Philistines, both horsemen and foot soldiers. He will hamstring their horses and throw their riders backwards.*

These Targum renderings emphasize the role of Samson as one who struggles against Philistine horsemen and foot soldiers. In the mosaic of the synagogue of Wadi Hamam Samson is depicted as a big and strong man who tramples foot soldiers while one Philistine horseman escapes him. This scenario is probably related to the episode in Judg 15:15–17 where Samson kills Philistines with a jawbone.[47] However, as Grey has noted, the presence of the Philistine horseman indicates that the scene is also related to a targumic interpretation of Gen 49:16–18 (see translations

---

[45] See the translation in Martin McNamara, *The Targum Neofiti 1: Genesis,* The Aramaic Bible 1A (Edinburgh: Clark, 1992), 221–22. All details in the text not attested in the Masoretic text are in italics.

[46] See the translation in Michael Maher, *The Targum Pseudo-Jonathan: Genesis,* The Aramaic Bible 1B (Edinburgh: Clark, 1992), 160.

[47] See Shulamit Miller and Uzi Leibner, "The Synagogue Mosaic," in *Khirbet Wadi Ḥamam: A Roman-Period Village and Synagogue in the Lower Galilee,* ed. Uzi Leibner, Qedem Reports 13 (Jerusalem: The Hebrew University of Jerusalem, 2018), 144–86, esp. 157–64.

above).[48] A similar scene is found in the fragmentary mosaic of the synagogue at Huqoq where in one fragment Samson is depicted as bearing the gate (Judg 16:1–3 is clearly behind the picture) and the horseman is in another fragment.[49] If we assume that the mosaic scene in Huqoq has also received inspiration from Gen 49:16–18—as the horseman seems to indicate—then it is clear that Judg 16:1–3 has been understood as Samson having struggled with the Philistines and using a city gate as a weapon. This is exactly the interpretation found in *LAB* 43:2–4.

Josephus emphasizes Samson's abnormal power by interpreting the meaning of his name which signifies "strong" (*Ant.* 5.285).[50] However, Josephus is critically inclined towards the Samson story because he did not want to depict the heroic soldier as an ideal for his readers—a tendency which becomes understandable after the tragic end of the Jewish revolt. Christopher Begg has noted a demythologizing tendency in Josephus. Josephus does not retell any biblical passage where reference is made to God's spirit.[51] This tendency has also led to his omitting the prayer of Samson in Judg 16:28. While Begg does not speculate on the consequences of such an omission in Judg 16, Tessel M. Jonquière does have an opinion here. She notes that by mentioning only that Samson's hair had begun to grow back Josephus would have argued that "Samson's strength is his own."[52] This conclusion is hardly valid, however. As already mentioned, Josephus interprets the name of Samson as "strong" and calls him "a prophet" (*Ant.* 5.285). That Josephus had in mind that Samson's abnormal power was from God also becomes clear in *Ant.* 5.301–303. In that passage Josephus emphasized that Samson became proud and, therefore, God had to teach him with a strong thirst that he needed God's help.[53] Josephus's

---

[48] Grey, "Redeemer to Arise from the House of Dan," 575.

[49] See Jodi Magness et al., "The Huqoq Excavation Project: 2014–2017 Interim Report," *BASOR* 380 (2018): 61–131, esp. 87; Jodi Magness et al. "Inside the Huqoq Synagogue," *BAR* (May/June 2019): 24–38.

[50] For this strange etymology, see more closely Louis Feldman, *Josephus's Interpretation of the Bible*, HCS 27 (Berkeley: University of California Press, 1998), 465–66.

[51] See his comments in Begg, *Antiquities 5–8*, 72 n. 796 and 79 n. 891. So also Koskenniemi, *Old Testament Miracle-Workers*, 255–58.

[52] Jonquière, "Of Valour and Strength," 122.

[53] This important detail is also noted in Jonquière, "Of Valour and Strength," 121.

final characterization of Samson (*Ant.* 5.317) also contains positive elements when he refers to his "strength" which is a clear allusion to his name "strong" as Begg rightly notes.[54] This implies that Josephus regarded Samson's abnormal power as being a gift from God. Josephus's tendency to censor all references to the spirit of God may be explained better as Koskenniemi posits, that "the political side of the man was unpleasant to him."[55]

Samson as an Abnormal Lover with Foreign Women

Samson's affairs with foreign women are *expressis verbis* commented on in the story by his parents in a negative way (Judg 14:3): "Is there not a woman among your kin, or among all our people, that you must go to take a wife from the uncircumcised Philistines?" However, the storyteller, in turn, comments that Samson's parents did not understand what was going on in Samson's life (Judg 14:4): "His father and mother did not know that this was from the Lord; for he was seeking a pretext to act against the Philistines." The importance of Judg 14:4 in understanding the story of Samson is rightly emphasized by Stuart Foster.[56] That this verse was indeed regarded as one of the key passages in understanding the story of Samson becomes evident from Josephus's account in *Ant.* 5.286. Josephus tells how parents opposed Samson's marriage without understanding the plan of God: "Though they refused because she was not a compatriot he succeeded in betrothing the virgin, God viewing the marriage as advantageous to the Hebrews."

The story connects Samson's supernatural powers with his desire towards Philistine women. Therefore, the question is whether this erotic desire is an important constitutive element in the story. Because of Samson's problem with Philistine women, the Philistines themselves had to meet the anger of Samson (and Yahweh). Samson's riddle to the Philistine bestmen illustrates well the erotic dimension of the story (Judg 14:14): "Out of the eater came something to eat. Out of the strong came

---

[54] Begg, *Antiquities 5–8*, 79 n. 894.

[55] Koskenniemi, *Old Testament Miracle-Workers*, 258.

[56] Stuart J. Foster, "Judges 14:4—Yahweh Uses Samson to Provoke the Philistines," *OTE* 25/2 (2012): 292–302.

something sweet." Such a riddle told at a marriage festival contains the key terms "eat," "sweet" and "strong" all of which can be found elsewhere in the Hebrew Bible in erotic contexts (Prov 5:15–18; 30:20; Cant 4:12, 15).[57]

The solution to the riddle is related to Samson's supernatural behavior when he killed the lion earlier in the story. The lion episode was told in the story in order to illustrate how the Philistines desperately attempted to find a solution to something which they believed belonged to the erotic sphere, but which, in fact, illustrates another kind of potency of Samson, which quickly showed its fatal consequences against the Philistines.

Another woman with whom Samson fell in love was Delilah. She managed to cut Samson's hair and in this way eliminated his supernatural powers. The name Delilah is probably related to the Hebrew word "night." At least Delilah managed to close Samson's eyes forever so that he could no longer see the light of the sun. As previously mentioned, Samson's own name, in turn, may have been a diminutive of Shemesh, "the sun" and thus related to the Yahweh war as indicated in Judg 5:31: "So perish all your enemies, O Lord! But may your friends be like the sun as it rises in its might." As the story continued, Samson's hair began to grow again. The blinded Samson, who was not expected to show his power as "the sun which rises in its might," received new strength from God, who then demonstrated his mighty power over the Philistines by allowing the hero to kill many thousands of enemies. If the inhabitants of the Jebusite Jerusalem said to David "even the blind and the lame will turn you back" (2 Sam 5:6) but failed to show that their reliance was true, the situation in the case of Samson was different. As "the blind" unable to see and as "the lame" put in chains, Samson was able to kill the Philistines.

This analysis indicates that Samson's desperate and problematic love affairs with Philistine women, in fact, were the vehicles through which the catastrophe fell upon the Philistines. Such a story may very well have been an old Israelite version of a "James Bond" figure, who combined loving and killing potencies with each other. The story was an example of entertainment in old Israelite society and apparently for those reasons preserved in Jerusalem's royal archive.

---

[57] For this analysis, see especially Crenshaw, *Samson*, 99–120.

As time runs in the clock of history, the humorous aspects of the story were no longer stored in the cultural memory and Jews began to evaluate the life of Samson in negative terms as the reception history shows. Samson's life was understood in later reception as immoral and not being in line with the instructions of the Mosaic Torah. This critical attitude becomes especially clear in the Hellenistic sermon *De Sampsone*[58] and in rabbinical writings.[59] Josephus's evaluation of Samson also contains criticisms as becomes clear when he begins to deal with his affairs with Delilah (*Ant.* 5.306): "He had, however, already violated the ancestral [customs] and altered his own manner of life by his imitation of foreign ways, and this was the beginning of his calamity." Nonetheless, the final evaluation of Josephus reveals that Samson for him, after all, was a positive figure (*Ant.* 5.317): "He is deserving of admiration for his valor and strength as well as the sublimity of his death and for his wrath against his enemies until the end. His being captivated by women should be ascribed to human nature that easily gives in to offenses; in all other respects, the abundance of his valor is a testimony to him."

Conclusions

The aim of this article was to discuss Samson's abnormal behavior as it is presented in Judges 13–16, and how the story has been understood in early Jewish reception history. I argued that the chronology and the structure of the Deuteronomistic History indicate that the Samson story was an integral part of the pre-Deuteronomistic version. In that version Samson was regarded as a Nazirite who was a military hero consecrated to the Yahweh war. The key-verse in understanding the Samson story is Judg

---

[58] See this sermon in Folker Siegert, *Drei hellenistisch-jüdische Predigten: Ps.-Philon, "Über Jona" (Fragment) und "Über Simson". 2, Kommentar nebst Beobachtungen zur hellenistischen Vorgeschichte der Bibelhermeneutik*, WUNT 61 (Tübingen: Mohr Siebeck, 1992), 51–83.

[59] See especially Ronit Nikolsky, "Rabbinic Discourse about Samson," 105–08. Another critical aspect of Samson found in rabbinical literature is his heroism without the right loyalty. For this see also Richard G. Marks, "Dangerous Hero: Rabbinic Attitudes Toward Legendary Warriors," *HUCA* 54 (1983): 181–94. Feldman, "Josephus' Version of Samson," discusses several rabbinical passages and their critical attitude towards Samson.

14:4. Yahweh sought conflicts between the Philistines and Israelites through Samson's affairs with women.

Samson's abnormal behavior becomes visible in four different themes: 1 Samson's birth; 2 Samson as a Nazirite; 3 Samson's supernatural powers; 4 Samson's affairs with foreign women. While all four of these themes were an integral part of the Samson story and interpreted in a positive way, the later reception history shows an ambivalent attitude toward the story itself. Two of the themes of Samson's abnormal life in particular, (i.e. Samson as a Nazirite and his relationships with women) led to criticism of him in later reception history. On the other hand, Samson's superpowers continued to be a positive theme in the Jewish reception history. The blessing of Jacob in Gen 49:16–18 was related to Samson's abnormal power and this connection was probably also reflected in the mosaic iconography of the synagogues of Huqoq and Wadi Hamam.

The Deep Sleep of Adam and Abram in the Book of Jubilees

Topias K. E. Tanskanen

1 Introduction

The book of Jubilees is a treasure chest of early biblical interpretation of the books of Genesis and Exodus. The author[1] of this book, which was written around the 2nd century BCE,[2] uses and adapts different exegetical traditions connected to Genesis and Exodus, offers own exegesis on texts and has also added a chronological layout. The author, however, was not merely a collector of traditions: he used them for a specific purpose. He wanted to give a right interpretation of the book of Genesis.[3]

Given the intention of the author to portray the patriarchs—not least Jacob and Abraham—in the most favorable light, it is interesting to see how the author dealt with sections in Genesis and Exodus which may have been perplexing and even abnormal for the ancient reader of Genesis. In this article, I analyse how the author tackled with two instances of 'deep sleep' (תרדמה) in Genesis: The case of Adam (Gen 2:21) in Jubilees 3 and the case of Abram (Gen 15:12) in Jubilees 14.[4]

---

[1] The coherence of the work is currently disputed. See, e.g., the articles in *RevQ* 104 (2014) and James C. VanderKam, *Jubilees: A Commentary*, Hermeneia (Minneapolis: Fortress Press, 2018), 25–28. My own view agrees with that of VanderKam, namely that there was (mostly) one author.

[2] The dating of Jubilees is still a matter of dispute, but most of the scholars tend to agree that it was written during the 2nd century BCE. On different proposals for dating, see VanderKam, *Jubilees*, 28–38. For the purpose of this article, the precise dating of Jubilees is unnecessary.

[3] That is, the author did not intend to replace Genesis, but to accompany it in an authoritative way. See Hindy Najman, *Seconding Sinai: The Development of Mosaic Discourse in Second Temple Judaism*, JSJSup 77 (Leiden: Brill, 2003), 43–44, 47–50.

[4] See also the articles of Lukas Bormann and Eva-Maria Kreitschmann in this volume, 119–140 and 225–256.

Some methodological problems need to be raised first. Since only a fraction of the book survives in the original Hebrew in many different forms of manuscripts at Qumran, one needs to depend on ancient translations of Jubilees.[5] The book was first translated into Greek, but sadly this has not survived to us. From Greek, it was translated to Ge'ez (classical Ethiopic) and Latin. The work is preserved to us in full only in Ge'ez, of which over 50 mediaeval or later manuscripts have been identified to date. One fifth century CE Latin palimpsest preserves a third of the work we know from the Ethiopic Jubilees.[6] In the case of chapters 3 and 14, no versions have been preserved to us other than the Ethiopic Jubilees in the Ge'ez translation.

This leads to the problem of different layers of interpretation. It is often emphasized in translation studies that a translation is always an interpretation. This is also the case with what we call 'literal' translations, such as the Ethiopic Jubilees.[7] So, for example, if the words that are most probably used to interpret the original תרדמה of Genesis 2:21 and 15:12 differ on the Ge'ez layer of Jubilees, that interpretation is not always the same as the interpretation made on the Greek layer, not to mention it may differ from what the original Hebrew author of Jubilees meant. In other words, there are three different layers of interpretation (The Ge'ez translator of Greek, the Greek translator of Hebrew, and the Hebrew author who interpreted and rewrote Hebrew Genesis–Exodus) and it is only the last of these to which we have direct access.

---

[5] Not all of the Qumran manuscripts contained the whole work we call Jubilees. See Matthew P. Monger, "The Many Forms of Jubilees: A Reassessment of the Manuscript Evidence from Qumran and the Lines of Transmission of the Parts and Whole of Jubilees," *RevQ* 112 (2018): 191–211.

[6] Generally on the textual history of Jubilees, see VanderKam, *Jubilees*, 1–16; Matthew P. Monger, *4Q216: Rethinking Jubilees in the First Century BCE*, PhD. diss. (Oslo: MF Norwegian School of Theology, 2018), 48–75; and the articles on Jubilees in *Textual History of the Bible, vol 2: The Deuterocanonical Scriptures*, ed. Frank Feder and Matthias Henze (Leiden: Brill, 2020). On the new Ethiopic manuscripts, see further Ted Erho, "New Ethiopic Witnesses to Some Old Testament Pseudepigrapha," *BSOAS* 76.1 (2013): 75–97; on Latin, see the website of the *Jubilees Palimpsest Project*, https://jubilees.stmarytx.edu/ (checked 22/04/2021).

[7] On the 'literality' of the Ge'ez translation in comparison with the Hebrew fragments in Qumran, see James C. VanderKam, *Textual and Historical Studies in the Book of Jubilees*, HSS 14 (Missoula: Scholars Press, 1977), 18–101.

In order to dig through these layers of interpretation to get to the original Hebrew one, it is necessary to build a suitable model to see how the same kind of interpretation through the translations has been done. A suitable model for comparison can be built by seeing how Genesis 2:21 and 15:12 have been interpreted and translated from the Hebrew original (roughly the MT) through the Greek version (roughly the LXX) to the Ge'ez of the Ethiopic Old Testament.

Before this, however, in order to build a background for the reception of 'deep sleep' of Adam and Abram in Jubilees, a short survey of the connotations of תרדמה in the Hebrew Bible is offered.

2 תרדמה in the Hebrew Bible

The Hebrew noun תרדמה is found seven times in the Hebrew Bible. In 1 Samuel 26:12, David can act without Saul and his men noticing, because the deep sleep which had fallen upon them had rendered them unconscious. In Isaiah 29:10, God had poured a 'spirit of deep sleep' (רוח תרדמה) upon Israel which put their prophets and seers out of commission, so they were unable to act. A negative view of 'deep sleep' is also found in Proverbs 19:15.

On the other hand, the book of Job seems to propagate the idea that the state of תרדמה is precisely the state in which God visits the human (Job 4:12–21; 33:14–18). In Job 4 this state of תרדמה is when nocturnal visions happen, and it also causes fear (4:14 פחד ורעדה / φρίκη καὶ τρόμος / *fərhat, dəngāḍē wa-rāʿad*[8]). The same aspect of fear caused by the visitation of God is also found in 33:16 (אז יגלה אזן אנשים ובמסרם יחתם / τότε ἀνακαλύπτει νοῦν ἀνθρώπων, ἐν εἴδεσιν φόβου τοιούτοις αὐτοὺς ἐξεφόβησεν / *wa-sobēhā yəkaśśət ləbbo la-sabʾ kama yərʾay gərmā wa-yəfrāh*) although there the fear is more related to the warnings uttered by God so that humans would

---

[8] The transliteration/transcription of Ge'ez is according to the SBL Handbook of Style and Thomas O. Lambdin, *Introduction to Classical Ethiopic (Ge'ez)*, HSS 24 (Missoula: Scholars Press, 1978; repr. Winona Lake: Eisenbrauns, 2006). On the challenges of transcribing Ge'ez and different systems of transcription, see Maria Bulakh, "Some Problems of transcribing Geez," in *150 years after Dillmann's Lexicon: Perspectives and Challenges of Ge'ez Studies*, ed. Alessandro Bausi, Supplement to Aethiopica; International Journal of Ethiopian and Eritrean Studies 5 (Wiesbaden: Harrassowitz, 2016), 103–37.

turn away from evil (33:17). The use of תרדמה in a positive sense in Job and its connexion with vision, the visitation of God and fear makes it a suitable background for the interpretation of תרדמה in Genesis.

The verb רדם in niphal is found seven times in the Hebrew Bible (Judg 4:21; Jonah 1:5, 6; Ps 76:7; Prov 10:5; Dan 8:18; 10:9–10). The unconscious aspect of 'deep sleep' is found in Judg 4:21; Jonah 1:5–6 and Prov 10:5. Daniel, on the other hand fell into a sleep due to the magnificence of the visions he saw but was then subsequently raised up again and shaken (awake?) (Dan 8:18; 10:9–10).[9]

To conclude, תרדמה can be either positive or negative. It causes either total unconsciousness or makes a visitation of God possible.

3 Genesis 2:21 and 15:12 in the LXX and in the Ethiopic Old Testament

Since the Ethiopic Old Testament (most probably including Jubilees) was translated by Christians during the Aksumite Era (300–700 CE), and presumably from a Greek version, it is important to investigate two translational phases: Hebrew => Greek; and Greek => Ge'ez, or actually *vice versa*. This task becomes somewhat complicated because the textual tradition of the Ethiopic Old Testament has had its fair share of different phases too.[10] The initial findings of the Textual History of the Ethiopic Old

---

[9] In the case of Eth Dan 8:18 and 10:9 the verb *dangaḍku* in Q perfect 1st singular is used along with G *wadaqqu* "I fell."

[10] See Daniel Assefa et al., "The Textual History of the Ethiopic Old Testament Project (THEOT): Goals and Initial Findings," *Textus* 29 (2020): 80–110. Scholars have discussed whether there was also a Syriac or even Hebrew *Vorlage* in use before the Solomonic reformation in the Middle Ages, from which period our extant manuscripts derive. On different opinions among older scholarship, see Edward Ullendorff, *Ethiopia and the Bible*, The Schweich Lectures of the British Academy 1968 (London: Oxford University Press, 1968), 31–62. Ullendorff is of the opinion that the situation was much more complex than is often thought, and that the Greek, Syriac and Hebrew influences were already there during the Aksumite Period. Recently, Michael A. Knibb, *Translating the Bible: The Ethiopic Version of the Old Testament*, The Schweich Lectures of the British Academy 1995 (Oxford: Oxford University Press, 1999), 1–46, argued convincingly that the Old Testament was translated almost exclusively from Greek sources. He writes that some Syriac influence during the Aksumite period is possible too, though unlikely.

Testament Project (THEOT) show that three distinct phases can be discerned in the textual history of the Ethiopic Old Testament:

(1) A distinct supercluster can be formed from earliest manuscripts from 14th to 16th centuries, within which two forms may compete. One of them attempts to improve the other ("Transitional Text").[11]

(2) A distinct number of the younger manuscripts forms a second supercluster, in which the 16th and 17th century manuscripts form a major subcluster ("Standardized Text"), which often has a connection to the "Transitional Text" form.[12]

(3) A third cluster is found in the 19th and 20th century manuscripts ("Textus Receptus") which may have distinctive readings to the "Standardized Text."[13]

Contact with the Hebrew (MT) text form is sporadic and found in younger manuscripts. Most contacts are via daughter translations (Arabic).[14] This means, too, that where the Ge'ez version is distinct from the LXX, it may actually stem from a later version in textual history. Although important for textual historical considerations, this does not help our survey here when trying to create a suitable model to understand possible translational choices the translator(s) faced for the text of Jubilees.

I now offer an analysis of the MT, LXX and Ethiopic versions of Genesis 2:21 and 15:12. This forms a background to our investigation of Jubilees 3 and 14, at least in terms of penetrating beneath the Ge'ez layer of the Ethiopic Jubilees.

3.1 Genesis 2:21

MT	LXX	Ethiopic OT
ויפל יהוה אלהים תרדמה על האדם ויישן ויקח אחת מצלעתיו ויסגר בשר תחתנה	καὶ ἐπέβαλεν ὁ θεὸς ἔκστασιν ἐπὶ τὸν Αδαμ, καὶ ὕπνωσεν· καὶ ἔλαβεν μίαν τῶν πλευρῶν αὐτοῦ	*wa-fannawa ʾəgziʾabḥēr dəqqāsa lāʿla ʾadām wa-noma wa-našʾa ʾaḥada ʾəm-ʿaṣma gabohu wa-*

---

[11] Assefa et al., "Textual History," 87–88.
[12] Assefa et al., "Textual History," 89.
[13] Assefa et al., "Textual History," 89–90.
[14] Assefa et al., "Textual History," 90–91, 107–08.

Topias K. E. Tanskanen

	καὶ ἀνεπλήρωσεν σάρκα ἀντ' αὐτῆς.	mal'a šəgā makāno

תרדמה in the LXX is rendered as ἔκστασις, but in Ge'ez as *dəqqās* 'sleep, slumber, drowsiness.'[15] Here, the meanings of the words differ greatly between the LXX and Ethiopic versions. *Dəqqās* is used for example in Eth Ps 131:4 (LXX Ps 131:4 νυσταγμός; MT Ps 132:4 תמונה)[16] and Luke 9:32 (ὕπνος).[17]

It is possible, however, that the Greek word behind the Ge'ez translation may be different. Symmachus has κάρος 'heavy sleep' and some other Greek witnesses ὕπνος.[18] It may be that the Greek *Vorlage* of the Ethiopic OT has had a different reading here, or that the Ethiopic OT was modified later with the help of other witnesses.[19]

3.2 Genesis 15:12

MT	LXX	Ethopic OT
ויהי השמש לבוא ותרדמה נפלה על–אברם והנה אימה חשכה גדלה נפלת עליו	περὶ δὲ ἡλίου δυσμὰς ἔκστασις ἐπέπεσεν τῷ Αβραμ, καὶ ἰδοὺ φόβος σκοτεινὸς μέγας ἐπιπίπτει αὐτῷ.	wa-soba ya'arrəb ḍaḥāy dəngāḍē maṣ'o la-'abrām wa-nāhu gərum ṣəlmat wa-'abiy maṣ'a lā'lēhu

In Genesis 15:12, תרדמה is also rendered as ἔκστασις in the LXX. In Ge'ez it is rendered as *dəngāḍē*, 'terror, amazement, stupor, dismay.' The word

---

[15] Wolf Leslau, *Comparative Dictionary of Geʿez (Classical Ethiopic): Geʿez-English / English-Geʿez with an Index of the Semitic Roots* (Wiesbaden: Harrassowitz, 1987), 140.

[16] LXX Eth Ps 131:4 have three lines whereas MT Ps 132:4 two.

[17] August Dillmann, *Lexicon Linguae Aethiopicae: Cum indice latino* (Leipzig: Weigel, 1865), 1099.

[18] John W. Wevers, ed., *Genesis*, Septuaginta Vetus Testamentum Graecum Auctoritate Academiae Scientiarum Gottingensis editum 1 (Göttingen: Vandenhoeck & Ruprecht, 1974), 88; John W. Wevers, *Notes on the Greek Text of Genesis*, SCS 35 (Atlanta: Society of Biblical Literature, 1993), 33. I thank Christian Seppänen for bringing this detail to my attention.

[19] Given the semantic difference between κάρος and ὕπνος, the latter referring to sleep in general, it is possible that the Ge'ez reflects the latter here. Compare this with the reading of *hədmat* in Jub 3:5, resembling a deep sleep in comparison with the lighter sleep of *dəqqās*, and the discussion below. This is of course hypothetical.

refers to a panic and a tumult in the mind, one which can cause terror or even amazement or astonishment.[20] Dillmann also gives the Latin gloss *ecstasis*.[21] Although Symmachus again witnesses the reading κάρος,[22] it does not seem to be reflected here.

Because *dəngāḍē* is also used in Jubilees 14:13 concerning Abram, one should see which words and phrases are rendered as *dəngāḍē* in the Ethiopic Bible. Firstly, this helps us to see different options for Greek words that may lurk behind *dəngāḍē* in Ethiopic Jubilees. Secondly, it helps us to define the semantic range of *dəngāḍē* and its use more closely and see how much it differs from the Greek ἔκστασις.[23]

3.3 dəngāḍē *in the Ethiopic Bible*[24]

The Ethiopic translators rendered at least seven different Greek terms as *dəngāḍē*, namely θάμβος 'amazement' (at least 6x)[25], τρόμος 'trembling' (2x)[26], ἔκστασις 'displacement, distraction of mind, trance, ecstasis'

---

[20] Leslau, *Comparative Dictionary*, 137.

[21] Dillmann, *Lexicon*, 1120.

[22] Wevers, ed., *Genesis*, 169; Wevers, *Notes*, 210 n. 18. According to him, it seems to be so that the reading of Aquila here is corrupted by the reading of Symmachus. I thank Christian Seppänen for alerting me to this observation.

[23] Concerning the semantics of ἔκστασις in ancient literature, see the articles of Lukas Bormann and Eva-Maria Kreitschmann in this volume, 119–140 and 225–256.

[24] The text editions of the Ethiopic Bible in use are two Accordance-program modules, namely the Ethiopic Old Testament (which presently contains Genesis-Ruth, 1 & 2 Samuel and Psalms) and Ethiopic Mahibere Hawariyat Canonical and Pseudepigrapha. It is to be borne in mind that the Ge'ez texts, especially the Mahibere Hawariyat version, are not critical editions, as such an edition is lacking overall in the case of the Ethiopic Bible. The survey that follows is made with the help of the computer program Accordance and August Dillmann's *Lexicon*. It is not exhaustive but is, nonetheless, extensive enough.

[25] 1 Sam 26:12; Qoh 12:5; Ezek 7:18; Song 3:8; 6:10 [Eth Song 4:19]; Luke 5:9. See also Song 6:4 [Eth Song 4:12] where *madangəḍ* (participle of causative CQ *'adangaḍa* 'terrify, strike with fear, amaze, astonish') is used.

[26] Job 4:14 and Judith 2:28 [Eth Judith 2:27–28]. Often in the LXX the words τρόμος and φόβος seem to have been used as hendiadys and are translated with different noun or verb forms of roots *f-r-h* and *r-'-d* (e.g. Gen 9:2; Exod 15:16; Deut 2:25; 11:25; Ps 2:11; LXX Ps 54:6 [Eth Ps 54:5]; Judith 15:2). Eth Judith 2:27–28 seems to be unique in this way, as there τρόμος seems to be translated with *dəngāḍē*. When standing alone, τρόμος is most often glossed with *ra'ād* (e.g. LXX Ps 47:7 [Eth Ps 47:6]; Isa 33:14; 54:14; Jer 15:8; Hab 3:16) or some other form of the same root (e.g. Isa 64:2 [Eth Isa 64:3]; Sir 16:19).

(14x)²⁷, φόβος 'fear' (6x of which one is as the negated adverb ἀφόβως),²⁸ δειλία 'timidity' (2x),²⁹ πτόησις 'excitement' (1x)³⁰ and θραυσμός 'breaking' (1x)³¹. Moving through the LXX layer all the way to the Hebrew original, 13 different Hebrew terms are rendered as dəngāḍē, namely תרדמה 'deep sleep' (Gen 15:12; 1 Sam 26:12; Job 33:15), חתחתים 'terror' (Qoh 12:5), פלצות 'shuddering' (Ezek 7:18), רעדה 'trembling' (Job 4:14, cognate of the Ge'ez ra'ād), שמה 'horror, appalment' (Jer 5:30)³², זועה 'trembling, terror' (2 Chr 29:8), חרדה 'trembling' (Gen 27:33; 1 Sam 14:15 [2x]; Ezek 26:16; Dan 10:7; the same root is also probably behind the Hebrew Vorlage of the LXX in Isa 41:2), אימה 'terror, dread' (Deut 32:25; Ps 55:5; Song 6:4, 10 [here as an adjective]), פחד 'dread' (2 Chr 14:13; Prov 1:33; Song 3:8; Jer 49:5), מרך 'weakness, timidness' (Lev 26:36), תמהון 'bewilderment' (Deut 28:28; Zech

---

²⁷ Gen 15:12; 27:33; Deut 28:28; 1 Sam 14:15 [2x]; 2 Chr 14:13 [Eth 2 Chr 14:14]; 29:8 [Eth 2 Chr 29:7]; Jer 5:30; Ezek 26:16; Zech 12:4; 14:13; Mark 5:42; 16:8; Acts 10:10. Furthermore, in Isa 41:2 the LXX ἐκστήσει reflects, according to BHS, the hiphil form יחרד of חרד 'to drive in terror.' The Ge'ez formula is yāmaṣṣaʾ dəngāḍē 'to bring dəngāḍē.'

²⁸ Deut 32:25; Job 33:15; LXX Jer 30:21 [MT Eth Jer 49:5]; Dan 10:7 [ra'ād wa-dəngāḍē]; Prov 1:33 [Eth Prov 1:34]; Sir 40:2 (a verse lacking in Hebrew and probably a later gloss according to Timo Veijola, Sirakin kirja hepreankielisen alkutekstin mukaan: Pohjakäännös eksegeettisin ja filologisin kommentein apokryfikomiteaa varten [Manuscript, 2003], 184). The Ge'ez farhat is the most often used gloss for φόβος (e.g. Gen 31:42, 53; 35:5; Exod 15:16; 20:20; 23:27; Deut 28:67; Josh 2:9; 2 Sam 23:3; 2 Chr 19:7, 9; Esth 8:17 [Eth Esth 10:29]; 9:3 [Eth Esth 11:3]; LXX Ps 5:8 [Eth Ps 5:7]; Prov 14:26; Jonah 1:10, 16; Mal 2:5; Isa 2:10; 7:25 [Eth Isa 7:26]; 24:17–18; 33:18; LXX Jer 31:43–44 [Eth Jer 48:43–44]; Lam 3:47 [Eth Lam 3:44]; Ezek 27:28; 32:32; Bar 3:7); also some other form of the same root f-r-h is used (e.g. 2 Chr 26:5; Neh 5:9, 15; LXX Ps 33:12 [Eth Ps 33:11]; Prov 1:7; 8:13 [Eth Prov 8:12]; Sir 1:11–12, 18, passim). The root g-r-m is used in some instances (e.g. Gen 15:12 on which see below; 1 Chr 14:17; Neh 6:16; LXX Ps 30:12 [Eth Ps 30:11]; LXX Ps 52:6 [Eth Ps 52:5]; Isa 2:19, 21 [cf. 2:10]; 33:7–8; Ezek 32:30; Wis 17:6 [Eth Wis 17:8].

²⁹ Lev 26:36; LXX Ps 54:5 (MT Ps 55:5; Eth Ps 54:4).

³⁰ 1 Petr 3:6.

³¹ Nah 2:11 (Eth 2:10), where actually the Q perfect verb form dangaḍa is used for nouns in both the MT and the LXX.

³² In Jer 5:30, שמה and שערורה are hendiadys, connected with ו and having the predicate in the singular. The same is true with the LXX ἔκστασις καὶ φρικτά and the Ge'ez dəngāḍē wa-našoṭāṭ ('horror, shuddering').

12:4), מהומה 'tumult, confusion' (Zech 14:13) and נמס 'melting' (Nah 2:11, the niphal participle of מסס).[33]

In some cases, *dəngāḍē* functions as one of two terms used to translate one term in the probable Greek original. Such cases are how φόβος is rendered in Dan 10:7 (*ra'ād wa-dəngāḍē*) and in Sir 40:2 (*dəngāḍē yəʾati wa-fərhata ləbb*), and τρόμος in Job 4:14 (*dəngāḍē wa-ra'ād*).[34] Additionally, the verb *dangaḍa* is used to render ἐταράχθη/חיל in Ps 55:5 [LXX Eth Ps 54:5].

There are two Greek terms that are most often rendered as *dəngāḍē:* ἔκστασις (11 of 28 times in the LXX) and θάμβος (6 of 6 times rendered as some form of the root *dngḍ*). This can be compared, for example, with the much more common term φόβος, which is rendered only 5 times as *dəngāḍē* even though it occurs 198 times in the LXX.[35]

The noun *dəngāḍē* is also used in Jubilees 30:26, which rewrites Genesis 35:5: *wa-kona gərmā ʾəgziʾabḥēr wəsta kʷəllon ʾahgur za-ʾawdā la-Saqimon wa-ʾi-tanšaʾu la-sadida wəludo la-Yāʿqob ʾəsma dəngāḍē wadqa lāʿlēhomu* "Fear of God came over all the cities that surrounded Shechem. They did not rise up to pursue after the sons of Jacob, because *dəngāḍē* had fallen upon them." Here *gərmā* 'fear' and *dəngāḍē* 'terror, tumult' seem to be synonymical.[36] The Latin palimpsest uses *timor* in both instances. Interestingly, φόβος in the LXX Job 4:13 is rendered as *gərmā*, but in a very similar text, LXX Job 33:15, it is rendered as *dəngāḍē*. This proves that the semantic fields of these two Ge'ez terms overlap.[37]

Further, the Q verb *dangaḍa* in its different forms is used in various cases, such as in Exod 23:27 (MT והמתי; LXX ἐκστήσω; Eth *wa-ʾadanaggəḍ*), Deut 28:67 (אשר תפחד פחד מפחד לבבך / ἀπὸ τοῦ φόβου τῆς καρδίας σου, ἃ φοβη-

---

[33] The glosses are of course of only approximate value. The glosses for the Greek terms are taken from the online version of *LSJ* (in *Thesaurus Linguae Graece*, stephanus.tlg.uci.edu) and for the Hebrew from *BDB*.

[34] In the case of Job 4:14, another possibility is that there could have been two terms in the Greek *Vorlage* of the Ge'ez translator too, and τρόμος is rendered as *ra'ād* as in Mark 16:8.

[35] The numbers are according to the word search of the Rahlfs edition in Accordance.

[36] Also the root *g-r-m* 'fear, amazement' has been used to render the Greek ἔκστασις, such as *garəmt* in Eth Num 13:33 [MT LXX Num 13:32]. Other options are *maʿāt* 'anger, wrath, calamity' in 2 Chr 15:5 and root *f-r-h* 'fear' in Ezek 27:35; 2 Chr 17:10.

[37] See also the discussion of תרדמה in Job 4:13; 33:15 above.

67

θήσῃ / *ʾəmanna fərhata ləbb za-tədanaggəḍ*), Judith 14:3 (καὶ ἐπιπεσεῖται ἐπ᾿ αὐτοὺς φόβος, καὶ φεύξονται / *wa-ʾəmzə yəfarrəhu wa-yədanaggəḍu wa-yəgʷayyəyu*). Often it is the Greek ἐξίστημι which lurks behind different forms of the verb *dangaḍa* (e.g. Gen 27:33; 42:28; Exod 18:9; 19:18; Lev 9:24; Josh 2:11; 10:10; Judg 4:15; 5:4; Ruth 3:8; 1 Sam 14:15[38]; 16:4; 17:11; 28:5; 2 Chr 15:6; Isa 10:31 etc.).[39] In Eth Job 21:8 (MT LXX 21:9), the Greek φόβος δὲ οὐδαμοῦ is rendered with *wa-ʾalbo za-yādanaggəḍomu* 'and there is nothing that would cause *dangāḍē* for them.' In Isa 21:4, the LXX ἡ ψυχή μου ἐφέστηκεν εἰς φόβον is translated with *wa-dangaḍani nafsəya* 'and my soul was dismayed.' These examples show that the connotation of fear is present in the root *dngḍ*.[40]

This survey confirms that *dangāḍē* is connected to a tumult in the mind, a terror which makes one numb and unable to fathom out what is happening or to be able to do anything. There is clear connotation to fear that makes one passive. The semantic field can also include a kind of ecstasis or trance. This is, however, relatively uncommon from a lexical point of view. This is reflected in Leslau's *Comparative Dictionary* in comparison with Dillman's *Lexicon*, since Leslau does not give the gloss 'trance' or 'ecstasis' at all.[41] That *dangāḍē* can cause an unconscious state (sleep) must be inferred from the context, as in 1 Sam 26:12, where *dangāḍē* is the reason for the sleeping (*yənawwəmu*).

Having constructed a model to understand how the different translators may have tackled the text of their *Vorlagen* and having investigated the use of *dangāḍē* in the Ethiopic Bible in order to form a background for the investigation of the reception of 'deep sleep' in Jubilees, it is finally time to turn to the book of Jubilees itself.

---

[38] Also θαμβέω in 1 Sam 14:15 is rendered as *dangaḍa*.

[39] Other renderings of ἐξίστημι include *farha* 'fear' (1 Kgs 1:49), *taḥazzaba* 'think,' but also 'fear' (1 Sam 4:13), and, interestingly, *zakkara* 'bring to memory' (Hos 3:5).

[40] See also Dan 4:2 (LXX 4:5); 5:6; Sir 4:17, where the noun φόβος is rendered using a verb form of *dangaḍa*.

[41] Of course 'ecstasy' itself can be a problematic term, since it is used to refer to many different phenomena. This was pointed out already by Alfred Guillaume, *Prophecy and Divination Among the Hebrews and Other Semites: A Study of Man's Intercourse with the Unseen World*. The Bampton Lectures for 1938 (London: Hodder and Stoughthon, 1938), 290–91.

4 Genesis 2:21 and Jubilees 3

3:1[42] During six days of the second week we brought to Adam, on the Lord's orders, all animals, all cattle, all birds, everything that moves about on the earth, and everything that moves about in the water—in their various kinds and various forms: the animals on the first day; the cattle on the second day; the birds on the third day; everything that moves about on the earth on the fourth day; and the ones that move about in the water on the fifth day. 3:2 Adam named them all, each with its own name. Whatever he called them became their name. 3:3 During these five days Adam was looking at all of these—male and female among every kind that was on the earth. But he himself was alone; there was no one whom he found for himself who would be for him a helper who was like him. 3:4 Then the Lord said to us: "It is not good that the man should be alone. Let us make him a helper who is like him." 3:5 The Lord our God imposed a sound slumber on him and he fell asleep. Then he took one of his bones for a woman. That rib was the origin of the woman—from among his bones. He built up the flesh in its place and built the woman. (*wa-wadaya ʾəgziʾabḥēr ʾamlākəna ḥədmata lāʿlēhu wa-noma wa-našʾa la-bəʾsit ʾəm-māʾkala ʾaʿṣəmtihu ʿasma ʾaḥada wa-yəʾati gabo fəṭratā la-bəʾsit ʾəm-māʾkala ʾaʿṣəmtihu wa-ḥanaṣa šəgā ḥəyyantēhā wa-ḥanaṣa bəʾsita*) 3:6 Then he awakened Adam from his sleep (*wa-ʾanqəho la-ʾadām ʾəm-nəwāmu*). When he awoke, he got up on the sixth day. Then he brought (him) to her. He knew her and said to her: "This is now bone from my bone and flesh from my flesh. This one will be called my wife, for she was taken from her husband." (*zāti təssammay bəʾsitəya ʾəsma ʾəmənna bəʾsihā tanašʾat*) 3:7 For this reason a man and a woman are to become one, and for this reason he leaves his father and his mother. He associates with his wife, and they become one flesh. (*bəʾənta-zə yəkun bəʾsi wa-bəʾsit ʾaḥada wa-baʾəntə-zə yəhaddəg ʾabāhu wa-ʾəmmo wa-yəḍḍāmmar məsla bəʾsitu wa-yəkawwənu šəgā ʾaḥada*). 3:8 In the first week Adam and his wife—the rib—were created, and in the second week he showed her to him. Therefore, a commandment was given to keep (women) in their defile-

---

[42] The English translation of Jubilees used in this article is based on the English translation by VanderKam, *Jubilees*, with some modifications made by me. The translation of the commentary differs somewhat from VanderKam's first translation in James C. VanderKam, *The Book of Jubilees*, CSCO 511; SA 88 (Leuven: Peeters, 1989). The critical edition of the Ethiopic Jubilees in use is based on 27 manuscripts and edited by James C. VanderKam, *The Book of Jubilees: A Critical Text*, CSCO 510; SA 87 (Leuven: Peeters, 1989). According to VanderKam, *Jubilees*, 14–16, the new manuscripts show no significant new information.

ment seven days for a male (child) and for a female two (units) of seven days. 3:9 After 40 days had come to an end for Adam in the land where he had been created, we brought him into the Garden of Eden to work and keep it. His wife was brought (there) on the eightieth day. After this she entered the Garden of Eden.

First, it is to be noted that the Ge'ez word here for Adam's sleep is *ḥadmat* (or *hadmat*)[43], not *daqqās* as in Eth Gen 2:21. The D verb *haddama* could be translated, according to Leslau, as 'sleep, slumber,' and the noun *hadmat* as 'deep sleep, numbness, torpor, absurdity.'[44] The 'deep sleep' here is causing a numb state where one does not feel or react to anything. *Hadmat* thus suits the almost surgical operation much better than *daqqās*, which lacks the connotation of as deep a sleep or the unconscious state of a mind that *hadmat* carries.[45]

Of course, since no Greek manuscripts are available to us, we do not know the specific Greek word that lurks behind the translational choice. Presumably, it could be ἔκστασις, and in the Hebrew *Vorlage* תרדמה. However, the Greek word could be different, too, since *dangāḍē* is not used here nor in Eth Gen 2:21. As noted above, Wevers documented κάρος or ὕπνος as antique Greek readings of Gen 2:21, and *hadmat* could very well be a rendering for either. Hypothetically it can be surmised that κάρος—connotating a deeper sleep than ὕπνος—would lie behind *hadmat* in Jubilees, since also it connotates a heavier sleep than *daqqās* in Eth Gen 2:21. In this layer, the interpretation of the original (Hebrew) author is not reflected. He probably understood תרדמה to mean a deep sleep, nothing else.

Thus, God put Adam into a very deep sleep where he was unconscious and numb. Next, God took one bone from Adam's bones, which contained

---

[43] In Ge'ez manuscripts the various *h*'s are often confused.
[44] Leslau, *Comparative Dictionary*, 214. Dillmann, *Lexicon*, 17, gives the following renderings for the noun *ḥadmat*: (1) *somnolentia, sopor, somnus gravis, torpor* [with reference to Jub 3]; (2) *deliratio*.
[45] Dillmann, *Lexicon*, 1099, gives Latin *sopor levis* for *daqqās*. Umberto Cassuto, *A Commentary on the Book of Genesis: From Adam to Noah*, trans. Israel Abrahams (Jerusalem: The Magnes Press, 1961), 133–34, comments on Gen 2:21 in a way which resembles the Ge'ez in Jub 3:5: "The act could not have been performed unless the man was unconscious, and to this end a deep sleep was cast upon him."

the (prototype) woman, 'built' the flesh on the place of the bones and then also 'built' the woman from that one bone, the rib. Then God woke Adam from his sleep (*wa-'anqəho la-'adām 'əm-nəwāmu*), which is an addition to the version in Genesis. This explication of how long the sleep lasted is interesting in relation to the analysis of the reception of Abram's sleep below. The sleep, and the situation itself, is of course abnormal or supernatural (from a modern perpective) and remains so.

The author's axe to grind is, however, elsewhere. He modifies the order of events. The utterance of Genesis 2:18 ("It is not good that the man should be alone") *before* the creation of the animals or the bringing of them to Adam—as it is in Genesis—could indicate that God created or brought animals to Adam in order to see whether Adam would find a (sexual) partner from among them.[46] The possibility for such a horrible interpretation is omitted in Jubilees. As Jacques van Ruiten points out, the animals are brought to Adam for a pedagogical purpose: By observing them, male and female, Adam understands his loneliness. Only then does God utter "It is not good that the man should be alone" (Jub 3:4).[47]

The author also makes the near bond between the creation of humanity and marriage even more explicit.[48] This is seen when one compares the wordings of Genesis 2:23b with Jubilees 3:6, where the Ge'ez usage of *bə'si* and *bə'sit*—although both have the general meaning of 'man' and 'woman'—connotates 'husband' and 'wife': *zāti təssammayt bə'sitəya 'əsma 'əmənna bə'sihā tanəš'at* (Jub 3:6) retroverted to Hebrew would be זאת תקרא אשתי כי מאיש לקחה.[49] Purity in marriage and in sexual relations is one

---

[46] James L. Kugel, *A Walk through Jubilees: Studies in the Book of Jubilees and the World of its Creation*, JSJSup 156 (Leiden: Brill, 2012), 37; Jessi Orpana, *Reception of the Creation of Humanity: Transmission and Interpretation of the Creation Traditions in Late Second Temple Jewish Literature* (PhD diss., Helsinki: University of Helsinki, 2016), 98. Cf. the discussion of some problematic modern interpretations of Gen 2:19–20 in Claus Westermann, *Genesis 1–11: A Commentary*, trans. John J. Scullion S.J. (Minneapolis: Augsburg, 1984), 227–29.

[47] Jacques T. A. G. M. van Ruiten, *Primaeval History Interpreted: The Rewriting of Genesis 1–11 in the Book of Jubilees*, JSJSup 66 (Leiden: Brill, 2000), 79–82; See also William Loader, *Enoch, Levi, and Jubilees on Sexuality: Attitudes towards Sexuality in the Early Enoch Literature, the Aramaic Levi Document, and the Book of Jubilees* (Grand Rapids: Eerdmans, 2007), 239–41.

[48] Cf. Loader, *Sexuality*, 244–45. Cf. Tobit 8:5–8 in the context of Tobit's marriage with Sarah.

[49] Cf. VanderKam, *Jubilees*, 213–14. Of course, this retroversion remains somewhat hypothetical. Eth Gen 2:23b actually has *zāti la-təkunani bə'sitəya 'əsma 'əm-mətā waḍ'at*

of the main focuses of many halakic additions in Jubilees. Having this trait in mind, VanderKam points out that it is somewhat interesting that the author does not exploit the opportunity to elaborate on such matters here.[50] Instead, the author has other halakic matters (the impurity at birth) in mind which he connects to the story. Perhaps the Garden of Eden, which according to the author is a sanctuary, made this matter important for the author.[51]

The author also connects the first creation narrative of Gen 1:1–2:3 and the second in Gen 2:4ff. to one another. What modern exegetes call the first creation narrative took place during the first week of creation, whereas Gen 2:4ff. happened during the second week. As humankind (male and female in Jub 2:16) was created on the sixth day of the first week, so is the creation of woman perfected on the sixth of the second week (Jub 3:5). This, in turn, gives the author the possibility to elaborate on halakic matters regarding purity and impurity in Jub 3:8–14.[52]

To summarize the reception of Adam's sleep in Jubilees, the following can be noted. In the Ge'ez layer, the unconsciousness of Adam is highlighted in comparison to the Ethiopic Genesis. This can also have been the case in the Greek version, which is lost to us. The reception in the original Hebrew layer remains close to the Hebrew of Genesis too. The author was not that interested in תרדמה, other than clarifying when it ended (Jub 3:6). Instead, his main focus was on the harmonization of the creation

---

yaʾati "…in order for her to become to me my wife, for she came forth from her husband." Also the Sam, LXX and Latin have the genitive suffix "from her man."

[50] VanderKam, *Jubilees*, 214.

[51] The importance of Eden as a sanctuary and Adam as a priest also had their fair share of influence on how the author tackled the nudity of Adam and Eve and their awareness of it. On this, see Jessi Orpana, "Awareness of Nudity in *Jubilees* 3: Adam Portrayed as a Priest in the Garden," in *Crossing Imaginary Boundaries: The Dead Sea Scrolls in the Context of Second Temple Judaism*, eds. Mika S. Pajunen and Hanna Tervanotko, Publications of the Finnish Exegetical Society 108 (Helsinki: The Finnish Exegetical Society, 2015), 241–58.

[52] Michael Segal, *The Book of Jubilees: Rewritten Bible, Redaction, Ideology and Theology*, JSJSup 117 (Leiden: Brill, 2007), 47–58, is of the opinion that the halakic addition of Jub 3:8–14 "stands in tension with the surrounding story with regard to the dating of events" (57). It also contains specific terminology not found in the surrounding narrative. The issue regarding specific terminology can be explained by specific discourse. Jub 3:8–14 is legal discourse, whereas 3:1–7 and 3:15ff. is narrative. On arguments against Segal's view, see VanderKam, *Jubilees*, 223–24.

narratives, playing out the possible dubious interpretations, highlighting the connection between creation and marriage, and explicating purity regulations related to the sanctuary.

5 Genesis 15:12 and Jubilees 14

14:1 After these things—in the fourth year of this week [1964], on the first of the third month—the word of the Lord came to Abram in **a dream** (*baḥəlm*): "Do not be afraid, Abram. I am your protector; your reward will be very large." 14:2 He said, "Lord, Lord, what are you going to give me when I go on being childless? The son of Maseq—the son of my maidservant—that is Damascene Eliezer—will be my heir. You have given me no descendants. Give me descendants." 14:3 He said to him, "This one will not be your heir but rather someone who will come out of your loins will be your heir." 14:4 He brought him outside and said to him, "Look at the sky and count the stars if you can count them." 14:5 **When he had looked at the sky and seen the stars,** he said to him, "Your descendants will be like this." 14:6 He believed the Lord, and it was credited to him as something righteous.

14:7 He said to him, "I am the Lord who brought you from Ur of the Chaldeans to give you the land of the Canaanites to occupy forever and to be God for you and your descendants after you." 14:8 He said, "Lord, Lord, how will I know that I will inherit (it)?" 14:9 He said to him, "Get for me a three-year-old calf, a three-year-old goat, a three-year-old sheep, a turtledove, and a dove." 14:10 He got all of these in the middle of the month. He was living at the oak of Mamre that is near Hebron. 14:11 **He built an altar there and sacrificed all of these. He poured their blood on the altar** and divided them in the middle. He put them opposite one another, but the birds he did not divide. 14:12 Birds kept coming down on what was spread out, but Abram kept preventing them and not allowing the birds to touch them. 14:13 At sunset, a terror fell on Abram; indeed a great, dark fear fell on him. (*wa-kona soba ʿərbata ḍaḥay dəngāḍē wadqa lāʿla ʾabrām wa-nāhu gərmā ʿabiy ṣəlmat wadqa lāʿlēhu*) It was said to Abram: "Know for a fact that your descendants will be aliens in a foreign land. They will enslave them and oppress them for 400 years. 14:14 But I will judge the nation whom they serve. Afterwards, they will leave from there with many possessions. 14:15 But you will go peacefully to your fathers and be buried at a ripe old age. 14:16 In the fourth generation they will return to this place because until now the sins of the Amorites have not been completed." 14:17 **When he**

awakened and got up (*wa-naqha 'əm-nəwām*[53] *wa-tanśə'a*), the sun had set. There was a flame and an oven was smoking. Fiery flames passed between what was spread out. 14:18 On that day the Lord concluded a covenant with Abram with these words: "To your descendants I will give this land from the river of Egypt as far as the great river, the Euphrates River: that of the Kenites, the Kenizzites, the Kadmonites, the Perizzites, the Rephaim, the Phaorites, The Hivites, the Amorites, the Canaanites, the Girgashites, and the Jebusites."
14:19 It passed (along), and Abram offered what had been spread out, the birds, their (cereal) offering, and their libation. The fire devoured them. 14:20 During this day we concluded a covenant with Abram like the covenant that we concluded during this month with Noah. Abram renewed the festival and the ordinance/covenant for himself forever.

When compared with Genesis 15, the first change that catches one's eye is that, whereas in the MT LXX Eth Genesis 15:1 God's word comes to Abram 'in a vision' (במחזה / ἐν ὁράματι / *ba-rā'y*), in Jubilees 14:1 it comes *ba-ḥalm* 'in a dream.' The word *ḥalm* is a cognate to the Hebrew חלום and often found in the Ethiopic OT where the MT has חלום and the LXX ἐνύπνιον (e.g. Gen 37:6; 41:1; Jer 23:27)[54] and has the meaning of a dream which one dreams when sleeping rather than being a vision that one can also see when awake. This change, of course, is interesting, because Jubilees (or Genesis) does not explicitly state that Abram was sleeping or—if he is indeed sleeping—when he awakens from this *ḥalm*. This is in contrast with Jubilees 3:6 where God explicitly wakes Adam up from *nəwām* 'sleep' (but see Jub 14:17). Possibly the first discourse in a dream happens in Jub 14:1–9, since 'the word' came to Abram on the first of the third month (Jub 14:1). After this, he gathered all the animals "in the middle of the third month" (14:10), referring to the Festival of Weeks, and prepared the sacrifice (14:11). Thus, in Jubilees there were 14 days between the dream and the ritual. It would be odd to consider that the dream lasted that long and, moreover, that everything which happened in Genesis 15 / Jubilees 14 took place in the dream. Van Ruiten is of the opinion that the word *ḥalm*

---

[53] Many Ethiopic mss. (9, 12, 20, 38, 39, 42, 47, 48, 58, according to VanderKam's edition) include the possessive suffix -*u* (3. sg. m.), thus "from his sleep." Cf. Jub 3:6 above.
[54] Cf. Job 7:14, where MT reads בחלמות ומחזינות, LXX ἐνυπνίοις καὶ ἐν ὁράμασιν, Eth *ba-ḥalm ba-rā'y*.

(which might be a gloss of the original חלום via Greek intermediary), was chosen "because this is used more often in connection with theophanies."[55] This is plausible. All in all, מחזה (in the sense 'a vision') is found only four times in the Hebrew Bible.

This brings us to the second addition. Jubilees 14:11 states that Abram built an altar and sacrificed the animals that God had commanded in the dream. This makes the actual situation of Jubilees 14:11–20 different from Genesis 15:10–21, the latter being peculiar and in a sense an abnormal ritual both for a modern reader and an ancient Jewish one.[56] It is explicitly mentioned that "he poured their blood on the altar," (Jub 14:11). This makes the ceremony explicitly a sacrifice which is connected to the concluding of the covenant (14:19–20).[57] The connection between the pieces of the animals and the covenant is found in Genesis too.

The most interesting case regarding the task at hand comes in Jubilees 14:13: the terror (*dəngāḍē*) or great, dark fear (*gərmā 'abiy ṣəlmat*) that fell (*wadqa*) on Abram when the sun had set.

---

[55] Jacques T. A. G. M. van Ruiten, *Abraham in the Book of Jubilees: The Rewriting of Genesis 11:26–25:10 in the Book of Jubilees 11:14–23:8*, JSJSup 161 (Leiden: Brill, 2012), 123–24 (citation 124).

[56] The contrast can be seen in how Nahum M. Sarna, *Genesis*; The JPS Torah Commentary (Philadephia: The Jewish Publication Society, 1989), 114, comments on Gen 15:9–17: "The text does not explain the elaborate ritual that is followed. *Clearly no sacrifice is involved, for there is no altar, no mention of the sprinkling of blood as in Exodus 24:8, and no suggestion that the animals are either eaten or burnt.* The meaning of the ceremonials is to be sought elsewhere." (my emphasis) So also Gerhard von Rad, *Genesis: A Commentary*, OTL, rev. ed. (Philadelphia: The Westminster Press, 1972), 186: "It is not certain whether the killing of the animals is to be understood as a sacrifice, but the fact that the pieces of meat were neither burned nor eaten but covered with earth as something accursed speaks against the notion of sacrifice." Sarna understands the cutting of animals along with analogous practices (e.g. Mari texts 'to kill a donkey foal') and concludes: "All these analogues demonstrate that the cutting up of the animal was a crucial element in the treaty-making procedure" (Sarna, *Genesis*, 114). This is clear for modern exegetes, but the author of Jubilees had other hermeneutic grounds on which he gave his interpretation to the text, and most probably had no knowledge of Mari texts. The detail in Jer 34:18, however, shows that the meaning of the ritual was still known during the later biblical period. Nevertheless, the author wanted to connect this odd ritual with such sacrificial practices that were also otherwise known.

[57] Cf. van Ruiten, *Abraham*, 129–30.

MT Gen 15:12	LXX Gen 15:12
ויהי השמש לבוא ותרדמה נפלה על אברם והנה אימה חשכה גדלה נפלת עליו	περὶ δὲ ἡλίου δυσμὰς ἔκστασις ἐπέπεσεν τῷ Αβραμ, καὶ ἰδοὺ φόβος σκοτεινὸς μέγας ἐπιπίπτει αὐτῷ.
Eth Gen 15:12	Eth Jub 14:13
wa-soba yaʿarrəb ḍaḥāy dəngāḍē maṣʾo la-ʾabrām wa-nāhu gərum ṣəlmat wa-ʿabiy maṣʾa lāʿlēhu	*wa-kona soba ʿərbata ḍaḥay dəngāḍē wadqa lāʿla ʾabrām wa-nāhu gərmā ʿabiy ṣəlmat wadqa lāʿlēhu*

Eth Gen 15:12 and Eth Jub 14:13 are quite similar to one another, except that *gərmā* is a noun 'terror, dread, fear, magnificence,' and *gərum* is often used as an adjective 'terrible, dreadful,' although it also can have the value of a noun 'a terrible thing, terror.' In the Ethiopic Genesis, *gərum* is clearly an adjective attribute to *ṣəlmat* 'darkness,' along with *ʿabiy* 'big.' This is different from the LXX, where φόβος is the noun and σκοτεινὸς μέγας are attributes. On the other hand, in Jub 14:13, *gərmā* is most probably in *status constructus* and *ʿabiy ṣəlmat* in *status absolutus*, meaning literally 'a fear of great darkness.' The phrase in Jub 14:13 could thus be retroverted as אימת חשכה גדלה in Hebrew (if one follows the construct structure). However, *gərmā* could also be in the absolute state, since a word in absolute state ending with -*ā* retains it in the construct state.[58] The phrase could then be translated as 'a fear, (that is) a great darkness.'[59] This would be similar to the MT Gen 15:12.

Regarding the word *dəngāḍē*, Jubilees follows the tradition of the LXX OL and Eth Gen 15:12.[60] *Dəngāḍē*, as previously pointed out, generally refers to a tumult in the mind that causes one to be unable to act and carries an aspect of fear. According to Jubilees 14:17, however, Abram was certainly sleeping when God spoke with him since he later wakes up from the sleep. In this sense, *dəngāḍē* here causes a sleepy or unconscious state

---

[58] Josef Tropper, *Altäthiopisch: Grammatik des Ge'ez mit Übungstexten und Glossar*, Elementa Linguarum Orientis 2 (Münster: Ugarit, 2002), 77 (§42.53).

[59] The phrase has led to different solutions in textual history. Ms. 9 has *gərmā ʿabiya ṣəlmat* 'a great fear of darkness,' ms. 20 *gərmā ṣəlmat* 'fear of darkness' or 'fear, (that is) darkness'; mss. 17, 38 *gərmā ʿabiy wa-ṣəlmat* 'a great fear and darkness.' The manuscript numbers are according to the numbering of mss. in VanderKam's critical edition.

[60] VanderKam, *Jubilees*, 497.

of mind. The use of *dəngāḍē* in Eth Job 4:14 and 33:15 in relation to nocturnal visions should also be noted.

The most likely Greek term to be behind *dəngāḍē* is ἔκστασις which itself is a translation of Hebrew תרדמה. The survey of different Greek terms in the Ethiopic Bible rendered as *dəngāḍē* in Ge'ez above demonstrated that ἔκστασις is the most probable option, since it is found in Gen 15:12 and nearly half the time it is used, it is glossed with the root *dngḍ*. The addition of the author in Jubilees 14:17 makes it clear that Abram was not sleeping when the fiery flames moved between the cut-in-half animals: it does not belong to the sleepy state caused by *dəngāḍē* / ἔκστασις / תרדמה.[61] Abram regained his consciousness back and was able to act again. This addition is similar to the addition of God waking Adam up in Jubilees 3:6.

Whereas in the Genesis account a reader can interpret the whole event as happening in a dream, or at least so that Abram is in a 'deep sleep' or 'ecstasy' for the whole time and only God performs the ceremony (this alluding to the one-sidedness and unconditionality of the covenant), in Jubilees, Abram takes an active part. He offers the sacrifices at the end (14:19). The 'deep sleep' or 'tumult/ecstasy/disturbance' in the mind is— with the help of the addition in Jubilees 14:17—restricted to the revelatory speech of God to Abram.

To summarize, the 'deep sleep' of Abram mattered to the author, as he was interested in the whole chapter of Genesis 15. With minor additions, the author makes explicit that the dream at the beginning was restricted to the duration of God's speech alone. Similarly, the 'deep sleep' of Abram was restricted to the time of God's speech. In this way, Abram is given a more active role in concluding the covenant, and the odd ritual in Genesis

---

[61] Kugel, *Walk through*, 96. That one can interpret Gen 15:12–17 in such a way that everything happens in a dream can be seen in the reading of Gen 15:17 by Carl F. Keil, *The Pentateuch*, K&D 1 (Edinburgh: T & T Clark, 1866; repr., Peabody: Hendrickson, 2011), 138: "a description of what Abram saw in his deep prophetic sleep, corresponding to the mysterious character of the whole proceeding." In other words, in the Greek and Ge'ez layers of interpretation, one interprets *explicitly* that Abram was sleeping during God's speech only because of Jub 14:17. In the most probable original Hebrew layer, the word itself had this connotation already in 14:13. Perhaps the Hebrew author wanted to specify that Abram's state of תרדמה had ended before his act of sacrifice.

15 itself is interpreted along the lines of the more common sacrificial rituals.

6 Conclusions

In this article I have analysed the reception of the 'deep sleep' (תרדמה) of Adam and Abram in Jubilees 3 and 14. The text of Jubilees is preserved only in Ge'ez, which is a translation of a lost Greek translation of the original Hebrew text, and thus a suitable model to understand translational choices was built with the help of the Hebrew (MT), Greek (LXX) and Ethiopic Genesis 2:21 and 15:12. This model enabled us to see which Greek and Hebrew words could be reconstructed with the help of the Ge'ez translation of Jubilees. Moreover, since the root *dngḍ* plays a role in Jubilees 14, a further analysis of that word in the Ethiopic Bible along with a short survey of the Hebrew תרדמה in the Hebrew Bible was conducted. With the help of this background information, an analysis of Jubilees 3 and 14 was undertaken. The results are as follows.

The 'deep sleep' of Adam and Abram differ in Jubilees, at least in its Ge'ez layer. The same may be true even in the Greek layer, which can reflect other Greek readings (κάρος or ὕπνος instead of ἔκστασις) of תרדמה in the case of Adam. Whereas the wording in Jubilees 3:5 (*ḥadmat*) implies a surgical-like sleep which renders one numb and unconscious, the word *dangāḍē* in Jubilees 14:13 does not reflect sleep at all, but rather refers to an awestruck state during which one is unable to act and which is caused by fear. A similar distinction is found in Philo's reading of Gen 15:12, as he makes a distinction between the ἔκστασις of Adam and Abram and understands the ἔκστασις of Adam as a deep sleep, but that of Abram as a prophetic state (*Her.* 257–258).[62] Philo, however, does use the word ἔκστασις even in the case of Adam's state. Most probably, in the Hebrew Jubilees, the original term in both instances was תרדמה.

In Jubilees 3:5, the deep sleep of Adam remains 'abnormal' or 'supernatural,' as does the terror or tumult of Abram in 14:13. In other respects, the author has changed the abnormal situations. In Jubilees 3, the author

---

[62] On this, see more closely the contribution of Eva-Maria Kreitschmann in this volume, 225–256.

makes some dubious and harmful interpretations (taking a sexual partner from among the animals) impossible and highlights the aspect of marriage. Overall, he is not that interested in the sleep of Adam, except in clarifying when it ends. In Jubilees 14, Abram does not have a 'vision,' but 'a dream' (Jub 14:1) when he is sleeping, and that sleep is restricted to the time of God's revelatory speech. The 'deep sleep' of Gen 15:12 is also made explicit: it contains only God's dialogue in Jub 14:13–16. The ceremony does not happen in a dream, nor is Abram sleeping when the covenant is being concluded. Instead, it is Abram who offers the animals as sacrifices, taking an active part in concluding the covenant. The ceremony is explicitly interpreted as a sacrifice along the lines of otherwise known rituals.

What is common in the reception of the deep sleep of Adam and Abram in Jubilees is that in both cases the author clarifies when the state of תרדמה ends.

Early Jewish Struggle with the Violent Moses in Exodus 2

Pekka Lindqvist

1 Introduction

For any reader of the Bible it seems obvious that, at least on a couple of occasions during his long life, Moses loses his temper. "No wonder, having this neurotic people around him!" a Jewish stand-up comedian might say. Many second temple, late-antiquity and talmudic era authors, however, had another way of handling these texts. Many did feel troubled by Moses's behavior. One can easily highlight their burning questions: Is this the way the well-tempered noble leader of Israel acts? Is this not willful murder? Was there any justification for what he did? This needed to be made clear for every Israelite so that there was no room for any misconceptions; probably, the thinking was also that it would not be a good idea to let misinterpretations spread amongst outsiders either, especially among those who eagerly spread stories about Jews and their leader.[1]

The anger of Moses blasts openly in Exodus chapters 2 and 32. Of these, I have already discussed the latter incident elsewhere.[2] There the nucleus of the problem was the act of smashing the tablets of the Law, but also, as may be seen e.g. in the energy which Philo puts into it, the bloodshed on

---

[1] On this last problem, see especially John Gager, *Moses in Greco-Roman Paganism* (Nashville: Abingdon Press, 1972). I have earlier discussed the problem of Moses's reputation in connection to Philo's rewriting of his life. See Pekka Lindqvist, *Sin at Sinai: Early Judaism Encounters Exodus 32*, SRB 2 (Turku/Winona Lake: Åbo Akademi University/Eisenbrauns, 2008), 121–28.

[2] Lindqvist, *Sin at Sinai.*

Moses's command. The first incident, the violent incident recorded in Exodus 2, i.e. Moses slaying an Egyptian, is the focus of this article.[3] Another case where Moses's behavior caused unrest in the minds of later readers is found in Num 16:28-33, which narrates the fates of the rebels Korah, Dathan and Abiram, and their followers.[4] The incident of Num 16 was obviously troubling for both Philo and Josephus. Philo summarizes the rebellion in *De praemiis et poenis* 77-78, and uses considerable energy to explain how Moses attempted to persuade the rebels in every way "without loss of temper, which indeed was alien to his nature."[5] In Josephus's *Jewish Antiquities* 4.51, Moses, after his failed attempts to persuade them, even wept over their destruction. There are other men of God, the violent deeds of whom have also troubled later interpreters: Elijah who called down the fire from heaven (2 Kings 1:9-12) leading to 250 victims, and even more so Elisha in 2 Kings 2:23-24, who summoned bears to kill a group of 42 boys. In the latter case Feldman has detected an apologetical tendency in Josephus, and the same tendency is visible in e.g. b. Soṭah 46b as well.[6]

---

[3] The reception of the slaying of the Egyptian has been discussed e.g. by Brevard S. Childs, "Moses' Slaying in the Theology of the Two Testaments," in *Biblical Theology in Crisis* (Philadelphia: Westminster Press, 1970), 164-83. Later Childs collects the viewpoints of this essay in his commentary on Exodus. Brevard S. Childs, *Exodus. A Commentary*, OTL (London: SCM Press, 1974). See esp. 27-46. Avi Sagi, "'He Slew the Egyptian and Hid Him in the Sand': Jewish Tradition and the Moral Element," *HUCA* 67 (1996): 55-76. Aaron Rosmarin, *Moses im Lichte der Agada* (New York: Goldblatt, 1932), follows much the same tradition as Ginzberg's *Legends* (cf. n. 12 below), but as a collection which goes far beyond the talmudic era until the middle ages, it is useful for a modern scholar.

[4] This incident is referred to in many post-biblical texts, see listing in Dale C. Allison, "Rejecting Violent Judgment: Luke 9:52-56 and its relatives," *JBL* 121/3 (2002): 459-78, esp. 461.

[5] See also *4 Macc.* 2:17 according to which Moses "did nothing against them in anger, but controlled his anger with reason" and *Tanhuma* Korah 6 according to which Moses spoke to them "politely and appeasingly". A reader might also note a striking similarity between Num 16:13 and Exod 2:14: in both cases Moses is challenged in a similar way with the question: "you want to be lord over us?"

[6] Louis H. Feldman, *Studies in Josephus' Rewritten Bible*, JSJSup 58 (Leiden: Brill, 1998), 339. I will shortly return to *b. Soṭah* 46b in the section 3.2. For this and further references, see Allison, "Rejecting," 470.

Pekka Lindqvist

2 The Biblical Episode and the Questions it Gives Rise to

The biblical account (Exodus 2:11–12) in focus in this article reads as follows[7]:

> [11] One day, after Moses had grown up, he went out to his people and saw their forced labor. He saw an Egyptian beating a Hebrew, one of his kinsfolk. [12] He looked this way and that, and seeing no one he killed the Egyptian and hid him in the sand.

For the sake of clarity concerning the intrigue, we may also add the following two verses, 13–14, which bring the open thread of the preceding account to its conclusion and show its significance for the subsequent turning point in Moses's life.

> [13] When he went out the next day, he saw two Hebrews fighting; and he said to the one who was in the wrong, "Why do you strike your fellow Hebrew?" [14] He answered, "Who made you a ruler and judge over us? Do you mean to kill me as you killed the Egyptian?" Then Moses was afraid and thought, "Surely the thing is known."

While the focus of this article is not in the exegetical analysis of the biblical text, a few observations by modern commentators regarding the narrative turns and benchmarks in the story should be made before turning to the early reception. The account fills a function in its biblical context. It bridges the story from Egypt to Midian, or is the starting point for the hero's desert years[8]. It may also be characterized as an introduction to Moses's marriage tale[9], or an incident opening the eyes of "a disillusioned prince."[10] The larger narrative framework of the incident is somewhat surprising. A reader of the beginning of the book of Exodus finds themself, with no preparation, thrust into the middle of the adult life of Moses. This

---

[7] All quotations from the Bible follow The New Revised Standard Version (NRSV).
[8] John I. Durham, *Exodus*, WBC 3 (Waco: Word Books 1987), 18–20.
[9] George W. Coats, *Moses: Heroic Man, Man of God*, JSOTSup 57 (Sheffield: Sheffield Academic Press, 1988), 49.
[10] William H.C. Propp, *Exodus 1–18. A New Translation with Introduction and Commentary*, AB (New Haven and London: Yale University Press, 1998), 165.

gives rise to questions such as: Where did he come from, and how he did know where to find his own people? What are his ties to these people anyway? The brevity of the narrative from childhood to manhood and the beginning of Moses's mission has been noted by modern commentators[11] and the huge gaps in the story have been eagerly filled by early commentators too.[12] In these we learn about Moses's childhood and his later years in the Egyptian court, his education there, his extraordinary character and skills, his beauty, his success in the service of the army of Pharaoh[13]—not to mention his learning of his authentic Hebrew identity which, in the account of Exodus 2:11–12, develops into a zeal for his own nation. Modern commentators have studied the dynamic of the story and pointed out, for example, the tension between the poles Egypt/Egyptian vs. Hebrew. The main figure becomes aware of the Egyptian oppression and intervenes on behalf of his brother, then intervenes in the fight between two of his brothers, although in this particular instance they are not called "brothers" (as the Hebrews collectively in verse 11), and is, thus, faced with a threat from both camps. Concerning the violent act itself, George W. Coats stresses that a close reading of the story excludes any need for interpreting Moses's act as a cold-blooded murder. Moses is aware of the risks of intervention—in the end the story depicts the act as heroic. By "looking this way and that" he is not portrayed as a wily hooligan trying to hide his deed, but rather shows himself to be cautious. There is not a hint of doubt concerning the opinion of the God of Israel. Moses seems to act in full confidence.[14] Coats also highlights the fact that the story between the lines indicates that the rescued Hebrew (who was the only witness to the deed on site) actually violated Moses's confidence. Betrayed by this, and threatened by others, and eventually faced with the threat of Egyptian power, Moses flees from his own people.[15] The story has a tension: a reader knows that the main figure is the chosen one, but—as e.g. Propp

---

[11] See e.g. Durham, *Exodus*, 18–19.

[12] On the latter, see Louis Ginzberg, *Legends of the Jews*, 2 (Philadelphia: The Jewish Publication Society, 1911). The notes are in volume 6 (1939). See also Rosmarin, *Moses*, 56–59.

[13] According to tradition, he had grown up to an age of forty-two (*Jub.* 47:1. 48:1) or forty (Acts 7:23–24). According to *Exod. Rab.* 1:27 he was twenty, although "some say forty."

[14] Coats, *Moses*, 49.

[15] Coats, *Moses*, 50. For similar observations, see Propp, *Exodus*,

comments—"the story sets up Moses' appointment in the next chapter. It shows the futility of attempting to rescue Israel without divine aid. Moses cannot kill each taskmaster individually." [16]

Naturally, the early interpretation simultaneously answers the unanswered questions predicated by the violent account cited above. Several unvoiced questions can be detected although never written down by any of the early interpreters: Was the killing of an Egyptian righteous or not? Did the Egyptian deserve it, and if he did, how did Moses know? Was there a problem with Moses's self-control? Was the hiding of the deed really fitting for an exemplary and noble law-giver?

Even though the main focus in this article will be on the early Jewish material, a word on the early Christian matters may be given by means of an introductory comment. The story gained some interest in the New Testament as well as amongst the patristic writers. In its retelling in the New Testament, by Stephen in Acts 7:23–29, the incident marks the beginning of the fulfilment—God is about to deliver his people. Acts also reviews the deed and Moses's inner thoughts: "He supposed that his kinsfolk would understand that God through him was rescuing them, but they did not understand." Hebrews 11:24–28 has a description of the same phase in Moses life, leaving out, however, the killing itself.[17] Among Church fathers, Basil the Great (*Exegetic homilies* 1:1); Gregory of Nazianzus (*Ep.* 76); Tertullian (*Marc.* 4:28); Ambrose (*Off.* 1:36); and Clement of Alexandria (*Strom.* 1.153.4–154.1) all give a positive evaluation, with differing nuances, of Moses's deed. Augustine differs. He compares Moses to Peter who also sinned in his zeal. Moses did not have an authority to do so—yet (*Faust.* 22:70; *Quaest. Exod.* 2). In the latter text Augustine however seems to ponder based on Acts 7:25 that maybe God had called him to act. He however is not able to find a direct scriptural proof for this.[18]

---

[16] Propp, *Exodus*, 168.

[17] On both of these (Acts and Hebrews), see Childs, *Exodus*, 33–40.

[18] According to Sagi's ("He Slew the Egyptian," 75) evaluation, from Augustine onwards the Church fathers strongly condemned Moses's deed. See also Timo Nisula's article in the present volume.

In the following, early Jewish texts will be opened, most of them rabbinic. A natural progression would be to follow the chronological sequence of these and, thus, aim at presenting the development of a tradition. Doing this, however, works poorly when there is a web of traditions ranging from a number of different sources, most of which are difficult to date. Scholars can seldom determine who cites whom, or indeed whether all cite a common source; moreover, some of them do not reproduce just one tradition but combine them into anthologies of interpretations. To be sure, the chronological order of the sources ought to be sought, where possible, although in this case I deem it as being of minor importance. In part the sources can be arranged in sequence: Naturally, Philo and Josephus, which I will deal with first, as well as the New Testament, mentioned already above, are the oldest. Putting the rest of the sources into a chronological order is, however, more difficult. *Leviticus Rabbah* is probably the earliest (between 400–500 CE).[19] It is followed by *Tanhuma*, the date of which, particularly those of its single homilies, is far from clear, but it is obvious that it has taken some of its traditions from *Leviticus Rabbah*.[20] *Deuteronomy Rabbah* does not fall far from *Tanhuma*.[21] The development of *'Abot de Rabbi Nathan* is unclear so no exact date for it can be given. Although its core is often assumed to stem from the early Amoraic era, the final form, especially version "A," which includes the tradition focussed on here, and which is later, may be contemporaneous with the major editing of the *Babylonian Talmud*, i.e. 500–600 CE. *Exodus Rabbah I* (i.e. chapters 1–14) is post-talmudic.[22]

---

[19] Günter Stemberger, *Einleitung in Talmud und Midrash*, Neunte, vollständig neubearbeitete Auflage (Munich: C.H. Beck, 2011), 319–23.

[20] Stemberger, *Einleitung*, 335–39. Marc Bregman, "Tanhuma Yelammedenu," in *EJ* 15 (2007), 503–04.

[21] Stemberger, *Einleitung*, 339–41. Moshe David Herr, "Deuteronomy Rabbah," in *EJ* 5 (2007), 620–21. Moshe David Herr, "Exodus Rabbah," in *EJ* 6 (2007), 624.

[22] Stemberger, *Einleitung*, 341–43. Menahem Kister, "Avot de-Rabbi Nathan," in *EJ* 2 (2007) 750–51. Jacob Neusner, *Introduction to Rabbinic Literature* (New York: Doubleday, 1994), 591.

Pekka Lindqvist

3 Apologetical Perspectives in Early Jewish Sources

We begin our survey of some early Jewish texts dealing with this incident with the two first century witnesses, Philo of Alexandria and Flavius Josephus. The former rewrites it, the latter omits it.[23] In the version recorded by Josephus (see *Jewish Antiquities* 2.254–256), Moses, after a campaign against Ethiopia, marries the Ethiopian princess and leads his troops back to Egypt. There is, however, a group hostile towards him and they inform the king about Moses who, in his daze of success, is plotting to start a revolution. After learning of the plot to eliminate Moses, sanctioned by the king, Moses subsequently escapes—in secret—to Midian. In other words, the entire episode of Exodus 2:11–14 is omitted. Only in mentioning Moses's fear of the king's revenge does the story superficially touch on the biblical narrative. Bearing in mind the problem of reading automatically-apologetic reasons into omissions, one may here join Feldman in suggesting such a motivation. The omission is conspicuous.[24] Philo (see *De vita Mosis* 1.40–44), on the other hand, does not hesitate to mention the death of the Egyptian at the hands of Moses, but goes to the extreme in describing the demonic character of this man. Prior to this Philo has, in a lengthy introduction, painted a picture of the sufferings of the Israelites and praised the extraordinary nobility of Moses.[25] In 1.44 we read:

> One of these, the cruelest of all, was killed by Moses, because he not only made no concession but was rendered harsher than ever by his exhortations, beating those who did not execute his orders with breathless promptness, persecuting them to the point of death and subjecting them to every outrage. Moses considered that his action in killing him was a right-

---

[23] Here we may note that this is exactly the same policy of handling as they have with Exodus 32—another violent act by Moses. See Lindqvist, *Sin at Sinai*, 117–46.

[24] Louis H. Feldman, *Judean Antiquities 1–4. Translation and Commentary*, Flavius Josephus. Translation and Commentary, 3rd ed. by Steve Mason (Leiden: E.J. Brill, 2000), 205. I have discussed the "omission policy" of Josephus in Lindqvist, *Sin at Sinai*, 141–46.

[25] For a discussion, see Louis H. Feldman, "Philo's View of Moses' Birth and Upbringing," *CBQ* 64:2 (2002): 258–80.

87

eous action. And righteous it was that one who only lived to destroy men should himself be destroyed.[26]

His conclusion is categorical, understandable for both a Torah-reading Jew and a Hellenistic non-Jew. The incident also gets a mention in *Legum Allegoriae* 3.12.37–39 and *De fuga et inventione* 26.148 where elements of it serve to give lessons by means of allegory: the Egyptian depicts the passion against which one has to fight. In *Leg.* Moses takes his refuge in God. While the death of Egyptian does not seem to be a great dilemma for Philo, he does, however, skip over the biblical incident in Exodus 2:13–14 about the two Hebrews fighting. Here too Feldman reads an apologetical motivation: "such an account would not redound to the credit of the Israelites."[27]

Before moving on to the apologetically-oriented midrashic expansions, I will briefly refer to a talmudic saying. While not apologetical interpretation *per se*, but focusing on another aspect, it lifts the violent incident into a position of a *halachic* precedent in a way, which does not leave much room for reading in it a criticism against Moses. *Bavli* states a *halacha*, or confirms a *halacha* found in the Scripture, through rabbinic interpretation, and then shows that Moses acted according to this. In *b. Sanh.* 58b, in a context in which the focus is on the profound differences between a Jew and non-Jew (e.g. a neighbour or a slave), we find a short reference to Exodus 2:11. *Bavli* reads:

> R.Hanina said: If a heathen smites a Jew he is worthy of death, for it is written, "And he looked this way and that way, and when he saw that there was no man, he slew the Egyptian."[28]

R. Hanina neither explains Moses's act nor justifies it: nor is the severity of the Egyptian's fault speculated upon. Whether he is about to kill or not, is

---

[26] The translation is that of Francis Henry Colson in Philo; with an English Translation by Francis Henry Colson and George Herbert Whitaker in ten volumes (and two supplementary volumes) 5, LCL (London: William Heinemann Ltd., 1966–1971).

[27] Feldman, "Moses Birth and Upbringing," 277.

[28] Translations here are those of Harry Freedman in *Sanhedrin*, Hebrew-English Edition of the Babylonian Talmud (London: Soncino Press, 1994).

of no interest here. In the immediate following context, however, we find the following, also attributed to R. Hanina, which allows us to draw the conclusion that the rabbi (or editor) does not think that the Egyptian was trying to kill the Israelite. What was happening was, in fact, far more severe.

> He who smites an Israelite on the jaw is as though he had assaulted Divine Presence (הסוטר לועו של ישראל כאילו סוטר לועו של שכינה), for it is written, "One who smiteth man attacketh Holy One!"

The concluding words, which in the excerpt above follow the translation of Freedman in the Soncino-Talmud, quote Proverbs 20:25 *verbatim*. The phrase מוקש אדם ילע קדש should be read in its biblical context in the way we read e.g. in NRSV: "It is a snare (מוקש) for one (אדם) to say rashly (ילע), 'It is Holy.'" The rabbinic interpretation, however, derives מוקש from נקש (smite), and combines the verb ילע with לועה (jaw, cheek). Thus, Proverbs 20:25 becomes the scriptural proof for the words attributed to R. Hanina. A man who hits an Israelite on the jaw, slaps no one else than God himself. The focus of these excerpts is not in the content of the incident itself, but rather it is in the essentially different status of a Jew and a non-Jew. One should pay attention to that in Hanina's halachic maxim אדם of Proverbs 20:25 means an Israelite. In this light, the biblical words of Exodus 2:12, quoted by Hanina, also get a new color: When Moses looked around, he saw "no man." And yet the Egyptian was there.[29]

I now turn to the midrashic narrative expansions in *Leviticus Rabbah*, *Midrash Tanhuma*, *'Abot de Rabbi Nathan* and *Exodus Rabbah*, each of which aim at filling in the gaps of the biblical story and giving needed explanations. I will present *three exegetical motifs*—in the second case with variant motifs—and how these are dealt with in the texts enumerated above, partly with sample passages, but mostly through paraphrase.[30] For

---

[29] See Sagi, "He Slew the Egyptian," 58–59, for the lively post-talmudic discussions concerning this halacha. It is, perhaps, needless to say that this talmudic passage, together with some others in its near context, has become to be cited very much by the latter day anti-Semites.

[30] The technical vocabulary (exegetical motif, variant motif, narrative expansion) is borrowed from James L. Kugel. See e.g. James L. Kugel, *In Potiphar's House. The Interpretive Life of Biblical Texts* (Cambridge, MA / London: Harvard University Press, 1990).

the sake of convenience I use the following descriptive titles for the motifs: "The Sin of the Egyptian," "Moses *looks* for a solution" and "Killing by the Name." Additionally, the targumic evidence (*Targum Neofiti* and *Pseudo-Jonathan*), as well as a slightly different approach found in *Deuteronomy Rabbah*, will be touched upon.

3.1 The Sin of the Egyptian

In order to justify the killing of the Egyptian, one ought to find the facts which show that he deserved it. *Leviticus Rabbah, Tanhuma,* and *Exodus Rabbah* share the same lengthy narrative expansion with only slight deviations. The core narrative is that the Egyptian supervisor enters the house of an Israelite foreman, rapes the wife of the latter and when caught by the husband, intends to kill him. It is at this point that Moses enters the scene, sees what is happening and understands, by the inspiration of the Holy Spirit, what had happened earlier. The context in which this story is placed varies.

Leviticus Rabbah 32:4 gives an exposition of the word "Whose father was an Egyptian" in Lev 24:10. The entire verse reads as follows, "A man whose mother was an Israelite, and whose father was an Egyptian … started to blaspheme the Name in a curse." In verse 11 he is identified as the son of a certain Shelomith, the daughter of Dibri, from the tribe of Dan. Whether the young man, soon to be stoned, should halachically be considered a bastard or not, divides the anonymous majority of the rabbis and R. Levi. According to the former, he could be classified as such, although halachically he was not. R. Levi says, with emphasis, that he was a bastard. The midrash poses the question: How is this to be understood? This leads to a repetition of the chain of events in Egypt.

> The taskmasters were Egyptians and the officers were Israelites. One task-master was in charge of ten officers and one officer was in charge of ten men. Thus a taskmaster had charge of a hundred men. On one occasion, a taskmaster paid an early visit to an officer and said to him: "Go and assemble me your group." When he came in, the other's wife smiled at him. Thought he: "She is mine!" So he went out and hid behind a ladder. No sooner had her husband gone out than he entered and misconducted himself with her. The other turned around and saw him coming out of the house. When the taskmaster realized that he had seen him, he went to him

and kept beating him all that day, saying to him: "Work hard, work hard!" The reason was that he wanted to kill him.[31]

The link to the original question about the blaspheming man in the Israelite camp in the desert (Lev 24:10), is—while not explicitly stated in the midrash—that his Egyptian father was the evil taskmaster killed by Moses. *Tanhuma Exodus* 9:167 (printed ed.) and *Exodus Rabbah* 1:28 reproduce the same story with minor variants. They both identify the Egyptian with a reference to Leviticus 24:10–11, and both do so by mentioning that the woman was Shelomith, mentioned in Leviticus 24:11.[32] *Tanhuma* tells the following:

> And he saw an Egyptian smiting a Hebrew (Exod 2:11). Who was this Egyptian? He was the father of the blasphemer, concerning whom it is said: "And the son of the Israelitish woman blasphemed the Name" (Lev 24:11). The Egyptian was beating the Hebrew who was the husband of Shelomith the daughter of Dibri.[33]

Only *Exodus Rabbah* explicitly states that the Israelite woman became pregnant.

3.2 Moses Looks for a Solution

The emphasis in the title is intentional, since the next logical step in these midrashic texts is to explain how Moses gained insight into what he should do. According to the biblical story, his first reaction to the violence he

---

[31] Mordecai Margulies, *Midrash Wayyikra Rabbah. A Critical Edition Based on Manuscripts and Genizah Fragments* ... 3, 2nd printing (Jerusalem: Wahrmann Books, 1972). The translation is that of Judah Slotki in *Leviticus*, Midrash Rabbah translated into English ... 4 (London: Soncino Press, 1983).

[32] I have some difficulty in reading Lehrman's suggestion that *Exod. Rab.* 1:28 would want to tell that Shelomith was the only adulterous woman in Israel, but that there was then this other woman, who was not, but yet was raped. See Simon Maurice Lehrman, *Exodus*, Midrash Rabbah translated into English ... 3 (London: Soncino Press, 1951), 36. In light of what *Lev. Rab.* and *Tanh* state it would be an unlikely opinion.

[33] Chanok Zundel, *Midrash Tanhuma 'al hamishshah humshe Torah 'im ha-perushim ha-mefursamim* (Jerusalem: Lewin-Epstein, 1973). The translation is that of Samuel A. Berman in *Midrash Tanhuma-Yelamedenu. An English Translation of Genesis and Exodus from the Printed Version of Tanhuma-Yelammedenu...* (Hoboken: KTAV, 1996).

witnesses, is to "turn this way and that way" (וכה כה), i.e. to *look*. What he notices is that there is no one else around. In one way or other this leads him to kill the man. While the most natural way to understand the phrase would be that he "looked around"[34], the midrashist do not contend with this. The wording is interesting, bi-partite and, moreover, without a direct parallel in the same sense in the MT.[35] Several variant motifs concerning what he looked at, emerge. Firstly, Moses either becomes aware of what had happened in the Israelite man's house and what is happening in front of him—i.e. the Egyptian is trying to kill the Israelite (*Lev. Rab., Tanh.*); or, secondly, after having looked around he understands that he is the only person present to take necessary action for the sake of God (opinion of R. Judah in *Lev. Rab.* and *Exod. Rab.* 1:29)[36]; or, thirdly, he did this to pronounce the Tetragrammaton against the Egyptian (opinion of R. Nehemiah in *Lev. Rab.* and *Exod. Rab.* 1:29); or, fourthly, he looks into the future (in addition to the past or present; therefore the bi-partite expression "this way and that way"!) and understands that there will never be any righteous offspring rising from this Egyptian (opinion of the Rabbis in *Lev. Rab.* and *Exod. Rab.* 1:29), and therefore he should be slain.

This last motif is also found in the targumic tradition.[37] *Targum Neofiti* Exod 2:11–12 has a literal translation with no additions. However, in its

---

[34] Or "to the left and to the right" as in Cornelis Houtman, *Exodus*, 1, A Historical Commentary on the Old Testament (Kampen: Kok, 1993), 292.

[35] To be sure, the phrase וכה כה is well-attested (see e.g. Num 11:31, 23.15 etc.), as for example Childs points out; see *Exodus*, 28. But in the sense *look around* it is not.

[36] Lehrman comments upon this: "so he acted on the Rabbinic advice 'Where there is no man, be thou the man.'" Lehrman, *Exodus*, 37, n.1. The advice is the famous maxim of Rabban Gamaliel, the son of Judah haNasi, found in *m. 'Abot* 2:5.

[37] Here we may also pick up b. Soṭah 46b and its discussion on Elisha and the bears—the incident in 2 Kings 2:23–24, briefly referred already above in fn 6. A series of explanations for the rage of Elisha, conspicuously similar to the defense of Moses, is given in *Bavli*. According to 2:24, Elisha "turned around and saw them" and then curses them. What the prophet saw is explained in four different ways: he saw that their mothers had conceived them on the Day of Atonement, or that they were half-gentiles (aping the ways of Amorites), or that "there was no sap of commandments in them." This last argument is then questioned. Perhaps, after all, he should not have destroyed them, since there might have risen some God-fearing men from among them in the future. Rabbi Eleazar, however, rejects this option: "Neither in them nor in their descendants unto the end of all generations." See *Sotah: Translated into English with Notes, Glossary and Indices by Abraham Cohen*, Hebrew-English Edition of the Babylonian

two marginal glosses it shows an acquaintance with the motif. To the phrase "he looked this way and that way" marginal gloss 1 attaches the following addition "in a spirit of prophecy in this world and in the world to come and saw, and behold, no just man was coming forth from him and he struck the Egyptian and buried him in the sand." Gloss 2 has a slightly differing, although substantially similar, version, as do the manuscripts V, N and P.[38] *Targum Ps-J.* Exod 2:12 expands the biblical original in a similar way:

> And Moses, in the wisdom of his mind, looked and considered every gener-
> ation, and he saw that no proselyte would arise from that Egyptian, and
> that no one from his children's children would ever repent. So he struck
> down the Egyptian and hid him in the sand.[39]

Exodus Rabbah (1:29) introduces its discussion with a unique interpretation of "seeing no one" (literally "that there was no man"). This does not
only mean that there were no others present, but also that Moses
understood that the Israelite was dying, i.e. that the only other Jewish man
would soon be taken away. Sample texts of the three midrashic excerpts
discussed above, now follow. *Leviticus Rabbah* reads:

> Thereupon the Holy Spirit began to stir in Moses; hence it is written "And
> he looked this way and that" (Exod 11:12). What is the signification of the
> expression "this way and that"? That he saw what the taskmaster had done
> to the officer in the house and in the field. He thought: "Not enough that he
> misconducted himself with his wife but he must seek to kill him!" Instantly,
> "When he saw that there was no man, he smote the Egyptian." (11:12) R.

Talmud (London: The Soncino Press, 1994). It should be also noted, for the sake of clarity,
that Elisha's "looking back and seeing them" and Moses's "looking this way and that" have no
obvious link with each other. b. Soṭah 46b includes a saying attributed to Rab and Rabban
Simeon ben Gamaliel, interpreting the glance of Elisha as akin to what might be called the
"fatal glance of a Sage," known from other talmudic stories. "Rab said: He actually looked
upon them, as it has been taught: Rabban Simeon b. Gamaliel says: 'Wherever the Sages set
their eyes there is either death or calamity.'"
[38] Martin McNamara. *Targum Neofiti 1: Exodus*, The Aramaic Bible 2 (Edinburgh: T&T. Clark,
1994), 16.
[39] Michael Maher, *Targum Pseudo-Jonathan: Exodus*, The Aramaic Bible 2 (Edinburgh: T&T.
Clark, 1994), 165.

Judah, R. Nehemiah, and our Rabbis differ on the interpretation of this. R. Judah says: "He saw that there was no one to stand up and display zeal in the name of the Holy One, blessed be he, so he slew him himself." R. Nehemiah says: "He saw that there was none to stand up and utter the Ineffable Name against him, so he slew him." Our Rabbis say: "He saw that there was no prospect of anything good emanating from him or from his children, or from his children's children to the end of all generations, so he instantly "smote the Egyptian."

Tanhuma Exodus 9:167 reads:

> Moses perceived through the Holy Spirit what the Egyptian had done to the man's wife and that now he was beating her husband as well, and he said to him: "Is it not enough that you violated his wife, must you then smite him also?" He became enraged at the Egyptian, And he looked this way and that way (Exod 2:12). Obviously, he was aware that the Egyptian had violated the woman and was now smiting her husband. When he saw that there was no man there, (he knew) that the man was destined to die at his hands: And he smote the Egyptian (ibid., v. 12).

Exodus Rabbah 1:29 reads:

> *And when he saw that there was no man*—for he saw that the smitten man would no longer live. R. Judah said: He saw *that there was no man* who would be zealous for God and slay him. R. Nehemiah says: He saw that there was none who would mention over him God's name and slay him. The Sages said: He saw that there was no hope that righteous persons would arise from him of his offspring until the end of generations.

Finally, *'Abot de Rabbi Nathan* (A) 20 (§96) presents one more interpretation of the phrase "there was no man." Since there was no man present, Moses was not able to consult other Israelites, even less to gather a *Sanhedrin*, which would have had the authority to pass a sentence. Therefore he set up a heavenly *Sanhedrin* of angels to decide:

What do the words that there was no man imply? They teach that Moses had set up a Sanhedrin of ministering angels and said to them, "Shall I kill this man?" They replied, "Kill him." [40]

Moses's consultation with the angels also occurs in *Exodus Rabbah* 1:29 with a somewhat different idea. Since the only man present was Moses, and he obviously was of the opinion that the man deserved death, the biblical text says "there was no man (to defend the man)."

> When Moses saw this, he took counsel with the angels and said to them: "This man deserves death." They agreed; hence it says: "and when he saw that there was no man" to say a good word for him. "And he smote the Egyptian."

The conclusion from both texts cited here is that Heaven agreed: The man deserved to be sentenced to death. Moreover, Moses cannot be viewed as an uncontrolled zealot: rather than acting short-temperedly, he consulted the heavenly court.

3.3. Killing with the Name
The midrashic tradition also briefly discusses the way in which Moses killed the Egyptian. Two of them may be called brutal, although easily imaginable, i.e. "with the fist" (R. Isaac in *Lev. Rab.* 32:4, R. Abyathar in *Exod. Rab.* 1:29), as well as the method suggested by some anonymous sages, namely that "he took a trowel full of clay and smashed his skull" (*Tanh.*; almost identically in *Exod. Rab.*). A third opinion is recorded in these two midrashes as a continuation of the preceding, more violent manner. According to *Tanhuma* "others say, that he invoked the Divine Name and slew him, as it says: 'Sayest thou to kill me?'" (Exod 2:14). *Exodus Rabbah* gives an identical explanation in the name of *the Rabbis*. However *'Abot de Rabbi Nathan* provides us with some additional words making the meaning plain:

---

[40] The translation is that of Abraham Cohen in *The Minor Tractates of the Talmud*, Hebrew-English Edition of the Babylonian Talmud (London: Soncino Press, 1965).

And do you think he killed him by the sword? No, he killed him with speech, as it is stated, Dost thou say to kill me as thou didst kill the Egyptian, proving that he killed him by [pronouncing] the Name.

The peculiar formulation in the Masoretic text, with a parenthetical participle אמר, uttered on the following day by one of the quarrelling Israelites[41], thus gave a clue to the midrashic interpreters that the power of the word, i.e. Tetragrammaton, was involved.[42]

4 A Non-Apologetical Aspect

The only rabbinic text judging the deed of Moses less favorably is *Deuteronomy Rabbah*, and even here we must leave the printed standard edition. According to *Deuteronomy Rabbah* 2:27–28, Moses's own experience as a murderer was the reason for his deep commitment to the creation of the cities of refuge. The following excerpt (lacking in the printed edition) has Moses himself flee into a city of refuge when he leaves Egypt. Moses feels remorse for what he had done.

> Since he killed him, he fled to a city of refuge, as it is said, "But Moses fled from before Pharaoh ... and he sat down by a well." What is "sat by a well?" He sang a song, as it is said, "Then sang Moses." And why did he sing? Because he knew the sorrow of a murderer, as the ordinary man would say, "he who has eaten of the dish knows its taste" and when the Holy One,

---

[41] The translation of the biblical phrase has been particularly difficult. Durham suggests the following: "Are you to kill me, say, as you killed that Egyptian?" (Durham, *Exodus*, 18). Propp translates: "Who set you as a man, ruler and judge over us? To kill me, do you say, as you killed the Egyptian." He comments further, that the verb אמר "often connotes mental action." To express thinking, when introducing indirect speech of a person, MT uses "say." (Propp, *Exodus*, 161, 165).

[42] On the deadly power and use of the Name in rabbinic literature, see Ephraim E. Urbach, *The Sages: Their Concepts and Beliefs*, translated from the Hebrew by Israel Abrahams (Jerusalem: The Magnes Press, 1975), 124–34. Already before the Common Era Artapanus (whose "On the Jews" we know fragmentarily via Eusebius) mentions Moses using the Name against the Pharaoh. Cf. John J. Collins, "Artapanus," in *The Old Testament Pseudepigrapha 2* (ed. James H. Charlesworth; London: Darton, Longman and Todd, 1985), 901.

blessed be He, told him the remedy, Moses began singing, as it is said, "Then sang Moses."[43]

This midrash builds a rather surprising bridge from the well in the land of Midian about which we read in Exodus 2:15 ("and he sat by a well") to Deuteronomy 32, where we meet the Song of Moses, his final words. According to the midrashist the promise of remedy was already present by the well in Midian in the midst of his sorrow, fear and remorse over the violent act, or alternatively, he had to bear the burden of sorrow through-out his career until he heard the liberating words from the Lord, and began singing his powerful swan song and last will. As a result, despite the fact that Moses felt "the sorrow of a murderer" neither here should we speak of any condemnation of the act of Moses.[44]

5 A Final Word

The early Jewish attitude towards the violent deed of Moses in Exod 2:11–12 is dominantly apologetical and the strategies vary from censorship to the rewriting the story with narrative expansions. Two characteristics in the biblical story have contributed to this: First, the sparse wording leaves gaps which ask to be filled. Secondly, there are details in the biblical texts which invite the midrashist to seize them and make use of them as evidence about what really happened. The narrative expansions given by the rabbis make it clear that Moses was in the right and he had every reason to kill the man. Above I divided these explanations into three classes. For the first, the rabbis simply state the wickedness of the Egyptian, for the second, Moses gains deeper insight by "looking this way and that," which is interpreted in various ways, and for the third, he uses the holy name of the Lord as his sword. In the last case, there is in a fact no

---

[43] See Lieberman's edition based on the Oxford manuscript 147 (a corrected 2nd edition: Lieberman, *Midrash Debarim Rabbah* (Jerusalem: Shalem Books, 1992). Cited according to Sagi, "He Slew the Egyptian," 74.

[44] Again, we may refer in passing to another "violent" figure, Elisha, in b. Soṭah. We have already seen above that his summoning of the bears is defended (b. Soṭah 46b) in a way which resembles the defense of Moses in *midrashim*. On the other hand, however, in 47a he is said to have been afflicted with three illnesses. One of these was laid on him because "he stirred up the bears against the children."

violence at all as far as Moses is involved. It is clear that the wickedness of the Egyptian is naturally a precondition in these two latter "strategies" too.

In passing two additional observations were made: The approaches of the two first century Hellenistic Jewish writers, Philo and Josephus, are similar to their treatment of another violent moment in Moses's life, i.e. the golden calf episode. Philo rewrites both, while Josephus skips the incidents altogether. Their different approaches can be explained by their intended, or potential, audiences. The great law-giver and leader of the Jews should not be shown in an unfavorable light before a potentially ill-willed readership. Rabbis, on the other hand, can be presumed to have their own flocks in mind. Attention was also paid to a certain level of similarity between the rabbinic ways of treating the two figures, Moses and Elisha. It is of importance for the Sages that one can find and show the mitigating circumstances surrounding the incident—the search is done with the tools of midrash—and that this results in the irrefutable conclusion: what was done was correct and just.

Qoheleth's Reality: Absurd or Not?

Mikael Nouro

Introduction

Surveying commentaries on Qoheleth, one cannot help noticing the peculiar position and sentiments of oddity set in motion by this enigmatic book. It is "the Bible's strangest book"[1]. "A less conventional preacher than [the author of the book] would be hard to find!"[2] "Perhaps no other book in the Bible has so steadfastly defied analysis and refused to be typed … Qoheleth remains as mysterious as his name, as the wisdom he sought (and failed, 7:23) to capture."[3] Qoheleth's message has been called "oppressive"[4] and his God "despotic."[5] It is as if the book itself, along with its main character, appears abnormal[6], an anomaly in the current of wisdom literature[7], accepted reluctantly in the canon only because of its

---

[1] James L. Crenshaw, *Ecclesiastes*, OTL (Philadelphia: Westminster, 1987), 23.

[2] Robert Gordis, *Koheleth—The Man and his World. A Study of Ecclesiastes*, 3rd ed. (New York: Jewish Theological Seminary of America, 1968), 5.

[3] Roland E. Murphy, *Ecclesiastes*, WBC 23A (Dallas: Word Books, 1992), Preface.

[4] Crenshaw, *Ecclesiastes*, 23.

[5] Crenshaw, *Ecclesiastes*, 30; Aarre Lauha, *Kohelet*, BKAT 19 (Neukirchen-Vluyn: Neukirchener, 1978), 17.

[6] The character Qoheleth has not been able to escape a psychological or even a psychoanalytical scrutiny, see e.g. Frank Zimmerman, *The Inner World of Qohelet* (New York: Ktav 1973). See also Michael V. Fox, *Qohelet and his Contradictions*, JSOTSup 71 (Sheffield: Almond, 1989), 11.

[7] Recently, the meaningfulness of "wisdom literature" itself as a designation for certain biblical books belonging to such a genre has been challenged, see e.g. Will Kynes, *An Obituary for "Wisdom Literature": The Birth, Death, and Intertextual Reintegration of a Biblical Corpus* (Oxford: Oxford University, 2019). This discussion, however, goes beyond the scope of this article.

supposed orthodox glosses.[8] Even in the book of Job, considered to be another dissenting voice, the causal connection between deed and consequence, implicit in Proverbs but attacked by Qoheleth, seems presupposed in the end. Why does this man complain all the time and declare everything to be 'vanity' or 'worthless'? What is Qoheleth's constructive theological message?

In Qoheleth scholarship it is common to have widely different, sometimes even diametrically opposite, opinions on matters ranging from the date, genre and composition of the book to questions concerning its message and purpose. In this article I will approach the normality/abnormality of Qoheleth by juxtaposing my own reading of the book with that of Michael Fox, who portrays a picture of a sage declaring that human existence is 'utterly absurd.' This is not to say that 'absurdity' or 'abnormality' mean the same thing, even if these words may be said to bear a certain family resemblance. In fact, Fox posits Qoheleth more firmly in the 'normal' Jewish wisdom tradition than many other commentators.[9] Nonetheless, I find Fox's position, particularly his understanding of the meaning and function of the book's key concept *hebel*, symptomatic for challenging the 'normality' of Qoheleth.

Qoheleth's language and modes of expression are indeed peculiar. In this article I argue that we should pay more attention to Hellenistic philosophy in order to understand the purpose and message of the book better. Doing this would also affect our views about the 'inner life' of its main character.

The Meaning of *hebel* and its Function as a Hermeneutical Key to the Understanding of the Book of Qoheleth

Hebel is the most central keyword in the book of Qoheleth. How we translate and understand *hebel* will largely determine how we will read the book as a whole. Conversely, and more importantly, our understanding of the entire book will most likely determine the way we translate and understand the term. Either way, when pressed for a translation of *hebel*

---

8 Thus e.g. Lauha, *Kohelet*, 6–7 and 20–21.
9 Fox, *Qohelet and his Contradictions*, e.g. ch. 3.

Mikael Nouro

the interpreter of this complicated book is already forced to show much of his hand.

Of the 73 attestations of *hebel* in the Hebrew Bible, 38 are found in Qoheleth. The importance of the word is highlighted not only because of its frequency, but also through its location in central places in the composition. After the introductory verse 1:1, a cluster of *hebels* are thrown at the reader/hearer right at the beginning of the exposition, stressing the evocative function of the word. Verse 1:2 appears again, in a slightly less intensive form, in 12:8, forming an inclusio with 1:2.[10]

The literal meaning of *hebel* is breath, vapor. Through its history of interpretation, alongside its concrete meaning *hebel* has always also been understood in an abstract or metaphorical way.[11] In the Vulgate, Jerome translated *hebel* as 'vanitas' ('vanity,' 'emptiness,' 'falsity,' 'futility'). *Vanitas*, however, lacks the connotations of temporality and the concrete imagery of breath. Thus, while early Jewish interpreters mainly understood *hebel* in its metaphorical sense of temporality or brevity, early Christian interpreters understood it primarily as a value judgement.[12]

In Western Christianity Jerome's commentary on Ecclesiastes constituted the more or less undisputed interpretation of the book for more than a millennium, and 'vanity' remained the overwhelmingly dominant translation of *hebel* up to the end of the 19th century. The 20th and 21st centuries have seen a plethora of suggestions of numerous different individual translations as well as different interpretative models for understanding the word. Translations such as 'fleeting' or 'transitory'

---

10 12:8 seems to have a double function in forming an inclusio with both 11:7 and 1:2. Most commentators separate the epilogue 12:9–14 (or even a first and second epilogue in vv. 9–11 and 12–14 respectively) from the rest of the book. While not taking a definitive stand on whether the epilogue was written by the same person or not, Fox sees no contradiction between the epilogue(s) and the rest of the book and introduces his idea of a frame-narrator adopting the persona Qoheleth in 1:2–12:8, Michael V. Fox, "Frame-Narrative and Composition in the Book of Qohelet," *HUCA* 48 (1977): 83–106. I agree with Fox on the high degree of unity of the book.
11 For an overview, see Gregory R. Vruggink, *Hbl in Ecclesiastes: Abel as Symbol Referent* (Master Thesis, Calvin Theological Seminary, 2016), 4–21, https://digitalcommons.calvin.edu/cts_theses/18/
12 Russell L. Meek, "Twentieth- and Twenty-first-century Readings of Hebel in Ecclesiastes," *CBR* 14 (2016): 280–84.

highlight the temporal connotations of *hebel*, 'emptiness' or 'nothingness' its derogatory functions.[13] A major divide in the understanding of *hebel* is whether the term is to be understood axiologically, expressing value judgement, or epistemologically.[14]

One suggestion that seems to evoke strong opinions for and against, is the translation of *hebel* as 'absurd.' This was suggested by Michael Fox in an article in 1986.[15] In his book *Qoheleth and his Contradictions* from 1989, Fox explored further Qoheleth's thinking, guided strongly by this particular understanding of *hebel*.[16] In *A Time to Tear Down and a Time to Build Up*, Fox modified some of his ideas, but his basic ideas about *hebel* as absurd have remained largely intact, as Fox himself stated.[17] Fox's main argument is that *hebel* expresses Qoheleth's view of human existence, one which, in essence, appears to him to be absurd.

Fox's suggestion has been highly influential.[18] In this paper I first sketch an overview of Fox's argument and then comment on it critically. Fox's treatment of Qoheleth is comprehensive, but I will mainly focus on the aspects of absurdity. I argue that for Qoheleth *hebel* is not descriptive of reality in the way Fox argues, and even if it were, 'absurd' would be too strong a rendering. I offer an alternative understanding of *hebel*, connected to a comparison with Hellenistic philosophy.

Although the basic question I try to answer in this article is whether Qoheleth really perceived reality or human existence as fundamentally

---

[13] For a useful and accessible overview of different interpretations of hebel, see Meek, *Readings of Hebel*.

[14] For an epistemological interpretation, see e.g. Graham Ogden, *Qoheleth, Readings. A New Biblical Commentary.* (Sheffield: Phoenix, 1987), 22; Craig G. Bartholomew, *Ecclesiastes* (Grand Rapids: Baker Academic, 2009), 104–07, "enigmatic." For a critical view, see Norbert Lohfink, "Ist Kohelets הבל-Aussage erkenntnistheoretisch gemeint?" in *Qohelet in the Context of Wisdom*, ed. Anton Schoors, BETL 136 (Leuven: Leuven University, 1998), 41–59.

[15] Michael V. Fox, "The Meaning of Hebel for Qohelet," *JBL* 105 (1986): 409–26.

[16] Fox, *Qohelet and his Contradictions*.

[17] Michael V. Fox, *A Time to Tear Down and a Time to Build Up: A Rereading of Ecclesiastes* (Grand Rapids: Eerdmans, 1999); idem, "On הבל in Qoheleth: A Reply to Mark Sneed," *JBL* 138 (2019): 559–63.

[18] E.g. Diethelm Michel, *Untersuchungen zur Eigenart des Buches Qohelet*, BZAW 183 (Berlin: De Gruyter, 1989), 40–51 ("sinnlos"), Anton Schoors, *Ecclesiastes*, HCOT (Leuven: Peeters, 2013), Crenshaw, *Ecclesiastes*, 57. The translation *absurdité* was suggested already by André Barucq in *Ecclésiaste*, Verbum Salutis, Ancien Testament 3 (Paris: Beauchesne, 1968).

Mikael Nouro

absurd, it is evident that such an undertaking is intimately linked to the way we understand and choose to define and translate *hebel*. Nonetheless, I am confident that these two questions can be kept sufficiently apart, thus avoiding a completely circular reasoning.

Qoheleth's Contradictions (and their Solutions)

Any reader of the book of Qoheleth is puzzled by what inevitably seems to be its internal inconsistencies. These have been noted from very early on in Jewish exegesis. According to b. Šab 30b, "The sages sought to suppress the book of Qoheleth because its statements contradict each other."[19]

Wisdom seems to be denigrated in 1:17–18, 2:15–16, but affirmed as an advantage in 2:13, 7:11,19, 9:16–18 and 10:10. The significance of pleasure is questioned in 2:2–3,10–11, but repeatedly commended in 2:24–26, 5:17–19 and 8:15. Qoheleth hates life in 2:17, but affirms life in 9:4–6,10 and 11:7. In 4:2–3 and 6:3–6 even non-being is preferred. God does not seem to intervene in human affairs in 8:10,14,17 and 9:2–3 but divine retribution is implied in 3:17, 5:5, 8:12–13, 11:9 and 12:13.[20] Verses such as 2:24–26, 6:10, 8:8 and 9:1 which seem to presuppose a predetermined existence clash with the numerous admonitions in the book: 4:17, 5:1-2, 5:3, 5:5, 5:6, 5:7, 7:2, 7:9, 7:10, 7:14, 7:16, 7:17, 7:21–22, 8:2, 8:3, 9:7, 9:8, 9:9, 9:10, 10:4, 10:20, 11:1, 11:2, 11:6, 11:8, 11:9aa, 11:9ab, 11:10 and 12:1a.[21] Moreover, verses such as 8:5,11 barely fit into a rigoristic deterministic scheme.

Fox notes at the outset, that the Tannaim did not deny the contradictions in the book, but the assertion that "it begins with words of Torah and it ends with words of Torah"[22] was enough to neutralize the book's

---

[19] Fox, *A Time to Tear Down*, 1–2, explains that this report by the Tannaim had nothing to do with doubts about the status of Qoheleth as inspired or canonical literature, but rather whether it was suitable and "safe" for general use. Qoh. Rab. compared verses such as 2:2 with 7:3, 8:15 and 4:2 with 9:4 respectively. See also Qoh. Rab. 1:3.

[20] My listing here is based on Choong-Leong Seow, *Ecclesiastes*, AB 18C (New York: Doubleday, 1997), 39, with some additions.

[21] Concerning the *Mahnworte*, see Christian Klein, *Kohelet und die Weisheit Israels. Eine formgeschichtliche Studie*, BWANT 132 (Stuttgart: Kohlhammer, 1994), 105–14.

[22] b. Šab 30b (cf. above).

103

internal contradictoriness.[23] The majority of commentators, however, has found the contradictions in the book disturbing, and consequently employed various strategies to eliminate them, in part or in full. Fox recounts different hermeneutical techniques for resolving the inconsistencies in the book, as well as pointing out the problems connected with these techniques.[24]

Harmonization is the traditional approach. Apparently conflicting statements are shown to use words differently or deal with different matters. An example is found in b. Šab 30b: "I praised *simchah*" (8:15) is said to pertain to the happiness that comes from fulfilling commandments, whereas "and *simchah*—what does this accomplish?" (2:2) speaks of pleasure that does not proceed from the commandments. Fox considers a certain measure of harmonization necessary for the reading process, but rejects appeals to extraneous factors, such as divine commandments as mentioned above and forced *ad hoc* definitions.

One solution to ease the tensions is to assign problematic propositions to a later hand. Fox observed that by removing the proposed redactional layers, a) the syntactical and logical problems tend to increase rather than decrease, b) supposed glosses do not follow the statements they are supposed to correct, e.g. in 2:12-16, 3:17, 8:5-7,10-14 the "skeptic" is allowed the last word, c) proposed glosses do not fulfill the purposes ascribed to the glossators, e.g. in 8:10-14 the tension is not solved in a satisfactory "pious" way and d) even with the supposed additions, the skeptical and pessimistic character of the book remains blatant.

One popular strategy is the identification of quotations in the text, and the supposed rebuttal of them by Qoheleth. The quotation hypothesis was advocated by Levy and has later been put to use by Gordis and Michel, among others.[25] Fox does not deny the existence of quotations in the book, but does not consider the identification of them as crucial. He points to the lack of specific markers for distinguishing supposed quotations. The use of

---

[23] Fox, *Contradictions*, 19. The book's consistency with Torah is also a prominent theme in Qoh. Rab.

[24] Fox, *A Time to Tear Down*, 14–26. Here only a few examples will be given.

[25] Ludwig Levy, *Das Buch Qohelet. Ein Beitrag zur Geschichte des Sadduzäismus* (Leipzig: Hinrichs, 1912); Gordis, *Koheleth*; Michel, *Untersuchungen*.

the quotation theory is also vulnerable to a certain degree of arbitrariness, which is evidenced by the variegated different reconstructions. Fox opines that if the author considered it important that we recognize that another person is speaking this or that sentence, he could have let us know, but he does not.[26] The view of the book being constructed as a dialogue faces similar problems.

Fox's solution to the question of contradictions in Qoheleth is different. Instead of harmonizing or explaining the book's contradictions away, Fox rather takes them as symptomatic of Qoheleth's understanding of human existence, which he considers in essence absurd. Relying on Albert Camus, Fox understands the essence of the absurd as a disparity between two terms that are supposed to be joined by a link of harmony or causality but are, in fact, disjunct. The absurd is an affront to reason, which seeks order in the world. Absurdity is inherent in the tension between a certain reality and a framework of expectations. Fox finds the same kind of connotations ("highly congruent," even if not completely identical) of the absurd in Camus as in Qoheleth's *hebel*: alienation, frustration, resentment, a stale taste of repeated and meaningless events, even resentment at the "gods."[27]

Fox also notes some differences between Qoheleth and Camus. Qoheleth does not advocate "rebellion" to push against the restraints placed on him, but rather recognizes that embracing life's limited possibilities is in accordance with God's will. However, Fox considers the similarities between the two thinkers to be deeper than their divergences. Thus, although Qoheleth firmly believes in God, this "incomprehensible master" is not far from the Camusian void.[28]

> Underlying Qohelet's hebel-judgements is an assumption that the system *should* be rational, which, for Qohelet, means that actions should invariably produce appropriate consequences. In fact, Qohelet stubbornly expects them to do so, see 3:17, 5:5, 7:17, 8:12b–13. Qohelet believes in the rule of divine justice. That is why he does not merely resign himself to injustice. He

---

[26] I share Fox's caution against an excessive use of the quotation theory. However, the lack of specific markers could be explained through the fact that some quotations were easily identified as such by the book's contemporary readers.

[27] Fox, *The Meaning of Hebel*, 409.

[28] Fox, *A Time to Tear Down*, 11, my quotation marks.

is shocked by it: it clashes with his belief that the world *must* work equitably. Injustices are offensive to reason. And the individual absurdities are not mere anomalies. Their absurdity infects the entire system, making "everything" absurd.[29]

As Qoheleth's use of *hebel* seems to be marked by a high degree of ambiguity[30], translating *hebel* has proven to be a complicated task. Fox rejects the alternative of using various translations, as Qoheleth's summary "everything is *hebel*" would then be meaningless. The thematic declaration and the formulaic character of the *hebel*-judgements show that for Qoheleth there is a single quality that is an *attribute of the world*.[31] Foregoing some of our counterarguments, this last point is problematic. According to Braun, when compared with the preceding literature, we can see a shift towards a more anthropological interpretation of *hebel* in Qoheleth. The implied meaning of emptiness or nothingness (Nichtigkeit) is no longer applied to the description of foreign Gods, but rather to the human condition.[32] According to Lohfink, all occurrences of *hebel*, except 1:2 and 12:8, clearly belong in the anthropological sphere.[33] Hence the הַכֹּל הֶבֶל in 12:8 cannot be interpreted in any other way. The case of 1:2 remains. While Lohfink acknowledges the openness of 1:2, he sees the immediately following sentence, מַה־יִּתְרוֹן לָאָדָם בְּכָל־עֲמָלוֹ שֶׁיַּעֲמֹל תַּחַת הַשָּׁמֶשׁ, as pointing to an anthropological interpretation and, thus, as the most suitable also for 1:2. Fox himself clearly limits *hakkol hebel* to human

---

[29] Fox, *Qohelet and his Contradictions*, 47.

[30] See also Doug Ingram, *Ambiguity in Ecclesiastes*, Library of Hebrew bible/Old Testament studies 431 (London: T&T Clark, 2006), 109.

[31] Fox, *Qohelet and his Contradictions*, 36–37, my emphasis. The LXX uses a variety of terms to translate *hebel*; κενός Job 7:16, καταιγίς Isa 57:13, εἴδωλα Jer 16:19 and μάτην Ps 38:7, 39:7. However, in Qoh exclusively ματαιότης, 'emptiness,' 'transitory,' 'vanity,' 'breath,' is used. The use of one word only probably reflects the recognition of *hebel* as a *Leitwort* for Qoheleth. Translating *hebel* with one single word is the preferred solution in most Bible translations.

[32] Rainer Braun, *Kohelet und die frühhellenistische Popularphilosophie*, BZAW 130 (Berlin: de Gruyter, 1973), 45–46. Braun nevertheless acknowledges also a cosmological meaning for *hebel*, reflecting the empiricism of the Hellenistic philosophical schools.

[33] Norbert Lohfink, "Koh 1,2, 'alles ist Windhauch'—universale oder anthropologische Aussage?" in *Der Weg zum Menschen: zur philosophischen und theologischen Anthropologie für Alfons Deissler*, ed. Rudolf Mosis and Lothar Ruppert (Freiburg: Herder, 1989), 201–16.

events, actions and experiences. Even within the range of the events of human life "everything" is not truly universal:

> It is not absurd ... that wisdom saved a city (9:13–15)—only the subsequent treatment of the wise man was absurd. It is not absurd that "God will judge the righteous and the wicked" (3:17), the absurdity lies in the delay in the execution of the sentence. *Hakkol* refers not to every event but to events in general, to life's occurrences taken as a whole. A bad day is made so by a few things—sometimes even one—going wrong, though most of what happens that day may be satisfactory. Similarly, within the totality of events many things are not absurd—some important values stand, some fundamental rules are valid—but the absurdities spoil everything.[34]

While Fox on the one hand clearly posits *hebel* (and explicitly also the expression *hakkol hebel*) in the anthropological sphere, he has created some confusion by treating *hebel*/absurd as an independent quality of the world too. *Hebel* implies a "violation of the rationality of the world."[35] According to Fox, Qoheleth's statement "Everything (that happens in life) is absurd" grasps most of what Qoheleth says, even in passages where the formulaic *hebel*-judgement is not used, e.g. 9:13–15, 10:5–7.[36] Fox further distinguishes between an action's performance and its outcome. A performance may be absurd, but when we believe the performance to be, in principle, ethically good but it, nevertheless, fails to yield the expected results, it is not the action that is absurd but the fact that there is a disparity between rational expectations and the actual consequences.[37] Considering Fox's own clear relativizations of Qoheleth's *hebel*-absurdity, a relevant question seems to me to be: simply *how much* "absurdity" is required for us to call the whole system absurd (see also below)?

Fox has of course recognized the complexity in Qoheleth's use of *hebel*. Fox does not claim universal validity for the translation of *hebel* as absurd in all instances but considers it to fit most cases. Fox does admit that in some cases other meanings may be primary, e.g. "ephemeral" in 3:19,

---

[34] Fox, *Qohelet and his Contradictions*, 44–45.
[35] Fox, *Qohelet and his Contradictions*, 46. See also Fox, *A Time to Tear Down*, 138–39.
[36] Fox, *Qohelet and his Contradictions*, 44.
[37] Fox, *Qohelet and his Contradictions*, 46–47.

11:10, 6:12, 7:15, 9:9. Fox, nonetheless, thinks that the connotation of absurdity carries over even into these cases.[38]

"Everything is absurd" is finally a complaint against God. Fox reads the "twisting" עוותו in 7:13 "no one can straighten what God has twisted" as God's distortion, the severance of deed from consequence, which strips human deeds of their significance.

> For Qohelet the reliability of the causal nexus fails, leaving only fragmented sequences of events, which, though divinely determined, must be judged random, and thus meaningless from the human perspective—and any other perspective does us no good.[39]

Counterarguments

Of course, Fox's views have also been met with criticism. Interestingly, we have a critique by Sneed, responded to, albeit in brief, by Fox himself.[40] Sneed gives three reasons why he considers Fox's notion of *hebel* as absurd to be misguided. Firstly, it is anachronistic, secondly, it fails on lexical-semantic grounds and thirdly, it downplays Qoheleth's central *carpe diem* ethic. I will deal with the last of these in the next section.

Fox lists several ancient Egyptian, Mesopotamian and Syrian texts which, according to him, express the notion of the absurd.[41] I will not go into the details of Sneed's and Fox's debate here. Suffice to say that Sneed rejects, while Fox insists on, the absurdist ideas present in these texts. Instead I focus on another problem. Fox has failed to show a specific word expressing the absurd in any of these texts. A "general sense" of absurdity might be too easily found. Considering Qoheleth, an understanding of his thinking as expressing the absurd cannot be found in early reception history, or even in later commentaries before Fox, for that matter.[42]

---

[38] Fox, *Qohelet and his Contradictions*, 42–43.

[39] Fox, *Qohelet and his Contradictions*, 47–48.

[40] Mark Sneed, "הבל as 'Worthless' in Qoheleth: A Critique of Michael V. Fox's 'Absurd' Thesis," *JBL* 136 (2017): 879–94; Fox, "On הבל in Qoheleth."

[41] Fox, *A Time to Tear Down*, 11–14.

[42] It is interesting to compare this with Fox, *Qohelet and his Contradictions*, 9: "Qohelet's message is not a mystery waiting for its solution until the twentieth century, or rather, always waiting for the next scholarly study to solve it."

Sneed also criticizes Fox for arguing for a meaning of *hebel* that is not found elsewhere in the Hebrew Bible. Fox is right in asserting that Qoheleth's use of *hebel* need not be dictated by the earlier use of the word in the Hebrew Bible. However, it does form a kind of semantic starting point, from which Qoheleth develops his characteristic *Leitwort* further. Schwienhorst-Schönberger, stressing the narrative aspect, concludes that the reader/hearer of 1:2, not yet knowing the directions Qoheleth will take, will have encountered the word with an understanding of it based on this context.[43] According to Seybold, Qoheleth uses the word in a way that shows that he is aware of all the possible meanings and connotations it has in the OT.[44] Qoheleth's use of *hebel* amounts to a semantic broadening of the word, but not to a completely new semantic innovation.[45] One might claim, as Fox does[46], that the idea of the absurd is somehow close to other meanings *hebel* might have. In that case we may ask whether not the concept of 'absurdity' is watered down.

Hebel as Devaluation: Qoheleth and the *eudaimonia* of Hellenistic Philosophy

While 'absurd' as a meaning for *hebel* might be too far from other meanings it has in the Hebrew Bible, it is evident that with Qoheleth we have an innovative semantic broadening of the word. What were the impulses for this new and peculiar use of *hebel*? I suggest that we should

---

43 Ludger Schwienhorst-Schönberger, *"Nicht im Menschen gründet das Glück" (Koh 2:24). Kohelet im Spannungsfeld jüdischer Weisheit und Hellenistischer Philosophie*, HBS 2 (Freiburg: Herder, 1994), 16–17.

44 Klaus Seybold, *TDOT* 3 (1978), 318.

45 Sneed, "הבל as 'Worthless,'" 889, invokes Weeks, who claims that "hebel does not have this meaning [absurd] elsewhere, and it is difficult to see either how 'breath' could have come to mean 'absurd,' or how the original readers were supposed to deduce this meaning. To put it another way, if hebel were a completely unknown word, then Fox would have supplied an excellent understanding from its use in the context of Ecclesiastes, but it is not, and his definition jars with the meanings and connotations established from numerous other contexts." Stuart Weeks, *An Introduction to the Study of Wisdom Literature*, T & T Clark Approaches to Biblical Studies (London: T & T Clark, 2010), 81. This is slightly puzzling, as Weeks' argument on the one hand seems to affirm Fox's thesis, finding the idea of absurdity strongly featured in the book.

46 Fox, *Qohelet and his Contradictions*, 42–43.

seek answers by looking at currents in contemporary Hellenistic philosophy rather than modern existentialism.[47]

In his Nicomachean Ethics Aristotle considered happiness the highest good for man. In the Hellenistic philosophies the eudaimonistic emphasis is intensified still further. The quest for happiness is the underlying question and the ultimate goal of all philosophy.[48]

Two differences in comparison with Aristotle can be noted. For Aristotle ethics was subordinated to politics. The questions about the well-being and right conduct of man was seen through the background of his role as a citizen in the *polis*. In the Hellenistic philosophies we can note a radical shift to an individualistic thinking.

Secondly, Aristotle considered virtuous action according to reason as central for *eudaimonia*. Additionally, Aristotle considered some amount of external goods as a prerequisite for happiness, for example health, friends and at least a certain amount of wealth. The Hellenistic philosophers took one radical step further. Finding the idea that happiness was dependent on external circumstances less than satisfactory, they declared that (almost) all external goods were a matter of indifference, ἀδιάφορα. Eudaimonia was dependent solely on man's own mental disposition and was to be reached through one's own strength. The extremity of this position can be seen in the statement that the wise man is happy even while being tortured.[49] It is easy to see that the notion of *adiaphora* and the individualism of Hellenistic philosophy go hand in hand.

The extent and classification of things that counted as *adiaphora* was an issue debated particularly in Stoicism.[50] A list of things which are

---

[47] Even if I believe there was an influence from Hellenistic philosophy on Qoheleth, it is not possible to argue for it at length here. However, even if this connection is historically rejected, I consider a comparison between Qoheleth and Hellenistic philosophy illuminating from a purely systematic point of view. I also consider this to be a strong argument in itself in favour of Hellenistic influences.

[48] According to Schwienhorst-Schönberger, *Nicht im Menschen gründet das Glück*, 246, *eudaimonia* is also the central theme in the book of Qoheleth. Schwienhorst-Schönberger argues forcefully, that Qoheleth picked up the theme from Hellenistic philosophy.

[49] Diogenes Laertius 10.22.

[50] 'Things' here are understood as objects of human concern. See Brad Inwood, "Stoic Ethics," in *The Cambridge History of Hellenistic Philosophy*, eds. Keimpe Algra, Jonathan Barnes, Jaap Mansfeld, and Malcolm Schofield, (Cambridge: Cambridge University, 1999), 691.

indifferent is given by Diogenes Laertius 7.102: life and death, health and illness, pleasure and discomfort, good looks and ugliness, physical strength and weakness, wealth and poverty, good and bad reputation, high and low birth; further in 7.106: natural ability, skill, even moral progress and their opposites. As if this were not enough, Diogenes Laertius concludes this second list with an additional 'etc.'

Qoheleth also builds up an impressive list of what can be considered *hebel*. Seybold notes that the dominant use of *hebel* in a nominal statement shows that for Qoheleth too it serves a purpose of evaluation, or *devaluation*, with critic-polemic intentions. The totality of human activity 1:14, 2:17, Qoheleth's own work 2:11, all living things 3:19, the future and youth 11:8,10, striving after wisdom 2:15 (1:17), laughter and pleasure 2:2, the life work of the wise 2:19, 21, 23, 26, energy exerted by the skillful 4:4, wealth 4:8, 5:9, the career of the wise 4:16, zeal 6:9, criticism of the wise, 7:6, decisions by the mighty 8:10, confidence in the law of just retribution 8:14 can all be characterized by *hebel*.[51] The expression *gam-seh/hu-hebel* is repeated fourteen times: 2:1,15,19,21,23,26, 4:4,8,16, 5:9, 6:9, 7:6, 8:10,14. Moreover, in 1:2 and 12:8 we are told that 'everything' is *hebel*. While of course not identical, when comparing the lists I think the similarity between what Qoheleth lists as *hebel* and the things that were customarily singled out as *adiaphora*, particularly in Stoic philosophy, is notable. The respective lists can be seen to comprise the totality of human concern and striving.

While using 'indifferent' as a definition for *hebel* may not match every occurrence in Qoheleth perfectly, it is certainly semantically closer to other uses of *hebel* in the Hebrew Bible than 'absurd.' Yet Qoheleth's usage of *hebel* is so distinct that the assumption of an outside influence is certainly plausible. 'Indifferent' is a clear value judgement, firmly anchored in Qoheleth's own time.

Things indifferent constitute the huge class between what is good and bad. Apart from utterly meaningless things, such as whether the number of hairs on one's head is odd or even, the Stoics distinguished between preferred and dispreferred indifferents, which could be described as having either a positive or a negative value. Preferred indifferents are

---

[51] See Seybold, *TDOT 3*, 319.

'according to nature.' For Qoheleth, wisdom, though *hebel*, seems to have a relative value 1:13–14.[52]

Adiaphora is a relative concept. That which makes a difference or is seen as a matter of indifference can only be understood with respect to something else. The indifferents are things which make no contribution to a happy or unhappy life.[53] For the Stoic, the road to happiness consists of the virtuous life. For Qoheleth, the surest way to achieve happiness is to enjoy the creation in this worldly life to the fullest.

Fox's main argument rests on his understanding of *hebel* as 'absurd' and his corresponding understanding of Qoheleth's perception of reality. It is true that the word *hebel* dominates and permeates almost the whole exposition, although we can note a few concentrations of the term. In addition we are informed that 'everything'[54] is *hebel* in 1:2 and 12:8. We can, however, offer a counter-proof here: is there anything that is excluded from the *hebel*-domain? We may note that the *carpe diem* theme of Qoheleth, 2:24–26, 3:12–13,22, 5:17–19, 8:15, 9:7–10, 11:9–12:1 is never considered to be *hebel*. As Lohfink points out, the works of God are never valued as *hebel* either.[55] All *carpe diem* passages are intimately connected to God and specifically the gifts that he bestows on man[56]. As the *carpe diem* motive is clearly connected to Qoheleth's creation theology, the character of life itself as a gift from God is emphasized. Here we may also see the different preconditions of Qoheleth compared to the more individualistic Hellenistic philosophy. What Qoheleth shares with the Hellenistic philosophers, however, is the understanding of happiness clearly as a subjective experience, mainly unconnected to externals. Humankind can distinguish between what is *hebel* and what is not, however, only by understanding that not only is (the temporary) life and the whole (lasting) creation a gift from God but so is also the enabling to enjoy the creation[57].

---

[52] Cf. also the *tob*-sayings in ch 7.
[53] Inwood, "Stoic Ethics," 692.
[54] On the meaning of *ha-kol*, see above.
[55] Lohfink, "Koh 1,2, 'alles ist Windhauch,'" 213–14.
[56] See also 12:7.
[57] For a contrasting view, see Fox, *A Time to Tear Down*, 7 n.13.

Mikael Nouro

Grasping what *hebel* is not also gives us a clue to a better understanding of the seemingly contradictory statements of pleasure by Qoheleth. As Fox notes, Qoheleth presents both a positive and negative evaluation of pleasure. Fox rightly rejects attempts to ease this tension by distinguishing between trivial forms of amusement and "deeper" pleasures, or between reflective and unreflective pleasures, pleasures deliberately sought after or not actively pursued[58] but he fails to notice the ethical imperative implicit in man's understanding of life and its pleasures as a gift. The different evaluations of pleasure do not necessarily imply a contradiction but rather offer a presentation of a twisted contra well-guided attitude to pleasure.[59] Pleasure is not principally an anodyne to life's misery or the pain of consciousness.[60] Qoheleth underpins the ontological significance of creation.[61] Through the enjoyment of creation man can enter into dialogue with God. This is also fully compatible with Qoheleth's central exhortation to fear God. *Carpe diem* becomes an expression for the fear of God. This possibility of dialogue with God through His creation seems to be absent from Fox's understanding of the book. Qoheleth's God is a hard and unpredictable ruler, running the world like a distant monarch ruling a minor province. God may have created an orderly world, that is, according to His own understanding, but one beyond human reason.[62]

There is a concentration of *hebel*-sayings in Qoh 2, the part of the so-called royal experiment, where different kind of pleasures are tried out. This passage is marked by the endeavor by the kingly figure Qoheleth, in Solomonic guise, to gain pleasure in the same vein as a king might acquire

---

[58] Fox, *Qohelet and his Contradictions*, 68–77.

[59] "Die *hbl*-Aussage ist keine universale Aussage, die alles Seiende als sinnlos qualifiziert, sondern eine anthropologische Aussage, die falsche Wertsetzungen aufdeckt und die Bestimmung des wahren Gutes via negationis vollzieht. Das wahre Gut selbst unterliegt nicht dem *hbl*-Sein. Hier zeigt sich eine Strukturparallele zur hellenistischen Philosophie." Schwienhorst-Schönberger, *Nicht im Menschen gründet das Glück*, 293.

[60] Fox, *Qohelet and his Contradictions*, 73.

[61] See also Schwienhorst-Schönberger, *Nicht im Menschen gründet das Glück*, 109: "Das Carpe-diem Motiv ist also bei Kohelet kein resignatives Trotzdem gegen eine als sinnlos und finster erfahrene Welt, sondern die ethische Konsequenz einer sich aus der biblischen Schöpfungstheologie inspirierenden Anthropologie."

[62] Fox, *A Time to Tear Down*, 136–37.

wealth, wives and luxury.[63] Trying to acquire pleasure in life like one acquires a possession is doomed to failure, and is subsumed under *hebel*.

Granted, even after softening or explaining away some of Qoheleth's contradictions, some do remain. I would prefer to call these 'paradoxical' rather than 'absurd.' The distinction between the absurd and a paradox is, however, not altogether clear. A paradox, according to Schufreider, is an idea which, while having all the marks of an ordinary contradiction, insists upon being treated as a distinctive category since included within it is the claim that its contradictory character is not sufficient to dismiss the idea in question. We may consider the absurd as 'the most extreme form of paradox,' defying even such claims.[64] Qoheleth partly accepts the limitations of human understanding and the reality of a human and fundamentally different divine perspective which can never be bridged fully, and he partly protests against it. The problem of injustice remains, despite his convictions of a just order. He believes in retribution, but still wonders at the speed of execution of judgement. Qoheleth recognizes paradoxes of human existence, but never questions the meaning of life to the point of perceiving reality as absurd, even not with modification—the supposed consolation of pleasure. In the larger picture even the paradoxes he perceives and struggles with can be subsumed under the limitation of human understanding, 3:11.[65]

---

[63] In 2:7 Qoheleth's enterprise is expressed with קָנִיתִי. In Gen 4:1 Cain's name is derived from this very same form, and it is possible in Qoh 2 there is an allusion to the story of Abel—הבל ! —and Cain in Gen 4. In anthropological theory various forms of nomadic and agricultural lifestyles and their characteristics are contrasted. Due to its more permanent features, an agricultural lifestyle, represented in Gen 4 by Cain, is naturally characterized by an accumulation of possessions. See also Gerhard von Rad, *Das 1. Buch Mose*, 12th ed. (Göttingen: Vandenhoeck & Ruprecht, 1987), on the two creation accounts in Gen 1-2.

[64] Gregory Schufreider, "The Logic of the Absurd," PPR 44/1 (1983): 61–83. Schufreider's article is a systematic exploration of the concept of the absurd, with special reference to Kierkegaard's understanding of the absurd. While a comparison with Kierkegaard is interesting, I do not see Qoheleth expressing a passionate Kierkegaardian call to faith, expressed in the idea that "the absurd is the proper object of faith," Søren Kierkegaard, *Concluding Unscientific Postscript to the Philosophical Fragments*, trans. David Swenson and Walter Lowrie (Princeton: University Press, 1941), 189; similarly Fox, *A Time to Tear Down*, 9. It is evident, that Kierkegaard and Camus view the absurd in different ways.

[65] See Fox, *Qohelet and his Contradictions*, 11, for a differing view.

Countering Fox and his view that Qoheleth sees reality as absurd and the concomitant notion that his key term *hebel* should be accordingly translated as 'absurd,' I have employed two different strategies. These are partly complementary and interrelated but, for the sake of conceptual clarity, should be distinguished from each other. The first has been to soften the sense of absurdity in the book. This does not negate Fox's fundamental assumptions but demonstrates that, nonetheless, the notion of *hebel* as absurd is difficult to maintain. The second strategy has been to argue for *hebel* as expressing a predominantly negative evaluation of the externals in human life, not a quality of the world itself. In addition, we have noted anachronistic and semantic problems.

Human effort is *hebel* when it seeks to obtain that which by its very nature is unobtainable. The word יתרון also functions for Qoheleth in this way, albeit negatively. For Qoheleth this word, meaning profit or surplus, carries the meaning (lasting) gain.[66] Directly following the *hebel*-cluster in 1:2 comes a programmatic question concerning man's possible *yitron* in life 1:3 מַה־יִּתְרוֹן לָאָדָם בְּכָל־עֲמָלוֹ repeated in 3:9 מַה־יִּתְרוֹן הָעוֹשֶׂה בַּאֲשֶׁר הוּא עָמֵל. In 2:23 the days of a man seeking *yitron* are described as an arduous business עִנְיָן. This does not mean that human activity is *a priori* absurd. Granted, this seeking for a lasting gain where it is not to be found is very *typical* of human behavior, Qoheleth had tried it himself!

We may compare this with Stoic anthropology. The Stoics set the standards for the wise man so high that practically no one could achieve them, but living according to *logos* was never lost sight of as an ideal. Underlying these conceptions is the understanding of the universe as a completely orderly whole. While Qoheleth certainly does not adhere to this rigoristic Stoic scheme, see especially 7:16–20, his evaluation of humans in general in this respect is admittedly rather pessimistic. But there is no logical necessity to succumb to a life dominated by *hebel*. Here Qoheleth's more life-affirming traits come to the fore. Pleasure is more

---

[66] Fox, *Qohelet and his Contradictions*, 60–62, gives "adequate gain" as one meaning of *yitron*, i.e. a reasonable return for the strain invested, but this cannot be right. Qoheleth addresses *yitron* as a qualitative, not quantitative question. Man should not attach himself to that which is, in essence, indifferent.

than making the best of a bad situation[67]—a common perception by commentators—but there is a fundamental possibility to enter into a dialogue with the one who is in heavens while man is on earth 5:1, who is stronger than man 6:10, whom man should not make an object 4:17–18.[68]

Qoheleth recognizes human weakness, or rather folly, the desire to control and obtain that which cannot be obtained. To be sure, this is a limitation, both epistemologically and practically, but Qoheleth's point is rather that this limitation is something that it is futile to lament. However, he also shows an alternative, to accept open-mindedly these limitations as being the human condition and thus freeing one's energy in a more constructive direction. Qoheleth paints the possibility of a good life that involves work, good sleep, food, drink and marital relations: a steady, happy life with its share of pleasure, albeit not in excessive form.[69] He also accepts the hardships that inevitably accompany this life, 7:14.

Various readings of Qoheleth produce vastly different results. In this paper I have argued that calibrating our lenses to interpret him in the light of typical themes and questions in Hellenistic philosophy is an important hermeneutical key for understanding the book. The sharpened and explicit quest for meaning and purpose in life, combined with the fervent degrading of externals in one's life, finds a better parallel in Hellenistic philosophy than in Qoheleth's own, more familiar Jewish tradition. A reading of Qoheleth that takes into account some underlying structures in Hellenistic thinking enables us to picture him as a relatively normal chap. He struggled not only with modes of Hellenistic thinking, however, but also the expression of these philosophical ideas in the Hebrew language, at times creating an obscure impression.

---

[67] Even in this restricted capacity Fox calls pleasure Qoheleth's *summum bonum*, Fox, *Qohelet and his Contradictions*, 68.

[68] See Schwienhorst-Schönberger, *Nicht im Menschen gründet das Glück*, 136–38, for Qoheleth's critique of religion.

[69] See above all 5:17–19. Norbert Lohfink, *Kohelet*, NEB (Würzburg: Echter, 1980), considers this passage as one of the most central in the whole book. Fox's reading here is rather nihilistic: God distracts man with pleasures, that dull the pain of consciousness! Fox, *Qohelet and his Contradictions*, 217.

Part II: New Testament

Being Close to God: "Deep Sleep" (*tardēmāh*) and "Ecstasy" (*ekstasis*) in the Reception History of Gen 2:21 and 15:12

Lukas Bormann

1 Introduction

The first book of the Bible, the book of Genesis, reports that two of its main protagonists experienced the same extraordinary state of mind: "deep sleep" or "trance" (*tardēmāh*; תַּרְדֵּמָה).[1] When God removes the rib from which he decided to form Eve, Adam falls into this extraordinary state. Abraham, the patriarch of Israel, is placed in the same condition when God makes a covenant with him by accepting the sacrificial animals that Abraham slaughtered, shared, and offered. In the course of the translation of the Pentateuch into Greek, the Hebrew word *tardēmāh* was translated as ecstasy (*ekstasis*; ἔκστασις) meaning "to be outside."[2] As a result, the history of the reception of these two most significant *tardēmāh* scenes is therefore divided into two branches, the reflection on the Hebrew word *tardēmāh* and that on the Greek *ekstasis*.[3] But these two branches are also linked. Although influenced by Plato's analysis of *mania* in the four modes of ecstasy, Philo decides to justify exegetically his list of the four modes of ecstasy. The similarities between Philo's pre-rabbinical interpretation of four different types of ecstasy based on the exegetical interpretation of the

---

[1] See the seven occurences of the noun in: Gen 2:21, 15:12, 1 Sam 26:12, Job 4:13, 33:15, Prov 19:15, Isa 29:10. Manfred Oeming, "רדם," *ThWAT* 7: 358–61; Manfred Görg, "Tardemā—'Tiefschlaf', 'Ekstase' oder?," *Biblische Notizen* 110 (2001): 19–24.

[2] See *ekstasis* (ἔκστασις) in the LXX Pentateuch: Gen 2:21, 15:12, 27:33; Num 13:33, Deut 28:28.

[3] On the reception of *tardēmāh* in the book of Jubilees, see the contribution of Topias K. E. Tanskanen in this volume, 59–79.

*"Deep Sleep" (*tardēmāh*) and "Ecstasy" (*ekstasis*)*

Bible and the four types of *tardēmāh* reflected in the early Midrash Genesis Rabbah are striking and demonstrate a transcultural reflection on being close to God. Luke-Acts, which covers more than 26% of the Greek New Testament, reflects both lines of reception by using ecstasy as the mode that demonstrates a human anthropological response to the closeness of God.

2 When God Acts, the State of Human Beings Changes

The phenomena of deep sleep and being outside of oneself differ fundamentally in the empirical and anthropological assumptions they presuppose about the relationship between body, mind, and soul. They also belong to two different languages and cultures. Yet both the Hebrew author and the translator into Greek had to imagine the same challenging situation: God's extreme physical closeness to a human being. To give expression to this narrative constellation, the authors of Gen 2 and 15 decided to transfer humans into an extraordinary or abnormal human condition.

The Hebrew Bible pictures a state of abnormality when the protagonists are very close to God in a physical sense. In these cases, it seems to have been necessary to demonstrate the abnormality of the situation with a special state for the human being. The word *tardēmāh* is used for this purpose in the Hebrew Bible several times (Gen 2:21, 15:12, 1 Sam 26:12, Job 4:13, 33:15; Isa 29:10). Its origin and basic meaning are not entirely clear. Manfred Oeming emphasizes a biological meaning. Deep sleep is the third state of sleep following light sleep (*nûmāh*; נוּמָה) and a middle form of sleep (*šēnāh*; שֵׁנָה).[4] Manfred Görg states that the origin is unclear, but proposes three possible original meanings: a) a special physical state of deep sleep without Rapid Eye Movement (REM), b) a more psychological meaning in the sense of being depressed, and c) based on sources from Egypt a form of an incubation sleep used during a healing ceremony.[5] Zobel states that *tardēmāh* is combined with *'ēymāh* (אֵימָה) in Gen 15:12 to

---

[4] Oeming, "רדם," 359.
[5] Görg, "Tardemā," 19–24.

Lukas Bormann

underline the importance of theophany.[6] Horst Seebass also emphasizes a theological meaning of *tardēmāh* in the Hebrew Bible: God causes *tardēmāh* and the word includes the notion that the state is God-given:

> V. 21 *tardēmāh* ist nicht das übliche alttestamentliche Wort für Schlaf. Es hat etwas Gottgewirktes an sich, sei es zugunsten einer Offenbarung (Gen 15,12; Hi 4,12ff.; 33,15ff.), sei es zur Verstockung (Jes 29,10), oder sei es, ähnlich wie hier, als Ausschaltung aller Wahrnehmungen (1 Sam 26,12;...).[7]

The etymology and the origin of the word give some hints to its meaning, but to understand the term it is important to analyze the semantic context in which it is used. In Gen 2:21 this *tardēmāh* induced by God means that all of Adam's senses are switched off by God before the creation of Eve out of Adam's rib:

> Gen 2:21–22 (NRSV): 21 So the Lord God caused a deep sleep (*tardēmāh* / תַּרְדֵּמָה) to fall upon the man, and he slept; then he took one of his ribs and closed up its place with flesh. 22 And the rib that the Lord God had taken from the man he made into a woman and brought her to the man.

Hermann Gunkel pointed to the rationale behind Adam's deep sleep: he should not be the witness of God acting as creator, because the work of God should always be kept as a mystery.[8] Claus Westermann is sceptical of Gunkel's interpretation, which he considers as much too reflected and rational. The deep sleep is to him a very old motif. The act of creation out of a part of Adam's body requires a physical state without sensory awareness in order to avoid harm and pain.[9] Seebass points to the narrative structure of Gen 2. The plot is to bring Adam from his dissatisfaction with creation to the joyful cry "At last!" Adam was unsatisfied with God's creation until he found "bone from my bone" (Gen 2:23).[10] The narrative

---

[6] Hans-Jürgen Zobel, "אמיה," *ThWAT* 1:235–38, see 236.
[7] Horst Seebass, *Genesis 1: Urgeschichte*, 2nd ed. (Neukirchen-Vluyn: Neukirchener, 2007), 117.
[8] Hermann Gunkel, *Genesis*, 3rd ed. (Göttingen: Vandenhoeck & Ruprecht, 1910), 12: "Gottes Schaffen und Wirken bleibt stets sein Geheimnis."
[9] Claus Westermann, *Genesis 1* (Neukirchen-Vluyn: Neukirchener, 1974), 314.
[10] Seebass, *Genesis 1*, 117.

motif of deep sleep was chosen to maintain the tension of the story. In sum, the state of *tardēmāh* has a physical meaning but is used to express the extraordinary state of Adam's closeness to God himself, a situation without comparison in daily life. The human being is without a sensory perception of what is happening and this state cannot be changed even by such drastic measures as taking out parts of the body. *Tardēmāh* means the completely numb state of the senses, deep sleep and narcotic lethargy, deemed necessary for the narrative of the creation of the woman from man's rib.

The Greek translation of the Hebrew Bible may have its starting point in Alexandria of the third century BCE, for at least the letter of Aristeas (ca. 127–118 BCE) points to this location and date when naming Demetrios of Phaleron (ca. 350–280 BCE) as *spiritus rector* and facilitator of the translation of what is called the "Jewish law."[11] The group of translators had to consider both, the original Hebrew meaning and the horizon of understanding of the target audience of the translation, those who read Greek. They decided to translate *tardēmāh* in such a way that the connection to "sleep"—which is important for the Hebrew—is no longer present in the Greek translation. In the Septuagint, *tardēmāh* is translated as *ekstasis*.

> Gen 2:21–22 (based on NRSV): God brought an ecstasy (ἔκστασις) upon Adam, and he slept; and he took one of his ribs and filled up flesh on its place. 22 And Lord God built the rib, which he had taken from Adam, into a woman and brought her before Adam.

The Septuagint underlines also that Adam is without sensory perception when God touches his body. However, it is not called deep sleep or trance but rather ecstasy. As noted above the Greek *ekstasis* means "to be or to become outside" and also "moving outside oneself." The semantic key content is "movement outward" or "displacement."[12] The Septuagint and the Hebrew insist that Adam does not recognize or feel what is happening

---

[11] Michael Tilly, *Einführung in die Septuaginta* (Darmstadt: wbg, 2005), 27–30; Norbert Meisner, "Aristeasbrief," *JSHRZ* 2:35–87, see 43.
[12] *LSJ* 520; cf. Friedrich Passow, *Handwörterbuch der griechischen Sprache* (Darmstadt: wbg, 1970), 832–33.

Lukas Bormann

when God is very close to him. The Hebrew text imagines the presence of Adam who is fully numb, in a nearly narcotic state, unable to perceive, feel or experience anything. His senses are switched off. On the other hand, the Septuagint underlines the senselessness of Adam with ecstasy, moving his senses and his mind outside of the body. Deep sleep is not enough to secure distance between God and Adam. Therefore, Adam's senses and his mind have to be outside, moved outwards from the body which will be touched and manipulated by God.

The second occurrence of *tardēmāh* in the book of Genesis is in Gen 15, the narration of God making a covenant with Abraham:

> Gen 15:12 (NRSV): As the sun was going down, a deep sleep (*tardēmāh* / תַּרְדֵּמָה) fell upon Abram, and a deep and terrifying darkness (*'ēymāh* / אֵימָה) descended upon him.

The Hebrew text of Gen 15 is assigned to the post-priestly Abraham tradition, together with Gen 14 and Gen 22 as well as Gen 26:3–5, and is dated by Schmid roughly to the late Persian period in the 4th century BCE.[13] Gen 15 tells how the covenant was performed as a cultic act. Certain animals were slaughtered and accepted by God. His acceptance of the sacrifice is demonstrated by a fire passing through the pieces of the slaughtered animals. Again the narrative seems to be led by the assumption that the closeness of God requires a distance of the human being at least in so far as his senses are numb. However, some details are different: God is not present himself but mediated through the "fire" and, most importantly, in v. 13 God speaks to Abraham who is in the state of *tardēmāh*: "Then the Lord said to Abram." On the one hand, it is stated that Abraham is in deep sleep and without a perception of what is going on; on the other hand, God is speaking to him not only delivering a short remark but even a complex promise of a covenant for generations.

Exegetes struggled with this contradiction. For Gerhard von Rad the whole speech of God in vv. 13–16 was an insertion and should be

---

13 Cf. Konrad Schmid, "Remembering and Reconstructing Abraham: Abraham's Family and the Literary History of the Pentateuch," in *Abraham's Family. A Network of Meaning in Judaism, Christianity, and Islam*, ed. Lukas Bormann, WUNT 415 (Tübingen: Mohr Siebeck, 2018), 9–31, see 15–19.

123

deleted.[14] Westermann was more cautious and deleted only v. 13a, the address to Abraham, and argued these words are not necessary because Abraham is in the state of deep sleep.[15] Seebass proposes vv. 13–16 as an insertion and assumes that v. 12 was followed by v. 17 in the original. Therefore, to Seebass there was no speech of God as part of the *Vorlage* but only the cultic act of slaughtering and the acceptance of the offer by God.[16]

The narration of the covenant between God and Abraham underlines with the state of the *tardēmāh* that the theophany taking place is concealed from human perception. While the connection between v. 12 and v. 17 regards the acceptance of the cultic sacrifice and the associated divine presence in the flames of fire as the climax of the narrative, which requires Abraham to be asleep, the continuation of the text inserts a sermon-like historical overview at precisely this point of the narration. It seems the second narrator uses the arc of tension in the original narrative to provide a historical-theological perspective on the future of the people of Israel. Regardless of the connection between Abraham's deep sleep and theophany, a speech from God is inserted which is aimed at Abraham on the narrative level but actually goes beyond the narrated situation and is instead directed to the readers of the text. It is quite probable that the speech of God was rewritten and some parts were added. Seebass concludes that the speech of God in vv. 13–16 is a word from the formative phase of the Hebrew Bible and called it a "canonical saying about Israel."[17]

In the story of the making of God's covenant with Abraham, a statement is inserted that looks back on the entire history of Israel. The speech is placed at a certain point of the narrative order of the context. The climax of the story was the report about Abraham's deep sleep. Then a speech of God was inserted and changed the storyline. Now, the sermon-like historical-theological speech of God, which itself shows development, appears as the climax of the story. The state in which Abraham finds

---

[14] Gerhard von Rad, *Das erste Buch Mose*, 6th ed. (Göttingen: Vandenhoeck & Ruprecht, 1961), 158.

[15] Claus Westermann, *Genesis 2* (Neukirchen-Vluyn: Neukirchener, 1980), 268.

[16] Cf. Horst Seebass, *Genesis 2/1* (Neukirchen-Vluyn: Neukirchener, 1997), 77.

[17] Seebass, *Genesis 2/1*, 77.

himself has lost its importance and is no longer fundamental for the understanding of Gen 15, and even contradicts somewhat the plot of the story. In the Hebrew reception of Gen 15:12 the state of "deep sleep," *tardēmāh*, was rarely reflected upon. The word is not found in the Dead Sea Scrolls and, as we will see later, was interpreted even in the Rabbinic tradition under the influence of the Greek translation as ecstasy.[18]

The translators of the Septuagint continued the development of the biblical text. In the Septuagint, *tardēmāh* is translated as *ekstasis*:

> Gen 15:12 (based on NRSV): As the sun was going down, an ecstasy (ἔκστασις) fell upon Abram, and a deep and great fear (φόβος) fell upon him.

As in Gen 2:21, the Hebrew *tardēmāh* is translated into Greek as *ekstasis* to define the state of the human being in a situation of closeness to God. The state of ecstasy, being outside, has a different connotation to deep sleep. As *tardēmāh* is a physical and biological state of the whole human being and means a numbness including a total exclusion of the senses, ecstasy is a psychological state of the human mind and means "to be outside." In ecstasy the human being can hear the speech of the gods. Moreover, ecstasy is an excellent state of mind for receiving and accepting the word of God. In the Septuagint, no contradiction can be seen between Abraham's ecstasy in v. 12 and the speech of God to Abraham in vv. 13–16. Abraham himself hears the words of God in ecstasy, which defines the highpoint of the story.

With the use of the word *ekstasis*, a meaning is now brought into the biblical statement that is foreign to the Hebrew text. The physical state of complete insensibility and unconsciousness is now expressed with the more complex idea of being outside of oneself, which presupposes a distinction between body, mind and soul. This tripartite anthropology is alien to Hebrew thought and ancient near eastern anthropology as a whole.[19] Through the translation of *tardēmāh* as *ekstasis*, Hellenistic Bible exegesis was able to emphasize the philosophical quality of the Torah. Also, the Church Fathers of the 3rd century took up the line of argument

---

[18] Oeming, "רדם," 361.
[19] Bernd Janowski, *Anthropologie des Alten Testaments* (Tübingen: Mohr Siebeck, 2019), 12.

from Jewish-Alexandrian exegesis that the books of Moses already contained Plato's philosophy when they underlined the philosophical quality of the scriptures.[20]

The use of *ekstasis* in the Bible allows readers with philosophical interests to draw a connection to Plato's interpretation of the four forms of *mania* in the tractate Phaidros, of which the last, god-given madness and divine *ekstasis*, is the state of mind appropriate to the true and perfect philosopher.

3 Plato's Ambiguous Theory of μανία

Plato's dialogue Phaidros was written in the years between 369 and 362 BCE.[21] The dialogue has an unusual structure. In the first part Phaidros, a historical figure of the city of Athens, re-narrates a speech of the sophist Lysias in which Lysias argues that it is better to have friendship or relationship with people without the influence of erotic desire and attraction (ἔρως). According to Lysias, erotic desire is an abnormal state of mind and therefore one should avoid being led by this desire. Moreover, the state (πόλις) has to act to prevent an "erotic lover" (ἐραστής) from causing public disorder or even crimes. A friendship or relationship is preferable based on rational decision or reflection and, in modern terms, the rational choice. For Lysias, only friendship that is not forced by erotic love should be allowed in the Greek state. It should be mentioned as a matter of clarity that the dispute is about paederasty, the erotic love between a male citizen of the polis and a young and beautiful boy or

---

[20] Cf. Jaroslav Pelikan, *What has Athens to do with Jerusalem? Timaeus and Genesis in Counterpoint,* Jerome Lectures 21 (Ann Arbor/Michigan: Univ. of Michigan Press, 1997), 68; David T. Runia, *Philo of Alexandria and the 'Timaeus' of Plato,* Philosophia Antiqua 44 (Leiden: Brill, 1986), 524.

[21] Madayo Kahle, "Parallelen zwischen der Katha Upanisad und der Palinodie des Sokrates in Platons Phaidros," in *Interkulturalität in der Alten Welt: Vorderasien, Hellas, Ägypten und die vielfältigen Ebenen des Kontakts,* ed. Robert Rollinger, Philippika 34 (Wiesbaden: Harrassowitz, 2010), 361–81, see 361; cf. Thomas Paulsen and Rudolf Rehn, "Einleitung," in *Phaidros,* by Platon, trans. and ed. Thomas Paulsen and Rudolf Rehn (Hamburg: Felix Meiner, 2019), VII–XLIV, see X.

Lukas Bormann

teenager and that the erotic desire is caused by "the beauty of the boy" (251C: τὸ τοῦ παιδὸς κάλλος).[22]

Socrates responds to Lysias's argument in two speeches. In the first, he elaborates further on the main topic of Lysias's speech (231A–234C). It seems that he supports the view that a relationship without erotic love is better. However, in his second speech, Socrates goes further or even contradicts what he has said before. This sequence of two contradictory speeches is seen as a rhetorical technique called *palinode*, a retraction of the first speech.[23] Socrates develops further the idea that erotic love is a form of "madness" (μανία). This *mania* or "madness" however, is presented as a positive state of the mind, god-given, and important to gain knowledge which is hidden to rational understanding (σωφροσύνη), normally presented by Socrates as a virtue of the soul (250B).[24]

The "madness" as a god-given, positive, and desirable abnormality is differentiated by Socrates into four sorts, the last of which is the most beautiful and desirable, namely the erotic love of the beautiful that transforms the human being into what was denigrated in the first speech, a lover: "He who loves the beautiful, partaking in this madness, is called a lover (ἐραστής)." (249E).

The idea of a god-given and positive madness opens the door to religious thinking, to theology, to the area in which people have the experience that religion does not contradict the rational mind (σωφροσύνη), rather opens the way to a knowledge that is not available under the condition of an understanding limited or defined by common social expectations.[25] To challenge these common social expectations through a divine gift, Socrates surprisingly develops a god-given and beneficial "madness" in his second speech. Four positive and god-given sorts of "madness" are superior to reasonable thinking (σωφροσύνη). The first is

---

[22] Manfred Geier, Die Liebe der Philosophen. Von Sokrates bis Foucault (Hamburg: Rowohlt, 2020), 19–44.

[23] Fabio Serrantino, "A somewhat unconvincing start. The first three kinds of beneficial μανία in the Palinode," in *In the Mirror of the Phaedrus*, ed. Mário Jorge de Carvalho, Lecturae Platonis 9 (Sankt Augustin: Academia, 2013), 77–111, see 83–87.

[24] Friedrich Pfister, "Ekstase," *RAC* 4:944–87, see 960–61; Herbert Preisker, "μαίνομαι," *TDNT* 4:363–65, see 363.

[25] Serrantino, "Unconvincing start," 105.

"Deep Sleep" (tardēmāh) and "Ecstasy" (ekstasis)

prophetic madness. To demonstrate the connection between madness and prophecy (*mania* and *mantike*) Socrates states that people had inserted falsely the letter tau (τ) in *mantike*, prophecy (μαντική), which was from the beginning also *maniē* (μανίη) and based on the same word as *mania* (244C: μανία). The gift or the madness of prophecy is from the gods and "a divine madness" (244D: μανία ἐκ θεοῦ). The second is more complicated and somewhat obscure but may be named religious madness. Socrates gives some explanations which hint at the madness which occurs when people who suffer from a serious illness flee to temples and beg the gods intensively for healing (244D: μανία καταφυγοῦσα πρὸς θεῶν εὐχάς τε καὶ λατρείας). The third one is the madness of poetry or the madness given by the Muses (245AB: μανία Μουσῶν, ἀπὸ Μουσῶν μανία) which is also a madness given by gods (μανία γιγνομένη ἀπὸ θεῶν). If a man writes poetry and is inspired by this madness, he experiences one of the greatest gifts and his poetry is not only superior to the poetry of reasonable men who followed the "learned art" (τέχνη) but will also demonstrate their insignificance (245A). Madness from God is the greatest "gift and happiness" (εὐτυχία) for men (245B). At this point, Socrates interrupts his explanations of the god-given madness and begins an excursus about the immortality of the soul, the last judgement, and the return of the soul (245B–249C). This excursus is necessary to develop further the fourth and most important type of madness connected to the soul and leading to eternal knowledge of beauty. This madness is the madness of the philosophers (249D) and the best inspiration of all. The philosopher has to distance himself from social reality and the expectations placed on him. When he reaches this state of freedom and independence, he will experience an extraordinary enthusiasm and the greatest happiness in viewing "reality" (τὰ ὄντα). Through this sort of madness, the philosopher is "enthusiastic" (ἐνθουσιάζω) and is removed from empirical reality (ἐξιστάμαι). At this point he has reached the most desirable state of the soul and is "perfect" (τέλεος). However, this state of the soul is dangerous:

Plato, *Phaidr.* 249D (Fowler): Now a man who employs such memories rightly is always being initiated into perfect mysteries and he alone becomes truly perfect (τέλεος); but since he separates himself (ἐξιστάμενος) from human interests and turns his attention toward the divine, he is re-

128

Lukas Bormann

buked by the vulgar, who consider him mad (παρακινῶν) and do not know that he is inspired (ἐνθουσιάξων).

The enthusiastic philosopher being outside of himself and at a distance to the social world can understand and acknowledge the beauty of being and the idea of the good. However, he is alone and alien to his social world which reacts with aggression and hostility. They see in the philosophical, perfect man a madman who does not fulfil the expectations of the social world and attracts aggression, hatred, and anger.

4 Philo's Interpretation of Genesis 2:21 and Genesis 15:12

Whereas in Israel the genre of rewritten Bible endures and dominates religious writing, in the Jewish community of Alexandria the authority of the Pentateuch is highly esteemed and the five books of Moses are seen as the law, history, and most important philosophical literature of the Jewish people. These books were no longer rewritten in a plain sense but commentated using the philological expertise of the famous Alexandrian exegetes. In this tradition, Philo of Alexandria (ca. 20 BCE–40 CE) interprets the book of Genesis carefully verse for verse in his allegorical commentary.[26] Philo's allegorical commentaries are aimed at an informed readership that is well-read in the Bible.[27] This audience has detailed knowledge of the complicated or even contradictory content of the Pentateuch and is seeking solutions to tricky exegetical questions. Furthermore, Philo's audience had a philosophical education and was trained in interpreting the Bible against the background of Greek philosophy and poetry.

In his tractate "Who is the heir of the divine things?" (*Quis rerum divinarum heres?*) Philo interprets Gen 15:2–18.[28] His interpretation aims to demonstrate in an analysis of the story of the covenant between God and Abraham an underlying allegorical meaning, namely how someone

---

[26] Maren Niehoff, *Philo of Alexandria: An Intellectual Biography* (Yale: Yale University Press, 2019), 173–91.

[27] James R. Royse, "The Works of Philo," in *The Cambridge Companion to Philo*, ed. Adam Kamesar (Cambridge: Cambridge University Press, 2009), 32–64, see 33.

[28] Philo, *Her.* 249–63.

129

"Deep Sleep" (tardēmāh) and "Ecstasy" (ekstasis)

inspired by God can reach wisdom and perfect virtue. Philo starts his commentary with the quotation of Gen 15:12 (transl. Colson): "About sunset an ecstasy fell upon Abraham and lo a great dark terror falls upon him." Philo immediately concentrates on the word ecstasy. The term occurs in this part of his tractate more often than in Philo's other writings.[29] He elaborates that four different sorts of ecstasy are present in the Pentateuch. The first is "a mad fury producing mental delusion (μανιώδης παράνοιαν) due to old age or melancholy or other similar cause." This negative ecstasy can be seen in the behaviour of disobedient people transgressing the commandments of God (250). These people are cursed and will experience blindness and madness (Deut 28:28–29). The second is not positive but at least ambiguous: the reaction of a human being to an unexpected event causes "terrible consternation" (σφοδρὰ κατάπληξις). Philo lists many examples of this state of mind (251–256). He starts with Isaac, who experienced a "great ecstasy" (ἔκστασις μεγάλη) when he recognized the betrayal of Jacob (Gen 27:33). Many more examples of this reactive ecstasy are listed by Philo (e.g. Jacob in Gen 40:26, the people of Israel in Exod 19:18 and Lev 9:24). Philo interprets this ecstasy caused by consternation as a challenge and demonstrates how biblical figures succeeded in overcoming this state of mind through education, wisdom, and virtue.

The third sort of ecstasy is the "passivity of mind" (ἠρεμία διανοίας) which befell Adam during the creation of the woman in Gen 2:21 (257).[30] According to Philo, Moses wrote about it to give an example for the importance of passivity of the "mind" (νοῦς) as a precondition for true "understanding" (διάνοια). The fourth sort of ecstasy is "the best one the divine possession or frenzy" (249: ἡ δὲ πασῶν ἀρίστη ἔνθεος κατοκωχή τε καὶ μανία). It is striking that Philo now uses the word *mania* for his interpretation of ecstasy.[31] The philosophically-informed reader knows

---

[29] See Philo, *Leg.* 2:19; 2:31 [2x]; *Cher.* 69, 116; *Plant.* 147; *Ebr.* 15; *Spec.* 3:99, *Contempl.* 40, *QG* 1:24, 4:79b. In most cases, ecstasy is used by Philo to describe the state of the mind without reason and controlled by drunkenness.

[30] Gen 2:21 is also quoted and discussed in *Leg.* 2:19,31. Philo emphasizes in *Leg.* 2:31 that Moses chose the word ecstasy "correctly" (ὀρθῶς).

[31] Pfister, "Ekstase," 948, argues that the Septuagint never uses ecstasy for the prophetic charisma. Cf. Folker Siegert, *Zwischen hebräischer Bibel und Altem Testament: Eine Einführung*

130

Lukas Bormann

very well that Plato interprets several forms of *mania* as "divine madness" (e.g. 244D: μανία ἐκ θεοῦ) in the tractate Phaidros discussed above. At this point the allegorical interpretation as inspired by Plato and applied to the Bible is obvious.[32] Abraham is pictured as a recipient of the most important and very best inspiration by God (258). He is inspired by God and enthusiastic. In this state he can act as a prophet. For Philo, the prophets are nearest to God and connected through wisdom to the wisdom of God. Only just and wise people can act as God-inspired and even God-bearing prophets and become "an instrument of God" (259: ὄργανον θεοῦ). The list of these great people in the Bible is very long, since Philo lists under the fourth sort of ecstasy all biblical figures who were also prophets, including Noah (260), Isaac and Jacob (261), and Moses (262). Philo's commentary is in the end not only interested in these great people but is eager to demonstrate that not only the prophets but every good man can also reach this state of mind. He concludes his allegorical interpretation of Gen 15:12 by analyzing the true meaning of the "sunset" and addresses the audience: the setting of the sun in Gen 15:12 means the retreat of reason from the human being (263). The sun means the mind (ὁ νοῦς); when the sun sets the mind leaves the man and every day the wise man may experience ecstasy and God-given beneficial madness (264: ἔκστασις καὶ θεοφόρητη μανία) caused by the divine spirit (265: τὸ θεῖον πνεῦμα) which leads him to knowledge and experiences which are otherwise not available to him. The state of this sort of ecstasy is the highest form of knowledge. The biblical heroes had reached this state, but it is also open to every human being searching for true knowledge.[33]

In sum, Philo merges the four positive forms of divine madness presented by Plato, the mantic, religious, poetic, and philosophical-enthusiastic *mania*, into a single divine madness, combining all positive characteristics and ascribing these to the biblical wise men and prophets as well as to the pious follower of the biblical God. They are all able to

---

in die Septuaginta, Münsteraner judaistische Studien 9 (Münster: Lit, 2001), 258, who posits that ἔκστασις/ἐξίστασθαι are used only as psychological terms in the Septuagint.

[32] Cf. Leopold Cohn, "Sachweiser zu Philo," in vol. 7 of *Philo von Alexandria: Die Werke in deutscher Übersetzung*, ed. idem (Berlin: De Gruyter, 1964), 407.

[33] Cf. Ellen Birnbaum, *The Place of Judaism in Philo's Thought: Israel, Jews, and Proselytes*, Brown Judaic Studies 290 (Atlanta: Scholars Press, 1996), 229.

attain the extraordinary and abnormal state of closeness to the divine in ecstasy, with the human mind leaving the body and the divine spirit entering.

5 "Deep Sleep" and "Ecstasy" in Other Ancient Jewish Literature

In ancient Jewish literature besides Philo, the idea of deep sleep or trance is reflected upon only in some writings. Josephus mentions in his *Antiquities* the creation of Eve out of Adam's "ribs" (πλευρά). He does not reflect on the unusual description of the state of Adam described in the Septuagint as *ekstasis* (ἔκστασις) but chooses the ordinary Greek word for "sleeping" (κοιμᾶσθαι).

> *Ant* 1.35 (transl. Thackeray): "He extracted one of his ribs while he slept (αὐτοῦ κοιμωμένου) and from it formed woman."

And when Josephus re-narrates the famous scene of God's promises to Abraham from Gen 15:1–21, he does not mention the deep-sleep scene at all. Josephus is much more interested in Abraham as a political and military leader and presents the story of Gen 14 about Abraham and his military success in great detail (*Ant*. 1.171–182) and devotes only a few sentences to the promises to Abraham (*Ant*. 1.183–185), which are presented as rewards for Abraham's "good deeds" (εὐπραγίαι). When a "divine voice" (γωνὴ θεία) proclaimed to Abraham the promises of land and an heir, the patriarch was fully conscious. When looking at the works of Josephus, it is obvious that for Josephus *ekstasis* is not a desirable state. The word is only used once in the writings of Josephus. In *Ant*. 17.247 the phrase ὡς μανίαν καὶ λογισμῶν ἔκστασιν means a state of despair, madness and loss of reason. In *Bell*. 6.210 παρέκστασις is used to render an even increased state of despair and madness combined with horror and stupor in a story about the cannibalism of a mother who killed, cooked and ate her child. In sum, for Josephus, the state of ecstasy is not of any significance for an encounter with God.

Some more interest in the idea of "deep sleep" can be found in the Testament of the Twelve Patriarchs (2nd century CE) and Fourth Baruch

Lukas Bormann

(70–135 CE).[34] The Testament of the Twelve Patriarchs alludes in several instances to the creation and the sleep that was brought upon Adam in Gen 2:21. In the second chapter of the *Testament of Reuben* seven spirits are named which are given to humankind at creation. The list is inspired by the idea of five senses in Greek philosophy and adjusted to the biblical expectation of the importance of the number seven.[35] Therefore, *T. Reu.* lists seven spirits or senses: the spirits of life, seeing, hearing, smell, speech, taste, procreation and intercourse. After this list of seven he proceeds to even more spirits beginning with the "spirit of sleep":

> *T. Reu.* 3:1 (Kee): In addition to all is an eighth spirit: sleep, with which is created the ecstasy of nature (ἔκστασις φύσεως) and the image of death.

In the following, *T. Reu.* adds six more spirits and forms an additional list of seven: sleep and error, insatiability, strife, flattery and trickery, arrogance, lying, and injustice. These seven spirits are combined:

> *T. Reu.* 3:7 (Kee): With all these the spirit of sleep forms an alliance, which results in error and fantasy (ὅ ἐστι πλάνης καὶ φαντασίας).

Neither "sleep" nor "ecstasy" is seen here as something positive but more or less connected with evil. The connection of "sleep" and "ecstasy" with evil spirits points to a less favourable understanding than that in Gen 2:21 and 15:12.

In the *Testament of Simeon*, the eponymous author of the writing retells how Joseph loved his brothers as much as his own life even though they had sold him as a slave. He was, however, filled with envy and zeal. Simeon describes the conflict of his soul and body caused by evil forces as ecstasy when awake and as a struggle with evil during sleep:

> *T. Sim.* 4:8–9 (Kee): For that attitude makes the soul savage and corrupts the body; it foments wrath and conflict in the reason, excites to the shedding of blood, drives the mind to distraction (εἰς ἔκστασιν ἄγει τὴν διάνοιαν),

---

[34] Howard Clark Kee, "Testaments of the Twelve Patriarchs," in *OTP* 1:775–828; Stephen E. Robinson, "4 Baruch," in *OTP* 2:413–25.
[35] Aristotle, *De an.* 418a–424a.

arouses tumult in the soul and trembling in the body. Even in sleep some passion for evil fills his fantasy and consumes him; by evil spirits it stirs up his soul and fills his body with terror. In distress it rouses his mind from sleep, and like an evil, penetrating spirit, so it manifests itself to human beings.

Again ecstasy and sleep are related to evil spirits and undesirable, morally wrong influences on humanity. In *T. Jud.* the warnings are directed against the love of money and idolatry, both are connected with ecstasy:

> *T. Jud.* 19:1 (Kee): My children, love of money leads to idolatry, because once they are led astray by money, they designate as gods those who are not gods. It makes anyone who has it go out of his mind (εἰς ἔκστασιν ἐμπεσεῖν).

In the Testament of the Twelve Patriarchs, ecstasy is seen as entirely negative. This state of mind is connected with immoral behaviour and irrational deeds.

A more positive meaning of ecstasy is presented in Fourth Baruch, an expansion of the book of Jeremiah. The figure of the Ethiopian Abimelech from Jer 38 is used to retell the story of the destruction of Jerusalem and the exile. Based on what is told about him in Jer 38 and what is known to the reader, Abimelech has rescued Jeremiah by pulling him out of the cistern and was lauded for this deed (Jer 38:7-13). In Fourth Baruch, this Abimelech falls to sleep for 66 years, wakes up and thinks he has had a short slumber. When he enters Jerusalem he does not recognize the city and again and again reflects that a "great ecstasy" (μεγάλη ἔκστασις) has fallen upon him.

> *4 Bar.* 5:8-9 (Robinson): And he said: "Blessed the Lord, for a great stupor has befallen (μεγάλη ἔκστασις ἐμπέπεσεν) me today. This is not the city of Jerusalem! I got lost because I came by the mountain road after getting up from my sleep, and since my head was heavy from my not getting enough sleep, I got lost!"

After looking around Jerusalem and searching in vain for those he expected to find in the city, he decided that this city is not Jerusalem.

Lukas Bormann

4 Bar. 5:16 (Robinson): And he puts the basket down, saying, "I'm sitting right here until the Lord takes the stupor away from me (τὴν ἔκστασιν ταύτην ἀπ' ἐμοῦ)."

Abimelech experiences ecstasy as a negative state and hopes for rescue from this state of mind. When he is sitting outside of the city an old man comes to him and starts a dispute with him about the city and Abimelech's understanding of the situation. The old man understands very well Abimelech's misunderstanding and interprets his state of mind as a God-given ecstasy:

> *4 Bar.* 5:28–29 (Robinson): O my son, you are a righteous man, and God did not want you to see the desolation of the city, so he brought this stupor upon you (ταύτην τὴν ἔκστασιν ἐπὶ σέ).

Fourth Baruch uses the word ecstasy to describe a certain disconnect from reality. Abimelech expects to see Jerusalem as he had known it. When recognizing a different city, his first guess is that ecstasy has come over him and has distorted his senses. However, he learns from the old man to see this differently: his senses were not distorted, rather his 66-year sleep was a God-given and beneficial ecstasy to allow him to avoid pain and grief. In both cases, ecstasy is related to sleep. It is also in dispute whether the ecstasy is God-given or caused by spirits or demons.

The Rabbinic literature only seldom reflects on *tardēmāh* as a state of mind. In Bavli the word is interpreted as "sleep" without deeper interest in differentiating various sorts of sleep.

Moreover, the state of sleep is problematized in discussions with opponents of rabbinic Judaism. In *Sanh.* 39a and *Gen. Rab.* 17:17 (Gen 2:21) a polemical discussion is reported in which the opponents call the God of Judaism a "thief" because he had created the woman out of one of Adam's ribs while he was sleeping:

> *Sanh.* 39 a (transl. Neusner): Said the emperor to Rabban Gamaliel, "Your God is a thief, for it is written, 'And the Lord God caused a deep sleep to fall upon Adam, and he slept, and he took one of his ribs.'" (Gen 2:21).

"Deep Sleep" (tardēmāh) and "Ecstasy" (ekstasis)

In *Genesis Rabbah* the provocative statement is uttered by a "noble lady" (transl. Neusner): "A noble lady asked R. Yose, saying to him, 'Why was it through theft [for a rib]?'"[36] The answer to this question points to the outcome of the act of God which is far from theft, but should be seen as a gift: God took a rib but returned Eve, which cannot be seen as theft but a gift. The discourse in *Gen. Rab.* turns to the problem that the creation of Eve was done "in secret" and emphasizes that secrecy was important so as not to endanger Adam's attraction to her in his seeing her blood during her creation. In this story, the special state of mind caused by deep sleep is not reflected upon. In *Gen. Rab.* 44:17 (Gen 15:12) *tardēmāh* is discussed based on its occurrences in Gen 2:21; 15:12; 1 Sam 16:12 and Is 29:10. Three kinds of "repose" are listed and a fourth added:

> *Gen. Rab.* 44:17 (transl. Neusner): Rab said, "three kinds of repose (שלש תרדמות): there is the repose of sleep (Gen 2:21), the repose of prophecy (Gen 15:12), and the repose of unconsciousness (1 Sam 16:12)" ... "also there is the repose of silliness (Is 29:10)."[37]

The reflection distinguishes between ordinary sleep and the state of mind called *tardēmāh* understood as a form of passive lethargy not necessarily related to sleep.[38] The listing of exactly four sorts of *tardēmāh* here may recall Plato's and Philo's reflections on the four sorts of *mania* and ecstasy. Particularly the "repose of prophecy" is near to Plato's gift of prophecy as "a divine madness" (*Phaedr.* 244D: μανία ἐκ θεοῦ) and Philo's "ecstasy and God-given madness" (*Her.* 264: ἔκστασις καὶ θεοφόρητη μανία) of the prophet.

The possibility that Greek thinking has influenced this Rabbinic idea is underlined by the use of the Greek loanword μαρμαρωτός in *Genesis Rabbah* 44:17 as מרמוטא for a state of petrification, translated by Neusner

---

[36] Jacob Neusner, *Parashiyyot 1 through 33 on Genesis 1:1 to 8:14*, vol. 1 of *Genesis Rabbah: the Judaic Commentary to the Book of Genesis: A New American Translation* (Atlanta: Scholars Press, 1985), 186.

[37] Jacob Neusner, *Parashiyyot 34 through 67 on Genesis 8:15 to 28:9*, vol. 2 of *Genesis Rabbah: the Judaic Commentary to the Book of Genesis: A New American Translation* (Atlanta: Scholars Press, 1985), 138.

[38] Jacob Levy, "תרדמה," *Wörterbuch über die Talmudim und Midraschim* 3:669.

as "unconsciousness." The concept of the three or four forms of sleep is not developed further in Rabbinic literature. In the early Medieval Pirqe Rabbi Eliezer Gen 15:12 is interpreted allegorically.[39] The unusual term *tardēmāh* is quoted in *Pirqe R. El.* 28 but rendered in a more understandable form together with "sleep" (*šēnāh*; שֵׁנָה) in the construct state as "sleep of *tardēmāh*" (שנת תרדמה). It seems that the meaning of *tardēmāh* is no longer immediately understood by itself and requires explanation.

6 New Testament

The narrative of the creation of Adam and Eve is well known by New Testament authors and is discussed in various ways. Most famous is Paul's interpretation of Gen 2:18–22 in 1 Corinthians 11:8–11. He discusses the relation and in some way the hierarchy between men and women in connection to the sequence of creation. Adam was created first and then Eve. Paul argues that in this sequence there is also a hidden meaning:

> 1 Cor 11:8–12 (NRSV): 8 Indeed, man was not made from woman, but woman from man. 9 Neither was man created for the sake of woman, but woman for the sake of man. 10 For this reason a woman ought to have a symbol of authority on her head, because of the angels. 11 Nevertheless, in the Lord woman is not independent of man or man independent of woman. 12 For just as woman came from man, so man comes through woman; but all things come from God.

Paul points to a somewhat unclear subordination of the woman when pointing to the "symbol of authority on her head" but his conclusion in v. 11–12 emphasizes equality and interdependence in the relationship between man and woman "in the Lord." The result of his argumentation is much more inclusive and equal than the beginning of the section would lead one to expect. Paul reflects on how men and women were exposed to the power of angels in a different way. Whereas women have to be protected against the power of the angels, men seem to be safe and secure. A plausible explanation for this idea is that an interpretation of the plural

---

[39] Dagmar Börner-Klein, *Pirke de-Rabbi Elieser,* Studia Judaica 26 (Berlin: De Gruyter, 2004), XXXVII; Moshe David Herr, "Pirkei de-Rabbi Eliezer," *EncJud* 16:182–3.

in Gen 1:26 ("Let us make") is in the background. Ancient interpretation of the plural in Gen 1:26 was that the plural points to the cooperation of God and angels in creation. Therefore, during the creation of Adam, Adam saw angels and is now protected against their power. Paul's turn to equality and interdependence in his interpretation of Gen 2:18–22 may be supported also by the detail of the creation narrative that Adam was not active in giving life to Eve but was overwhelmed by a deep sleep which made him unable to cooperate in her creation. This detail is not mentioned in 1 Corinthians. However, since the creation narrative is not quoted by Paul but paraphrased, it is very plausible that the idea of Adam's passivity during the creation of Eve in 1 Cor 11:8–12 is an echo of the biblical narrative about deep sleep.

Abraham is an important figure in the New Testament. Gen 15 is well attested in New Testament discussion, and Gen 15:6 is quoted in particular in the context of debates about justification by faith in Paul and James (Rom 4:3.9; Gal 3:6; Jas 2:23). However, for Gen 15:12 the *loci citati vel allegati* of the Greek New Testament note only one allusion of the verse in Acts 10:10, the famous episode about Peter's vision of the unclean animals and God's commandment "Kill and eat!" In this episode, the mental state of Peter is described using the same word as in Gen 15:12 with which the Hebrew *tardēmāh* is translated by the Septuagint, namely *ekstasis*. The NRSV translates this *ekstasis* with "trance," which underlines that Peter is present physically but his mental state is in some way absent.

> Acts 10:9–16 (NRSV): 9 About noon the next day, as they were on their journey and approaching the city, Peter went up on the roof to pray. 10 He became hungry and wanted something to eat; and while it was being pre-pared, he fell into a trance (ἐγένετο ἐπ' αὐτὸν ἔκστασις). 11 He saw the heaven opened and something like a large sheet coming down, being low-ered to the ground by its four corners. 12 In it were all kinds of four-footed creatures and reptiles and birds of the air. 13 Then he heard a voice saying, "Get up, Peter; kill and eat." 14 But Peter said, "By no means, Lord; for I have never eaten anything profane or unclean." 15 The voice said to him again, a second time, "What God has made clean, you must not call profane." 16 This happened three times, and the thing was suddenly taken up to heaven.

Lukas Bormann

In Acts 11 the episode is re-narrated by Peter. He tells his audience, the Jerusalem community, the following:

> Acts 11:5 (NRSV): I was in the city of Joppa praying, and in a trance (ἐν ἐκστάσει) I saw a vision. There was something like a large sheet coming down from heaven, being lowered by its four corners; and it came close to me.

The wording in Acts 10:10 and 11:5 does partially resemble the wording of Gen 15:12. In the context of Gen 15:12, some more similarities occur (animals, a dialogue with God), but no significant textual link is included in Acts 10 and 11 to inform the reader to have Gen 15 in mind. In Acts, *ekstasis* is God-given, beneficial and even necessary for receiving an important message from God or the exalted Christ (cf. Acts 3:10; 22:17).[40]

7 Conclusion: When God Acts

Gen 2:21 and 15:12 reflect the situation of an extraordinary physical closeness of God to a human being. This physical closeness has serious consequences. The state of the human being has to correspond to the closeness of God. The authors of the book of Genesis define this corresponding state as *tardēmāh*, deep sleep. The human being is without sensory perception of the empirical world. The Septuagint transforms the physical state to a mental state: *ekstasis*, ecstasy. The state of mind of the human being allows an exchange between God and the human being. Abraham in ecstasy can hear the voice of God including the promises God makes to him, his heir and the people of Israel. Plato and Philo develop the closeness of God further and elaborate on a mediated closeness to God. Some sort of *mania*, "madness," is God-given and allows a much deeper and more meaningful contact with God. For Philo, the Hebrew prophets are examples of this, but any wise man can reach the state of extraordinary mental closeness to God. The enduring ambiguity of *ecstasy* can be seen in the writings of ancient Judaism. Josephus omits deep sleep and ecstasy from his re-narration of the book of Genesis. The Testaments of the

---

[40] On ecstasy in Acts, see the contribution of Eva-Maria Kreitschmann in this volume, 225–256.

*"Deep Sleep" (*tardēmāh*) and "Ecstasy" (ekstasis)*

Twelve and Fourth Baruch include ecstasy as negative and morally destructive, caused by evil spirits during sleep, but can also understand it as God-given and a blessing. The Acts of Apostles has a positive view of this state of the mind. Ecstasy allows a mediated closeness to and dialogue with God and it is assumed to be produced by God himself.

In sum, being close to God causes an ambiguous state for a human being. To correspond with the close presence of God requires a special state for the human. The Hebrew version of Gen 2:21 and 15:12 is based on the assumption of the unity of soul and body. The human as unity has to correspond to the closeness of God and therefore a severe "deep sleep" (*tardēmāh*) is necessary. The influence of Greek philosophy on ancient Judaism changes anthropological assumptions and introduces the body-soul dichotomy into the history of biblical reception. The narration and re-narration of the biblical accounts of the creation of man and woman as well as the promises to Abraham and his heirs are reflected upon with more complexity. The human mind, its ecstasy, madness, and also inspired God-given state is discussed in ancient Judaism and New Testament. As a high point of this discourse about ecstasy, Philo—inspired by the more elitist concepts of Plato—develops the democratic ideal of a God-given ecstasy for every wise man which is achievable every day of his life.

·

140

Labeling Jesus as "Glutton and Drunkard": Abnormality and Social Norm in Jewish Legal and Sapiential Discourses

Guido Baltes

The designation of Jesus as "glutton and drunkard" (Matt 11:19 par. Luke 7:34) is frequently classified as part of a recurring literary motif of Jesus's inclusive table fellowships with tax collectors, sometimes also as a reflection of an excessive meal practice of the historical Jesus.[1] This reading, however, is questionable on two grounds: First, the designation has the form of a polemical, external ascription in the mouth of Jesus's enemies and should therefore not be read as the evangelists' own characterization of Jesus. Second, the construction of a recurring motif of "inclusive table fellowships with tax collectors" has little textual basis.

It has therefore been suggested that the deuteronomic legislation concerning the "rebellious son" (Deut 21:18–21) should be viewed as the main reference point of the ascription. Especially in the light of the legislation's reception history in early Jewish and rabbinic literature, the designation "glutton and drunkard" would not necessarily refer to the actual eating habits or meal practices of Jesus, but rather function as a conventional *label*[2] for abnormal behaviour, marked as deviant by dominant groups in society and sanctioned accordingly. The label would then stand closer to comparable allegations of mental illness (Mark 3:21;

---

[1] Michael Labahn, "Jesus als 'Fresser und Weinsäufer,'" in *Jesus-Handbuch*, ed. Jens Schröter, Christine Jacobi and Lena Nogossek (Tübingen: Mohr Siebeck, 2017), 455–60, 459; Christina Eschner, *Essen im antiken Judentum und Urchristentum. Diskurse zur sozialen Bedeutung von Tischgemeinschaft, Speiseverboten und Reinheitsvorschriften*, AJEC 108 (Leiden: Brill, 2019), 466 and 516–19; János Bolyki, *Jesu Tischgemeinschaften*, WUNT 2/96 (Tübingen: Mohr Siebeck, 1998), 79.

[2] On the sociological term *label* and the concept of *labeling* cf. below p. 165–7.

Matt 11:18 par.; 1 Cor 14:23), demonic possession (Mark 3:22; John 10:20) and drunkenness (Acts 2:13), raised against Jesus and his followers, than to the synoptic meal traditions.

After a short analysis of the literary context (1.), this story will examine the popular classification of the label as part of a larger motif of "inclusive meals" (2.) and then argue for an intertextual connection with the "rebellious son" legislation instead (3.). A survey of the reception history of the legislation in late biblical, early Jewish and later rabbinic tradition (4.) will show that the text was used far beyond its original legal setting as a reference point for the designation of deviant behaviour. Modern sociological concepts of deviance and abnormality (5.) can therefore foster greater understanding of the polemical ascription as "glutton and drunkard" as reflection of a conflict in which deviant behaviour is designated as abnormal by dominant groups of society, thereby providing a basis for legal sanctions in the later course of the narrative (6.).

1 Transmission, Literary Context and Historical Authenticity

The designation "glutton and drunkard " (ἄνθρωπος φάγος καὶ οἰνοπότης) is paired with "friend of tax collectors and sinners" in Matt as well as Luke (τελωνῶν φίλος καὶ ἁμαρτωλῶν, Matt 11:19 par. Luke 7:34).[3] In both versions, the double charge is part of a larger composition commonly identified as Q material (Matt 11:2–19 par. Luke 7:18–35; 16:16), with minor redactional additions.[4] Some features of the text however suggest an overlap with Markan and/or Johannine material or a shared pre-synoptic tradition.[5]

---

[3] The order of words varies in Luke.
[4] Joseph A. Fitzmyer, *The Gospel according to Luke I–IX*, AB 28.1 (New Haven: Yale, 1986), 662–63, identifies Matt 11:12–13 as Q material, 14–15 as a Matthean addition. Joachim Gnilka, *Das Matthäusevangelium*, HThKNT 1.1 (Freiburg: Herder, 1986), 412–13, identifies 12–15 as Matthean. Luke 7:29–30 is widely seen as a Lukan addition. Cf. William Foxbury Albright and Christopher Stephen Mann, *Matthew. Introduction, Translation and Notes*, AB 15 (New York: Doubleday, 1971), 140; François Bovon, *Das Evangelium nach Lukas, Teilbd. 1*, EKKNT 3/1 (Zürich: Benzinger, 1989), 372 and 378: "redaktionelles Summarium"; Joel B. Green, *The Gospel of Luke*, NICNT, 4th ed. (Grand Rapids: Eerdmans, 2004), 294 and 299–300; Luke T. Johnson, *The Gospel of Luke*, SP 3 (Collegeville: Liturgical Press, 1991), 125.
[5] Cf. below p. 167–8.

In both gospels, the unit is placed at the transition from introductory accounts of Jesus's teaching and healing ministry (Matt 5–7 and 8–9; Luke 6 and 7:1–17) and emerging conflicts about his purported messianic identity and role (Matt 11:25–12:50; Luke 7:36–9:50).[6] The motif of diverging role ascriptions, especially in comparison with the Baptist, is the bracket that holds together the three (or four) original pieces of tradition: The Baptist's inquiry, Jesus's testimony to the Baptist, the parable of the quarreling children and possibly also Luke 16:16. The first set of role ascriptions is mutually applied by both figures to each other. John's designation of Jesus as "the coming one" (ὁ ἐρχόμενος) is posed as a question, while Jesus cites popular expectations about John (prophet, Elijah, "a reed swayed by the wind" and "a man dressed in fine clothes"). The next set of ascriptions is applied by Jesus to unspecified groups of opponents, designated pejoratively[7] as "this generation," and then figuratively as "playing children." At the end of the unit, another pair of ascriptions is applied to John and Jesus, this time by their opponents. However, the logic of the two parallel accusations however is asymmetric: while the inference from abnormal diet to demonization might follow conventions, the inference from normal diet to gluttony and drunkenness is surprising. John is accused precisely *because* of his abnormal eating behaviour, while Jesus is accused *in spite of* his normal eating behaviour.

The double charge against Jesus is usually rated with a high probability of historical authenticity,[8] based not only on the criterion of embarrass-

---

[6] Cf. Green, *Luke*, 294: "...firmly grounded in the portrayal of the character of Jesus's ministry [...], this section presents us with an interpretive recapitulation of Jesus's identity as God's agent of salvation." Similar Matthias Konradt, *Das Evangelium nach Matthäus*, NTD 1 (Göttingen: Vandenhoeck & Ruprecht, 2015), 183.

[7] Cf. Friedrich Büchsel, "γενεά κτλ.," *TWNT I*, 1933, 660–61, similarly Konradt, *Matthäus*, 184 ("...trägt einen abschätzenden Ton ein"). In view is not the whole nation, but dominant groups.

[8] Labahn, "Fresser," 455; Fitzmyer, *Luke*, 678; Heinz Schürmann, *Das Lukasevangelium*, HThKNT 3.1, 4. Auflage (Freiburg: Herder, 1990), 425–427.; Hans Klein, *Das Lukasevangelium*, KEK I/3 (Göttingen: Vandenhoeck & Ruprecht, 2006), 288; Yair Furstenberg, "Zöllner und Sünder als Adressaten des Wirkens Jesu," in Schröter, Jacobi, and Nogossek, *Jesus Handbuch*, 348–56, 348. For an extended survey of the discussion cf. Stefan Witetschek, "The Stigma of a Glutton and Drunkard: Q 7:34 in Historical and Sociological Perspective," *ETL 83* (2007): 135–54, 138–46.

ment,[9] but also on the unusual parallelization of Jesus and John, unique in the synoptic tradition.[10] The unit might therefore reflect historical conflicts between Jesus and his opponents. Conversely, it might also reflect later conflicts between the tradents of the Jesus tradition and their surroundings.

2 Jesus's Table Fellowships as Underlying Motif?

The formula "glutton and drunkard" is regularly categorized by commentators as part of a larger motif of "table fellowships with tax collectors and sinners."[11] These table fellowships are said to provoke the criticism of opponents, not only because they include sinners,[12] but also because they presumably violate purity laws,[13] express *joie de vivre*,[14] include excessive indulgence[15] and lead to gluttony.[16] A person who enjoys what is being offered at a table can presumably not be a holy person.[17] In addition, Jesus's meals are often labeled as "feasts."[18] The meals are interpreted as

---

[9] An interpretation of the charge as deliberate self-stigmatization would eliminate the aspect of embarrassment and could therefore corroborate an origin in early groups of Jesus-followers. Cf. however Witetschek, "Stigma," 151.

[10] Cf. Gnilka, *Matthäus*, 421: "Das ist einmalig in der synoptischen Tradition."

[11] Gnilka, *Matthäus*, 424 and 426; similar Hermut Löhr, "Mahlgemeinschaften Jesu," in Schröter, Jacobi, and Nogossek, *Jesus Handbuch*, 292–98, 293.

[12] Cf. Löhr, "Mahlgemeinschaften," 293; Eschner, *Essen*, 517.

[13] Bruce Malina and Jerome H. Neyrey, *Calling Jesus Names: The Social Value of Labels in Matthew* (Sonoma: Poleridge Press, 1988), 28; cf. Bolyki, *Tischgemeinschaften*, 73; Gnilka, *Matthäus*, 424; Klaus Berger, *Wer war Jesus wirklich?* (Gütersloh: Gütersloher, 1995), 44–45; Howard Clark Kee, "Jesus: A Glutton and a Drunkard," *NTS 42* (1996): 374–93, 384.

[14] Klein, *Lukas*, 290.

[15] Joseph B. Modica, "Jesus as Glutton and Drunkard: the 'Excesses' of Jesus," in *Who Do my Opponents say I Am? An Investigation of the Accusations Against Jesus*, ed. Scot McKnight and Joseph B. Modica, LHJS 327 (London: T&T Clark, 2008), 50–75. Gnilka, *Matthäus*, 424; Berger, *Jesus*, 45; Bovon, *Lukas*, 382.

[16] Bolyki, *Tischgemeinschaften*, 70.

[17] Wolfgang Wiefel, *Das Evangelium nach Lukas*, THKNT 1 (Berlin: Evangelische Verlagsanstalt, 1988), 151.

[18] Klein, *Lukas*, 290; similar Green, *Luke*, 303; Berger, *Jesus*, 44; Bolyki, *Tischgemeinschaften*, 106 and 109; Thomas Söding, *Die Verkündigung Jesu: Ereignis und Erinnerung* (Freiburg: Herder, 2011), 182; Mary J. Marshall, "Jesus: Glutton and Drunkard?" *JSHJ 3* (2005): 47–60, 47.

"enacted parable of the feast in the kingdom that was to come,"[19] the wine being a symbol of the Messiah.[20] Eating and drinking with Jesus would have been "wie ein Himmelreich"[21] for those in his company and would have invoked "die Erinnerung an uralte, ewig junge Bilder vollendeten Glücks."[22] Jesus's opponents are said to find fault with either his mere attendance at such feasts,[23] or with him being the host,[24] or with him regularly appearing as an uninvited guest at such feasts.[25] They presumably accused Jesus of "libertinism"[26] because he teared down "walls that had been built meticulously in order to protect one's own privileges."[27] However, on closer inspection, the construct of a recurring motif of inclusive table fellowships featuring excessive food consumption or festal joy lacks a solid textual basis, for several reasons:

a) The polemic ascription by Jesus's opponents should not hastily be taken as a reflection of historical reality: Just as the designation of John as being demon possessed should not be lumped together with other Baptist traditions to form an overall image of John the Baptist, the charge of gluttony and drunkenness should not be combined with meal traditions to form a conclusive image of Jesus's meal practice. Both charges are cited by the evangelists merely to be refuted. "Es wäre also dem historischen Jesusforscher nicht geraten, Jesus zu einem 'Fresser und Weinsäufer' zu erklären."[28]

---

[19] Bruce Chilton, "Method in a Critical Study of Jesus," *Handbook for the Study of the Historical Jesus. Volume 1: How to Study the Historical Jesus* (Leiden: Brill, 2011), 129–58, 135.

[20] Berger, *Jesus*, 44.

[21] Berger, *Jesus*, 45.

[22] Söding, *Verkündigung*, 182.

[23] Klein, *Lukas*, 290; similar Green, *Luke*, 303.

[24] Söding, *Verkündigung*, 182.

[25] Marshall, "Glutton," 47.

[26] Bovon, *Lukas*, 382; similar Josef Ernst, *Johannes der Täufer*, BZNW 53 (Berlin: De Gruyter, 1989), 76: "wegen seiner offenen Lebensform."

[27] Gnilka, *Matthäus*, 426 (translation mine); cf. Kee, "Glutton," 384: "those who are ethnically, occupationally, culturally, ritually beyond the traditional boundaries of God's people."

[28] Wolfgang Stegemann, *Jesus und seine Zeit* (Stuttgart: Kohlhammer, 2009), 98. More nuanced in Bovon, *Lukas*, 382: The terms "Libertinist" and "Exzess" are here presented merely as hostile ascriptions. Similar already Theodor Zahn, *Das Evangelium des Matthäus*, Kommentar zum Neuen Testament 1 (Leipzig: Dechert, 1903), 430.

b) The two parts of the double charge against Jesus should not hastily be combined into one image: Too often, the diverging accusations against Jesus of being a "glutton and drunkard" and a "friend of sinners and tax collectors" are lumped together into the image of Jesus eating and drinking *with* tax collectors,[29] thereby creating an alleged "double attestation" of a recurring motif in Q and Mark 2:13–17 (parr. Matt 9:9–13 und Luke 5:27–32).

c) In reality, Mark 2:13–17 parr. is the single one occurrence of a "meal with tax collectors" within the whole Jesus tradition. It can therefore hardly be called a recurring motif. Other texts, sometimes counted as additional evidence, do not contribute to such a motif: Luke 19:5–7 mentions a tax collector, but no meal. Luke 15:1–2 is a redactional expansion of Luke 5:27–32 and explicitly separates between the *fellowship* with tax collectors (Luke 15:1) and *meals* with sinners (Luke 15:2).

d) None of the synoptic meal traditions mentions excessive food consumption or drinking. As a matter of fact, Jesus himself is never pictured as eating or drinking, with only one exception.[30] In a survey of Jesus's table fellowships, Hermut Löhr has categorized the differing traditions as follows:[31]

1. Table fellowship with tax collectors
(Mark 2:13–17 parr.; cf. Luke 19:1–10)[32]
2. Other meal scenes
(Mark 14:3–9 parr.; Luke 14:1–24)[33]
3. Feeding miracles
(Mark 6:31–44 parr.; Mark 8:1–8 / Matt 15:32–39; John 2:1–11)

---

[29] Cf Löhr, "Mahlgemeinschaften," 293; Eschner, *Essen*, 517; Berger, *Jesus*, 44; Gnilka, *Matthäus*, 424.

[30] Cf. Löhr, "Mahlgemeinschaften," 293. The only exception is Luke 24:43, a scene that neither relates to sinners and tax collectors nor suggests excessive consumption.

[31] Löhr, "Mahlgemeinschaften," 292–93.

[32] Löhr counts Luke 19:1–10 among the "table fellowships with tax collectors," even though a meal or table is not mentioned. This turns a single table fellowship tradition (Mark 2:1–10) into a whole category of "table fellowships with tax collectors." The same happens in Wiefel, *Lukas*, 153.327 and Bolyki, *Tischgemeinschaften*, 109–12

[33] Luke 7:36–50 is probably counted as a synoptic parallel of Mark 14:3–9 (cf. Aland Nr. 114 and 306).

4. Post-resurrection meals
(Luke 24:13–35; 24:36–43; John 21:9–13)
5. Sayings about the meal practice of Jesus and his followers (Mark 2:18–22 parr.; 7:1–23 par.; Matt 11:19 par. Luke 7:34; Luke 15:2)
6. Other sayings about meals
(Luke 12:35–38; 13:29/Matt 8:11)

To these should be added the traditions about the last supper (7.) and images of meals in the parables (8.).[34] The survey shows that the narrative traditions about the meal practice of Jesus (categories 1, 2, 4 and 7) contain no images of excessive *joie de vivre*,[35] unholy indulgence[36] or "ewig junge Bilder vollendeten Glücks."[37] To the contrary, they depict very ordinary meals without even mentioning the amounts of food consumed. None of the narratives adress purity questions, neither with respect to the food nor to the persons partaking.[38] The focus of the narration is not on *what is consumed* but on *who is invited.* The feeding miracles (category 3), in contrast, focus on the amounts of food and beverage, however here there is no mention of either tax collectors or sinners. Jesus himself is not pictured as eating or drinking, and there is no mention of excessive consumption. Therefore, the miracle stories can neither contribute to an alleged motif of "provocative table fellowships" nor to the charges of gluttony and drunkenness. The controversy stories (category 5) do indeed focus on questions of purity, sabbath halakha and fasting. However, they again do not mention excessive consumption or provocative company and therefore do not relate to the ascription of Matt 11:19 par. And finally, the parable stories (category 8) adress festive joy as well as questions of legitimate participation. They, however, never describe excessive consumption. The motif of eschatological abundance (cf. e.g. Isa 25:6) is

---

[34] Both are treated in separate articles in Schröter, Jacobi, and Nogossek, *Jesus Handbuch.* Cf. Löhr, "Mahlgemeinschaften," 292.

[35] Cf. n. 14 above.

[36] Cf. n. 15 and 17 above.

[37] Cf. n. 22 above.

[38] Cf. n. 13 above and, more detailed, Eschner, *Essen,* 466–530.

not picked up in the synoptic meal traditions apart from the miracle stories.[39]

Upon closer analysis, the connections between the designation ἄνθρωπος φάγος καὶ οἰνοπότης and the meal traditions are therefore weaker than suggested by the assumed motif of (excessive) "table fellowships with tax collectors" which in fact is an artificial combination of very divergent meal traditions otherwise unrelated to the charge. Only one text shows Jesus himself eating. Only one text describes a meal with tax collectors. None of the texts mentions excessive consumption of food or beverage, or as it were festive joy or abundance. The meal traditions therefore provide no suitable background against which the origins of the charges of gluttony or drunkenness may be explained.

3 The Legislation of the "Deviant Son" as Alternative Background

Some commentators have suggested reading the formula "glutton and drunkard" as an intertextual allusion to the legislation of Deut 21:18–21:[40]

> (18) If someone has a stubborn[41] and rebellious son (בֵּן סוֹרֵר וּמוֹרֶה; υἱὸς ἀπειθὴς καὶ ἐρεθιστής) who will not obey his father and mother, who does not heed them when they discipline them, (19) then his father and his mother shall take hold of him and bring him out to the elders of his town at the gate of that place. (20) They shall say to the elders of his town, "This son of

---

[39] Löhr, "Mahlgemeinschaften," 298, identifies the main topics of the meal traditions as follows: (1) Jesus's non-ascetic lifestyle (2) Jesus's care for social and religious outcasts (3) meal and feast as an image for the end of time. The third topic however does not imply excess or abundance of food in the Jesus traditions.

[40] Cf. I. Howard Marshall, *The Gospel of Luke: A Commentary on the Greek Text*, NIGTC 3 (Exeter: Paternoster, 1978), 302; Craig S. Keener, *A Commentary on the Book of Matthew*, NICNT (Grand Rapids: Eerdmans, 1999), 342; John Nolland, *Luke*, WBC 35 (Waco: Word Books, 1989), 346; Kee, "Glutton," 390; Modica, "Glutton," 63; Gerhard Maier, *Das Evangelium des Matthäus, Kapitel 1–15*, Historisch Theologische Auslegung 1.1 (Witten: SCM Brockhaus, 2015), 627; Schürmann, *Lukasevangelium*, 427.

[41] The current translation follows NRSV. The traditional rendering of סוֹרֵר with "stubborn" however evokes a wrong image of active resistance. In other places however, the Hebrew סוֹרֵר rather carries the meaning "straying away from a path" (Isa 65:2; Jer 5:23; 6:28; Prov 7:11) or "to turn away from somebody" (Isa 30:1; Zech 7:11; Ps 68:7; 78:8; Neh 9:29). The modern term "deviant" therefore represents the semantic range of סוֹרֵר more accurately.

Guido Baltes

ours is stubborn and rebellious. (בְּנֵנוּ זֶה סוֹרֵר וּמֹרֶה; ὁ υἱὸς ἡμῶν οὗτος ἀπειθεῖ
καὶ ἐρεθίζει) He will not obey us. He is a glutton and a drunkard." (אֵינֶנּוּ שֹׁמֵעַ
בְּקֹלֵנוּ זוֹלֵל וְסֹבֵא; οὐχ ὑπακούει τῆς φωνῆς ἡμῶν, συμβολοκοπῶν οἰνοφλυγεῖ) (21)
Then all the men of the town shall stone him to death. So you shall purge
the evil from your midst; and all Israel will hear, and be afraid.

The suggestion to read Matt 11:19 par. Luke 7:34 as an allusion to this text
is often attributed to Joachim Jeremias,[42] but it already appears in Adolf
Schlatter's commentary on Matthew.[43] That such a connection was already
assumed in the late middle ages, is attested by the Hebrew rendition of
Matt 11:19 in the 14th-century work Even Bohan, written by Shem-Tob
ben-Isaak ben-Shaprut: The translator chose to render the Greek wording
ἄνθρωπος φάγος καὶ οἰνοπότης with a Hebrew citation of Deut 21:20 (זוֹלֵל
וְסֹבֵא).[44] However, it has been argued against such a connection that the
Matthean wording has virtually no resemblance with the Septuagint
wording of Deut 21:20 (συμβολοκοπῶν οἰνοφλυγεῖ) and therefore cannot be
an allusion to that text.[45] A possible intertextual relation is therefore
denied[46] or not even discussed[47] by many commentators.

Reliable criteria for the identification of intertextual allusions or echoes
in New Testament texts are a matter of intense debate.[48] As a general rule,

---

[42] Joachim Jeremias, *Die Gleichnisse Jesu*, 11th ed. (Göttingen: Vandenhoeck & Ruprecht, 1998), 160.

[43] Adolf Schlatter, *Der Evangelist Matthäus: Seine Sprache, sein Ziel, seine Selbständigkeit* (Stuttgart: Calwer, 1929), 373.

[44] George Howard, *Hebrew Gospel of Matthew*, 2nd ed. (Macon: Mercer, 1995), 50.

[45] Fitzmyer, *Luke*, I:681.

[46] Fitzmyer, *Luke*, I:681; Ulrich Luz, *Das Evangelium nach Matthäus. 2.Teilband: Mt 8–17*, EKK 1.2 (Zürich/Neukirchen-Vluyn: Benziger/Neukirchener, 1990), 188; Klein, *Matthäus*, 290–91; Johnson, *Luke*, 124; Gnilka, *Matthäus*, 424; Witetschek, "Stigma," 150; Bolyki, *Tischgemeinschaften*, 72.

[47] Bovon, *Lukas*, 382; Konradt, *Matthäus*, 184; Green, *Luke*, 303; Walter Grundmann, *Das Evangelium nach Matthäus*, THKNT 1 (Berlin: Evangelische Verlagsanstalt, 1975), 312; Petr Pokorný, "Demoniac and Drunkard: John the Baptist and Jesus According to Q 7:33–34," in *Jesus Research: The First Princeton-Prague Symposium on Jesus Research*, ed. by James H. Charlesworth and Petr Pokorný (Grand Rapids: Eerdmans, 2005), 170–81, 176–77; Str-B I:604 also does not refer to the passage.

[48] On the origins of the concept of intertextuality in the field of literary studies cf. Stefan Alkier, "Intertextualität—Annäherungen an ein texttheoretisches Paradigma," in *Heiligkeit und Herrschaft: Intertextuelle Studien zu Heiligkeitsvorstellungen und zu Psalm 110*, ed. Dieter

a certain amount of verbatim agreement (*volume*) is seen as a minimum requirement.[49] However, in certain cases even two words can suffice to establish an intertextual link,[50] even though such an identification should then be corroborated by additional observations such as the availability of the pretext for the intended reader,[51] the significance of the allusion for the referring text,[52] thematic coherence[53] or discernable markers (*Markierung*)[54] and signals of intertextuality (*Intertextualitätssignale*).[55]

Sänger, Biblisch-Theologische Studien 55 (Neukirchen: Neukirchener, 2003), 1–26 and Brisio J. Oropeza, "Intertextuality," in *The Oxford Encyclopedia of Biblical Interpretation*, ed. Steven L. McKenzie, Volume I (Oxford: University Press, 2013), 453–63. On criteria for the identification of intertextual links cf. Alkier, "Intertextualität," 16–21; Dietrich-Alex Koch, *Die Schrift als Zeuge des Evangeliums. Untersuchungen zur Verwendung und zum Verständnis der Schrift bei Paulus*, BHT 69 (Tübingen: Mohr Siebeck, 1986), 11; Richard Hays, *Echoes of Scripture in the Letters of Paul* (New Haven: Yale, 1989), 29–32 and idem, *Echoes of Scripture in the Gospels* (Waco: Baylor University, 2016), 10–14; Gregory K. Beale, *Handbook on the New Testament Use of the Old Testament* (Grand Rapids: Baker, 2012), 31–35; Lukas Bormann, "Psalm 110 im Dialog mit dem Neuen Testament," in Sänger, *Heiligkeit*, 171–205, 185–90; Joel White, "Identifying Intertextual Exegesis in Paul: Methodological Considerations and a Test-Case (1 Cor. 6:5)," in *The Crucified Apostle: Essays on Peter and Paul*, ed. Paul House and Todd Wilson, WUNT 2/450 (Tübingen: Mohr Siebeck, 2017), 167–88; Ruben Zimmermann, "Jesus im Bild Gottes: Anspielungen auf das Alte Testament im Johannesevangelium am Beispiel der Hirtenbildfelder in John 10," in *Kontexte des Johannesevangeliums: das vierte Evangelium in religions- und traditionsgeschichtlicher Perspektive*, ed. Jörg Frey (Tübingen: Mohr Siebeck, 2004), 81–116, 83–89; Marianne Grohmann and Hyun Chul Paul Kim, ed., *Second Wave Intertextuality and the Hebrew Bible*, RBS 93 (Atlanta: SBL Press, 2019).

[49] Hays, *Paul*, 30; Beale, *Handbook*, 33; Bormann, "Psalm 110," 190.

[50] Cf. e.g. σκότος and φῶς in 2 Cor 4:6 (Hays, *Paul*, 30) or ἐν ἀρχῇ in John 1:1 (Bormann, "Psalm 110," 190) as allusions to Gen 1.

[51] In the case of the allusions named in n. 50, a high degree of familiarity and availability can be assumed.

[52] In the case of 2 Cor 4:6 (n. 50): "Paul has placed the echo at the rhetorical climax of a unit in his letter" (Hays, *Paul*, 30).

[53] In the case of John 1:1 (n. 50): "...der gemeinsame Kontext der uranfänglichen Schöpfung" (Bormann, "Psalm 110," 190).

[54] Jörg Helbig, *Intertextualität und Markierung. Untersuchungen zur Systematik und Funktion der Signalisierung von Intertextualität*, Beiträge zur neueren Literaturgeschichte 3/141 (Heidelberg: Winter, 1996), 53.

[55] Susanne Holthuis, *Intertextualität: Aspekte einer rezeptionsorientierten Konzeption*, Stauffenburg-Kolloquium 28 (Tübingen: Stauffenburg, 1993), 32.

Questions of availability, significance and context of the formula זוֹלֵל וְסֹבֵא will be adressed in the upcoming paragraphs. As regards markers or signals of intertextuality, the introduction of ἄνθρωπος φάγος καὶ οἰνοπότης with the verb λέγουσιν marks the formula as a citation and therefore opens a wider horizon of meaning which the reader has to take into account when approaching the text,[56] in this case the use of the formula as a hostile ascription in the context of a conflict. The charge against Jesus differs from that against John by using nominal style and therefore has more the character of a *label*, a categorizing role ascription,[57] than the latter. The formulaic character of the expression is further underscored by the fact that Matthew and Luke are in verbatim agreement only here, while they vary in the introduction as well as in the wording of the second charge, the company of sinners and tax collectors. In addition, both core terms, φάγος and οἰνοπότης, are New Testament hapax legomena. The formula is therefore demarcated by features of *Störung* as well as *Überkodierung*,[58] two prominent signals of intertextuality according to Helbig. The heightened complexity of the formula therefore presumes a higher level of attention on the part of the reader to the nuances of the text.[59]

A search for possible pretexts yields verbatim use of the Greek formula neither in the LXX nor in any other contemporary sources. In the LXX, the term φάγος is absent altogether, οἰνοπότης is found only once (Prov 23:20), where it is combined, however, with an expression of excessive eating (μηδὲ ἐκτείνου συμβολαῖς κρεῶν τε ἀγορασμοῖς) in analogy to Matt 11:19 par. The Hebrew text uses the terms סֹבֵא and זוֹלֵל here, which is why an intertextual relation between Prov 23:20 and Deut 21:20 is frequently assumed by commentators, even if in this case the agreement is not verbatim. It is followed, though, by a quotation from Deut 21:20 (סֹבֵא וְזוֹלֵל) in the next verse. A look at other examples of a reception of Deut 21:20 suggests that the formula retained a relatively fixed form in Hebrew, while Greek translations could vary and no comparably fixed formula was generated in Greek (Table 1):

---

[56] cf. Bormann, "Psalm 110," 189.
[57] Cf. below p. 165–6.
[58] Bormann, "Psalm 110," 189.
[59] Helbig, *Intertextualität*, 65.

Deut 21:20	זוֹלֵל וְסֹבֵא	συμβολοκοπῶν οἰνοφλυγεῖ
Prov 23:20	אַל־תְּהִי בְסֹבְאֵי־יָיִן בְּזֹלֲלֵי בָשָׂר לָמוֹ	μὴ ἴσθι οἰνοπότης μηδὲ ἐκτείνου συμβολαῖς κρεῶν τε ἀγορασμοῖς
Spr. 23:21	סֹבֵא וְזוֹלֵל	μέθυσος καὶ πορνοκόπος
Spr. 28:7	זוֹלְלִים	ἀσωτία
Sir 18:33	זולל וסובא	πτωχὸς συμβολοκοπῶν ἐκ δανεισμοῦ

Table 1: The formula זוֹלֵל וְסֹבֵא and its derivatives in Hebrew and Greek

In his extensive treatment of the formula, Philo uses the LXX wording consistently,[60] while in Josephus's exposition of Deut 21:18–21 no influence of the LXX is discernible. He either made direct use of the Hebrew text or interacts with secondary halakhic discourses about the passage.[61]

A further look into the reception history of the formula זוֹלֵל וְסֹבֵא will show that it assumed a figurative meaning beyond its original legal context as a *label* for abnormal and deviant behaviour. The differing Greek renderings of the Hebrew formula attest to the fact that the Hebrew formula did not produce a similarly fixed expression in the Greek language, so that ad hoc translations had to be generated anew in different contexts.

Against this background it seems plausible that the expression ἄνθρωπος φάγος καὶ οἰνοπότης is yet another variant of such an ad hoc translation. Even if ἄνθρωπος φάγος does not exactly correspond to the semantic content of the Hebrew term זוֹלֵל, the LXX renderings of the term in Deut 21:20 and in Prov 23:20 demonstrate that the term זוֹלֵל was associated with eating at a banquet very early on. Later rabbinic discus-

---

[60] On Philo. cf. below p. 158–62.
[61] On Josephus, cf. below p. 162–3.

sions of the passage[62] and the rendering in Targum Neofiti read זוֹלֵל as an expression of excessive eating. A translation of זוֹלֵל with ἄνθρωπος φάγος is therefore plausible despite the lexical difference. For οἰνοπότης, a dependence on Prov 23:20 and therefore a relation to Deut 21:20 is more obvious. The verbatim agreement of the formula in Matt and Luke however suggests, however, that the Greek wording was not created by the evangelists but originates in an earlier pre-synoptic stage of the tradition. In view of the widely assumed historical authenticity of the tradition,[63] the charge against Jesus must have been worded in a Semitic language. It probably made use of the Hebrew formula from Deut 21:20[64] and then was translated into Greek in the later process of transmission. As in the case of Josephus, a direct use of the Hebrew scriptures,[65] an interaction with contemporary halakhic discourses[66] or the use of a non-

---

[62] Cf. below p. 163-4.

[63] Cf. p. 152 above.

[64] Cf. Targum Onkelos on Deut 21:20, where Hebrew loanwords are used to render the formula.

[65] Schlatter, *Matthäus*, 373; Kee, "Glutton," 390. On the relevance of the Hebrew scriptures for the question of intertextuality in New Testament texts cf. Jörg Frey, "'Wie Mose die Schlange in der Wüste erhöht hat' .... Zur frühjüdischen Deutung der 'ehernen Schlange' und ihrer christologischen Rezeption in Johannes 3:14 f.," in *Schriftauslegung im antiken Judentum und im Urchristentum*, ed. Martin Hengel and Hermut Löhr, WUNT 73 (Tübingen: Mohr Siebeck, 1993), 153-205, 190-96.203; Ulrike Mittmann, "Jesaja 53 LXX—ein umstrittener urchristlicher Referenztext. Zum traditions- und rezeptionsgeschichtlichen Hintergrund der Einsetzungsworte," in *Die Septuaginta und das frühe Christentum*, ed. Thomas S. Caulley and Hermann Lichtenberger (Tübingen: Mohr Siebeck, 2011), 217-32; Steven Notley, "Non-Septuagintal Hebraisms in the Third Gospel: An inconvenient Truth," in *The Language Environment of First Century Judaea*, ed. Randall Buth and R. Steven Notley, JCP 26 (Leiden: Brill, 2013), 320-46; Zimmermann, "Bild Gottes," 86-88.

[66] On the relevance of targumic and rabbinic reception of biblical traditions for the question of intertextuality in the New Testament cf. Leroy A. Huizenga, "Der Jesus des Matthäusevangeliums und der Isaak der antiken jüdischen Enzyklopädie," in Sänger, *Heiligkeit*, 71-91, 72-75; Dieter Sänger, "Das Alte Testament im Neuen Testament," in *Das Alte Testament als christliche Bibel in orthodoxer und westlicher Sicht*, ed. Ivan Z. Dimitrov, WUNT 174 (Tübingen: Mohr Siebeck, 2004), 155-203, 178-79; Frey, "Mose," 196-99.

septuagintal Greek version of Deuteronomy[67] could have provided the basis for the translation.

In sum, the origins of the polemical ascription Matt 11:29 par. Luke 7:34 in inner-Jewish conflicts around the Person of Jesus or at least in an early pre-synoptic phase of the Gospel transmission, its formulaic character, the semantic affinities with the Hebrew formula זוֹלֵל וְסֹבֵא and the signals of intertextuality support the plausible assumption that the ascription ἄνθρωπος φάγος καὶ οἰνοπότης is an intentional allusion to the legislation of the "deviant son" in Deut 21:18–21).[68]

4 Origins and Reception of the Legislation About a "Deviant Son"

The historical origins of the legal tradition in Deut 21:18–21 are uncertain. Elizabeth Bellefontaine assumes an ancient tribal ritual from the pre-state era, regulating the handling of socially deviant members in a society:[69]

> Most tribal societies were confronted at one time or another with dissolute or non-conformist individuals who were deemed incorrigible. Irreformable deviancy was almost always considered a crime and the criminal was put to death, thus ridding the community of his evil influence. ... Thus, the son's deviant behaviour not only corrupted himself but may have meant serious negative consequences for his neighbours. He was ... an undesirable member of society and he at last attained the status of the "finally intolerable."[70]

The passage probably combines two independent legal traditions, one (בֵּן סוֹרֵר וּמוֹרֶה) sanctioning disobedience against parental authority, the other (זוֹלֵל וְסֹבֵא) describing a legal procedure "by which a clan rid itself of irreformable and dangerous social deviants."[71] In noticeable contrast with

---

[67] Jens Schröter, "Das Alte Testament im Urchristentum," in *Das Alte Testament in der Theologie*, ed. Elisabeth Gräb-Schmidt and Rainer Preul, MTS 25 (Leipzig: Evangelische Verlagsanstalt, 2013), 49–81, 63–68.

[68] Cf. Helbig, *Intertextualität*, 45 f., for the distinction of different degrees of authorial intentionality and reader competence.

[69] Elizabeth Bellefontaine, "Deuteronomy 21:18–21: Reviewing the Case of the Rebellious Son," JSOT 13 (1979): 13–31, 23.

[70] Bellefontaine, "Rebellious Son," 21.

[71] Bellefontaine, "Rebellious Son," 23.

other casuistic legal regulations, the delinquent is not charged with any specific act that would constitute a violation of law.[72] Rather, a continuous pattern of behaviour is labeled as deviant and therefore sanctioned by the community.

In view of this legal opacity it is a matter of debate whether the law in its present form was ever justiciable or part of legal practice in Israel or whether it assumed a merely deterrent function in its present deuteronomistic context.[73] In biblical or post-biblical literature, there are no examples of an application of the law. Later rabbinic discussion explicitly classifies the legislation as a legal fiction.[74] Some commentators view the whole passage as a theological metaphor for Israel as the "deviant son" in the context of a deuteronomistic view of Israel's history.[75] The framing of the legislation in Deut 21:1 and 21:23 and the theological résumé in 21:21bc point to that direction. In non-legal biblical texts, the formula סוֹרֵר וּמֹרֶה ("deviant and disobedient") is used twice as a description of the people of Israel (Jer 5:23 and Ps 78:8), the root סרר in many more comparable contexts.[76] The latest monographical analysis of the passage combines legal and theological aspects and concludes that the harsh punishment of the deviant family member is due to the fact that cultic, non-Yahwistic eating and drinking rituals probably stand in the background of the accusation:

> Excessive consumption, the traditional understanding of the crime of the Rebellious Son, is not viewed as problematic behaviour in biblical terms. "Deviant" consumption, however, like other forms of non-Yahwistic practice, is deemed by biblical scribes to be a threat to the wider community and must be dealt with in such a way as to remove that threat from society.

---

[72] Attempts to reconstruct an actual violation of law by reference to other legal texts (e.g. Exod 20:12; 21:15.17) must remain hypothetical since Deut 21:18–21 does not relate explicitly to any violation of laws stated in these texts. Cf. Bellefontaine, "Rebellious Son," 15–16; Bruno J. Clifton, "What if Israel was God's Stubborn and Rebellious son? Deuteronomy 21:18–21, Jeremiah 5:23, Psalm 78:8," *ZABR 20* (2014): 115–26, 119.

[73] Clifton, "Rebellious son," 115.

[74] Cf. p. 163–4 below.

[75] Bellefontaine, "Rebellious Son," 13 and Clifton, "Rebellious son," 124.

[76] Isa 1:23; 65:2; Hos 9:15; Neh 9:29; for numerous additional texts cf. Bellefontaine, "Rebellious Son," 18.

... Death, throughout the Hebrew Bible, is Yahweh's typical response to sociability with other divine beings.[77]

For the purposes of the present analysis, however, the historical origins of the legislation are less important than its later reception in biblical and postbiblical literature. Examples of such a reception are found in Jewish wisdom literature, in Philo and in rabbinic discourses.

4.1 The Reception in Biblical Wisdom Literature

The occurrence of סֹבֵא וְזוֹלֵל (Prov 23:21) already mentioned above is part of an extended instruction on parental obedience (Prov 23:12–26). The expectation of listening obedience towards parents is addressed as well as the issue of physical punishment in cases of disobedience. The text infers that obedient children are a source of honour for parents while disobedience leads to dishonor, shame, poverty and eventually death. This connection of parental disobedience and death closely resembles the legislation of Deut 21:18–21. Obedience, on the other hand, is equated with a "wise heart" (אִם־חָכַם לִבֶּךָ, ἐὰν σοφὴ γένηταί σου ἡ καρδία, V. 15), "prudent talk" (לְאָמְרֵי־דָעַת, λόγοις αἰσθήσεως, V. 12), "straightforwardness" (מֵישָׁרִים, ὀρθά, V.16) und "fear of YHWH" (בְּיִרְאַת־יְהוָה, ἐν φόβῳ κυρίου, V. 17). In contrast to these, the consequences of unwise behaviour are illustrated, drawing on the vocabulary of Deut 21:18–21. In the center of the passage, the three motifs of wisdom, parental obedience and deviant eating and drinking are woven together: Framed by the inclusio of an exhortation to wisdom (A and A'), the two separate charges of Deut 21:18–21 (B: glutton and drunkard, cf. Deut 21:20; B': parental disobedience, Deut 21:18) form a second inclusio, while in the center, the consequences of poverty and social stigmatization (C and C') are laid out:

---

[77] Rebekah Welton, *He Is a Glutton and a Drunkard: Deviant Consumption in the Hebrew Bible* (Leiden: Brill, 2020), 291–92.

A (19) Hear, my child, and be wise, and direct your mind in the way.

B   (20) Do not be among winebibbers (אַל־תְּהִי בְסֹבְאֵי־יָיִן)

  or among gluttonous eaters of meat; (בְּזֹלֲלֵי בָשָׂר לָמוֹ)

C   (21) for the drunkard and the glutton (סֹבֵא וְזוֹלֵל) will come to poverty,

C′   and drowsiness will clothe them with rags.

B′   (22) Listen to your father who begot you,

  and do not despise your mother when she is old.

A′ (23) Buy truth, and do not sell it;

  buy wisdom, instruction, and understanding (NRSV).

In verse 20, the simpler formula סֹבֵא וְזוֹלֵל (V. 21) is expanded and shifts the focus from the *act* of eating and drinking to the *company* in which such eating and drinking takes place. In the Greek translation, the range of behaviour deemed as deviant is exspanded even further: μέθυσος καὶ πορνοκόπος shifts the focus from excessive eating and drinking towards intoxication leading to sexual transgression. The longer formula in V. 20, which already included bad company in the Hebrew original, is expanded to include banquets and (non-Israelite?) meat markets (μὴ ἴσθι οἰνοπότης μηδὲ ἐκτείνου συμβολαῖς κρεῶν τε ἀγορασμοῖς). The rationale behind both verses is the same: excessive eating and drinking is unwise because it includes bad company and leads to deviant behavior. In analogy with Deut 21:18–21, such behaviour is then combined with the notion of parental disobedience (V. 22), and both are framed with the motif of wisdom (V. 19 and 23).[78]

In another passage of Proverbs (Prov 28:7), the term זוֹלְלִים is used without its counterpart סוֹבָאִים and translated with ἀσωτία. However, here it is also combined with the motif of parental disobedience: Even the company of זוֹלְלִים is a cause of shame for the father. Tora obedience, on the other hand, is a characteristic of a "prudent son" (בֵּן מֵבִין). Finally, a third passage in Proverbs (Prov 20:1) contrasts wine drinking and wisdom, though without using the terms סֹבֵא or זוֹלֵל .

In Sir 18:33 (LXX), the expression μὴ γίνου πτωχὸς συμβολοκοπῶν ἐκ δανεισμοῦ (NETS: "Do not become poor by feasting out of borrowing") is

---

[78] In the LXX, an equivalent for V. 23 is absent. Instead, V. 24 is expanded: καλῶς ἐκτρέφει πατὴρ δίκαιος, ἐπὶ δὲ υἱῷ σοφῷ εὐφραίνεται ἡ ψυχὴ αὐτοῦ· References to wisdom therefore form an inclusion here as well.

used as a warning against poverty through feasting and financial debt. The term συμβολοκοπῶν is probably an echo of Deut 21:20. The Hebrew manuscript of Ben Sira (C 4r:3) found in the Cairo Geniza has אל תהי זולל [ה]וסובא ומאומ here.⁷⁹ If it reliably reflects the original Hebrew version, then the whole term πτωχὸς συμβολοκοπῶν ἐκ δανεισμοῦ is another translational variant of זולל וסבא. The context again is parental instruction to obedience (Sir 18:15), equating obedience with wisdom (18:27–28) and deviant behaviour with foolishness (18:18.27) and ridicule (18:31). Again, the formula זולל וסובא is used as a summarizing label for a range of deviant activities (Sir 19:1–3), such as intoxication, sexual trangression and bad company (ἄτης μέθυσος; οἶνος καὶ γυναῖκες; ὁ κολλώμενος πόρναις). The consequences of such behaviour are named as poverty (πλουτισθήσεται), social decline (πεσεῖται), loss of mental sanity (ἀποστήσουσιν συνετούς) and eventually death (ψυχὴ ἐξαρθήσεται).

4.2 The Reception in Philo

Philo dedicates large parts of his work *De Ebrietate* to an extended allegorical exposition of Deut 21:18–21.⁸⁰ His exposition of the passage is part of a larger treatise on phenomena of drunkenness and mental abnormality, spanning several of his exegetical works. The topical excursus is initiated by the narration of Noah's drunkenness (Gen 9:20–21) in the final chapters of *De Plantatione Noe* (140–177). Originally, it apparently included a further, no longer extant volume treating the various views of ancient medical and philosophical writers on the issue of drunkenness⁸¹ and then continues in *De Ebrietate*, where Philo uses the legislation on the "deviant son" as a basis to contrast wisdom and

---

⁷⁹ Pancratius C. Beentjes, *The Book of Ben Sira in Hebrew: A Text Edition of All Extant Hebrew Manuscripts and a Synopsis of All Parallel Hebrew Ben Sira Texts*, VTSup 68 (Leiden: Brill, 1997), 97.

⁸⁰ Philo, *Ebr.* 11–29. In fact, the following chapters (*Ebr.* 30–124) are based on the same passage, though explicit references to the actual wording of Deut 21:18–21 are rare here. Philo then returns to the topic of drunkenness in *Ebr.* 125–61.

⁸¹ The volume formed the first part of a double work called "On Drunkenness" (Περὶ μέθης), of which only the second part seems to have survived. Eusebius (*Hist. Eccl.* 2.18.2) and Hieronymus (*Vir. Ill.* 11) claim to have known both parts. Philo himself mentions the first part in *Ebr.* 1:1, and in *Plant.* 173–174 he mentions "tens of thousands" of works written by ancient authors on the issue of drunkenness.

Guido Baltes

drunkenness.⁸² The motif of parental obedience is used allegorically by Philo as an image for wise behaviour, which he argues to be a result of obedience to natural reason (father) and social norms (mother).⁸³ Philo's starting point is the question, "whether the wise man will get drunk" (εἰ μεθυσθήσεται ὁ σοφός, *Plant.* 142).⁸⁴ In summing up the attitudes of ancient writers towards drunkenness, he states that only few demand total abstinence,⁸⁵ while the majority differentiates between drinking and drunkenness. Philo himself follows the majority and distinguishes between two forms of μεθύειν, namely οἰνοῦσθαι and ληρεῖν ἐν οἴνῳ.⁸⁶ The translations offered by De Yonge ("being overcome with wine" and "behaving foolishly in one's cups") lack the appropriate precision here: ληρεῖν is a medical term regularly employed by ancient writers to describe "mental abnormalities, especially fevers."⁸⁷ Philo thus equates drunkenness with insanity. The border between wise alcohol consumption and drunkenness for him is crossed as soon as a person is no longer capable of using his or her reason (φρόνησις) in order to prevent harm (τοῖς βλάπτειν ἐπιχειροῦσιν).

After a general introduction into *De Ebrietate* (1–10) Philo commences a detailed exposition of the legislation concerning the "deviant son." He

---

⁸² For an extensive treatment of the interrelation of drunkenness and wisdom in the works of Philo cf. Thomas E. Phillips, "'Will the Wise Person Get Drunk?' The Background of the Human Wisdom in Luke 7:35 and Matthew 11:19," *JBL* (2008): 385–96.

⁸³ *Ebr.* 34.

⁸⁴ Unless stated otherwise, all English translations of Philo follow the edition of Charles Duke Yonge, *The Works of Philo: Complete and Unabridged.* 3rd revised ed. (Peabody: Hendrickson, 1995).

⁸⁵ *Plant.* 176–177 seems to ascribe this position to Zenon.

⁸⁶ *Plant.* 142–143.

⁸⁷ Steven Kidd, *Nonsense and Meaning in Ancient Greek Comedy* (Cambridge: University Press, 2014), 26. According to Xenophon (*Mem.* 3.9.6–7), Socrates defined abnormal behaviour as "not the sort of mistakes everyone makes, but those that only a few make" (translation by Kidd, *Nonsense*, 32). As examples, he relates the cases of a man who thought he was so tall that he had to bow his head when entering the city gates, and a man who thought he was so strong that he could lift a house. Hegesiander (3rd c. BCE) reports the case of a man who thought he was Zeus (fr. 5, FHG 4:414 / Ath. 7.289c–e). Heraclides Ponticus (4th c. BCE) writes about Thrasyllus, who in a delirious state (ὑπὸ μανίας) went to the harbour of Piraeus daily to count the ships since he was convinced that they all belonged to him (fr. 56 ed. Wehrli / Ath. 12.554c). Cf. Kidd, *Nonsense*, 32–35.

159

interprets the four core terms of the double accusation in Deut 21:20 (ἀπειθεῖ καὶ ἐρεθίζει and συμβολοκοπῶν οἰνοφλυγεῖ) as four levels of increasingly harmful influence of alcohol on a person's mind and behaviour:

> "Therefore, here the accusations are four in number—disobedience, and contentiousness, and love of revelling, and drunkenness; and the last of these is the greatest, deriving its growth from the first, namely, from disobedience; for when the soul begins to be restive it advances onward through contention and quarrelsomeness, and arrives at last at the furthest boundary, drunkenness (μέθη), the cause of alienation of mind (ἔκστασις) and folly (παραφροσύνη).[88]

Throughout his treatise on phenomena of drunkenness in *Plant.* and *Ebr.*, Philo closely connects intoxication and mental abnormality. Both are in turn contrasted with the semantic fields of wisdom, sanity and reasonable behaviour. Terms associated with "wise behaviour" include wisdom (σοφία, 22x), wise (σοφός, 32x), understanding (φρόνησις κτλ., 19x), virtue (ἀρετή, 54x) and thoughtfulness (σωφροσύνη, 3x). Terms associated with drunkenness, in contrast, include insanity (ληρεῖν etc., 10x), madness (μανία, 4x), erratic behaviour (ἔκστασις, 2x), unconsciousness (ἀναισθησία etc., 7x), ignorance (ἄγνοια etc., 16x; ἀπαιδευσία etc., 13x) and foolishness (ἀφροσύνη etc., 16x).

The same contrasts then appear in Philo's exegesis of Deut 21:18–21. After a short introduction on the issue of obedience towards parents, authorities and God (*Ebr.* 16–19) he turns to the terms συμβολοκοπῶν and οἰνοφλυγεῖ. He paraphrases the first expression with "to bring contributions and supplies in aid of an entertainment" (συμβολὰς καὶ ἐράνους φέρειν) and sees it as an allegory for "participation in ... prudence (φρόνησις)," which in itself would be honourable. If such contributions however aim "to the worst of all objects, folly (ἀφροσύνη)," then they must be rejected (*Ebr.* 20). Following this, Philo contrasts such "contributions of

---

[88] *Ebr.* 15. In *Her.* 249, Philo introduces four different meanings of the term ἔκστασις (insanity, shock, trance and divination). Here, he clearly uses the first of these (λύττα μανιώδης παράνοιαν ἐμποιοῦσα).

prudence" with "contributions of folly."[89] Positive contributions αἱ πρὸς τὸ ἄριστον συμβολαί) include desire for virtue (πόθος ἀρετῆς), imitation of good men (τῶν καλῶν ζῆλος), continued caution (μελέται συνεχεῖς), laborious practice (ἀσκήσεις ἐπίμονοι), incessant and unwearied labours, (ἄτρυτοι καὶ ἀκμῆτες πόνοι), health (σωτήρια), reason (φρόνησις), prudence (σωφροσύνη), manliness (ἀνδρεία), justice (δικαιοσύνη), the good (τἀγαθόν) and doing justice (δικαιοπραγεῖν).

In contrast, opposite contributions (αἱ δὲ πρὸς τὸ ἐναντίον) include relaxation (ἄνεσις), indifference (ῥᾳθυμία), luxury (τρυφή), effeminacy (θρύψις), complete alteration of habit (παντελὴς ἐκδιαίτησις), drinking competions (ἐπαποδυομένους πολυοινίᾳ), greediness (ἀπληστίᾳ γαστρός), injury to one's property, body and soul (ζημιουμένους ... χρήματα, σώματα, ψυχάς), giving up property (μειοῦσι τὴν οὐσίαν), luxurious way of life (ἀβροδίαιτος), breakdown of bodily powers (τῶν δὲ σωμάτων ... θρύπτουσι τὰς δυνάμεις), excesses of food (ἀμετρίᾳ τροφῶν), being swept away as from a flowing river (ποταμοῦ χειμάρρου τρόπον ἐπικλύζοντες), being forced to sink into an abyss (εἰς βυθὸν ἀναγκάζουσι δύεσθαι), cutting of one's sanity, understanding and self-control (ἀποκόπτοντες τὰ σωτήρια φρόνησιν καὶ σωφροσύνην), destruction of rationality (καθαίρεσις παιδείας), injuring one's perception (ζημιοῦσι διάνοιαν), cutting one's soul to pieces to the point of utter destruction (συγκόπτουσι μέχρι παντελοῦς φθορᾶς τὰς ψυχάς).

Philo concludes by stating that Moses purposefully chose the composite συμβολοκοπῶν, because by their harmful contributions (συμβολαί) people would eventually "wound and lacerate, and cut to pieces" (τιτρώσκουσι καὶ διαιροῦσι καὶ συγκόπτουσι) their own souls.

Turning to the term οἰνοφλυγεῖ, Philo designates it the "fourth and greatest of the accusations" (*Ebr.* 27). According to Philo, the law of Moses is in agreement with most ancient philosophers in that it does not require complete abstinence from alcohol, but a "wise" consumption (*Ebr.* 1), which avoids the loss of mental control. Close to the end of his lengthy excursus on drunkenness (*Ebr.* 161), Philo admonishes his readers:

---

[89] Translations within the following paragraphs largely follow Yonge, *Works of Philo.* In some instances, translations are mine for the sake of terminological clarity.

Let us, then, never drink unmixed wine in such quantities as to cause insensibility to our outward senses (ὡς ἀπραξίαν ἐμποιῆσαι ταῖς αἰσθήσεσι), nor let us alienate ourselves to such a degree from knowledge (ἐπιστήμης ἀλλοτριωθῶμεν), as to diffuse ignorance (ἄγνοια), that vast and dense darkness, over our souls.

This general attitude also surfaces in Philo's exposition of the term οἰνοφλυγεῖ in *Ebr.* 27, where he distinguishes between a mild form of drunkenness (ἀνειμένως) and a more advanced form (σφόδρα συντόνως) and then again contrasts reasonable and abnormal behaviour: In this passage, reasonable behaviour produces phenomena like justice (δίκη), purification of the mind (πάντα μοχθηρὸν τρόπον ἐκκαθαίρουσα διανοίας), separation from false thoughts (ἀποκόπτειν καὶ διαφθείρειν) , exhortation (νουθεσία), self-control (σωφρονισμός), sanity and safety (σῴζεσθαι). Excessive alcohol consumption (οἰνοφλυγεῖν) however brings forth the substance of stupidity (ἀφροσύνης φάρμακον), ignorance (ἀπαιδευσίαν), conflagration of the soul (τὴν ψυχὴν ἐμπιπρᾶσάν), inflammation of the soul (τὴν ψυχὴν πυρπολοῦσαν), an evil state of the mind (μοχθηρὸν τρόπον διανοίας), faulty and blameworthy thoughts (ὑπαίτιοι καὶ ἐπίληπτοι λογισμοί), destruction of what is good (καθαίρεσις τοῦ καλοῦ), inflammation with strong wine (ἀκράτῳ φλεγόμενον), raging in a drunken manner against virtue (καταμεθύοντα ἀρετῆς), and alienation by drunkenness (παροινίας ἐκτόπους).

For Philo, the legislation of Deut 21:18–21 therefore describes the fundamental contrast between wise and foolish behaviour. Wisdom expresses itself in obedience towards parental authority, social norms and divine laws. Disobedience eventually leads to a loss of control, which is illustrated with images of drunkenness, mental illness and madness. For Philo the formula συμβολοκοπῶν οἰνοφλυγεῖ describes symptoms of a deeper human disorder and therefore serves as an image for a life that lacks wisdom and understanding.

4.3 The Reception in Josephus
Josephus refers to the legislation of the "deviant son" in two places: While *C. Ap.* 2:206 is merely a short reference, *Ant.* 4:260–264 offers a summariz-

ing explanation of the passage from Deut 21:18–21.[90] Josephus paraphrases the text freely, so that no verbatim citations are discernible. The topical focus is on the issue of parental obedience, so that the expression υἱὸς ἀπειθὴς καὶ ἐρεθιστής is paraphrased and explained, but not the phrase συμβολοκοπῶν οἰνοφλυγεῖ. Either Josephus was not aware of any contemporary use of the law (e.g. halakhic discussions that surface in later rabbinic discourses) or he restricted himself deliberately to the aspect of parental obedience.[91] In any case, the way in which he relates to specifics of the legislation and discusses its application suggests however that he does not simply expound the biblical text but also draws from legal norms or discourses of his own time in which Deut 21 played a role.[92] In his exposition of the law, Josephus emphasizes the preference for verbal rebuke over physical punishment,[93] his aim being to underline the similarities between Jewish and Roman law. While his treatment of the passage cannot directly contribute to the question of reception history, it attests to the fact that the legislation of the "deviant son" was part of active Jewish legal discourses of his time.

4.4 The Reception in Rabbinic Literature
The legislation of the "deviant son" is discussed in several places and contexts in rabbinic literature.[94] It is listed among the three legal regulations that "never were (implemented) and never will be" (לא היה ולא עתיד להיות).[95] The legislation is thus treated as a fictional case with mere paradigmatic relevance. To substantiate this reading, the wording of the law is meticulously analysed and eventually rendered ad absurdum by an over-literal reading: In a first step, the scope of application is limited to a narrow group of persons. The formula "glutton and drunkard" is then

---

[90] For an extensive analysis of the passage, cf. Michael Avioz, "The Law of the Rebellious Son (Deut 21:18–21) According to Josephus," *ZABR* 22 (2016): 177–84.
[91] Avioz, "Josephus," 181, regards both options as plausible.
[92] Avioz, "Josephus," 183.
[93] Josephus interprets the phrase וְיִסְּרוּ אֹתוֹ (Deut 21:18) as verbal exhortation, whereas the term is understood in rabinical discourses (e.g. b. Sanh. 71a) as corporal punishment.
[94] m. Sanh. 8:1–5; Sifre Deuteronomy § 218; b. Sanh. 68a–71a.
[95] b. Sanh. 71a. In addition, cf. t. Neg. 6:1, t. Sanh. 11:6 and 14:1, and Gilad J. Gevaryahu and Harvey Sicherman, "What Never Was and Never Will Be: Rebellious Son—Subverted City—Infected House," *JBQ* 29 (2001): 249–54.

explained by way of a *gezerah shawa* from Prov 23:20 as referring *only* to the consumption of wine and meat—both at the same time and nothing else. The accusation itself can only be voiced by both parents together, at the same time and in unison (Deut 21:20). Neither of the parents must be blind, deaf or otherwise disabled, because both need to have admonished the son together, seen and heard his disobedience together and brought him before the court together. The expression "He will not listen to our voice" (Deut 21:20) is taken literally, so that both parents do not only need to speak at the same time, but also with the same voice, requiring an identical shape of body. In short: If all the regulations of the law are taken literally, they can never be fulfilled. The rabbis therefore infer that the law was never intended to be applied, but rather to serve as a paradigm for legal discussion: "There never has been a 'stubborn and rebellious son,' and never will be. Why then was the law written? That you may study it and receive reward."[96]

The question whether the rabbinic interpretation of the legislation distorts the original purpose of the text or perhaps even rightly detects a nuance inherent in the legislation from the beginning[97] may be left open here. What is important for the present analysis is the fact that Deut 21:18–21 was part of an ongoing legal discourse that left traces in so divergent contexts as biblical wisdom literature, the works of Philo, Josephus and rabbinic discussions. It is therefore plausible to assume that the text would provide the repertoire for charges of deviance and abnormality in the time of Jesus and the tradents of early gospel traditions.

---

[96] b. Sanh. 71a, ed. Epstein 483.

[97] As a matter of fact, large parts of rabbinic halakhic discourse are to be read as theoretical exercise. And even the intent of the original legislation in Deut 21:18–21 might have been to transfer unregulated family and clan jurisdiction into institutionalized forms, thereby preventing excessive violence. Therefore it remains in fact unclear if capital punishment was ever executed on the basis of this law. Cf. Gevaryahu and Sicherman, "What Never Was," 253.

Guido Baltes

5 Deviance, Abnormality and Social Control

Sociological theories of deviance and abnormality[98] have been applied to the field of New Testament studies since the 80s,[99] and also to issues of norm and deviance in the writings of Philo and Josephus,[100] Qumran[101] and in rabbinic literature.[102] "Sociologists refer to behavior that is widely condemned, which, if someone engages in it and is observed, is likely to attract or generate hostility, condemnation or punishment from others [as] *deviance* or *deviant behavior*."[103] While older theories defined such deviant behavior mainly with reference to the transgression of existing social, legal or criminal norms,[104] more recent theories increasingly refrain from doing so. Howard Becker, a key proponent of the so-called "labelling theory," has suggested that deviance is not constituted by the behavior of the person transgressing social boundaries, but rather by those who

---

[98] For an overview, cf. Erich Goode, *The Handbook of Deviance* (Chichester: Wiley & Sons, 2015); Lothar Böhnisch, *Abweichendes Verhalten: Eine pädagogisch-soziologische Einführung* (Grundlagentexte Pädagogik, Weinheim/München: Juventa, 1999); Helge Peters, *Devianz und soziale Kontrolle: Eine Einführung in die Soziologie abweichenden Verhaltens.* Grundlagentexte Soziologie, 3rd revised ed. (Weinheim/München: Juventa, 2009); Lamnek, Siegfried, *Theorien abweichenden Verhaltens I: "Klassische" Ansätze*, 9th revised ed. (Paderborn: Fink, 2013).

[99] Bruce Malina and Jerome H. Neyrey, *Calling Jesus Names: The social Value of Labels in Matthew* (Sonoma: Poleridge, 1988); John M. G. Barclay, "Deviance and Apostasy: Some Applications of Deviance Theory to First-Century Judaism and Christianity," in *Social Scientific Approaches to New Testament Interpretation*, ed. David G. Horrell (Edinburgh: T&T Clark, 1999), 289–307; McKnight and Modica, *Opponents.*

[100] Barclay, "Deviance," 298–300.

[101] George J Brooke, "Justifying Deviance: The Place of Scripture in Converting to a Qumran Self-Understanding," in *Reading the present in the Qumran library; the perception of the contemporary by means of scriptural interpretations* (Atlanta: SBL, 2005), 73–87; Lloyd K Pietersen, "'False Teaching, Lying Tongues and Deceitful Lips' (4Q169 Frgs 3-4 2.8): The Pesharim and the Sociology of Deviance," in *New Directions in Qumran Studies*, ed. Jonathan G. Campbell (London: T&T Clark, 2005), 166–81; Jutta Jokiranta, "Black Sheep, Outsiders, and the Qumran Movement: Social-Psychological Perspectives on Norm–Deviant Behaviour," in *Social Memory and Social Identity in the Study of Early Judaism and Early Christianity*, NTOA 116 (Göttingen: Vandenhoeck & Ruprecht, 2016), 151–74.

[102] Simcha Fishbane, *Deviancy in Early Rabbinic Literature: A Collection of Socio-Anthropological Essays* (Leiden: Brill, 2007).

[103] Goode, *Handbook*, 70; cf. Peters, *Devianz*, 19.

[104] Peters, *Devianz*, 19: "… ein Handeln, das gegen gesellschaftliche Normen verstößt und von negativen Sanktionen bedroht ist."

165

Labeling Jesus as "Glutton and Drunkard"

establish these boundaries and therefore create the label "deviant" for those who do not conform to these boundaries.

> Social groups create deviance by making rules whose infraction creates deviance, and by applying those rules to particular people and labeling them as outsiders. From this point of view, deviance is not a quality of the act the person commits, but rather a consequence of the application by others of rules and sanctions to an 'offender.' The deviant is one to whom that label has been successfully applied; deviant behavior is behavior that people so label.[105]

The question regarding which specific acts committed by the historical (or remembered) Jesus would have provoked the ascription ἄνθρωπος φάγος καὶ οἰνοπότης therefore regularly leads into aporia.[106] Rather, the designation should be understood as an attempt by opposing groups, specified by the expressions γενεά ταῦτα and λέγουσιν, to find ways of legally sanctioning for a behaviour that precisely did *not* violate specific law, but transgressed boundaries of social and religious convention. The conflict stories in the Jesus tradition regularly reflect the motif that Jesus is *labeled* by his opponents as a violator of law (John 5:18: "He violates the Sabbath"; Mark 2:7: "He is blaspheming!"), while his actions do not constitute halakhic norm violations.[107] Recourse to the legislation of Deut 21:18–21, using the formulaic charge ἄνθρωπος φάγος καὶ οἰνοπότης, might therefore reflect a differing conflict strategy, one that is also found in other

---

[105] Howard Becker, *Outsiders. Studies in the Sociology of Deviance* (New York: Free Press, 1963), 8–9; cf. Erich Goode and Nachman Ben-Yehuda, *Moral Panics: The Social Construction of Deviance* (Malden: Blackwell, 2009), 80.

[106] Even where the *labeling approach* is applied to Matt 11:19 par., authors try to find such factual violations of law: Modica, "Glutton," 73, sees violations of purity law. Rick F. Talbott, "Nazareth's rebellious son: deviance and downward mobility in the Galilean Jesus movement," *Biblical Theology Bulletin 38* (2008): 99–113, reads the ascription as a conscious act of "Self-Stigmatization"; cf. however Witetschek, "Stigma," 146, who rejects this reading: the concluding appeal to wisdom as witness to him is "just the opposite of Self-Stigmatization" (151). In sum, the very essence of the *labeling approach* should caution against attempts to locate the causes of such labels with those who are labeled and instead focus on the aims of those who apply the label, in this case the opponents of Jesus.

[107] Cf. Thomas Kazen, "Jesu Interpretation der Tora," in Schröter, Jacobi, and Nogossek, *Jesus Handbuch*, 402–16, 415: "Es gibt keinen Beleg, dass Jesus sich gegen die Tora gewendet hat."

166

places of the Gospel tradition: The attempt to equate deviant behaviour with phenomena of drunkenness, mental illness or demon possession. The charge of demon possession is found in the mouth of the same opposing groups, put forth against John the Baptist in the preceding verse (Matt 11:18 par.), and in Mark 3:22 it is applied to Jesus. Furthermore, mental illness is ascribed to Jesus in Mark 3:21 and John 10:20, and to his followers in 1 Cor 14:23. The charge of drunkenness is voiced against followers of Jesus in Acts 2:13. In addition, the ascription ἄνθρωπος φάγος καὶ οἰνοπότης is contrasted with wisdom in Matt 11:19 par., which is analogous to the contrasts of wisdom and drunkenness in Philo and biblical wisdom literature. It is therefore plausible to read the label ἄνθρωπος φάγος καὶ οἰνοπότης as a legal term for the designation of deviant and abnormal behaviour, clothed in the image of gluttony and drunkenness.

6 Drunkenness, Mental Illness and Demon Possession in the Early Jesus Tradition

The proximity of the formula "glutton and drunkard" to charges of demon possession, madness and drunkenness evokes the question of literary or pre-literary connections between the diverging traditions containing such charges. The Markan redactional composition Mark 3:20–22 combines the motifs of madness, demon possession and parental obedience. The Johannine narrative John 2:1–10 combines excessive consumption of wine with the motif of parental obedience and therefore possibly also with Deut 21:18–21.[108] In addition, several overlaps with Mark 1:1–7 suggest that parts of the Q materials from Matt 11:2–19 par. were also known to Mark[109] or originate in a pre-synoptic tradition used by Mark and Q.[110] The

---

[108] Adele Reinhartz, "A rebellious son? Jesus and his mother in John 2:4," in *The Opening of John's narrative (John 1:19–2:22); Historical, Literary, and Theological Readings from the Colloquium Iohanneum 2015 in Ephesus*, ed. R. Alan Culpepper and Jörg Frey, WUNT 385 (Tübingen: Mohr Siebeck, 2017), 233–47, 243.

[109] For the hypothesis of a Mark/Q overlap, cf. Schürmann, *Lukasevangelium*, 161; James M. Robinson, Paul Hoffmann and John S. Kloppenborg, *The Critical Edition of Q*. Hermeneia Supplement 1 (Minneapolis: Fortress Press, 2000), 4–7 and 134. For the hypothesis of a Markan usage of Q, cf. Jan Lambrecht, "John the Baptist and Jesus in Mark 1.1–15: Markan

redactional composition Mark 3:20–22 in turn corresponds with noticeable *minor agreements* in Matt and Luke which suggest that Mark 3:20–22 is a Markan addition into material from the triple tradition.[111] If Mark indeed knew the double charge of demon possession and drunkenness from Matt 11:18–19 par., then it seems likely that he used the material to create his own double charge of demon possession and madness in Mark 3:20–22, integrating also the motif of parental disobedience. John 2:1–2 might be another echo of the same pre-synoptic tradition, but the connections are less obvious here.

7 Conclusion

In conclusion, the present analysis substantiates the claim that the designation of Jesus as "glutton and drunkard" (Matt 11:19/Luke 7:34) should not be read as a description of his actual eating or drinking habits, but as an example of *labeling* by dominant groups of society, attempting to mark Jesus out as a deviant member of that society in the absence of specific criminal or halakhic charges. The *label* applied to Jesus makes use of terminology from an ancient biblical legislation about the "deviant son" (Deut 21:18–21), which apparently was a text frequently used in Jewish

---

Redaction of Q?" *NTS 38* (1992): 357–84, 372; David R. Catchpole, "The Beginning of Q: A Proposal," *NTS 38 (1992):* 205–21, 219, Harry T. Fledderman, *Mark and Q: A Study of the Overlap Texts* (Leuven: University Press, 1995), 26 and 29; Rudolf Pesch, *Das Markusevangelium, Band 1*, HThKNT II.1 (Freiburg: Herder, 1976), 78.

[110] Marie-Émile Boismard, "Évangile des Ébionites et problème synoptique (Mc I, 2–6 et Par.)," *RB 73* (1966): 321–52, 332 and 350; Léon Vaganay, *Le problème synoptique: une hypothèse de travail*, Bibliothèque de théologie III.1 (Tournai: Desclee & Cie, 1952), 353; Étienne Trocmé, *L'Évangile selon Saint Marc*, CNT 2 (Paris: Labor et Fides, 2000), 23 ; Basil Christopher Butler, *The Originality of St. Matthew: A Critique of the Two-Document Hypothesis* (Cambridge/New York: University Press, 1951), 110; Adolf Schlatter, *Das Evangelium des Lukas aus seinen Quellen erklärt*, Reprint of the 3rd edition, 1931 (Stuttgart: Calwer, 1975), 33; Guido Baltes, *Hebräisches Evangelium und synoptische Überlieferung*, WUNT 2/312 (Tübingen: Mohr Siebeck, 2011), 236–42.

[111] Matthew and Luke both have a short healing account, missing in Mark, in this same place. Both do not mention the intervention of the family and the charge of madness. The charge of demon possession (Βεελζεβοὺλ ἔχει), which is found in Matt 11:18 par. with regard to John, is a doublet in Mark 3:22, paralleling the charge of collaboration also found in Matthew and Luke.

sapiential and legal contexts throughout the Second Temple period and beyond. The formula allows for legal or at least social sanctions in cases where no specific criminal delinquency can be made out, but deviance from parental authority or societal norms is perceived by dominant groups of that society. In the case of Jesus, such charges of deviance and abnormality are attested elsewhere in the gospel tradition.[112] In the present context of Matt 11:19 par., the charges are contrasted purposefully with the question of Jesus's messianic role and identity. They serve to refute a claim to messianic identity by labeling Jesus as a glutton and drunkard, which refers not primarily to Jesus's table fellowship or eating habits, but to abnormal behaviour such as drunkenness and madness. Matthew and Luke however respond to this strategy of 'labeling' by contrasting the charges with Jesus's own reference to his future vindication by divine wisdom.

---

[112] Conflicts with parental authority are found, apart from Mark 3:20–22 and John 2:1–10, in Mark 10:29 par. Matt 19:29; Matt 10:35.37; 12:50; Luke 12:53; 14:26; 2:48. Transgressions of social and religious boundaries are reported in the meal tradition Mark 2:13–17, but also in more central aspects of Jesus's ministry, such as the announcement of imminent judgement, the temple action, and claims to messianic identity. In comparable cases, similar accusations of mental illness, drunkenness or magic practice are reported by Josephus, e.g. in the case of Jesus bar Ananus (Josephus, *B.J.* 6:305), Simon (*Ant.* 17:274), Theudas (*Ant.* 20:97), or the zealot movement as a whole (*Vita* 19).

Possessed by Demons and Spirits: Space and Gender of Non-normative Behavior in New Testament Figures

Aliyah El Mansy

1 Preliminaries

1.1 Possession—Madness—Disease

"But I saw people becoming mad and deranged from no visible cause, and at the same time behave unsuitably." (Hippocrates, *Morb. sacr.* 1)[1]

Society or groups try to find names, and explanations for behavior marked as deviant and then allocate a suitable space to it. The pattern of behavior I want to look at in this essay is labelled as "possession," "madness," "inspiration" or "disease." The explanations for such behaviors range from wrath of deities, possession by demons, spirits or deities to medical reasons.[2] Accordingly, the allocated spaces vary: people with such behavior patterns can live hidden away in their families, be cast out of their family, home town or village, they can be sent to deserted places, they can be part of a cult. It is characteristic for this kind of noticeable behavior that it is shown by all genders. At the same time, I noticed that gender biased tendencies can be found in specific descriptions. Therefore, my focus is firstly to uncover the gender bias in what is at first glance non-gendered behavior. Secondly, my aim is to understand in depth the function of spaces in the depiction of non-normative behavior.

As we will see later, symptoms interpreted as possession, madness or illness fall mostly in the categories of (1) loss of bodily or mental self-control—like motiveless laughing or weeping, uttering incomprehensible

---

*I wish to thank Lisa Walter for improving my English text.

[1] Translations are my own if not otherwise indicated.

[2] Strong emotional states like love or grief can cause a similar behavior pattern.

words, rolling eyes, spasms, hallucinations, falling to the ground, and (2) deviation from expected social behavior—like self-harm, violence, nakedness, disarrayed hair, and screaming. All in all, behavior patterns which are noticeable.[3] Especially, in Greek tragedy a fixed set of symptoms was developed from which later literature draws.[4] Very often people display symptoms from both categories. Medical explanations include both drunkenness and illness.[5] Cultural explanations include possession by a demon, visitation by ghost or punishment by deities. In the context of prophecy or art these symptoms are a sign for inspiration.[6]

Because of the similar symptoms, sources often don't distinguish between possession, madness or illness. So, it completely depends on the sources' context, how these patterns of symptoms are classified. We might find a description of mental or neurological disorder one source calls illness, another madness, and yet another possession or inspiration. Thus, I am going to use a more neutral term suggested by Anna Rebecca Solvåg: non-normative bodily state or behavior.[7] This also reflects the above cited description which can be found in the Corpus Hippocratum in the treatise on the "sacred disease": "But I saw people [ἄνθρωπος] becoming mad [μαίνομαι] and deranged [παραφρονέω] from no visible cause, and at the same time behave unsuitably [ἄκαιρος: ill-timed]." (Hippocrates, *Morb. sacr.*1) The writer shows an understanding that is not only about bodily reactions—which he elaborates on later—but also about behavior

---

[3] Cf. Christian Strecker, "Jesus und die Besessenen. Zum Umgang mit Alterität im Neuen Testament am Beispiel der Exorzismen Jesu," in *Jesus in neuen Kontexten*, eds. Wolfgang Stegemann, Bruce J. Malina, and Gerd Theißen (Stuttgart: Kohlhammer, 2002), 58.

[4] Eric Sorensen, *Possession and Exorcism in the New Testament and Early Christianity*, WUNT 2/157 (Tübingen: Mohr Siebeck, 2002), 99 lists: eye-rolling, sudden body movements, moving the head up and down, trembling, groaning, screaming, delusions, paranoia, froth at the mouth, making animal noises, laughing.

[5] Modern diagnosis often suggests epilepsy, mania, personality disorder or a multiple personality. Cf. Christian Wetz, "Dämonen/Dämonenbeschwörung (NT)," *Das wissenschaftliche Bibellexikon im Internet* (Oktober 2015, http://www.bibelwissenschaft.de/stichwort/46933/), 8.

[6] Plato, *Phaedr.* 244–245A distinguishes prophetic inspiration, mania as a punishment for wrongdoing, and artistic inspiration. Cf. Sorensen, *Possession*, 91.

[7] Cf. Anna Rebecca Solevåg, *Negotiating the Disabled Body. Representations of Disability in Early Christian Texts*, ECL 23 (Atlanta: SBL Press, 2018), 105. She also uses "bodily deviation" (112).

patterns which can be marked as unsuitable in the sense of "un-timely" rather than per se deviant in themselves.

1.2 Gender—Space

Gender can be understood as a cultural construct which is constantly reproduced in performative acts (*doing gender*).[8] Also, written texts contribute to establish (or sometimes challenge) categories like gender, which a society needs to cope with and manage their experiences of life.[9] In antiquity gender was constructed in a patriarchal and androcentric matrix with differences due to locality, culture, and period. As a result, Graeco and Roman gender constructs differ in detail as well as having features in common.[10] Caroline Vander Stichele and Todd Penner phrase it as follows: "Both men and women could display masculine and feminine characteristics, and the balance between the two determined where one ended up on the male to female scale. In this way, discipline and self-control were of utmost importance, as one's identity was scrutinized and could always be questioned on the basis of one's appearance and behavior."[11] They both allude to the fact that gender constructs are fluid and that a person's gender is judged on appearance and behavior patterns. The control of your own body and mind was connected to rationality and regarded as more male, whereas lack of control implied irrationality, being closer to nature and rather female.[12]

---

[8] Cf. Judith Butler, *Gender Trouble. Feminism and Subversion of Identity* (New York: Routledge, 1990); for a short introduction to gender in antiquity see Aliyah El Mansy, Elena Köstner and Urs Wohlthat, eds., *Frauen in Kulten der römischen Kaiserzeit. Interdependenz und Gender in Fallstudien* (Gutenberg: Computus Druck & Satz, 2019), 8–10.

[9] A survey of the use of the category Gender in classical studies and recent publications can be found in: El Mansy, Köstner, and Wohlthat, 4–8. Groundbreaking: Joan W. Scott, "Gender: A Useful Category of Historical Analysis," *AHR* 91,5 (1986): 1053–1075.

[10] Cf. Lambert Schneider and Martina Seifert, "Ehefrau—Fremde—Dämon: Konstruktionen des Weiblichen in griechischer Kultur," *Archäologie in Deutschland Sonderheft. Sphinx—Amazone—Mänade. Bedrohliche Frauenbilder im antiken Mythos* (2010), 9–11.14.

[11] Caroline Vander Stichele and Todd Penner, *Contextualizing Gender in Early Christian Discourse. Thinking beyond Thecla* (London/New York: T&T Clark, 2009), 67. On the next page they elaborate on the fact that these concepts can be found mostly in elite class literature and households.

[12] Cf. Solevåg, *Negotiating*, 100.102; Schneider and Seifert, "Ehefrau," 11–12.20.

Space can be regarded as social product, too, but a special one: "it subsumes things produced, and encompasses their relationships in their coexistence and simultaneity"[13]. The concept of space useful for the topic of non-normative bodily state is the space created by language and metaphor, the so-called "conceptualized space" (Henri Lefebvre).[14] Outside the text the conceptual space can also be a physical space, e.g. a space you can perceive with your senses and also live in with your body. Hence, categories of space are connected with each other.[15] Space is a valuable locative category to understand better how a society constructs permeable and non-permeable boundaries to protect their social cohabitation. The "demonic," "madness" or "disease" can also be regarded as a specific space.[16] It is the space a non-normative body state is assigned to. Therefore, different spaces can exist simultaneously. For example, a person who has fits can be located to the space of disease and then be physically placed in a domestic space, a medical space or a religious space—or even all of them. Things and persons need to be at their right place according to a specific social-cultural "map." Space is gendered, and hierarchical—in both a social and religious sense.[17] Xenophon, for example, assigns to (elite) women the inner space of the house and to men the outer space (Xenophon, *Oec.* 7,23–25). Something or somebody deviating from the assigned space is breaking boundaries and is very likely

---

[13] Henri Lefebvre, *The Production of Space* (Malden/Oxford/Victoria: Blackwell, 1991), 73. The number of spatial studies is abundant. Besides Lefebvre, the other most cited theorist is Edward W. Soja, *Postmodern Geographies. The Reassertion of Space in Critical Social Theory* (London/New York: Verso, 1989). Some critical reflections on biblical spatial studies are to be found in Christopher Meredith, "Taking Issue with Thirdspace: Reading Soja, Lefebvre and the Bible," in *Constructions of Space III. Biblical Spatiality and the Sacred*, ed. Jorunn Økland, J. Cornelis de Vos, Karen J. Wenell (London/Oxford/New York: Bloomsbury 2016), 75–103.

[14] Cf. Lefebvre, *Space*, 53.

[15] Cf. Christl Maier, *Daughter Zion, Mother Zion. Gender, Space, and the Sacred in Ancient Israel* (Minneapolis: Fortress Press, 2008), 11–12; Stephan Günzel, *Raum. Eine kulturwissenschaftliche Einführung* (Bielefeld: transcript, ^{3}2020), 85–97.

[16] Cf. Jonathan Z. Smith, "Towards Interpreting Demonic Powers in Hellenistic and Roman Antiquity," *ANRW* II.16.1 (1978): 429.

[17] Cf. Sybille Bauriedl, Michaela Schier, and Anke Strüver, eds. *Geschlechterverhältnisse, Raumstrukturen, Ortsbeziehungen. Erkundungen von Vielfalt und Differenz im spatial turn.* Forum Frauen- und Geschlechterforschung 27 (Münster: Westfälisches Dampfboot, 2010), 10–14.

so be stigmatized in a negative way.[18] To understand such deviant behavior, society creates explanations like disease, madness or prophecy. By labelling phenomena this way, it is possible to allocate a new space to them—you could say it puts deviancy back into set boundaries. Hence, such space is constructed by discursive practice inside a society respectively a text imagining social discourse.[19]

1.3 Approach
The New Testament presents different stories about people with non-normative bodily states and behavior patterns. Mark has the most detailed accounts of a possessed man in Kaphernaum (Mark 1:23–28), Gerasa (5:1–20), and a possessed boy (9:14–29). Matthew rather shortens the descriptions about the man in Gerasa and the boy (Matt 8:28–34; 17:14–18), and omits the scene in Kaphernaum altogether. Luke follows Mark more closely in picking up all three Markean stories (Luke 4:31–37; 8:26–39; 9:37–42), and shares some material with Matthew about a blind/mute man (Luke 11:14—Matt 12:22). There are only two female characters who are possessed—a Syrophoenician/Canaanite girl and a bent-over woman (Mark 7:24–30/Matt 15:21–28; Luke 13:10–13), the rest are men in the Gospels. In Acts there is only one description of a man being possessed by a demon (Acts 19:13–20) and of a woman with a spirit (Acts 16:16–22). Besides, different inspirations by the Holy Spirit respectively prophecy is being mentioned (Acts 2:4;13, 11:27–28, 21:4;9–11). I will only briefly touch upon inspiration in the letters of Paul.

I am interested in the presentation of people suffering from "possession," "madness" or the "sacred disease" and secondly the spaces offered to them. My paper aims at exploring the construction of gender and space in depictions of persons in a non-normative bodily state. My reference texts are to be found in medical, poetic, or prosaic literature where "possession," "madness," and "disease" frequently occur. Greek tragedy and also early historiography understand the patterns of possession

---

[18] Cf. Smith, "Demonic Powers," 429.
[19] Cf. Bauriedl, Schier and Strüver, *Geschlechterverhältnisse*, 12.

Aliyah El Mansy

depicted in the New Testament texts mostly as madness.[20] My starting point each time will be a text from the New Testament. I will then analyze aspects of space and gender and compare it to description in Graeco-Roman texts and some Acta literature. At the end, I will sum up the results.

2 Public Space and Loud Behavior (Mark 1:23;26/Luke 4:33;35)

In this episode, the possessed person is said to be in the synagogue, so he lingers at a central meeting point of the community in Kaphernaum. Mark describes the person as ἄνϑρωπος, so it is more likely that it is a man. The Lukan version is similar but makes some changes. The sequence in Luke is the same but he specifically says that it is a demon and he let the demon throw the man violently in the middle of the by standing crowd. Like in Mark the possessed person has no control over his own body. One of the signature signs of "possession" is loud screaming and addressing people out of the blue without the usually expected greeting etiquette. The effect is that the behavior seems rude, aggressive, unpredictable, and out of social control. We will see later, that the person in Gerasa is said to scream (κράζω) and to make loud sounds, too.[21] Luke stresses the social embarrassment by pointing out that there is a crowd watching. An audience is necessary to confirm that the person is behaving non-normatively and to acknowledge his being out of place. Therefore, the public plays a role in ascribing the afflicted person to the general space of "possession."

2.1 Public Space
The Greek philosopher and priest of Apollo Plutarch (45–125 CE) tells a story about a certain Nicias displaying unexpected and inappropriate behavior to escape an arrest. Nicias is one of the leading citizens of Engyium, which is famous for the appearance of deities called "the Mothers" (Plutarch, *Marc.* 20.2–3).[22] These deities are assumed to allude

---

[20] Cf. Everett Ferguson, *Demonology of the Early Christian World*. SymS 12 (Lewiston: Edwin Mellen Press, 1984), 51–52; Sorensen, *Possession*, 97, 124.

[21] Cf. Mark 5:5, 6; Matt 8:29; Luke 8:28.

[22] Engyum is located on Sicily according to Diodorus, *Bibl.* 4.79.5-7 and was founded by Cretans. The city was never found. Cf. Franco De Angelis, "Archaeology in Sicily 2001–2005," *Archaeological Reports* 53 (2006–2007), 175.

176

to the Cretan Rhea. Nicias is an important member of the city and tries to convince people to side with the Romans against Carthage, the city's ally (Plutarch, *Marc.* 20.3). Out of fear of Nicias's influence, the leading people of the city plan to arrest Nicias. But he learns of the plan and sets in motion his own scheme. In public he starts to talk ill about the city's deities, the Mothers (Plutarch, *Marc.* 20.4). Then, he shows the following symptoms (Plutarch, *Marc.* 20.5–6): falling down to the ground, moving his head around, speaking in a low and trembling voice, tearing his clothes, being half naked, and finally screaming and running away.

Nicias displays unexpected and inappropriate behavior. He seems to lose control over his body, he speaks not in his usual voice, even starts to scream. Without reason he takes off his clothes and then runs away. On top of all this he claims that he is pursued by deities Plutarch calls "the Mothers," hence seeing something nobody else can. Nicias is presented as a person who taps into the cultural patterns of "possessed" and "mad" persons' behavior, as is stated at the end of his performance (Plutarch, *Marc.* 20.6: δαιμονάω and παραφρονέω). His strategy illustrates that there is a cultural knowledge about these patterns and that they need an audience—that is to say they need interaction, recognition and acknowledgement.[23] He uses patterns which he knows society will understand as indicators for possession.[24] The effect on the audience is superstitious fear and shock. Nobody dares to touch him. This is a very important piece of information. Instinctively, the people shun away, because they grasp Nicias erratic behavior as something dangerous, even though he is not attacking anyone but only displaying self-shaming behavior. His running away serves the purpose of fleeing the city but is also regarded as typical behavior of possession or madness: the afflicted is trying to get away from

---

[23] For the performative nature of possession in general cf. Giovanni Bazzana, *Having the Spirit of Christ. Spirit Possession and Exorcism in the Early Christ Groups* (New Haven/London: Yale University Press, 2020), 168–72.

[24] Cf. Uta Poplutz, "Dämonen—Besessenheit—Austreibungsrituale," in *Die Wunder Jesu.* Vol. 1 of *Kompendium der frühchristlichen Wundererzählung,* ed. Ruben Zimmermann (Gütersloh: Gütersloher Verl.-Haus, 2013), 100 who explains: "In dramatischer Form inszenieren Besessene öffentlich bestimmte Rollenmuster, die in der jeweiligen Gesellschaft als Indiz für Besessenheit gelten. Dabei bestimmen kulturelle Muster das Verhalten und umgekehrt formt das Verhalten kulturelle Muster." Compare nearly the same statement: Strecker, "Jesus," 58.

other people and civilization running to a space outside the inhabited areas. Nicias prepared his scheme to make it believable and convincing that he believes the Mothers are punishing him. Mythology knows plenty of stories about people being punished with madness by scorned deities, especially female ones.

There are many stories about demonic possession in the various Acts of the Apostles. The Acts of Andrew (150–200 CE)[25] tell in a few verses the story of the son of Gratinus from Sinope who is possessed by a demon (Acts Andr. (Greg) 5). The son takes a bath in a women's bath and the demon causes him to faint. When Andrew is fetched to help Gratinus's son and enters the house, the son is being shaken and thrown down by the demon in front of the Apostle's feet. A women's bath indicates an inappropriate place for a young man. He is being washed there by women, so the whole scene is touched with immorality and indecency.[26] The demon causes the young man to enter an exclusively female space, except maybe small children of both genders being present. At the same time, it is a public place. Baths are places which are regarded with suspicion from a Jewish and Christian perspective, especially when it is a mixed male-female one.[27] It is also assumed that bathes are sometimes connected to prostitution.[28] Thus, a bath can be regarded in the context of the text and the Christian perspective as an indecent public space. Certainly, people will notice the young man and also that he is out of place. The demon provokes him to violate social boundaries in a public gendered space.

One very short description can be found in Mart. Andr. 2 in the Praetorium of Patras, where Stratokles, the brother of the proconsul, arrives. His slave Alkmanes is said to be possessed, he loses his mind and lies in his

---

[25] According to the revision of Gregory of Tours.
[26] Cf. Al-Suadi, Soham. "Geh weg von dem Diener Gottes! (Dämonenaustreibung und die Heilung einer ganzen Familie). ActAndr(Greg) 5," in *Die Wunder der Apostel*. Vol. 2 of *Kompendium der frühchristlichen Wundererzählung*, ed. Ruben Zimmermann (Gütersloh: Gütersloher Verl.-Haus, 2017), 790.
[27] Cf. Al-Suadi, "Dämonenaustreibung," 794.
[28] Cf. Bettina Stumpp, *Prostitution in der römischen Antike* (Berlin: Akademie, 1998), 68–70, 163–64.

feces.[29] Later he is frothing from the mouth and lies completely convulsed on the floor. These are all typical features of the phenomenon regarded as demon possession, madness or illness. The feces are a special feature to provoke revulsion and show clearly that the boy cannot control his body. It also keeps other people away from him. Again, possession happens in a domestic context as public space. It is telling that after the demon left the boy, he is said to be calm, standing securely on his feet, talking comprehensibly and looking with affection to his master. This shows that in the description of possession or madness, the cutting of social ties plays a crucial role—the person is not able to relate to other people.

2.2 Loud Behavior

Possessed people in the New Testament stories scream or shout (κράζω) often. Screams or other loud noises like laughter can be regarded as inappropriate in public space and in domestic space. In Mark 1:23–28 the screaming or shouting takes place in a synagogue and is used to address Jesus. Both are impolite if not inappropriate behavior regarding social and space conventions. It can be a sign of a person regarded as erratic as we will see later in the story about a possessed person in Gerasa. Laughter is not generally a "suspicious" behavior. So, it is a good example to observe why and how laughter is interpreted as non-normative behavior.

Herodotus (490/480–430/420 BCE) tells at length about King Kambyses's madness (Herodotus, *Hist.* 3.23.29–38). Beside killing his brother, sister, and the son of a trusted friend out of a whim (Herodotus, *Hist.* 3.30.1–2, 31.1–2, 34.1–4) Kambyses attracts attention with his laughter. Several times Herodotus mentions that Kambyses laughed about his insane deeds and that other people interpreted this as a sign of madness (Herodotus, *Hist.* 3.34.1–4).[30]

---

[29] Dennis R. MacDonald, "Stärker als Herkules! (Heilung des besessenen Sklaven des Stratokles) MartAndr 2–5," in Zimmermann, *Wunder der Apostel*, 849–52 compares the parallels to Euripides' drama *herculens furens*.

[30] It is noticeable that Herodotus ponders that Kambyses is suffering from the "sacred disease" and thus it should not come as a surprise that his mind was also afflicted (Herodotus 3,33,1). Herodotus offers this as another reason next to the opinion that Kambyses is being punished because he offended the Egyptian God Apis.

In the Acts of Peter 11 (180–190 CE) a short notice about a young man being possessed by a demon can be found. Peter recognizes the demon because the young man laughed and after being directly addressed, the man cannot control his body, he is violently thrust forward, thrown against a wall and screams a kind of prophecy with a loud voice. His behavior is ascribed to a vicious demon. Again, it is a young man who is laughing. Also, in non-Christian texts men are especially prone to laughter when they display non-normative behavior.

Flavius Philostratos (165–244 CE) presents a case of possession in chapter 4 part 20 of his book on Apollonius of Tyana. The Greek wandering philosopher and wonderworker (around 40–120 CE) journeyed through many countries according to Philostratos's fictional report. In Athens he encounters a young man who is known for his extravagant and licentious character. While Apollonius is lecturing about libations, the young man suddenly bursts out into a broad [πλατύς] and lewd [ἀσελγής] laughter. The text shows clearly, that it is a completely inappropriate situation to laugh at all. The philosopher is talking about sacred rituals and not making a joke. Apollonius concludes immediately that the young man is possessed by a demon. The text then gives several "proofs" for this diagnosis: "He laughed when nobody else did, and turned quickly to cry without having a reason, had discussions with himself and sung." (Philostratus, *Vit. Apoll.* 4.20). The young man's behavior is noticeable because he is the only one showing emotions. An indicator for non-normative behavior is also if others join in or not. Talking to himself and singing are also marked as suspicious. People think he is behaving like this because he is still young as the text explains. But Apollonius states that in truth he is possessed and thus seems like drunk. This last explanation shows how certain behavior patterns can be ascribed to age, drunkenness or possession. Obviously, especially because it is a young man, people are interpreting his behavior in the context of young manliness. Once more, the symptoms are displayed in public.

3 Liminal Space and Aggressive Behavior (Mark 5:1–6 parr. / Acts 19:16)

There are two occurrences in the New Testament addressing violent behavior, super-natural strength, and liminal spaces. The first one is the story taking place in Gesara or Gadara (Mark 5:1–20 parr.).[31] The other one is situated in or near Ephesus (Acts 19:13–20).

I want to focus on several aspects of the text's versions. First of all, the deviations from Mark in Matthew and Luke are noteworthy and also the length of the Markian version. Gerasa is a town in the Decapolis rather far away from the Sea of Galilee. Gadara is another town in the Decapolis, but only a few kilometers from the Sea of Galilee.[32] This might be the reason for the different location in Matthew The Decapolis is a non-Jewish area. From the perspective of the Jewish motherland it can be seen as more likely to encounter very bad demons and unclean spirits there.[33] It is in itself a liminal-space.

The protagonist in Mark is a person (ἄνθρωπος) with an unclean spirit. Luke calls him a man (ἀνήρ) with a demon and Matthew changes one to two persons and calls them "the possessed." Luke later copies Mark and also refers to the possessed as the person (ἄνθρωπος) with an unclean spirit (Luke 8:29). Also, Luke is the only one who specifically says that this person is from the city. So, in Luke there is an elaborated map of spaces. Before being possessed, the person lived in the town, in a house (Luke 8:27). Now, he is living among the tombs and being driven to the desert.[34] All these places are deserted, hostile environments where the living are not meant to linger and dwell. Mark furthermore mentions mountains.

---

[31] For information about the literary levels and redactional work of Matthew and Luke cf. Rudolf Pesch, *Der Besessene von Gerasa. Entstehung und Überlieferung einer Wundergeschichte*, SBS 56 (Stuttgart: Kohlhammer, 1972).

[32] Cf. Pesch, *Besessene*, 17–18; Robert Vorholt, "Böses flieht (Die Heilung der Besessenen von Gadara) Mt 8,28–34," in Zimmermann, *Wunder Jesu*, 410–11. Vorholt draws attention to the Jewish population in the Decapolis.

[33] Cf. Pesch, *Besessene*, 24.

[34] For information about the desert as place of demons cf. Otto Böcher, *Dämonenfurcht und Dämonenabwehr. Ein Beitrag zur Vorgeschichte der christlichen Taufe*, BWANT 90 (Stuttgart: Kohlhammer, 1970), 65–67.

Aliyah El Mansy

Mountains are regarded as wild and dangerous places.[35] Very often they are the space of specific deities—especially the ones close to the wilderness like Cybele or Pan.

The most significant symptom is above all the strength of the possessed person in Mark and Luke.[36] Nobody is able to bind him, he easily destroys all chains. Matthew might hint to this strength by saying that the two possessed are so dangerous, nobody dared to walk by them. Therefore, it seems the aggression is aimed at other people. The Greek word χαλεπός also means that somebody is hard to deal with. This facet leads to another aspect: social seclusion. In Matthew other people are afraid, in Mark the possessed is non-stop screaming, and Luke explicitly says that he is not wearing clothes and is not staying in a house.[37] In short, he is not any longer socially compliant. It would be hard to spend time with a person in such a state. Aspects like clothing and housing are replaced by living at the gravesite, in the wilderness, going to deserted areas, and not being properly clothed or naked (Mark 5:15/Luke 8:35). Mark even mentions self-harming behavior—the possessed is cutting himself continuously with stones (Mark 5:5). The Greek word κατακόπτω means literally to cut into pieces. Also, screaming and loud sounds or a loud voice are mentioned again. The figure presented in all three synoptics is either a danger to other people or himself or both. This also seems to be the reason why people tried to control him with chains and shackles. The texts do not say if the people chased the person away from town to where the graves are or if the demons drove him to these spaces connected to death, demons and unclean spirits.[38]

There are also other ways to separate people from family and society by the means of bodily dysfunction. Matthew reports about a mute or deaf (κωφός) person and a person who is both mute and blind (τυφλός), being possessed by demons (Matt 9:32–34, 12:22, Luke 11:14). Though, not all

---

[35] For information about mountains as place of demons cf. Böcher, *Dämonenfurcht*, 68–70.

[36] Compare the similarities to Isa 65:1–7, where assimilated Jews are accused to behave in a non-Jewish way. Cf. Martin Ebner, "Wessen Medium willst du sein? (Die Heilung des Besessenen von Gerasa) Mk 5,1–20 (EpAp 5,9–10)," in Zimmermann, *Wunder Jesu*, 272–73.

[37] Also, Mark presupposes nakedness when it is said in Mark 5:15 that the formerly possessed person is now dressed.

[38] Cf. the uncleanliness of burial sides Pesch, *Besessene*, 23; Vorholt, "Böses," 411–12.

blind persons are possessed (Matt 9:27–30). Unfortunately, Matthew does not list more symptoms, so that we could understand why specifically these mute and blind persons are understand to be possessed. A woman with a spirit causing a physical ailment, a curved back, is mentioned in Luke 13:10–13. The spirit is called "a spirit of weakness/illness" (Luke 13:11), but later Jesus says that she was bound by Satan (Luke 13:16).[39] Hence, this story is a good example that illness and possession are not always distinguished.[40] For 18 years the woman is restricted—her view is limited, her communication probably is handicapped, and her movement is complicated. Everyday life probably is a struggle and full of pain. Likely, she has neither husband nor children, because nobody is mentioned. But if she has a family of her own she probably cannot take care of them due to being limited in her working opportunities.[41] Jesus encounters her in a synagogue, so she is situated inside the village or town.

As already mentioned, the second text about aggressive behavior and super-natural strength can be found in Acts 19:13–20. The story goes that the seven sons of a Jewish High-Priest named Skevas are trying to use Jesus's name to cast out evil spirits in the area of Ephesus. One of these encounters and attempts of exorcism does not end well: The possessed man develops such strength that he manages to overpower seven other men. He beats them up, so they leave the house wounded and naked. On one hand the story is about the humiliation of exorcists, on the other hand the possessed person is shown as very dangerous. The event takes place in a house, probably the house the person is living in. It is not said explicitly if he is still living within his family. Nevertheless, it shows that at least at one point most of the possessed persons belonged into a family, lived with them in a house. It is the demons' or spirits' work to cause a behavior that

---

[39] Sandra Hübenthal, Sandra, "Umgekehrter Hexenschuss: Keine Heilung ohne Kontext (Heilung einer gekrümmten Frau am Sabbat) Lk 13,10–17," in Zimmermann, *Wunder Jesu*, 619–620 addresses the blending of those two aspects in the Lukan story.

[40] For some thoughts concerning the medical aspects of this affliction cf. Hübenthal, "Hexenschuss," 618–19.

[41] Some assume that it was hard bodily work in childhood like carrying heavy loads, pounding of grain or weaving that caused the curved her back—both women and men can be affected from heavy work in this way. Cf. Hübenthal, "Hexenschuss," 623–24.

families or societies cannot find a way to cope with and the affected person is sometimes cast out.

3.1 Liminal Space

Herodotus tells the story of the women of Argos who were driven mad. Their madness spreads like an infectious disease among the other women (Herodotus, *Hist.* 34.1–2). The library of Apollodor (1st century CE) gives a lengthier account. The daughters of Proetus and Stheneboea—Lysippe, Iphinoe, and Iphianassa—were driven mad either according to Hesiod by Dionysos because they did not want to participate in his rites or according to Acusilaus because they insulted an image of Hera (Apollodor, *Bibl.* 2.2:2). The madness drives the sisters to wander (πλανάω) around the Peloponnese mountains and to run quickly (τροχάζω) to the desert in a disorderly fashion (ἀκοσμία). The Greek word ἀκοσμία also signifies disorder in a moral sense. Not only are the women wandering around alone in the wilderness, they also do this in disorder. This could mean that their hair or their clothes are in disarray—a typical feature of the portrayal of women displaying non-normative behavior as we will see later. They are drawn to wild and deserted places like the possessed from Gerasa in Mark and Luke. The story about the three sisters goes on that their father refused the fee the seer Melampus asked for to heal his daughters. As a result, it gets worse. Now, other women are leaving their houses to join the sisters, they even kill their own children and run to the desert. It seems that nobody can prevent the women from their deeds. The text illustrates that the women are not themselves by using an antique feature of parental madness—murdering your own children. It needs several young and strong men to chase the women from the mountains to the city of Sicyon. The pictures being used remind more of a hunt of wild animals—the women are screaming and dancing in a possessed fashion. These symptoms of wilderness, screaming and dancing probably also occur because the myth is connected to Dionysus and the presentation resembles the account of the Bacchae by Euripides.[42]

---

[42] It is an important feature of the Dionysos myth, that the introduction of the cult was first rejected in Greece. The God uses the women to establish the cult and draws them away from domestic space and male control. Cf. Schneider and Seifert, "Ehefrau," 20; Schneider and

Philostratus presents another story about Apollonius encountering a demon. The Prophet arrives in India where he visits some wise men who are also exorcists. A mother reaches out to them on behalf of her 16 year old son who has been possessed by a "mocking and lying demon" for two years. The mother is asked by one of the wise men why she thinks that her son is possessed and she lists the following symptoms: he is not sensible, does not go to a teacher or an archer or stay at home, he goes to deserted areas, speaks with a deep and hollow voice, does not look with his own eyes and does not recognize his mother (Philostratus, *Vit. Apoll.* 3.38). The story goes on. The demon revealed to the mother that he was a ghost of a soldier fallen in battle whom his wife cheated on. This is why he hated women and chose to possess a boy. He promised the mother many wonderful things but never fulfilled the promises and instead controls the whole house. Even when she tried to get the son to see the wise men, the demon refused and threatened to kill the boy by throwing him off a cliff. The demon isolates the boy, he possesses and hinders him from living a normal life. The mother stresses that the demon prevents her son from getting an education and instead drives him out to deserted places. The demon wants the boy to be in liminal space. Another symptom is the loss of his own voice and look. He cannot talk or see for himself. His senses are directed by the demon. Eyes and voice are important body parts like in Matthew's stories about the blind and mute possessed persons. The boy does not even recognize his own mother. Through the boy the demon controls the mother and the whole house. Nothing is said of a father, so maybe she is a single parent.

This story also illustrates the ambiguity of demonic possession: the demon promised to help the boy with good things and the mother believed him. But she realizes then that the promise is only to control and stall her. So, in the end, the whole family is affected. The threat to get the boy to kill himself is a typical feature of demonic possession. The text also implies sexual connotations by using forms of ἐράω to describe the demon's motivation. He loved his wife, but because of her unfaithfulness he started

Seifert, "In Ekstase: Nymphen und Mänaden," *Archäologie in Deutschland Sonderheft* (2010), 91.

to abhor the love of women and turned towards boy-love. The fact that the boy is 16 and very beautiful emphasizes the sexual aspect and evokes the context of the Greek institution of Pederasty.

3.2 Aggressive Behavior
Super-human strength is a common feature of possession and madness in ancient texts. Herodotus in his History and especially Euripides (480–406 BCE) in his tragedies make use of it. For example, is it necessary to bind Heracles after he went mad (Euripides, *Herc. fur.* 1094–1097). Herodotus tells about Cleomenes that he was on the verge of madness (ἀκρομανής) (Herodotus, *Hist.* 5.42.1) and when mania befell him, he started to hit Spartan people indiscriminately with his stick in the face (Herodotus, *Hist.* 6.75.1). His relatives bound him in the stocks with a guard to watch over him (Herodotus, *Hist.* 6.75.2). Cleomenes threatens the guard into giving him a dagger which he uses to cut himself into pieces (Herodotus, *Hist.* 6.75.3). This self-harming behavior resembles the possessed in Gerasa who cut himself with a stone, but he did not commit suicide. Cleomenes madness is thought to have befallen him because he did nor respect the deities (Herodotus, *Hist.* 6.75.3).

Harming other people is one of the reasons why people with aggressive, non-normative behavior patterns are chained, locked up or chased out to non-inhabited places. Greek myths also narrate many cases of maddened parents murdering their children (Heracles, Agaue, Myniades, Athamas) or family members hurting other family members (Halia)[43]. The most famous one certainly is the story of Agave and her son Pentheus in Euripides's play *Bacchae*. The Bacchantes are presented as very dangerous and out of control.[44] They pursue men, tear apart cattle and plunder villages (Euripides, *Bacch.* 677–770). The peak of events is reached when Agave does not recognize her own son and tears him apart with other Maenads (Euripides, *Bacch.* 1124–1135). It is said that Agave is foaming (ἀφρός) at the mouth and her eyes are rolling backwards (διάστροφορος). She does not recognize her own son and tears out his shoulder—explicitly not by her own strength but because the God Bacchus made her hands

---

[43] Halia is being raped by her mad sons, cf. Diodorus, *Bibl.* 5.55.
[44] Compare also the account of the Bacchanalia Scandal (Livius, *Ab urbe condita* 39).

strong. The symptoms are similar to the possessed boy in Mark 9 as we will see later. It is stressed that a woman is stronger than she is supposed to be.

Ovid (43–17 CE) tells the story of Athamas and his wife Ino (Ovid, *Metam.* 4.464–542). The Goddess Juno is offended because the new God's Bacchus human aunt Ino praises him everywhere around Thebes. To punish her Juno instructs Tisiphone, one of the Furies, to drive Ino and her husband Athamas mad. In his madness Athamas believes that Ino and his two children are a lioness and her two cubs and he sets out to hunt them. He then kills the first son. Ino is described as howling either because of her husband killing their son or because of Tisiphone. She flees, insanely, tearing at her hair and with her other son in her arms and calling for help to Bacchus. Ino climbs a cliff—Ovid tells us that the madness gave her the strength to do it—and because of fear she throws herself with her son off the cliff. The Goddess Venus intervenes and Ino and her son are transformed into deities in the end.

Hallucinations are a common feature of madness in myth and tragedy.[45] Athamas is described in his madness as doing things associated with men: he goes hunting and kills his prey. Ino on the contrary is the hunted who flees. Again, her hair is mentioned as being in disarray. She even tears at it which can be seen as sign of grief and fear in this situation. She manages to climb a cliff. Her super-human strength is not a danger to other people but rather a super-female strength which enables her to manage a physical task a woman is regarded to be incapable of.

Another case of child-murder can be found in the myth of the Myniads. In Plutarch's (45–125 CE) account Mino's daughters Leucippe, Arsinoe, and Alcathoe (called Myniads) refuse to take part in Dionysos's festival and are punished.[46] The God drives them mad and they tear apart Leucippe's son (Plutarch, *Quaest. rom.* 38). Afterwards the sisters roam the mountains. So, it is known for both mothers and fathers to kill their own children and this is regarded as a sure sign of madness. The Myniads are driven into the mountains, a space of wilderness, and kill a family member

---

[45] Compare Aias/Ajax who kills a flock of sheep thinking they are Greek army commanders because of his madness (cf. Sophocles, *Aj.*).
[46] Compare also Antonius Liberalis, *Metam.*

Aliyah El Mansy

like the daughters of Proetus and Agave. All these stories are connected to the God Dionysos.

4 Domestic Space and Self-harming Behavior (Mark 9:17–18; 20–22; 26 parr.)

The symptoms mentioned in the story of the possessed boy (Mark 9:14–29 parr.) resemble the ones ascribed to the "sacred disease."[47] I will concentrate on the description of the symptoms. Again, Mark has the longest version with the most detailed description. All of the symptoms fall in the category of loss of bodily control: falling to the ground or into fire and water, spasms, frothing around the mouth, rolling around, and screaming. Most, if not all, can be life threatening. Thus, the father concludes that the spirit wants to kill his son. Matthew only copies the falling into fire and water and apart from that only mentions the boy's suffering (Matt 17:15). Luke adds screaming, which Mark only mentions during the exorcism (Luke 9:39). In general, Luke describes similar symptoms as Mark but sometimes uses other verbs—especially such with the meaning of crashing and shattering somebody (Luke 9:42). He stresses the severity by mentioning that those fits happen very often. It is striking that Luke leaves out the fire and water incidents.

In Mark the symptoms are caused by a mute spirit (τὸ ἄλαλον πνεῦμα) who is later specified as τὸ ἄλαλον καὶ κωφὸν πνεῦμα (Mark 9:25)—a speechless and mute spirit. Both words can be regarded as synonyms. Luke calls the spirit simply spirit (Luke 9:39) or demon and unclean spirit (Luke 9:42). Matthew implies a demon at the end (Matt 17:18), but in the beginning only speaks of the boy being moonstruck.[48] The afflicted person is a son, Luke even says the only son (Luke 9:38). The age is not mentioned, but he is called a child (Mark 9:24, Matt 17:18, Luke 9:42). The

---

[47] Modern research equals the described pattern to epilepsy. Martin Leutzsch, "Vermögen und Vertrauen, Dämonie und Exorzismus (Die Erzählung vom besessenen Jungen) Mk 9,14–29," in Zimmermann, *Wunder Jesu*, 354 concludes that some symptoms are the same but not all.

[48] Cf. for the relation to the moon Jutta Leonhardt-Balzer, "Warum nicht gleich so? (Heilung eines mondsüchtigen Jungen) Mt 17,14–20(21) (Lk 9,37–43a)," in Zimmermann, *Wunder Jesu*, 477–478.

mother in Philostratus, *Vit. Apoll.* 3.38 also calls her 16 years old son "a child" which stresses maybe a parent's perspective or that the afflicted person still needs care like a child. There is only one other story about a possessed child—the daughter of the Syrophoenician woman—but her symptoms are not depicted (Mark 7:24–30 par.). Both cases show that here, parents are concerned about their children and they remain part of the family even in a non-normative bodily state. They are no cast-outs.

4.1 Family Space

Another exorcism in the Acts of Andrews takes place in the house of Antiphanes in Megara, the harbor-city some 30 kilometers East of Athens. When Antiphanes comes home from a journey he finds his slaves and wife possessed by demons (Acts Andr. (Greg) 29). The slave who is responsible for guarding the gates is screaming fretfully, other young slaves are grinding their teeth, they attack their owner Antiphanes and they are laughing hysterically. His wife is lying exhausted and distraught by madness in her bedroom. Her hair is falling in front of her eyes and she cannot neither see nor recognize her husband.

Again, we encounter typical descriptions: the male slaves are laughing, screaming, grinding their teeth and even attacking their owner. To laugh and scream is out of place behavior, especially for slaves. Even more, that it happens without any reason. The first slaves mentioned are the gatekeeper and his family. He obviously cannot any longer attend to his task. Symbolically the house is therefore unguarded and open to in-truders.[49] The young slaves are said to attack Antiphanes. Attacking your owner turns the hierarchy upside down and is regarded as a serious crime. So, the slaves behave contrary to their social position. In contrast, the woman is lying down and not making any sounds at all. Her hair seems in disarray, falling loosely around her head and covering her eyes, so she cannot see. To describe the status of the woman the author refers especially to her hair. Hairstyle and hair in general convey social and moral status in antiquity. Loose hair for a grown-up woman, a wife and

---

[49] Cf. Anders Klostergaard Petersen, "Die Austreibung der Dämonen aus dem Haushalt des Antiphanes. (Dämonenaustreibung in Megara). ActAndr(Greg) 29," in Zimmermann, *Wunder der Apostel*, 834.

lady of the house is a sign that something is amiss. It seems indecent and is associated with uncultivated nature as opposed to culture.[50] Furthermore, she does not recognize her husband. Not recognizing close family is very often mentioned as a symptom that the person is not her- or himself.

In one of the satirist Lucian's (125–180 CE) writings—the Lover of Lies—he depicts in chapter 16 possessed persons (δαιμονάω participle) in general. Their symptoms are: falling down at moonlight, rolling (διαστρέφω) their eyes, and frothing (ἀφρός) at the mouth. The cause is said to be ghosts (φάσμα) and demons (δαίμων). All genders are affected. In the writing *Toxaris* Lucian presents Kydiache—a woman falling down at moonlight (Lucian, *Tox.* 24). No more symptoms are mentioned but her ailment comes on top of an unpleasant outer appearance which limits her chances for marriage. Still, her father's friend Zenomathes not only marries her, but also cherishes her and they have at least one healthy and beautiful child and a caring relationship (Lucian, *Tox.* 25–26). Her non-normative bodily state (including not fitting into beauty standards), does not prevent her from having a family of her own and thereby a space inside society.[51]

The Acts of Thomas (beginning of 3rd century) present a case of demon possession resembling the behavior pattern of the possessed boy in Mark. As is typical of the Acta literature, the story is elaborate and very detailed. In Acts Thom. 5.62–67 the wife and daughter of a high-ranking soldier of King Misdais's army are possessed by demons. At night on the way home from a wedding they attended without her husband, and the daughter's father, the two women and the accompanying slaves are attacked by a man and a boy who are later described as ugly, with white teeth and carbon black skin close to the water pipes (Acts Thom. 5.63–64). The slaves cannot do anything against the demons because the demons render their swords useless. The signs that something happened to the women are the following: they fall down, they gnash their teeth and their heads hit the ground (Acts Thom. 5.63). Immediately after hearing the story, the soldier

---

[50] Cf. Klostergaard Petersen, "Austreibung," 836–37.
[51] Aretaeus of Cappadocia (80/83–130/138 CE) comes to a very different conclusion by saying that people afflicted by the "sacred disease" are stupid, unsociable, not capable of having intercourse etc. Cf. Aretaeus, *Sign. diut.* 1.4.3.

leaves the house and finds his wife and daughter lying in the market place. His wife tells him the whole story but suddenly the demon throws her down again (Acts Thom. 5.64). From that time one, the story goes, both women cannot leave the house but are confined to it. Besides, they are regularly thrown down and exposed by the demons. For three years the family did not set up the table or have a meal together, the father concludes (Acts Thom. 5.64). Again, it is a father who seeks help for household members. Wife and daughter display some of the classical non-normative behaviors. Besides the spasms, there is a new aspect: they are being exposed. The Acts of Thomas also display in other stories sexual connotations of demonic possession (cf. Acts Thom. 5.43). The description of the demons as male, unnaturally black colored, strong and lingering at non-populated places feeds the stereotype of "dangerous foreign masculinity." Furthermore, they attack after sunset, even though the women encountered the demons already earlier on their way to the wedding. Sunset, evening and night can also be regarded as liminal spaces. The story draws special attention to the fact that the family cannot have meals together and that the women are locked up in the house. Mother and daughter can stay inside the family but they are separated from everybody else. Inside the family it seems not possible to spend time together normally. Again, the possessed persons are separated from other people and prevented to live a "normal" life.

4.2 Self-harming Behavior

In the story of the possessed man in Gerasa and in the story about the possessed boy, self-harming behavior is displayed. The man in Gerasa hurt himself with stones (or later the pigs drowned themselves) and the boy nearly fell into fire or water—both are seen as involuntarily behavior caused by demons. According to the geographer Pausanias (110–180 CE) Orestes is said to have bitten off his finger when he was maddened as a punishment for killing his own mother (Pausanias, *Descr.* 8.34). Attis castrates himself after being driven mad by Agdistis/Cybele (Pausanias, *Descr.* 7.17.12). According to Lucian, *Dial. d.* 12.1 the (male) Korybantes cut holes in their arm, and run around with flying hair in the mountains. The latter might be an allusion to the Maenads and illustrates that the

191

Korybantes are effeminate. Suicide can be regarded as the final stage of self-harm. In myth, madness sometimes drives people to kill themselves like Aglaurus and Herse who disobeyed Hera (Pausanias, *Descr.* 1.18). As punishment they are driven mad and throw themselves off the Acropolis. In Acts Andr. (Greg) 14 a demon causes the son of a Thessalonian to hang himself because the father asked to cure his son.

5 Religious Space and Inspired Behavior (Acts 2:4, 16:16–18)

Acts begins with inspiration by the spirit when Jesus-followers gathered in Jerusalem start to speak in different languages. It is noteworthy, that the neutral verb λαλέω is used. Nevertheless, "to speak in foreign tongues" certainly gets the attention of many people (Acts 2:5–12), because glossolalia is regarded as non-normative behavior. It is telling that some people interpret the events as caused by drunkenness (Acts 2:13). This is due to the possibility of ascribing these symptoms to different reasons, drunkenness being one of them. Depending on the translation of the term "followers" those affected might only be men (the apostle) or all people belonging to the Christ-group more generally. These events happen in a house (Acts 2:2), but when onlookers start to gather, it shifts to public space. From a Christian perspective inspiration by the holy spirit marks it as religious space, specifically connected to prophecy.[52]

In Philippi Paul and Silas and maybe some others encounter a prophet-ess possessed by a spirit (Acts 16:16–18). It certainly is not by chance that the spirit is called πνεῦμα πύθωνα. The Phytian prophetesses were famous and popular and obviously also outside the official oracle sites a good way to make money. It is actually not so easy to say if the prophetess is showing non-normative behavior patterns. She is marked as an inspired person by shouting—again κράζω is being used—divine messages in public space, and described as a slave and woman following a group of men. This is not to be expected of a female slave usually. But, it is to be expected from an inspired seer to scream or shout as we will see later.

---

[52] There are more cases of people prophesizing in Acts, but they do not show non-normative bodily or behavioral patterns: Prophet Agabus (Acts 11:27–28, 21:10–11), disciples in Tyrus (Acts 21:4), Philippus' prophetic daughters (Acts 21:9).

Also, to know and tell things inspired by divine knowledge to others. Noticeable other behavior is also part of the performance. The female slave's behavior as a Pythian seer might thus be non-normative in only one aspect: she is following Paul and the others for many days. Her owners expected and used her to give prophecies for money—probably at the market place or close to a temple where many people pass by. This can be regarded as a conventional space for a (slave-)woman with her gift. The deviant behavior is not shouting out divine messages, but stepping out of her assigned place as a "market seer" and following people for several days. This is maybe why Paul is not surprised by her message or behavior, but simply annoyed by her following them and probably also by the economic exploitation of religion.[53]

5.1 Religious Space

The two stories from Acts show that non-normative behavior can be assigned to religious space. Acts 16 conveys, that spirits can inspire people. In the preliminary remarks I already mentioned that non-normative behavior is often ascribed to deities in Graeco-Roman culture. On classic example stems from the Corpus Hippocratum. The document dismisses this interpretation of the "sacred illness" as superstition which its own treatise explains as the effects caused by phlegm or air-flow in the brain.[54] Each symptom is ascribed to a deity reflecting certain roles, qualities or aspects of the deity (Hippocrates, *Morb. sacr.* 4). Animal like sounds (βρυχάομαι, ὀξύς, εὔτονος) are ascribed to the "Mother of the Gods"—probably Magna Mater/Cybele—and Poseidon. The Mother of the Gods is also said to cause convulsion (σπάω). Excrements are ascribed to

---

[53] Cf. Friedrich Avemarie, "Warum treibt Paulus einen Dämon aus, der die Wahrheit sagt? Geschichte und Bedeutung des Exorzismus zu Philippi (Act 16,16–18)," in *Die Dämonen. Demons. Die Dämonologie der israelitisch-jüdischen und frühchristlichen Literatur im Kontext ihrer Umwelt. The Demonology of Israelite-Jewish and Early Christian Literature in Context of their Environment*, eds. Hermann Lichtenberger, Armin Lange, and K.F. Diethard Römheld (Tübingen: Mohr Siebeck, 2003), 570–71.

[54] Often the sacred disease is diagnosed today as epilepsy: Michael Wohlers, *Heilige Krankheit. Epilepsie in antiker Medizin, Astrologie und Religion*, Marburger Theologische Studien 57 (Marburg: Elwert, 1999). Solevåg, *Negotiating*, 98 warns to apply such modern terms.

Enodia, another epitaph of Hecate meaning "the one at the way," and Apollo Nomius, the shepherd. Maybe Enodia evokes the notion of passing by and Apollo Nomius of sheep and their excrements. The war deity Ares is responsible for froth around the mouth (ἀφρός) and kicking. Both can be regarded also as signs of anger and fury. Hecate and heroes are responsible for more psychological symptoms and reactions to being afraid. Hecate is a Goddess of liminal space and also of magic.

In general, it can be said that more female deities and divine beings cause "madness." One of the reasons is the imagination of menacing and dangerous women as a shared concept in the Mediterranean.[55] In one chorus of Euripides Hippolytos 141–145 addressed to Phaidra only Pan is mentioned as a male God causing non-normative behavior (here falling in love with her step-son Hippolytos). The verses go on and list: Hecate, the Corybantes, the demons accompanying Cybele[56] or Cybele herself, and Dictynna (Selene). Dictynna is said to haunt lakes, dry land and the eddies of the surf. You can find this Goddess in the wilderness and deserted or dangerous places. From other myths it is known that Hera, Aphrodite and Artemis punish by driving people mad respectively causing the "sacred disease."[57] Artemis Soteira and Artemis Orthia were believed to drive enemies mad. Sometimes, the deities instruct Erinnyen/Furiae to carry out the punishment, and they act as spirits of vengeance.[58] In the Roman context the Larvae are spirits causing madness. These divine beings are very often believed to live in the underworld and are therefore also called chthonic deities. Mania and Lyssa in Greek mythology are the personification of madness and can also be sent by deities. Besides Pan/Faunus, only Dionysos/Bacchus is said to drive people crazy.[59] Hence, there exists an imbalance: In mythology the non-normative behavior pattern regarded as madness is mostly caused by female deities and specific female spirits or demons driving people crazy. Some of the Goddesses and especially the spirits inhabit liminal spaces connected with death or wilderness.

---

[55] Cf. Schneider and Seifert, "Ehefrau," 7–8.

[56] Later on her priests are called by the same name.

[57] Hera: Euripides, *Her.* 830–42, Artemis: Callimachus, *Aet.* 75.12, Selene: Aretaeus, *Sign. diut.* 1.4.2.

[58] Also cf. Sorensen, *Possession*, 85–86.90–91.

[59] Sorensen, *Possession*, 78–80 also mentions Eros and maybe Ares in Sophocles' dramas.

Some of the myths are simultaneously the aetiology for rituals. We already took a look at the fate of the daughters of Minos who killed Leucippes's child and roamed the mountains. Plutarch records a spring feast for women, called Agriona. The women display raving, maenadic behavior being pursued by a priest of Bacchus who was allowed to kill any of them (Plutarch, *Quaest. rom.* 38). It is known that women in the cult of Dionysos, called Maenads from μαίνας (mad woman) or Bacchantes, are honoring the God with frantic rituals. Their depiction is mostly influenced by Euripides's play *Bacchae*. The Bacchantes are said to be women driven mad out of their houses into the mountains where they sit on rocks, dance, scream etc. (Euripides, *Bacch.* 30–35, 75, 215). According to Ovid they run with loose hair decorated with vine tendrils, dressed in animal skin, playing flute, shouting and howling through the woods (Ovid, *Metam.* 4.1–30, 6.571). The Dionysos cult with its Bacchic rites seems to offer a space for women to let loose or literally "let their hair down." Euripides warned that only immodest women will be corrupted to participate in the rituals, implying that this behavior is not appropriate. Women are leaving their assigned space—the house—and thereby escape male control. Nevertheless, society offered women a space to dance, scream, and run wild if we follow Ovid's account. Besides, women who do not want to take part in the rites are punished by the God.

Already, Euripides connected Dionysus with Cybele (Euripides, *Bacch.* 75). Lucian describes the rites of the Cybele cult in his work *De Syria Dea*. The myth behind the cult is the one of Attis we already looked at. Lucian narrates that Attis, after being castrated, stopped living like a man and started to wear women's dresses, roaming the world spreading the cult of Cybele (Lucian, *Syr. d.* 15). When the priests, the Galloi, are performing the mysteries of the Cybele cult, they cut their arms and beat each other's back—but only outside the temple (Lucian, *Syr. d.* 50). The new recruits are sometimes bystanders who are infected by the music and rituals. Lucian reports such an instance: a young man was grabbed by the μανία of the Cybele priests, tear off his clothes, let out a loud cry (βοή), took one of their swords and castrated himself. Afterwards, he ran around and threw his penis in a random house. The inhabitants of the house now needed to provide him with female clothes and everything a woman needs to dress herself (Lucian, *Syr. d.* 51).

Part of the Cybele mysteries is self-harming behavior displayed by the priests. This is not allowed inside the temple but only outside. Symptoms of the cultic madness are tearing off the male clothes, castrating yourself and finally dressing as a woman. Like women can act out in the Dionysos cult, men are allowed to do so in the Cybele cult. But, it is important to note, that in order to become a priest and share the rituals, you need to self-mutilate yourself first. Men are giving up on secondary sexual characteristics and social male identity—the latter being emphasized by changing into women's clothes.[60] In order to be part of the cult men need to take steps to change their gender, specifically to become more female. In the context of the myth Attis did so because he was driven mad. In the cultic context it is part of the expected behavior to become a priest.

5.2 Inspired Behavior

A positive way to locate non-normative bodily behavior is divine inspiration. The link between the terms μαίνομαι and μανία show that madness and inspiration are two sides of the same coin. But that does not mean it is understood automatically, that mantic seers are displaying physically or psychologically non-normative behavior otherwise regarded as possession or madness. Actually, most do not. This kind of inspiration is mostly recorded of female mantic seers[61] and this is likely, due to cultural influence. At the sanctuary of Apollo at Didyma male prophets gave oracles but in Hellenistic times this changed, probably influenced by Delphi and its female prophetesses.[62] In general, there are more male seers mentioned in

---

[60] Epigraphical evidence and reliefs show more nuances in the dress code and significant differences to women's clothing. Cf. Susan Elliot, *Cutting Too Close for Comfort. Paul's Letter to the Galatians in its Anatolian Cultic Context* (London/New York: T&T Clark International 2003), 163–166.

[61] Which does not mean that male seers could not be inspired. Michael Attyah Flower, *The Seer in Ancient Greece* (Berkeley/Los Angeles: Univ. of California Press, 2008), 84–91 explains that there are no strict distinctions between the different mantic techniques. Still, it is noteworthy that inspiration and its non-normative bodily state is more often ascribed to female seers.

[62] Cf. Joan Breton Connelly, *Portrait of a Priestess. Woman and Ritual in Ancient Greece* (Princeton: Princeton University Press, 2007), 80; Wiebke Friese, *Die Kunst vom Wahn- und*

literature, even though the first person coming to mind might be the Pythia of the Delphic oracle.[63] Also well-known is Cassandra to whom Apollo taught the art of prophecy. Euripides depicts her as a frantic and frenzied prophetess using expressions like μαντιπόλος and Βάκχη (frenzied; Bacche; Euripides, *Hec.* 121), βακχεῖον and θεσπιῳδός (Bacchic revelry; singing in prophetic strain; Euripides, *Hec.* 676), ἐκβακχεύω and μαινάς (excite/filled with Bacchic frenzy; Maenad/mad woman; Euripides, *Tro.* 170) or ἔνθεος (inspired/possessed; Euripides, *Tro.* 365). The depiction of Cassandra alludes to Euripides's Bacchantes.

Herodotus tells of a male πρόμαντις and προφήτης in the temple of Ptoan Apollo in Thebes, who gave oracles in foreign languages (Herodotus 8.135.1–3). Nothing more is told about the divine inspiration. The shepherd Coretas is, according to Plutarch, the first one who discovered Apollo's mantic cave later known as Delphi (Plutarch, *Def. orac.* 42). This is the only instance that a man is being affected by the fumes: Coretas falls down and reveals ecstatically (ἐνθουσιώδης) future events. People do not notice him at first—maybe because he is a shepherd, or they regarded him as drunk. Anyway, they did not take him seriously. Finally, when his prophecies came to pass, they started to admire him. Coretas is losing control over is his body and speech. People only acknowledge him later and then assign him a space as a prophet.

It can be regarded as an exception that female mantics display a non-normative behavior pattern as can be seen by the descriptions of the Pythia giving oracles.[64] Most instances causing non-normative bodily

---

Wahrsagen. Orakelheiligtümer in der antiken Welt (Darmstadt/Mainz: Zabern, 2012), 41–42. In Claros prophetesses were inspired by Apollo. Cf. Friese, *Kunst*, 46.

[63] Flower, *Seer*, 2 speaks of 70 male seers. Female seers in Graeco-Roman literature are: The Pythia, the priestesses of Dodona, Cassandra, Manto, the Sibylles, Diotima, Veleda, Theoris, Asterie, Martha. For more information on female seers cf. Aliyah El Mansy, "Mantik als Raum religiöser Partizipation und Gestaltung von Frauen jenseits institutionalisierter Kulte. Die Darstellung mantisch begabter Frauen in der Apostelgeschichte und bei Plutarch," in El Mansy, Köstner, and Wohlthat, *Frauen*, 101–3.

[64] Compare Pausanias, *Descr.* 2.24,1, Diodorus, *Bibl.* 16.26, Plutarch, *Def. orac.* 5.8.50, *Pyth. Orac.* 6;7;17;21–22 (about the Sybil 9–10). Another example of a forced oracle session can be found in Plutarch, *Def. orac.* 51.

reactions are actually forced oracles and not the regular ones.[65] Lucan (39–65 CE) presents such an incident in vivid words (Lucan 5.121–216).[66] The events are set around 48 BCE. Appius Claudius Pulcher, who was an ally of Pompeius, wants to inquire about the outcome of the civil war at the oracle of Delphi. But the oracle site is closed down and the priestess is enjoying a walk in the groves of the sanctuary. When one of the priests tries to fetch her, she is unwilling to be possessed by the God Apollo. She is so afraid of the divine possession that she tries everything to discourage Appius Pulcher from getting an oracle. In the end, the priest forces her into the temple. In a last desperate attempt, she starts to act as if prophesying, but the fraud is obvious (Lucan 5.149–155): It is said that her "bosom is unstirred," her cries are not "inarticulate" or "tremulous (*tremo*) as sign of "divine frenzy" (*furor*) and the laurel wreath "was not raised off her head by the bristling (*horror*) hair."[67] Appius Pulcher explodes in anger and the prophetess is so scared that she seeks refuge by the tripod and is immediately filled with the divine power and possession (*bacchor*). The prophetess cannot control her body, sudden and uncontrolled movements make her stagger and jerk her head around (Lucan 5.169–174). Her eyes roll around (*torqueo; vagor*) and she froths at the mouth (*spumeus*). She is uttering screams (*ululatus*), groans (*gemitus*) and sighs (*anhelo*). She is described to be frantic (*demens*) and that the frenzy (*rabies*) has her in its grip (Lucan 5.189–193;208–216).

We already saw all of the mentioned non-normative bodily reactions in descriptions of people believed to be possessed or mad. She is not herself

---

[65] Cf. Breton Connelly, *Portrait*, 75–78.

[66] He might be inspired by Vergil (70–19 BCE) and his presentation of the Sibyl of Cumae (Vergil, *Aen.* 6.42–105). The oracle site is located in a mountain-grotto. The Sibyl is said to be a virgin (6.45) and called a seer (*vates*; Vergil, *Aen.* 6.65;78). While she is inspired by the God her face color changes, her hair is loose, she is panting, her heart beats fast due to frenzy (*rabies*), her figure seems to be taller than a human-being and her voice does not sound mortal (Vergil, *Aen.* 6.46–50). She is said to rave (*baccor*) in her cave and that there is froth at her mouth (Vergil, *Aen.* 6.77–80). She is said to be out of her mind (*furor*; Vergil, *Aen.* 6.100;102). Lucan uses very similar Latin expressions and also the motive that Apollo is forcing the prophetess (Vergil, *Aen.* 6.78–79;101). It would be worth to compare the description of divine possession of female seers with language used to describe sexual violence. More information about the Sibyl can be found in Friese, *Kunst*, 116–26.

[67] Translation by James D. Duff (Lucan. The Civil War LCL).

anymore and cannot later remember what the God showed her of the future because she is only the medium. Lucan emphasizes the strain and stress the divine possession is putting her under. The space of this mantic possession is a shrine in a temple built around the chasm causing these reactions and what are believed to be divine vapors. The oracle site is in the mountains. It is a very secluded and controlled space—even though the story shows that it can be violated.

There are also other deities inspiring people apart from Apollo.[68] Ovid presents Manto, the daughter of the famous blind seer Tiresias,[69] who conveys messages of the Goddess Latona, the mother of Apollo and Diana (Ovid, *Metam.* 6.157–164). She is described as being driven to walk through the streets, prophesy (*vaticinor*), saying that the Goddess speaks through her. Walking alone in the streets and conveying non-human messages can be regarded as non-normative female behavior outside the context of prophesy. It resembles the behavior of the slave with the python spirit in Acts.

6 Results

The following tendencies can be tentatively identified with the awareness that I presented a selection of available sources.

6.1 Space

In general—as already mentioned—loss of bodily and mental control is considered to be un-manly. Therefore, "possession," "madness," and "sacred disease" are per se more feminine connotated spaces. The analyzed texts reveal that there is a kind of mental map in which to locate this non-normative behavior. It includes the domestic space, the public space, the liminal space and the sacred space. A person affected by a non-normative body state can move or be moved between these spaces and actually exist in all of them. But, socially the person is foremost assigned to

---

[68] Still, Apollo is the most important one with most oracle sites. Veit Rosenberger, *Griechische Orakel. Eine Kulturgeschichte* (Darmstadt: WBG, 2001), 22–23 lists 20 places. Other deities and their oracle sites are listed in Rosenberger, *Orakel*, 24–25.
[69] Tiresas was blinded by Hera/Juno out of anger and Zeus/Jupiter hence gave him the gift of seeing the future. Cf. Ovid, *Metam.* 3,316–338.

liminal and sacred space. Inside the domestic and public space, they are stigmatized, because they are regarded as not fitting in.

In public and domestic space people with non-normative behavior or bodily state are tolerated as long as they are not endangering other people. But, they are very often locked away in domestic space and are not included in everyday life.[70] There was only one exception in the case of the woman afflicted by the "sacred disease."[71] The two spaces are also characterized by the wish of mostly relatives that the person might be healed, so they can participate again in everyday life.

There are different incidents when people can be found in liminal space: either the demon or deity or the frenzy drives them to the wilderness or society does.[72] Liminal space is foremost secluded, wild, deserted or hostile like mountains, the desert or burial sites. Places where people in a normative state only rarely go or with a reason like hunting or to perform rituals for deceased people.

Sacred space is ambivalent. In the case of inspired seers their non-normative bodily state and behavior is expected and accepted.[73] It even is a sign of the integrity for the inspired person. Adherents of cults with non-normative behavior are on one hand accepted in the limits of cultic rituals but on the other hand are always watched with suspicion (Bacchantes, Galloi).

6.2 Gender

Most symptoms of non-normative behavior or bodily state are not gender specific. This is a very important result. These symptoms are froth around the mouth,[74] falling to the ground,[75] distorted eyes,[76] screaming,[77]

---

[70] Acts Thom. 5.62–6, Philostrus, *Vit. Apoll.* 4.20.
[71] Lucian, *Tox.* 15–26.
[72] Philostrus, *Vit. Apoll.* 3.38, Apollodorus, Bibl. 2.2.2, Plutarch, *Quaest. rom.* 38, Ovid, *Metam.* 4.464–542.
[73] Euripide, *Hec.* 121, 676, *Tro.* 170;365, Plutarch, *Defect. orac.* 42, Ovid, *Metam.* 6.157–164, Vergil, *Aen.* 6.42–105, Lucan 5.121–216.
[74] Euripides, *Bacch.* 1124–1135, Vergil, *Aen.* 6.77–80, Lucan 5.189–193, Lucian, *Pseudol.* 16, Mart. Andr. 2.
[75] Plutarch, *Marc.* 20.5–6, Lucian, *Pseudol.* 16, *Tox.* 24.
[76] Euripides, *Bacch.* 1124–1135, Lucian, *Pseudol.* 16.
[77] Plutarch, *Marc.* 20.5–6, Vergil, *Aen.* 6, Lucan 5, Acts Petr. 11.

unintelligible speech,[78] aimless wandering or running,[79] not recognizing family members,[80] and being naked.[81] Still, it is crucial to be aware that this condition is gendered as "un-manly" in general. Mainly, this is because losing control over one's own body is regarded as "unmanly." Still, the descriptions show sometimes gendered tendencies.

More men are said to show self-harming behavior[82] and commit suicide more often.[83] Also, super-human strength is more often mentioned in regard to men. This strength is mostly threatening other people.[84] Men also seem more prone to hallucination which leads them to mistake human-beings for animals or the other way around.[85] Obviously, this feature has to do with activities ascribed more often to men like hunting or fighting. Especially striking was that men are more often presented as laughing inappropriately.[86]

Women also can show super-human strength but mostly this is mentioned to explain why they manage an activity like climbing a cliff.[87] So, it is used for activities women are usually thought to be not strong enough for. Women are more often said to wander alone in the wilderness.[88] Both genders are seen killing their own children as a sign of non-normative behavior, but especially in myth there are more women to do so.[89] Very often female hair is mentioned and described to be in disarray.[90] As well, in the presentation of non-normative female behavior there is sometimes a sexual connotation, especially when it is about male demons or deities

---

[78] Lucan 5.
[79] Plutarch, *Marc.* 20.5–6, Philostratus, *Vit. Apoll.* 3.38.
[80] Euripides, *Bacch.* 1124–1135, Philostratus, *Vit. Apoll.* 3.38, Mart. Andr. 2, Acts Andr. (Greg) 2, Plutarch, *Marc.* 20.5–69.
[81] Plutarch, *Marc.* 20.5–6, Acts Thom. 5.62–67.
[82] Lucian, *Syr. d.* 50, *Dial. d.* 12.1, Pausanias, *Descr.* 8.34, 7.17, Philostratus, *Vit. Apoll.* 3.38.
[83] Herodotus, *Hist.* 6.75.3, Pausanias, *Descr.* 1.18, Acts Andr. (Greg) 14.
[84] Herodotus, *Hist.* 3.30;31;34, 6.75. Euripides, *Herc.* 1094–1097, Acts Andr. (Greg) 29.
[85] Sophocles, *Aj.*, Ovid, *Metam.* 4.464–542.
[86] Herodotus, *Hist.* 34.1–4, Philostratus, *Vit. Apoll.* 4.20, Acts Petr. 11, Acts Andr. (Greg) 29.
[87] Euripides, *Bacch.* 1124–1135, Ovid, *Metam.* 4.464–542.
[88] Euripides, *Bacch.*, Apollodorus, *Bibl.* 2.2.2, Plutarch, *Quaest. rom.* 38.
[89] Euripides, *Bacch.*, Ovid, *Metam.* 4.464–542, Plutarch, *Quaest. rom.* 38, Apollodorus, *Bibl.* 2.2.2.
[90] Apollodorus, *Bibl.* 2.2.2; Ovid, *Metam.* 4.1–30;464–542, 6.571.

possessing women.[91] Non-normative behavior in cultic contexts also seems to be more often told of women or if it is told of men, they need to become effeminate (Corybantes, Galloi).[92] Also, in myth and religion there is a connection of femininity and non-normative behavior, because most deities and spirits causing such behavior are female. More female seers are presented in a non-normative bodily state or behavior patterns (Cassandra, Pythia, Sibyl, Manto).

6.3 Space and Gender of Non-normative Behavior in New Testament Figures
The New Testament assigns people with non-normative bodily states and behavior to demonic space. Only Matthew sometimes uses the language of disease, but the remedy is always an exorcism.[93] The afflicted persons are found mostly in domestic space, sometimes in public space like synagogues, and liminal space like the graveyard.[94] In Acts the female slave with the Python spirit is explicitly located in public space. The Acta Literature is taking up on this. Non-normative bodily state and behavior is assigned to demonic space and people need to be transferred to non-demonic space. They are adding especially central public space of Graeco-roman cities like the Praetorium, the market place, or a female bath which also marks the crossing of gendered spaces.[95] The Christian sacred space is limited to prophetesses and inspiration caused by the Holy Spirit. Both can happen in public space, but mostly within the community. But the inspired do not show symptoms like the Pythia or Sibyl, only "speaking in foreign languages" is mentioned.[96]

The New Testament narrates in more detail the symptoms of male characters. This changes in the Acta Literature. Symptoms are presented at length in both male and female characters. They resemble a lot more the

---

[91] Vergil, *Aen.* 6, Lucan 5, Acts Thom. 5.62–67.

[92] Lucian, *Dial. d.* 12.2, *Syr. d.* 15;51.

[93] Matt 17:14–18.

[94] Synagogue: Mark 1:23–28 par., Luke 13:10–13; street: Matt 9:27; house: Mark 7:24–30 par., 9:14–29 parr., Acts 19:13–20, graveyard: Mark 5:1–20 parr.

[95] Mart. Andr. 2; Acts Andr. (Greg) 5.

[96] Paul talks about speaking in tongues in 1 Cor 14:1–33.39, too. He labels it as προφητεύω, but remarks that "non-believers" will understand it as μαίνομαι—being out of your mind (1 Cor 14:23). For 1 Cor 12–14 cf. Bazzana, *Spirit*, 172–205.

narrative practice in Graeco-Roman literature as shown.[97] In some instances the afflicted person is said to be a male slave. Slaves are also regarded as non-men, so they already are socially effeminate.[98]

Differing from Graeco-roman narrative patterns, women are less often presented as possessed in the New Testament and when they are, their outer appearance is not described. Women are also not found to be lingering in the wilderness. Only in one case a possessed male person inhabits a liminal space and it is implied that he is not properly dressed.[99] Possessed men can show socially aggressive behavior, a typical symptom also found in Graeco-roman texts.[100] A shared feature of both genders is social exclusion. This is mostly caused by a non-normative bodily state like blindness, muteness, fits or curvature.[101] Or sometimes by non-normative behavior.[102] Thus, it is very often family or other people taking the afflicted to be transferred to a normative state to be able to live in society again.[103] The Acta Literature also concentrates on reintegrating people in families and social life. This is also important in Graeco-roman literature but in tragedy and myth this is not central to the genre. Furthermore, in myth and tragedy it is mostly women leaving the domestic and male-controlled space. Possession in the New Testament is not sexualized by gender specific descriptions in contrast to Graeco-roman and Acta Literature. Especially, inspired persons do not display any frantic behavior but are only speaking in tongues or are simply foretelling the future.[104] Thus, both male and female prophets are presented but explicitly not according to mantic inspired ideal.

On one hand, non-normative bodily behavior in the context of possession or madness leads to a blurring of gender boundaries. The loss of self-

---

[97] Laughing: Acts Petr. 11, Acts Andr. (Greg) 29; not recognizing people: Acts Andr. (Greg) 29, Mart. Andr. 2; hair in disarray: Acts Andr. (Greg) 29; aggressive behavior: Acts Andr. (Greg) 29; suicide: Acts Andr (Greg) 14

[98] Acts Andr. (Greg) 19, Mart. Andr. 2.

[99] Mark 5:1–20 parr.

[100] Mark 1:23–38 par., 5:1–10 parr., Acts 19:13–20.

[101] Matt 12:22 par., 9:32–34, Mark 9:14–29 parr., Luke 13:10–13.

[102] Mark 1:23–28 par., 5:1–20.

[103] Mark 7:25–26 par., Mark 9:17 parr., Matt 9:32, 12:22.

[104] Acts 2:4, 1 Cor 12–14, Acts 11:27–28, 21:4, 9–11.

control and discipline is regarded as rather female. On the other hand, in the midst of this vagueness there are distinct features of gendered depictions of such persons. They are ascribed mostly to liminal spaces. Some cults offer a religiously controlled space to live out one's deviant gender parts. They create spaces for a "regulated escape." The New Testament and later Christian literature emphasize the effect of non-normative behavior: loneliness, loss of relationship and participation, and self-harm. The suffering of the inflicted and their relatives or communities is stressed. The healing performed by Jesus is more than the curing of an ailment. It is a return to communal space and a return of self-control—so to say a re-location and re-gendering.

Dreams and Visions as Signs of a New Era: The Role of Joel 3:5 in Romans 10:13 and in Acts 2:17–21

Bart J. Koet

Does an article on dreams and visions fit into a volume on "Understanding abnormalities"? Are they even abnormal? And, if so, what is abnormal about them? Since Kant wrote his book against dreams, there has been, especially and probably only in the West, a great suspicion among enlightened thinkers that dreams convey any form of knowledge and, hence, ascribing meaning to dreams has been seen as abnormal.[1] In so many cultures, however, this is thought of differently and dreams are seen as a special form of knowledge. This was also true of the Jewish and Christian traditions in late antiquity. So whether you consider dreams and visions to be "abnormalities" depends on which world-view you adhere to. Without having to choose too quickly between dreams as wisdom or as deception, it seems to me worthwhile to take a closer look at the phenomenon of dreams in the New Testament (=NT) precisely because in this tradition references to dreams could legitimize new realities. Thus, dreams and visions as a possible way of revealing and legitimizing new realities may ultimately prove to have something to contribute to "Understanding abnormalities."

In an earlier article on the relationship between Paul's autobiographical statements in Gal 1:13–16 and the Paul of Acts, I observed that the revelation Paul refers to in Gal 1:16 is open to quite different interpretations. Was it a visible disclosure or an inner process?[2] While in

---

[1] Immanuel Kant, *Träume eines Geistersehers, erläutert durch Träume der Metaphysik* (Stuttgart: Reclam 2002; first published in 1766).

[2] Bart J. Koet, "Paul, a Light for the Gentiles? Paul as Interpreter of Scriptures in Galatians 1:13–16 and in the Acts of the Apostles," in *Paulinische Schriftrezeption. Grundlagen—*

Galatians this remains ambiguous, in Acts it is clear that Paul receives revelations in the form of dreams and visions or a voice from heaven. Luke is one of the NT authors, who, in line with ideas about dreams and visions we can find in the Old Testament (=OT), presents these phenomena as a possible form of divine revelation and he does so in the book of Acts.[3] In this article, we examine how Luke uses the Joel quote in Acts 2:17–21 to legitimize dreams and visions in Acts as divine revelations. Just like in the above-mentioned article, we will compare Luke's interpretation of a text from the OT with Paul's references to that text in his letters. In doing so, this article will be able to make a modest contribution not only to the research into the relationship between the Paul of his letters and the Paul in Luke's Acts[4] but also to the assessment of "irrational" phenomena such as dreams and visions in the days of the Second Temple.[5]

Regarding the relationship between Pauline Letters and the Paul of Acts, in an influential article, Philipp Vielhauer argued in the early 1950s that the theology as embodied by the Paul of Acts is far removed from that

---

Ausprägungen—Wirkungen—Wertungen, ed. Florian Wilk and Markus Öhler, FRLANT 268 (Göttingen: Vandenhoeck & Ruprecht, 2017), 249–74, esp. 249–51, 256, and the conclusion.

[3] For the fact that there are no dreams in Luke's Gospel, see Bart J. Koet, "Why does not Jesus dream? Divine Communication in Luke-Acts," in: idem, *Dreams and Scripture in Luke-Acts. Collected Essays* (CBET 43; Leuven: Peeters, 2006), 11–24.

[4] For a short summary of the problems regarding the relationship between the Paul of his epistles and the Paul according to Luke's Acts, see Bart J. Koet, "Paul, a Light for the Gentiles?," 249–51. Cf. Daniel Marguerat, "Paul after Paul: A (Hi)story of Reception," in: idem, *Paul in Acts and Paul in his Letters,* WUNT 310 (Tübingen: Mohr Siebeck, 2013), 1–21. See also idem "The image of Paul in Acts," in: idem, *Paul,* 22–47. See Marguerat, ("The image of Paul in Acts," 27–32) for a description of his model of Pauline reception. For him a question is of what kind of information did Luke have at his disposal? He argues that Luke works with the memory of Paul's life and teaching, such as it was preserved by his circle. Research focusing on Christian apocryphal literature lead to the realization that—outside and alongside the tradition fixed in the canonical texts—a number of both oral and partially written traditions existed. He qualifies these traditions as the reception of Paul and the Acts of the Apostles is only *one* of these traditions. See the survey of research in the dissertation of his pupil Odile Flichy, *La figure de Paul dans les Actes des Apôtres: un phénomène de réception de la tradition paulinienne à la fin du premier siècle* (Paris: Cerf, 2007), 15–34.

[5] For a summary of Biblical views on dreams and visions, see Bart J. Koet, "Divine Dream Dilemma's: Biblical Visions and Dreams," in *Dreaming in Christianity and Islam: Culture, Conflict and Creativity,* ed. Kelly Bulkeley, Kate Adams and Patricia M. Davis (New Brunswick, NJ–London: Rutgers University 2009), 17–31.

of Paul of his letters.[6] His thesis, however, was mainly based on a comparison of Paul's speeches only with quite specific theological themes in Paul's epistles (natural theology, Law, Christology and eschatology).[7]

Therefore, there is need for a new assessment of the question of the relationship between the two "Pauls." In the above-mentioned article about the relationship between the interpretation of Scripture by the Paul of Galatians and that of the Paul of Acts, I assessed whether the focus on interpretation of Scripture could shine new light on the perennial question about the relationship between the different "Pauls" in the canonical traditions.[8] Consequently, I argued that when one looks at Paul's interpretation of Scripture instead of looking at Paul's *theologia crucis*, there is more continuity between the Paul of Galatians 1 and the Paul in Acts. This continuity is evident in that what is implicit in Galatians is made explicit in Acts: the implicit reference to Isa 49:6 in Galatians becomes an explicit quotation in Acts 13:46–47.[9] Richard Hays also explores this continuity by looking at the use of Scriptural quotations both in Paul's letters and in Luke-Acts, which would serve to correct Vielhauer's overly bold thesis of the discontinuity between the two Pauls.[10] Hays looks at the OT passages in Acts and assesses whether there are connections with OT references in Paul's letters. He suggests that there are fewer differences between the Paul of Acts and the Paul of his letters than Vielhauer thought. He even argues that some of the most "Pauline theological" elements (*his typification!*) appear in that part of Acts where Peter is the protagonist. Thus, Peter can be an interpreter of those ideas that can be typified as Pauline.[11]

---

[6] Philipp Vielhauer. "Zum 'Paulinismus' der Apostelgeschichte," *EvTh* 10 (1950–51): 1–15; English translation: idem, "On the Paulinism of Acts," in *Studies in Luke-Acts. Essays Presented in Honor of Paul Schubert*, ed. Leander E. Keck and J. Louis Martyn (Nashville: Abingdon Press 1966), 33–50. See Odile Flichy and James D. Ernest, "The Paul of Luke: a survey of research," in *Paul and the Heritage of Israel: Paul's claim upon Israel's legacy in Luke and Acts in the light of the Pauline letters*, ed. David P. Moessner et al., LNTS 452, Luke the Interpreter of Israel 2, (London-New York: T & T Clark, 2012), 18–34.

[7] Vielhauer, "On the Paulinism of Acts," 34.

[8] See Koet, "Paul, a Light for the Gentiles?," 251.

[9] Koet, "Paul, a Light for the Gentiles?," 256–60 and 271–73.

[10] Koet, "The Paulinism of Acts. Intertextually reconsidered," in: Moessner, *Paul*, 35–48.

[11] Koet, "Paulinism," 37–38.

Like Hays, I think it is worthwhile to compare the interpretation of Scripture in Acts with that of Paul to reveal the continuity between them.[12] However, while Hays fleetingly discusses quite a few passages from Acts, in this article I will focus on the use of a Joel-text in Paul's letters and in Acts: What, then, are the similarities and differences between the use of Joel 3:5 in Rom 10:13 (and 1 Cor 1:1-10) and the use of Joel 3:1-5 in Acts 2:17-21?[13] When it comes to the Paul of the letters it is always questionable how far his ideas can be found in the image of Paul in Acts. In this article we will try to assess how much of Paul can be found in the image of Peter in Acts by comparing Paul's allusion to Joel 3:1-5 with the quotation by Peter of that passage in Acts 2:17-21. Because dreams and visions are mentioned in that longer quotation, the role of dreams and visions in the sequel of Acts will also be examined.

My starting point will be the Pauline texts where Paul alludes Joel 3:5.[14] I will then look at how Luke attributes Joel 3:1-5 to Peter. Subsequently, I will assess points of correspondence and points of difference between the interpretation of Joel by Paul in the Pauline texts and by Luke in Acts. However, because 3:1-5 is the text that plays a key role in the texts to be discussed, I will briefly discuss the book of Joel and the place of 3:1-5 within that book.

Joel 3:1-5 in its (Prophetic) Context

Joel is one of the Minor Prophets, since Sir 49:10 also referred to as "the Twelve." They are not necessarily twelve separate booklets, but they fit together in a certain way.[15] For example, locusts appear not only in the

---

[12] Koet, "Paulinism," 38.

[13] Chronologically and methodologically, I think this is the right way. It is surprising that in his thorough book, John Strazicich (*Joel's Use of Scripture and the Scripture's Use of Joel. Appropriation and Resignification in Second Temple Judaism and Early Christianity*, BibInt 82 [Leiden: Brill. 2007]), first discusses Acts 2 and only then the other references to the New Testament.

[14] In several translations Joel 3:1-5 is 2:28-32. I follow the versification of the Masoretic Text and the LXX.

[15] For connections between these prophets, see James D. Nogalski, *The Book of the Twelve and Beyond: Collected Essays*, (Atlanta: SBL 2017); Elena Di Pede and Donatella Scaiola, eds., *The Book of the Twelve—one book or many? Metz conference proceedings, 5-7 November 2015*,

first two chapters of Joel (1:4 and 2:25), but also in Amos, the book that follows Joel in the Hebrew Bible (4:9). Similarly, the Day of YHWH is a theme in Joel (1:15; 2:1.11; 3:4; 4:14) as well as in some other Minor Prophets (for example in Amos 5:18 [2x].20; Obad 15; Zeph 1:7.14–15[2x]; Zech 14:1; Mal 3:23, but see Isa 2:12; 13:6.9; and Ezek 13:5; 30:3 and 34:12).[16]

The book of Joel is usually divided into two parts, but there is much discussion about this division.[17] I am using the division of Thomas Lyons here.[18] After assessing various positions in the literature on the structure of Joel, Lyons argues for a two-part division 1:2–2:17 and 2:18–4:21. An important argument for him is that the primary governing semantic structure for Joel is positive cruciality.[19] Lyons defines cruciality as involving a "change of direction" centered on a pivot where elements on one side of the pivot differ from elements on the other side. He argues that one can see "the negative direction of Joel's lament in 1:2–2:17 followed by the pivot point at 2:18–19a and the ensuing positive expansion and redefinition of the Day of the Lord throughout 2:19b-4:21."[20] For us, his structure of the second part is relevant. Lyons argues that 2:18–19a serves

---

FzAT 91 (Tübingen: Mohr Siebeck, 2016); Rainer Albertz *et al.* (eds.), *Perspectives on the Formation of the Book of the Twelve: Methodological Foundations—Redactional Processes—Historical Insights*, BZAW 433 (Berlin: De Gruyter, 2012); Ray Clendenen, "Textlinguistics and Prophecy in the Book of the Twelve," *JETS* 46 (2003): 385–99. For the relationship between the Twelve Prophets (as a unity) and the New Testament, especially Acts, see Aaron W. White, *The Prophets Agree. The Function of the Book of Twelve Prophets in Acts*; BibInt 184 (Leiden/Boston: Brill 2020), 1–53; Lena-Sofia Tiemeyer and Jakob Wöhrle (eds.), *The Book of the Twelve: Composition, Reception, and Interpretation*, VTSup 184 (Leiden/Boston: Brill, 2020).

[16] The phrases "that day", "the day" or "the great day" can also refer to a / the Day of the Lord.
[17] Strazicich (*Joel's Use of Scripture*) divides the first part in two: 1:2–20 (communal calls for lamentation and individual lamentation) and 2:1-17 (imminent military threat and a call to repentance). For an assessment of different structures, see Thomas Lyons, "Interpretation and Structure in Joel," *The Journal of Inductive Biblical Studies* 1 (2014): 80–104.
[18] Lyons, "Interpretation and Structure in Joel." Joel Barker (*From the Depths of Despair to the Promise of Presence: A Rhetorical Reading of the Book of Joel*, Siphrut 11 Literature and Theology of the Hebrew Scriptures [Winona Lake: Eisenbrauns, 2014]) seems to follow this division and sees 2:18 as the beginning of the change for the better.
[19] Barker (*From the Depths of Despair*, 167–97) typifies 2:18–37 as "Reversing the Crisis" (167–97).
[20] Lyons, "Interpretation," 100.

as a narrative interlude to the material that follows as it introduces the second part of Joel (2:20–4:17). This part consists of three segments (2:19b–27; 3:1–5 and 4:1–17) and each of which somehow has a positive message for those in Judah who remained faithful to YHWH. Lyons argues that it is "the lament of Joel in 1:2–2:17 and the corresponding suffering of both the people and the land that evokes YHWH's zeal and pity in 2:18–19a and the ensuing mercy of 19b–27."[21] In 2:19b–27, the prophet announces that YHWH will restore the land and this restoration will compensate for what has been eaten by the locusts (2:25). After this positive change for the people and the land, the second segment (3:1–5) deals with deliverance for those who will call (ἐπικαλέσηται; 3:5) on the name of YHWH.[22] The third and longest segment (4:1–17) describes God's judgment of the other nations for what they did to Judah. Tyre, Sidon, and the land of the Philistines will get their deserved punishment (3:4).[23]

Therefore, when we take a closer look at how 3:1–5 fits into the whole text of Joel, we see that this passage contains a positive message for Judah and Jerusalem, which is at the same time a negative one for the nations. Between 3:1a and 3:5 Joel describes how God will inspire his people (3:1b-2) and how he will give signs in the heavens and on earth before the Day of the Lord comes (3:3–4). Where in 2:17–27 God promises material restoration, 3:1–2 is about a kind of spiritual awakening by the promise of the outpouring of the Spirit of God on all flesh:

3:1a The bestowal of God's Spirit "upon all flesh";

b   Sons and daughters will prophecy (προφητεύσουσιν);

c   The old will dream dreams (ἐνύπνια ἐνυπνιασθήσονται);[24]

d   The young will have visions (ὁράσεις ὄψονται);

3:2   The bestowal of God's spirit on "servants and handmaids."[25]

---

[21] Lyons, "Interpretation," 101.

[22] For the unity of Joel 3:1–5, see for example David C. Hymes, "Notes on Joel 3:1–5," AJPS 1/1 (1998): 83–103.

[23] Lyons, "Interpretation," 100; he sees 4:18–21 as a separate subunit that describes the result of the Day of the Lord.

[24] Most translations here translate with masculine words. That's not necessary. Given the fact that in the direct context we are talking about men and women, it is more obvious that old men and women and young men and young women are meant here too!

210

The outpouring of the Spirit and the activities of those who receive the Spirit are an indication that the people involved are God's agents. In 3:1a God's gift to his agents is described in general, while in 3:1b-2 the specific categories in the imagery are so complementary that they can be seen as depicting the outpouring on all flesh.

The first line of 3:1 describes how "all flesh" will receive God's Spirit. In the following, the recipients of that Spirit are described in an artfully constructed *parallelismus membrorum:* In 3:1b a first category is mentioned "your sons and daughters (thus m/f)" will communicate as prophets (προφητεύσουσιν) and thus the "future" generations will proclaim God's words. The following lines are a variation on this message: your old people will dream and the young ones will have visions. As mentioned in Num 12:6-8, God speaks to his prophets through dreams and visions and thus people who receive these complementary categories are depicted as agents of God.[26] Is the outpouring of the mind on handmaids and servants a new category in which social status is at stake or are God's agents always his servants (cf. Moses in Num 12; probably 'assistant' would be a translation more adapted to the 21st century)?[27] However, for the interpretation of this verse, when used in a NT context the important implied follow-up question is to whom or about whom Joel speaks here and in 3:5.

---

[25] "Servants and handmaids" as in the King James Version. Translations show quite a few differences when they translate the Hebrew words, but I can't go into this here. However, it is too easy to translate these words here with "slave (m/f)." For this problem see Bart J. Koet and Bert Jan Lietaert Peerbolte, "The Annunciation Narrative (Luke 1:27-38). Read in Times of #MeToo," in *BN* 192 (2021): 91-103.

[26] Num 12:6-8 is an important source for the relationship between prophecy and dreams and visions and the interchangeability of dreams and visions in biblical traditions. Also Barker (*From the Depths of Despair*, 205) refers to Num 12:6-8 as a text which establishes the validity of dreams and visions as tools for divine revelation. Cf. Koet, "Why does Jesus not dream?," 12; and idem, "Trustworthy Dreams? About Dreams and References to Scripture in 2 Maccabees 14-15, Josephus' *Antiquitates Judaicae* 11.302-347 and in the New Testament," in *Dreams and Scripture in Luke-Acts,* 25-50, 26 and the literature mentioned there.

[27] See footnote 25 above.

In Joel 3:3-4, the immediately following verses, cosmological signs as an indication of the day of the Lord are described.[28] Like in 2:19-27, in 3:1-4 YHWH is the principal actor.[29] However, in 3:5 there is a change of the perspective, when Joel explains who will benefit from God's faithfulness and who will be saved: "all, those who call upon the Name of the Lord."

Here, the question is: How inclusive is "all"?[30] The answer has to be deduced from the context of this verse. The positive message of 3:1-5 consists of at least three elements. Firstly, Joel 3:1-2 proclaims that God's people will become a prophetic people: thus they benefit from God's actions.[31] Secondly, all the signs in heaven and on earth are a clear threat to the nations that are the enemies of Israel. It is not for nothing that the signs of Joel are connected with the signs of the exodus from Egypt in the later Passover haggadah. Thus, it is again God's prophetic people who will benefit from God's actions. Thirdly, the assertion that anyone who invokes the name of the Lord will be saved applies (especially?) to those who are on Mount Zion and in Jerusalem (3:5). This supplies the answer to the question concerning to whom or about whom does Joel refer: to Jewish

---

[28] We have to note that in text of Joel there are reminiscents of earlier biblical traditions. Although Joel quotes only one earlier source (Obad 17 in 3:5) there are quite a few biblical motifs and allusions. Strazicich (*Joel's Use of Scripture*, 15) stresses that Joel is not so much a scripture interpreter but that he is more an appropriator and a resignifier of Israel's scribal traditions. This subtle distinction shows that dealing with older wisdom is not an unambiguous activity and has many facets. Because the activity of interpreting does not explicitly exclude updating, adapting and giving new meaning, we will continue to use the word "to interpret" in this article.

[29] And he is also a mighty one: YHWH will roar out at Zion and utter his voice from Jerusalem (3:16; see 3:5).

[30] For this, see already Paul-Émile Langevin, "Ceux qui invoquent le nom du Seigneur (1 Co 1,2)," *ScEs* 21 (1969): 71-122, 118: "Quelle ampleur donnait-il au mot 'tous'?" Langevin concludes that it must be God's people Israel, and then he observes (118): "Il serait donc difficile, en l'occurence, de prêter à Joël un universalisme du salut qui embrasserait tous les hommes." White (*The Prophets Agree*, 57.61-63) refers to some scholars who argue that Joel 3:1-5 contains some of the most universalistic themes "unparalleled in the Old Testament." While there is quite a stress on the fact that God will save his people, I agree with Langevin that it will be difficult to argue that Joel proclaims universal salvation. However, it will be not impossible for Paul, as we will see below!

[31] Langevin, "Ceux qui invoquent le nom du Seigneur," 118, argues that this is in line with the fact that in Num 11:29 Moses says, that he wishes all the Lord's people were prophets and that the Lord would put his Spirit on them!

212

sons and daughters, old and young people and all God's assistants. Therefore, 3:1-5 is mainly about salvation for Judah and Jerusalem and punishment and darkness for those peoples who oppressed Judah and Jerusalem. It is about the restoration of Judah and Jerusalem and this is confirmed in Joel 4, where the punishment for the nations that oppressed Israel is further elaborated.

Given that later in this article the focus will be on the use of Joel 3:1-5 in the NT, it is necessary to note here that the positive message includes a mutuality between God and all who call on his Name. This is signaled by the fact that the statement "Whosoever shall call on (ἐπικαλέσηται) the name of the Lord shall be saved" (3:5) can be linked by the use of the root καλέω to the phrase "those who are called (προσκέκληται) by the Lord" (3:5).

Paul's Use of Joel 3:5 in Romans 10:13

A discussion on the relationship of Israel to the peoples can also be found in Rom 9-11, but in a quite different perspective. This passage is one of the most discussed passages of Paul's letters. In Rom 1:16 Paul argues that the gospel is a power of God for salvation for everybody who believes/trusts: to the Jew first, and to the Greek! Rom 9-11 then takes that theme further, but the question is more specific: How to deal with those from Israel who are not Israel (9:6)? Rom 9:7-11:36 seems to deal with that question. This is not the place to discuss Paul's extensive argumentation. However, there are at least two things that are important to note. It is sufficient to mention that Rom 9-11 is rightly often seen as Paul's struggle to determine the place of his Jewish relatives (9:3), the Israelites (9:4), Abraham's seed (9:7) in the love of God, which is in Christ (Messiah) Jesus, our Lord (8:39). In 11:1 he makes it clear that God has not disowned his people, and in the following verses Paul presents the image of the olive tree and argues that in the end all Israel will be saved. In addition, it is important to note that Paul sets out the positive arguments regarding Israel using a whole series of references to scriptures. Nowhere in Paul can we find as many quotes from the scriptures as in this passage.[32] Even though the main focus of this passage is on the position of Israel and their childhood (9:4.9.27) and their relationship to the Law (9:31; 10:3–5), there is also the other side of that coin, namely the position of the Gentiles and it is on this element that I want to focus here. With Hosea (2:25 and 2:1), Paul shows that Gentiles can become the people of God (9:25–26). Precisely to elaborate on that aspect Paul uses a phrase from Joel 3:5 in chapter 10. In 10:9 Paul argues that if you shall confess with your mouth the Lord Jesus and if you believe/trust in your heart that God raised him from the dead, you will be saved. In 10:11 Paul adds a reference to Isaiah (28:16) as proof who believes/trusts in him.[33] In 10:12 Paul even says that there is no difference between Jew and Greek when they call upon Him.[34]

In 10:13, Paul is quoting a phrase from Joel 3:5 to support his statement in 10:12 that the offer of salvation is for both Jew and Gentile: "And it will come about that whoever calls on the name of the Lord will be saved." Paul's quote is just like the Septuagint translation of Joel 3:5.[35] However, there is a shift in meaning.[36] Long ago, Langevin remarked that the

---

[32] Dieter-Alexander Koch, *Die Schrift als Zeuge des Evangeliums: Untersuchungen zur Verwendung und zum Verständnis der Schrift bei Paulus*, BHT 69 (Tübingen: Mohr Siebeck, 1986); see also Folker Siegert, *Argumentation bei Paulus, gezeigt an Röm 9–11*, WUNT 34 (Tübingen: Mohr Siebeck, 1985).

[33] For Paul's text and the LXX, see Koch, *Schrift als Zeuge*, 115.

[34] Here he uses again the word "Greek" (Ἕλληνος), like in Rom 1:16

[35] Gert J. Steyn ("Observations on the Text Form of the Minor Prophets Quotations in Romans 9–11," *JSNT* 38 [2015]: 49–67, esp. 59–61) argues that Rom 10:13 contains here an identical reading to that of Joel 3:5 (LXX). Only γάρ has to be an extra word, which Paul uses to indicate that it is a reference to Scripture.

[36] Paul's free way of dealing with scripture is something that can also be found in Qumran and among the rabbis. Bruce Chilton and Jacob Neusner, *Judaism in the New Testament: Practices and Beliefs* (London-New York: Routledge, 1995), 62–71 extensively discuss Rom 9–11. Even though they object to the fact that some scholars characterize Paul's use of scripture here as a *midrash*, they do display that both Paul and the rabbis synthesize Scripture with their own sensibilities and their grasp of what Scripture as a whole means. There are more exegetical strategies to be found in this piece that can be compared to later rabbinic interpretation rules. For example, in Romans the quotations are partly linked by a technique that resembles the later *Gezerah shawah* rule; see for example Theo de Kruijf, "The Perspective of Romans 10," *Bijdr* 62 (2001): 170–89, footnote 38. In this context we cannot elaborate further.

214

Bart J. Koet

universal meaning as applied here by Paul is not Joel's primary meaning.[37] Although the sentence "anyone who invokes the name of the Lord will be saved" sounds universalistic, in Joel it was most probably about all Israel (men and women, young and old, etc.). So Paul seems to have radically reversed this meaning here.[38] Paul adds to this a change in accent, quite different from Joel. He does not hesitate to apply a text about calling upon YHWH to a new context: confessing that Jesus is Lord (10:9).

1 Corinthians 1:1–10

Simarly, at the beginning of 1 Corinthians, Paul seems to refer to the Joel-text about the idea that anyone who invokes the name of the Lord can be saved with reference to that such a person can be part of the ecclesia. The introduction to 1 Corinthians can be typified as a *paronomosia*, a word game with καλέω and its cognates (see the different variants with καλ- in 1:1–10).[39] By typifying himself in the second word of the heading as "called" (κλητὸς) Paul introduces "calling" as a theme of the letter's introduction. In 1 Cor 1:2c-d there are two explicit references to "calling": "the ones *called* saints, with all those who (in every place) *call upon* the name of Jesus Christ our Lord"[40]. A first point of comparison between Joel 3:5 and 1 Cor 1:2 is that the phrase "calling on the name of the Lord" is combined with (a form of) καλέω.

---

[37] See footnote 30 above.

[38] Mark Reasoner, "The Redemptive Inversion of Jeremiah in Romans," *Bib* 95 (2014): 388–404, shows that Paul uses a comparable strategy with the quotation from Jeremiah. He presents seven points of focused dissonance between Jeremiah and Romans and argues that Paul in Romans 9–11 inverts the judgment language of Jeremiah 1–20 against Judah. These inversions of Jeremiah highlight these chapters' positive stance toward corporeal, ethnic Israel.

[39] Bart J. Koet, "Conflict management in Corinth. A Comparison between the openings of 1 and 2 Corinthians," *Bib* 99 (2018): 75–92, esp. 81–2; cf. idem, "Ethics or Halacha? 'Calling' as a key to the Dynamics of Behaviour according to Paul in 1 Cor 1:1–11," in *Biblical Ethics and Application Purview, Validity, and Relevance of Biblical Texts in Ethical Discourse*, ed. Ruben Zimmermann and Stephan Joubert, Contexts and Norms of New Testament Ethics IX (Tübingen: Mohr Siebeck, 2017), 243–57; esp. 250–55.257.

[40] Anthony C. Thiselton (*The First Epistle to the Corinthians*, NIGTC [Grand Rapids, Mich.: Eerdmans, 2013], 56.64) rightly argues that Paul is being called to be an apostle provides a parallel with the adressees' being called to be a holy people.

215

A second comparable element is that in 1 Cor 1:1–10 there is, as in the Joel-text, a mutuality, where in 3:5 the statement "Whosoever shall call on the name of the Lord shall be delivered" (καὶ ἔσται πᾶς ὃς ἂν ἐπικαλέσηται τὸ ὄνομα κυρίου σωθήσεται) rhymes with "those who are called by the Lord" (οὓς κύριος προσκέκληται). In 1 Cor 1:1–12 God's calling (1:2.9) is answered by all those who call upon the name of our Lord Jesus Christ (1:2) and this leads to the fact that Paul can call the Corinthians to unity. Thus, there is, as in Joel 3:1–5 a connection between God's saving actions and human behaviour.[41] Thiselton argues that the reference to the day of the Lord (1 Cor 1:7–8) makes the allusion to Joel all the more probable.[42]

Although there are thus quite a few reminiscences of Joel and especially of Joel 3:5 in the beginning of 1 Corinthians, Paul, like in Rom 10:13, adds quite another accent by not hesitating to apply a text about calling upon YHWH to a new context: calling upon the name of our Lord Jesus, the Christ. In this way Jesus is inscribed into the Divine Name.

Paul's references to Joel 3:5 indicates that a new era has dawned with Jesus's death and resurrection. When Paul alludes to Joel in 1 Cor 1:1–10, especially in 1:2, he implies that everybody, Jew and non-Jew, can participate in such an act of being called. Although quite clearly not a quotation, but rather a short allusion, this is a reference to a biblical concept, the inclusion of the non-Jews into God's people, a concept that one can find for example in Isa 49:1–6.[43] According to Paul, Joel can be a testimony that for everybody one of the first steps can be to call on the name of the Lord. Although less explicit and radical than in Rom 10:13, in 1 Cor 1:2d Paul seems to adapt the original meaning of the Joel-text: it is not only Judah who is saved, but everybody, Jew and non-Jew alike by implication who can be saved in messiah Jesus.

---

[41] For Paul's use in 1 Cor 1:1–10 of several forms of the root καλέω to introduce the dynamics between him, the ecclesia in Corinth and God, see the conclusion of Koet, "Ethics or Halacha?," 256–57 and esp. the scheme on 257.

[42] Thiselton (*First Corinthians*, 78) notes that ἐκκλησία is also mentioned in Joel 2:16.

[43] In Gal 1:15–16 Paul refers to Isa 49:1–6 to show that within God's covenant with Israel there exists room for non-Jews to share in his promises; see Koet, "Paul, a Light for the Gentiles?"

In Rom 10 and 1 Cor 1:1-10 the reference to Joel is clearly used to legitimize the turn towards the non-Jews: "whosoever calls upon the Name of the Lord shall be saved."

In the next paragraph we will investigate how Luke uses the Joel-text.

The Function of Joel 3:1-5 in Acts 2:1-41

We saw above that Paul explicitly quotes Joel 3:5 in Rom 10:13 to legitimize the turn to the Gentiles with a scriptural text. The only other time that this text occurs elsewhere in the NT is in Peter's speech in Acts 2:17-21, albeit in an explicit and longer quotation. In Acts 1 we are told how Jesus is received into heaven (1:4-11) and how Matthias takes the place of Judas among the Twelve (1:15-26). On the Jewish feast of the fiftieth day, when all come together in unison (ἐπὶ τὸ αὐτό), a wind comes from heaven and all are filled with the Holy Spirit and all begin to speak prophetically (2:1-4). There is no further mention of a location in these verses after the apostles returned in the upper room (1:13). When Peter speaks for the first time to discuss the replacement of Judas (1:16-22), the suggestion is that a group of one hundred and twenty people meet in that hall (1:15). In chapter 2 there is no specific reference to the place where "all" are filled with the Holy Spirit (could "all the house" refer back to the place where the upper room is?).[44] However, a consequence of prophetic speaking (2:4) is that the spatial perspective broadens. Thus, it is told how the *whole* of Jerusalem is filled with Jews from "every nation under heaven" (for a list of several nations, see 2:9-11). All (again unspecified) are amazed and marvelled (2:7) and several questions arise (2:7b and 2:8), because the audience hears them speak in different tongues (2:11). That leads to a question ("What does this mean?" [2:12]) and a kind of blaming explanation ("These men are full of new/sweet wine." [2:13]).[45] The answer to that question and explanation is given by Peter who raises his voice and then delivers his second speech in Acts (2:14-36). As argued by Gert Steyn, among others, this speech is presented by Luke as direct

---

[44] I cannot discuss here why I think that the translation "in one place" for ἐπὶ τὸ αὐτό is not correct.

[45] For γλεῦκος, see *LSJ* 351.

speech.[46] Steyn shows how at the beginning of this second speech the same elements are found as at the beginning of the first: Peter arises (Καὶ ἐν ταῖς ἡμέραις ταύταις ἀναστὰς Πέτρος [1:15] and Σταθεὶς δὲ ὁ Πέτρος [2:14]), as an introduction of the direct speech and a comparable address.[47]

It is possible to divide up the speech by looking at the several address-es it includes (2:14.22.29.36). Peter refutes the accusation of drunkenness by arguing that another and special state of the human mind is at stake. It is a very specific human condition, once mentioned by the prophet Joel: the divine inspiration of prophecy. Peter's quotation is not just a phrase, but a rather long passage: an extensive quotation consisting almost entirely of Joel 3:1-5. As we now turn to assess the similarities and differences in the use of Joel 3:5 between Paul (and especially Rom 10:13) and the use of Joel 3:1-5 in Acts 2:17-21 we will focus on three themes:

1) As elsewhere in his work, Luke makes the quotation more explicit; in this case he quotes a longer piece and he mentions the source.
2) Related to this is the fact that while Paul's use of the Joel-text actually gives a meaning opposite to the text of the prophet himself, Luke here remains closer to the original intention of the text in terms of the message, namely that it is the Jews who invoke the name of the Lord and that they are then saved.
3) Ultimately, Luke uses data from the Joel-text in Acts to support the turn to the non-Jews; there is a special role for dreams and visions: they legitimize that new path as divine relevations.

1) The Quotation of Joel in Acts 2:17-21
In Romans Paul quotes Joel 3:5. Luke's quote in Acts 2:17-21 is longer and he explicitly mentions Joel as the source of this quotation. This fits the way Luke sometimes deals with quotations: where he has a quotation that also appears in an earlier source in the NT, Luke's text is sometimes longer and more explicitly marked as a quotation than in that source. For example, his

---

[46] Gert J. Steyn, *Septuagint Quotations in the context of the Petrine and Pauline Speeches of the Acta Apostolorum*, CBET 12 (Kampen: Kok, 1995), 68.
[47] Steyn, *Septuagint Quotations*, 68.

Bart J. Koet

quotation from Isa 40:3 (3:4–6) is two verses longer than in the composite quote in Mark 1:3. Moreover, in Luke's there is no reference to Malachi (cf. Matt 3:3), which makes the quotation more formal than in Mark. In Luke 8:10 we find that Luke shortens the allusion to Isa 6:9 in Mark 4:12, in particular by omitting the phrase μήποτε ἐπιστρέψωσιν καὶ ἀφεθῇ αὐτοῖς. However, in Acts 28:26–27 Luke uses the same text and there he is more explicit: he mentions Isaiah as the source and thus makes it a formal quotation and, again, he quotes a larger part of the text.[48] Given that in Acts 2 the reference to the prophetic text is longer and the prophet is mentioned by name, which makes the quotation more formal, the question that arises is whether such a quotation does more justice to the original text than to the reference in Paul. Before answering this question, we shall take a brief look at the text form of the quotation.

There are some differences between the Greek text, as received in the LXX for example and the Joel-quote in the Acts text.[49] Steyn has mapped the main differences in the text form of Joel 3:1–5 between the text of Acts 2:17–21 (NA[26]=the same as NA[28]), the current LXX, codex W and the MT.[50] Steyn mentions eight additions in Acts to the Joel-text, of which the following two are the most important.

First: the addition "so speaks God (λέγει ὁ θεός)." This addition is actually not an addition to the quotation itself but an introductory formula that makes the connection between the quoted text and its context. This makes

---

[48] In Bart J. Koet, "Luke and His Sources: Making Implicit Scriptural Allusions Explicit in Luke 3,4–6; 4,18–19 and Acts 28,26–27" (forthcoming), I will examine those quotations.
[49] It is well known that one can hardly speak of one LXX-text. In the first century CE there were recensions of the LXX. Often these recensions agree better with the Hebrew text which is common nowadays. See only Maarten J.J. Menken, *Matthew's Bible. The Old Testament Text of the Evangelist*, BETL 173 (Leuven: Peeters) 7–8. Several scholars have dealt with the question of which text Luke used for his quotations. See the history of research in: Steyn, *Septuagint Quotations*, 6–8. It is clear, that when investigating textual similarities between Luke's quotations and either the Greek or the Hebrew OT text, we observe that Luke normally quotes a text in its Greek form more or less according to what we have nowadays as the LXX; see Steyn, *Septuagint Quotations*, 232.
[50] For these differences, see Steyn, *Septuagint Quotations,* 74–90: Textual differences between MT and LXX (77); Textual differences between Acts and LXX (77–78); Additions (78–86); Substitution (86–88); Transposition (88), Case change (89).

it clear that God Himself speaks through the quoted prophetic text and the text to be quoted is formally introduced as a quotation.[51]

Second: in Acts 2:18 we find an addition to the Joel-text: καὶ προφητεύσουσιν.[52] In Acts 2:17 (which is largely the same as Joel 3:1[2:28]) it has already been said that God will pour out His Spirit on all flesh, immediately after that it is said that all sons and daughters will prophesy. Through the addition in Acts 2:18, the parallel that already exists between Joel 3:1 (in Acts 2:17) and Joel 3:2 (cf. Acts 2:18) becomes even clearer: sons and daughters will prophesy, but old and young, and all who are God's assistants (δοῦλος or δούλη), will prophesy. Joel's text shows that God's faithful become divine agents and thus can prophesy.

2) Salvation for the Jews

Luke has Peter proclaim that in the last days that dream of Joel will come true![53] The function of this quotation in Acts 2:17–18 can be interpreted in different ways.[54] The focus of this article is on who are the addressees of this quote and who is going to do what is promised here. There are a number of elements in Luke's reference to Joel that are closer to Joel's original text than in Paul's references. We saw above that according to Joel this breakthrough of prophecy will take place on Mount Zion and in Jerusalem. So it is in the spirit of Joel 3:1–5 that in Acts the outpouring of the Spirit happens in Jerusalem. The reference to a prophetic text gives a biblical legitimation to the fact that all were filled with the Holy Spirit

---

[51] Martin Rese, *Alttestamentliche Motive in der Christologie des Lukas*, SNT 1 (Gütersloh: Gütersloher Verlagshaus Gerd Mohn, 1969), 48–49. See Dietrich Rusam, *Das Alte Testament bei Lukas*, BZNW 112 (Berlin-New York: De Gruyter, 2003), 287–335, 291.

[52] Steyn (*Septuagint Quotations*, 82) mentions that this phrase is absent in quite a few manuscripts, but that witnesses supporting this insertion outweigh those who do not have it.

[53] The change from μετὰ ταῦτα to ἐν ταῖς ἐσχάταις ἡμέραις is important, see Steyn, *Septuagint Quotations*, 86–88. Steyn argues that ἐν ταῖς ἐσχάταις ἡμέραις could be reminiscent of Joel 1:2 (ἐν ταῖς ἡμέραις ὑμῶν ἢ ἐν ταῖς ἡμέραις τῶν πατέρων ὑμῶν). He stresses that it is not so easy to pinpoint the origin of the expression ἐν ταῖς ἐσχάταις ἡμέραις, but it is clear that it is an indication of a new era. In this article I cannot discuss what this means for the eschatology of Luke. Ulrich Busse ("Eschatologie in der Apostelgeschichte," in *Eschatology of the New Testament and Some Related Documents*, ed. Jan G. van der Watt, WUNT 2/315 [Tübingen: Mohr Siebeck, 2011], 141–78, esp. 158–60) argues that Luke plays down the urgency of the present eschatology.

[54] See White, *The Prophets Agree*, 57.61–63; see footnote 30 above.

(2:4), as promised by Jesus in Acts 1:8. It is that Spirit that will make possible what Simeon foretold in the beginning as the result of Jesus's life: the nations will share in the salvation brought about by Jesus. Still, this turn to the Gentiles is not so explicitly addressed in Acts 2—contrary to what is sometimes thought and certainly contrary to the way Paul uses Joel 3:5. After all, Peter's speech is addressed (only or mainly?) to the ἄνδρες Ἰουδαῖοι and οἱ κατοικοῦντες Ἰερουσαλὴμ πάντες, and in the foregoing, all kinds of countries and regions were mentioned where those Jews (mentioned in Acts 2:5) come from (2:9–11).

That Peter's speech seems to be mainly for Jews—although also with proselytes (cf. Ἰουδαῖοί τε καὶ προσήλυτοι in 2:10)—is corroborated by the last sentences of his speech (2:36):[55] "The *whole house of Israel* must know that (their) God made him (=Jesus) Lord and anointed." It seems that Luke does justice to the text of Joel by making the phrase "anyone who calls on the name of the Lord" in this passage mainly refer to a Jewish audience.[56] Thus, the use of this text by Luke seems to be different from that of Paul!

3) Salvation for the Non-Jews
Yet it is not the case that Luke completely ignores the possibilities offered by this text to make the turn to the non-Jews that Paul so emphatically propagated.[57] Peter quotes the passage that the young (m/f) will see dreams and the old (m/f) will have visions. It is this element of the Joel-text that will be fulfilled in the sequel of Acts and through which the turn to the Gentiles will be legitimized. The Joel-text shows in advance how in

---

[55] It is thus fitting that it is Peter as the apostle of the Jews is the one who quotes the Joel-text to a *Jewish* audience.

[56] Would Luke have known the rest of the Joel-text? A possible clue is the allusion to Joel 3:5 in Acts 2:39. Huub van de Sandt ("The Fate of the Gentiles in Joel and Acts 2: An Intertextual Study," *ETL* 66 [1990]: 56–77) argues that not only in Acts 2 Luke is in dialogue with Joel, but also in quite a few other places, like Acts 16,6–10 (59–60); 8:1–13 (60–61).

[57] Rese (*Alttestamentliche Motive*, 50) rightly notes that there is a certain tension between the omission of the phrase ὅτι ἐν τῷ ὄρει Σιων καὶ ἐν Ιερουσαλημ ἔσται ἀνασῳζόμενος and the fact that the speech is for Jews only.

Acts the disciples receive divine guidance through dreams and visions. Thanks to the Spirit of God they will have dreams and visions.[58]

Also, in view of the fact that, according to Num 12:6-8, dreams and visions are interchangeable, it follows that the statement of Joel on dreams and visions will be fulfilled in Acts. Quite a few visions/dreams are told in Acts (see 9:10-16; 10:3-7.11-16; 16:9; 18:9; 23:11; 27:23; cf. 7:55-56).[59] However, these manifestations show in one way or another that the turn to the non-Jews is legitimized by a divine communication.[60]

The visions of Peter and Cornelius pave the way for the turn to the non-Jews.[61] The visions of Paul legitimize a real proclamation among the non-Jews of Europe (cf. Acts 16) and especially in Corinth. (18:9).[62] However, it is not only protagonists like Peter and Paul who receive the gift of prophecy, the statement about the daughters who will prophesy (2:18)

---

[58] When his protagonist Paul in 16:6-10 enters the Hellenistic homeland, Luke mixes in his depiction some Greco-Roman elements with some Jewish ones, see Bart J. Koet, "Im Schatten des Aeneas: Paulus in Troas (Apg 16,8-10)," in: idem, *Dreams and Scripture*, 147-71.

[59] Acts 7:31 (τὸ ὅραμα in Stephen's speech, referring to Moses's vision in Exod 3); 9:10 (vision to Ananias); 9:11 (vision to Paul; 9:10 and 9:11 are a double vision); 10:3 (Cornelius); 10:17.19 and 11:5 (Peter); 16:9-10 (Paul) and 18:9 (Paul); see 12:9. We find the combination ἐνυπνίοις ἐνυπνιασθήσονται only in 2:17. The individual words cannot be found in the rest of the NT. For a list of "Dream and Vision Terminology" in Hebrew and Greek, see John R. L. Moxon, *Peter's Halakhic Nightmare: The "Animal" Vision of Acts 10:9-16 in Jewish and Graeco-Roman Perspective*, WUNT 2/432 (Tübingen: Mohr Siebeck, 2017), 351-61; for a list of divine message visitation forms (including dreams and visions), see 451-53.

[60] In this way Luke is in line with the dream conceptions of the OT and it shows that Oepke's views that dreams are no longer necessary since Jesus are false (*TWNT* 5:220-38, see 228-31). Perhaps his ideas are an example of the fact that sometimes in that dictionary there is a tendency to play off the Old Testament against the New. That propensity is linked to anti-Semitic tendencies.

[61] In this article I confine myself to the observation that the divine communications in these chapters pave the way for the turn to the non-Jews. For an assessment of the halachic issues involved in this story, see the in-depth discussions in Moxon, *Peter's Halakhic Nightmare*.

[62] For Acts 16:6-10, see Bart J. Koet, "Im Schatten des Aeneas," 46. For 18:9, see idem, "As Close to the Synagogue as Can Be; Paul in Corinth (Acts 18,1-18)," in *The Corinthian Correspondence*, ed. Reimund Bieringer, BETL 125 (Leuven: Peeters, 1996), 397-415, reprinted in: *Dreams and Scripture*, 173-93.

Bart J. Koet

will also be fulfilled. As mentioned in Acts 21:8-9: Philip's daughters possess the gift of prophecy.[63]

Perhaps the "slave-girl" in Acts 16:16 is another example of someone with a prophetic gift. References to concepts and words from Joel 3:1-5 that appear elsewhere in Acts, show how important the Joel-text is for the development of the mission among the non-Jews in this book.

For example, in Acts 10:45 and 16:10 we find concepts (e.g. "all who invoke the Name of the Lord") from that Joel-passage that express the universal dimension of the Jesus movement.[64]

Extensive references to Scripture are relatively rare in Luke-Acts and when they are included they have a special function: they underline an important element or announce a new phase.[65] The Joel-quotation in Acts 2 ultimately prepares for one of the more important themes of Acts: the turn to the non-Jews. [66]

Conclusions

The text in Joel 3 is about the salvation of the Jews from the oppression of the other nations. In 3:1-5 God promises that he will not only defeat enemies and materially restore Israel, but he will also shower them with spiritual gifts, specifically that they will receive His spirit and they will have contact with YHWH through dreams and visions. Joel 3:5 appears to have played an important role in the earliest tradition about Jesus.[67] Paul uses a phrase from that text to legitimize the turn to the Gentiles.

---

[63] Gerhard Dautzenberg (*Urchristliche Prophetie: Ihre Erforschung, ihre Voraussetzungen im Judentum und ihre Struktur im ersten Korintherbrief*, BWANT 104 [Stuttgart: Kohlhammer, 1975], 29) refers to the fact that often Acts 2:17-21 is seen as the fulfilment of the promise in Joel about the restoration of prophecy.

[64] Cfr. Strazich, *Joel's Use of Scripture*; Van de Sandt, ("The Fate of the Gentiles," 59-67), argues that there is a relationship between the use of the Joel-text and the proclamation of salvation to the Gentiles.

[65] See Koet, "Trustworthy Dreams?," 46.

[66] There is another way in which the fact that Luke quotes a larger part of Joel can resonate in the sequel of Acts. With the phrase καὶ δώσω τέρατα ἐν τῷ οὐρανῷ ἄνω καὶ σημεῖα ἐπὶ τῆς γῆς κάτω, Luke introduces the motif of signs and thus legitimizing the signs that the followers of Jesus in Acts will see as prophetic. In Acts, the apostles, Philip and Paul will do these signs. See Steyn, *Septuagint Quotations*, 85, and Busse, "Eschatologie," 158.

[67] The Joel-text plays an important role in early Christian literature, see for example Tertullian, *Marc*, 5,8, and *An* 47,2.

223

Where Paul interprets the Joel-text quite differently from what probably is the intent of the original text, Luke's use of the text is more fitting to the original use. He refers to Joel as the source by having Peter refer to Joel explicitly and even though he seems to make some changes in the Joel-text, his quotation is longer and therefore more in accordance with the source text.

We saw above that Joel has a positive message for Jews/Israelites who have remained faithful to God, so that Zion and Jerusalem will become places of salvation for them. When Peter quotes Joel 3:1–5a it is in Jerusalem, the place that plays a central role in the Joel-text. Since in Joel the salvation seems to be only for Judah, this concurs with the fact that Peter's audience is mainly typified as Jewish. This is more or less the opposite of Paul, who uses the text as the biblical basis for his acceptance of non-Jews.

It seems that Luke makes a less radical interpretation than Paul. Yet, as with Paul, Luke's use of the quotation is also ultimately related to the turn of the proclamation of the kingdom of God to non-Jews and Luke achieves this by using the Joel-text in a special way. Because Luke quotes Joel more extensively than Paul, he mentions that the new period involves God giving dreams and visions. It is those dreams and visions that will legitimize the turn to the Gentiles in the continuation of Acts. The Joel-text paves the way for dreams and visions that will legitimize in Acts 10, Acts 16 and Acts 18 the turn to the non-Jews. In this article we cannot elaborate on the question whether Luke was aware of the way Paul deals with the Joel-text.[68] What we can conclude here is that both in Pauline and Lukan circles the Joel-text has played an important role. Luke's uniqueness in handling that text is that he makes the reference to the text from the prophets more explicit and that he puts that quotation on the lips of Peter, thus making Peter "spokesman of Paul."

---

[68] I can't deal here with the question whether Luke speaks of memory or that he had a text in front of him. By the way, knowing a separation between texts from memory and having a written text is too modern a contradiction. Most likely the transitions between these two attitudes were much smoother in the period of the NT than in our time.

The ἔκστασις of Peter and Paul (Acts 10:9; 22:17) between Socio-Religious Innovation and Reintegration

Eva-Maria Kreitschmann

1 Introduction

Ecstatic experiences form part of nearly every religion or cult and seem to be a special means to transcend the human sphere and to come into contact with the divine. According to psychological definitions ecstasy can be described as "an experience of dissolution of ontological boundaries" of the self "leading to an intense affective experience of oneness or union"[1]. The sociological and anthropological perspectives on the phenomenon also point to this aspect of boundary transgression in ecstatic religious experiences but interpret it as a transgression of *social* boundaries. In states of trance, ecstatic hyperkinesia etc. everyday patterns of behavior are transcended, and accepted norms and values are challenged. For example, in the Reformation Era dreams and visions played an important role among some dissident religious groups, who also engaged in socially deviant practices such as shared property and bigamy.[2] In the first half of the twentieth century prophetic movements with ecstatic elements occurred among African indigenous tribes that propagated liberation from colonial powers, from suppression and economic distress.[3] These exam-

---

[1] See Jo Nash, "Ecstasy," *Encyclopedia of Psychology and Religion* (Boston, MA: Springer US, 2014), 572–74, see 572.

[2] See Dieter Fauth, "Träume bei religiösen Dissidenten in der frühen Reformation," in *Religiöse Devianz in christlich geprägten Gesellschaften: Vom hohen Mittelalter bis zur Frühaufklärung*, ed. Dieter Fauth und Daniela Müller (Würzburg: Religion und Kultur, 1999), 71–105, 83.

[3] See Vittorio Lanternari, *Religiöse Freiheits- und Heilsbewegungen unterdrückter Völker*, trans. Heinz Maus und Friedrich Fürstenberg (Berlin: Luchterhand, 1972), 29–110.

ples show that through ecstatic experiences alternative forms of reality can be imagined and former contexts of meaning can be destabilized and reconstructed anew. Thus, ecstasy as a deviant religious behavior can have a critical and creative potential.[4] It seems that this innovative character of ecstasy that leads to a new self-understanding and identity of the respective individual or group is particularly important in times of pressure and crisis,[5] as demonstrated by the aforementioned example of the African prophetic movements. We can observe the same in forms of ecstatic cults performed by indigenous North American tribes (ghost dance, Peyote-religion), practices that became important during their fight against European invaders[6], thus appearing as an expression of protest and resistance.[7] The definition of an ecstatic phenomenon as "abnormal" or deviant is of course dependent on the respective cultural frame of norms and values that mark the boundaries of the "normal."[8]

The texts of the New Testament provide evidence that there was a certain role in early Christian communities for ecstatic phenomena such as visions, raptures or speaking in tongues (Acts 2:1–4; 1 Cor 12–14; 2 Cor 12,2–4; Rev 1:10).[9] Against the background of the sociological insights outlined above, these ecstatic experiences can be explained in their function as transgressing the realm of the religious norm and allowing for alternative religious worldviews and ideas. This perspective on ecstasy is important when one takes into account that the texts of the New Testament in their original contexts constructed a sense of identity for their

---

[4] Gordon Blennemann, "Heiligkeit und Devianz in vormodernen Kontexten. Perspektiven einer möglichen Systematisierung," in *Sakralität and Devianz: Konstruktionen—Normen—Praxis*, ed. Klaus Herbers and Larissa Düchting, BzH 16 (Stuttgart: Steiner, 2015), 299–306, 303.

[5] Burkhard Gladigow, "Ekstase und Enthusiasmos. Zur Anthropologie und Soziologie ekstatischer Phänomene," in *Rausch—Ekstase—Mystik. Grenzformen religiöser Erfahrung*, ed. Hubert Cancik (Düsseldorf: Patmos, 1978), 23–40, see 40.

[6] See Lanternari, *Heilsbewegungen*, 111–84.

[7] See Gladigow, "Ekstase," 38.

[8] Blennemann, "Heiligkeit und Devianz," 302–03.

[9] See e.g., James B. Wallace, *Snatched into Paradise (2 Cor 12:1–10): Paul's Heavenly Journey in the Context of early Christian Experience*, BZNW 179 (Berlin: De Gruyter, 2011); Hans-Josef Klauck, "Von Kassandra bis zur Gnosis: im Umfeld der frühchristlichen Glossolalie," *ThQ* 179.4 (1999): 289–312.

intended audiences, as scholars today often emphasize.[10] Luke, who to our knowledge is the first author to write the history of the emerging Christian community, seems to be especially interested in ecstatic events such as dreams, visions and inspired prophetic speeches.[11] In the narrative world of Luke-Acts, God reveals his will to the protagonists through these extraordinary events. But divine epiphanies are known from the Tanakh and ancient pagan sources.[12] Thus, the question arises whether the supernatural events in Luke-Acts can really be seen as "deviant" against the background of a Jewish-Hellenistic frame of reference or whether it is not better to classify them as "conventional plot mechanism[s]"[13] that do not transcend but rather confirm a collective worldview and belong to the prevailing religious norms. This question can only be answered through a closer look at the narrative world of Luke-Acts itself. What is normal and deviant is defined by the norms and values that are effective throughout Luke's work. Considering the phenomena in Luke-Acts that can be classified as "ecstatic" it is striking that Luke presents a number of dreams or visions that he calls ὅραμα (e.g., Acts 7:31; 9:10; 12:9; 16:9–10; 18:9). Occurring often, these ὁράματα can indeed be seen as a conventional plot mechanism in Luke-Acts. They can be classified as "message dreams"[14] where God reveals his will clearly to the protagonists and shows them the next steps they are to undertake. But there are two visions that stand out against this background: Peter's vision in Acts 10:9–16 and Paul's temple vision recounted in Acts 22:17. Here, Luke does not use the conventional term ὅραμα but the term ἔκστασις, which is an unusual use of the term as the following analysis will show. Furthermore, Peter's vision is not a

---

[10] See Geir O. Holmås, "Prayer, 'Othering' and the Construction of Early Christian Identity in the Gospels of Matthew and Luke," in *Early Christian Prayer and Identity Formation*, ed. Reidar Hvalvik, WUNT 336 (Tübingen: Mohr Siebeck, 2014), 91–113, 91–92.

[11] See John B. F. Miller, *Convinced that God had Called Us: Dreams, Visions, and the Perception of God's Will in Luke-Acts*, BiInS 85 (Leiden: Brill, 2007); see in this volume the contribution of Koet, XX.

[12] See William V. Harris, "Greek and Roman Hallucinations," in *Mental Disorders in the Classical World*, ed. Harris William V, CSCT 38 (Leiden: Brill, 2013), 285–306, see 295.

[13] Harris, "Hallucinations," 290.

[14] For this designation see John B. F. Miller, "Exploring the Function of Symbolic Dream-Visions in the Literature of Antiquity, with Another Look at 1QapGen 19 and Acts 10," *PRSt* 37.4 (2010): 441–55, 443–44.

"message dream" but a "symbolic dream"[15] whose meaning is opaque to Peter (Acts 10:17). It is the only "symbolic dream" of the New Testament outside the Revelation. Commentators in general do not place any particular focus on the term ἔκστασις and they do not ask why Luke uses it only here and again for Paul's temple vision in Acts 22:17. They interpret Peter's vision as prophetic vision induced by fasting and parallel to Cornelius's vision[16], sometimes relating it to Gen 15:12.[17] Thus, the ἔκστασις of Peter and Paul is usually interpreted as a conventional experience with the background of prophecy and divine visitations in the Hebrew Bible. The following contribution takes a closer look at the semantics of the word ἔκστασις and its cognates in non-biblical Greek Literature, the LXX and the New Testament.[18] The analysis will show that Luke uses an unconventional term to emphasize the extraordinary and abnormal character of the visions. The content of the visions, the full inclusion of Gentile Christ-believers in the Christian congregation, is indeed something *innovative* and boundary-transgressive and it is revealed to the most important protagonists of Acts, Peter and Paul, at crucial points in the narrative. At the same time, Luke does not depict the ἔκστασις as completely outside a Jewish frame of reference but rather relates it to the Jewish religious world, especially by highlighting the time—prayer—and in Paul's case the place—the Jerusalem temple. Thus, it becomes apparent

---

[15] For this designation see Miller, "Symbolic Dream Visions," 443–44.
[16] Richard I. Pervo, *Acts. A Commentary*, Hermeneia (Augsburg Fortress, MN: Fortress, 2009), 269; Jacob Jervell, *Die Apostelgeschichte*, KEK 3 (Göttingen: Vandenhoeck & Ruprecht, 1998), 304–5; Johannes Munck, *The Acts of the Apostles: Introduction, Translation and Notes*, AncB (New York: Doubleday, 1967), 93; Rudolph Pesch, *Die Apostelgeschichte. Apg 1–12*, vol I of *Die Apostelgeschichte*, EKK V/1. (Zürich: Benziger, 1986), 338.
[17] Joseph A. Fitzmyer, *The Acts of the Apostles. A New Translation with Introduction and Commentary*, AncB (New York: Doubleday, 1998), 454; Charles K. Barrett, *The Acts of the Apostles: Preliminary Introduction and Commentary*, vol. I of The Acts of the Apostles, CECNT (Edinburgh: T&T Clark, 2003), 505.
[18] One recent publication, a comprehensive analysis of Acts 10:9–16 by John R.L. Moxon, *Peter's Halakhic Nightmare: The 'animal vision' of Acts 10:9–16 in Jewish and Graeco-Roman Perspective*, WUNT 2/432 (Tübingen: Mohr Siebeck, 2017), also takes a closer look at the meaning of ἔκστασις in Acts 10:9 and points to its non-prophetic background. However, Moxon does not analyze the term with the categories of normality, abnormality and deviance and does not include Acts 22:17. Nevertheless, his book has provided important background for the subject of this contribution, see below.

that his intention is to *integrate* this abnormal and boundary-transgressive experience into a known and recognized religious system.

2 The Meaning of ἔκστασις / ἐξίστασθαι in Non-Biblical Greek

The verb ἐξίστασθαι literally means "to displace" (trans.) or "to be beside oneself," "arise out of," "become separated," "cease from," "abandon," "depart from," "change one's position" (intrans.).[19] Recent publications that deal with the semantics of ἔκστασις point to the non-religious meaning of the term. Chiara Thumiger, who examines medical texts from the fifth- and early fourth centuries in her article on "early Greek medical vocabulary of insanity," also spends some time on ἔκστασις and its cognates and defines the basic meaning as follows: "ἐξίσταμαι and other compound verbs (and phrases) with ἐκ/ἐξ (alongside παρά, ἐν, ἐντός and ἐξ, ἐκτός) are expressions familiar from poetic sources to qualify mental soundness and its opposite."[20] This basic meaning of ἔκστασις as opposed to the "normal" state of mind was of course already seen by Friedrich Pfister in his comprehensive article on the word.[21] He points to expressions like ἔκστασις φρενῶν (Menander, *Com. Flor.* 80), ἐκ. τῆς φύσεως (Theophrastus, *Caus. Plant.* 3,1,6), ἐκ. δαινοίας (Philo, *Her.* 250; Deut 28:28) or ἐκ. λογισμῶν (Plutarch, *Sol.* 8). As Pfister notes, these expressions are not to be understood as genitives of the subject, i.e., that the φρήν "steps out" of the person. On the contrary, we are dealing with an ablative relationship, i.e., ἔκστασις φρενῶν means that someone steps out *from* her or his φρήν, φύσις, διάνοια etc., which means they move away from a state of sound mind, normal human nature or the normal capacity for thinking or understanding, and behave in a strange, "abnormal" way.[22] John R.L. Moxon, who in his comprehensive analysis of Peter's animal vision in Acts 10:9–16 devotes a chapter to the semantics of ἔκστασις, concludes: "In Luke's period the religious literature does not routinely use the term for

---

[19] See *LSJ* 595.
[20] Chiara Thumiger, "The Early Greek Medical Vocabulary of Insanity," pages 61–95 in *Mental Disorders in the Classical World*, ed. Harris William V, CSCT 38 (Leiden: Brill, 2013), 77.
[21] See Friedrich Pfister, "Ekstase," *RAC* 4: 944–87, 946.
[22] See Pfister, "Ekstase," 946.

divinely inspired states leading to prophecies."[23] He builds on the contribution of Thumiger and two other recent studies, "Greek and Roman Hallucinations" (2013) by William V. Harris and "Mental Disorders in Ancient Philosophy" by Marke Ahonen (2014), and describes the meaning of the word-group around ἔκστασις as follows: "ἐξίσταμαι and similar compounds are used in a relatively non-technical sense in medical discussions of temporary mental and behavioral aberrations."[24]

However, in my opinion Moxon puts too much emphasis on the non-religious meaning of the term and overlooks the fact that in antiquity the borders between medical and religious explanations are fluid. Nor does Thumiger really support Moxon's view but says that the word-group oscillates between a religious concept close to ἐνθεαστικά and mental illness or insanity that is reflected in ancient medical treatises.[25] Nevertheless, ἔκστασις is not first and foremost linked to cognition and the gaining of insight but rather to the opposite, namely bewilderment and disorientation.

To this general picture there are two important exceptions where ἔκστασις is related to a prophetic state. Philo in his treatise *Quis rerum divinarum heres sit* deals with Gen 15:12, Abraham's extraordinary experience, which the LXX renders as ἔκστασις (Philo, *Her.* 249–266).[26] Philo describes four different meanings of the term. But before he is concerned with Abraham's ἔκστασις as prophetic experience, he discusses at length its non-prophetic meaning: Firstly, ἔκστασις can be "a mad fury (λύττα μανιώδης) producing mental delusion (παράνοιαν) due to old age or melancholy (μελαγχολίαν) or other similar cause"[27] (Philo, *Her.* 249). Secondly, it can mean "great amazement" (σφοδρὰ κατάπληξις), as expressed by Isaac or Jacob (Gen 27:33; 45:26) (249). The third meaning is that of a deep sleep as experienced by Adam (Gen 2:21) (257). Only the fourth meaning is related to a specifically prophetic experience. By commenting on the Greek text of Gen 15:12 (Philo, *Her.* 249: περὶ δὲ ἡλίου δυσμὰς ἔκστασις ἐνέπεσεν τῷ Ἀβραάμ), Philo interprets the ἔκστασις of

---

[23] Moxon, *Nightmare*, 357.
[24] Moxon, *Nightmare*, 359.
[25] See Thumiger, "Insanity," 77.
[26] See in this volume Lukas Bormann, 119–40; Albrecht Oepke, "ἔκστασις, ἐξίστημι," ThWNT 2:447–57, 451.
[27] Translation by Colson and Whitaker, LCL.

Abraham as the state of mind of one who is ἐνθουσιῶν ("in God") and θεοφόρητος ("God-bearing") (Philo, *Her.* 258), i.e., someone who is in close contact with God, for example the prophets. ἔκστασις for Philo means a state of mind where the human spirit leaves the body so that the light of God can take its place (Philo, *Her.* 265). In this state the prophet is God's sounding instrument (Philo, *Her.* 259: ὄργανον θεοῦ ἐστιν ἠχεῖον). Via this instrument God can give his messages. This can be seen from the case of Abraham: After Abraham falls into an ἔκστασις God speaks to him and reveals his plans to him (Philo, *Her.* 266). Philo apparently makes an effort to show that Abraham's ἔκστασις was of the highest quality (ἀρίστη; Philo, *Her.* 249), the prophetic or indeed "divine possession" (ἔνθεος κατοκωχή; Philo, *Her.* 249–50). Here, he picks up the idea of ἔκστασις we find in Plato's Phaedrus where Plato deals with "divine madness" (Plato, *Phaedr.* 245B: μανία γιγνομένης ἀπὸ θεῶν), the state of the inspired prophet, with very similar wording (Plato, *Phaedr.* 249D: ἐξιστάμενος; ἐνθουσιάζων; the "divine madness" as "the best of all inspirations" (Plato, *Phaedr.* 249E: πασῶν τῶν ἐνθουσιάσεων ἀρίστη).[28]

Philo uses the word ἔκστασις for a prophetic revelation only in the aforementioned treatise.[29] In connection with his labored comment on the different meanings of the word it seems he was struggling with the term in the context of God making a covenant with Abraham as the honored ancestor of the Jewish people. But of course, the term was given by the LXX, and Philo could not or did not want to pass over it in silence. At least, Philo seems to feel the need for broader explanations about the meaning of ἔκστασις. But what Philo does here is to link the concept of ἔκστασις to the well-known and honored Jewish concept of prophecy.[30] ἔκστασις as prophecy is—according to Philo—a gift only for the wise (σοφός) and just (δίκαιος) man (Philo, *Her.* 259–260). And so, it is not remarkable, as Philo puts it, that just men like Noah, Isaac, Jacob and Moses prophesied under

---

[28] On this text see Julija B. Ustinova, *Divine Mania: Alteration of Consciousness in ancient Greece* (Abingdon: Routledge, 2018), 1–2.57.294–98; Marke Ahonen, *Mental Disorders in Ancient Philosophy*, Studies in the History of Philosophy of Mind 13 (Heidelberg: Springer, 2014), 37–40.

[29] See Moxon, *Nightmare*, 358.

[30] See Moxon, *Nightmare*, 360.

"divine possession" (κατεχόμενος) und were "inspired" (ἐνθουσιῶντος) (Philo, *Her.* 261–262).[31]

Plato and Philo combine ἔκστασις / ἐξίστασθαι with ἔνθεος or ἐνθουσιασμός, thus linking the state of "being outside oneself" explicitly to divine inspiration.[32] Apart from Plato und Philo this theological meaning of ἔκστασις / ἐξίστασθαι can also be found in other Jewish and non-Jewish texts. Josephus comments on the spirit-induced speech of Balaam that he was "not in himself" (οὐκ ὢν ἐν ἑαυτῷ) while he was calling upon God (ἐπεθείαζεν), but he was overwhelmed by the spirit of God (τῷ δὲ θείῳ πνεύματι ... νενικημένος) (Josephus, *A.J.* 4,118). Plutarch also describes someone who is θεοφόρητος as ἐστερημένος νοῦ (Plutarch, *Quaest. rom.* 5b), i.e., deprived of their mind. In Euripides's *Bacchae* ecstatic states play an important role in the context of the Dionysus cult. Here, the god Dionysus puts his mortal adversary Pentheus into a state of madness. He decides to cause him "to go out of his mind" (ἔκστησον φρενῶν) (Euripides, *Bacch.* 950), so that Pentheus dressed in women's clothes enters the territory of the Bacchae. These women form an ecstatic frenzy and kill Pentheus by tearing him apart. Here, we have an example for ἐξίστασθαι being used as a divinely induced state, but it is the work of a malevolent god, who seeks revenge for not being worshipped properly.[33] Harris in his insightful contribution on attitudes towards and interpretations of hallucinations in Greek antiquity puts Euripides's *Bacchae* in the context of other Athenian tragedies, such as Sophocles's *Ajax*, Aeschylus's *Choephori* or another play of Euripides, *Heracles furens*. In these plays, the protagonists show abnormal behavior which is clearly depicted as "signs of ill health"[34], of

---

[31] Moses is explicitly named a "prophet" in the Hebrew Scriptures (Num 12:6.8; Deut 34:10), as Philo states. In the case of Noah, Isaac and Jacob Philo has to deduce their acting as prophets. Concerning Noah Philo refers to the "curses which [Noah] called down on subsequent generations, the prayers which he made on their behalf, [...] uttered by him under divine possession" (transl. by Colson and Whitaker, LCL). Concerning Isaac and Jacob Philo interprets Jacob's farewell discourse as having taken place under divine inspiration (see Gen 49:1).

[32] See Pfister, "Ekstase," 955.

[33] See the introduction to the play the edition by Colson and Whitaker, LCL, 2–10; on Euripides's Bacchae see also El Mansy, 171–204 in this volume.

[34] Harris, "Hallucinations," 294.

madness. It can be induced by "divine ill-will"[35] as in the case of Ajax and Orestes or by the dispositions of the character as in the case of Heracles, whose "madness arises from the extreme violence of his character."[36] Harris concludes that these explanations of hallucinations as negative and confusing states of mind reveal the attitude of the "thinking members of the Athenian audience"[37] towards what they consider abnormal behavior. Harris also provides some evidence of classical writers whose attitudes to hallucinations, divine dreams and visions were ambivalent or even critical.[38] Thus Plutarch in his *Life of Brutus* reports of a late-night supernatural apparition of a demon-like figure to Brutus while he is in a military camp preparing for battle. When Brutus tells his colleague Cassius about the apparition, Cassius, who is an Epicurean, reacts with the words: "perception by the senses is a pliant and deceptive thing.... As for daimones, it is incredible that they exist...."[39] Cassius also finds a natural explanation for Brutus's vision: "In your case too the body is under stress, which naturally excites and deceives your mind." (Plutarch, *Brut.* 37). The "stress" Brutus experiences is apparently a lack of sleep (Plutarch, *Brut.* 36), i.e., an exceptional bodily condition.

These examples of course do not all include references specifically to ἔκστασις and its cognates. The use of ἔκστησον φρενῶν to describe a state of divinely induced madness in Euripides's *Bacchae* forms the starting point for an examination of ambivalent attitudes towards ecstatic states in the cultural context of the New Testament. To be "out of one's normal state of mind" and/or to experience hallucinations, dreams or visions was not in every case assessed as something positive or "normal" which corresponds to conventional expectations of divine epiphanies or revelations. But as the examples of Plato, Philo and Josephus show, the word-group around ἔκστασις can *also* refer to a prophetic experience that provides the prophet with knowledge about otherwise hidden things. In sum, the term ἔκστασις appears to be an ambivalent, multifaceted notion, whose meaning depends

---

[35] Harris, "Hallucinations," 294.
[36] Harris, "Hallucinations," 293.
[37] Harris, "Hallucinations," 294.
[38] Harris, "Hallucinations," 296.297–98.
[39] Translation by Perrin, LCL.

on the specific author's interpretation of the event he is describing. Is the experience a dissociation of the mind that leads to confusion or even madness, and thus causes the person to fall out of the "normal" state of having a sound φρήν, διάνοια, φύσις or λογισμός? Or is the person used "as God's instrument" as Philo puts it and by "being out of himself" receives higher knowledge thus transcending the human capacity of φρήν, διάνοια, φύσις and λογισμός?

3 The Use of ἔκστασις / ἐξίστασθαι in the LXX

In the LXX the translators use the word-group to translate 29 different Hebrew words and its basic meaning is "to be frightened" or "to tremble," albeit with different nuances.[40] It belongs to the vocabulary of psychology the LXX translators tend to use instead of Hebrew terms that are more related to physical organs (such as heart, kidneys etc.).[41] It can designate different stages of emotions ranging from astonishment and awe (Gen 43:33; Job 26:11; 1 Macc 15:32; Sir 43:18), to joy (Exod 18:9; Isa 60:5), anger and fury (Jer 2:12), fear (Gen 27:33; 1 Sam 13:7; Jer 4:9), shock, terror and dismay (Gen 42:28; 1 Kgs 9:8; 2 Chr 7:21).[42] But it can also have "a suggestive religious meaning"[43] when it describes a state of mind which is induced by God or by the presence of God. In prophetic literature one finds the idea that people "will be terrified" (ἐκστήσονται) when the day of judgement is near (Isa 13:8). When Israel sees God descending in fire on Mount Sinai, all the people "trembled greatly (ἐξέστη ... σφόδρα)" (Exod 19:18). This so-called "Gottesschrecken" can also be a state of madness. In Deut 28:28 ἔκστασις διανοίας is paralleled with παραπληξία (madness) and ἀορασία (blindness). ἔκστασις is thus not the ability of the prophets to see, but clearly the opposite, the *inability to see* or even unconsciousness (Gen 2:21).[44] In Zech 12:4 we also find this meaning, here in a combination with παραφρόνησις. In Dan 10:7 (LXX [Th]) the meaning of ἔκστασις as a state of

---

[40] See Ceslas Spicq, "ἐξίστημι (ἐξιστάνω)," *TLNT* 2:25.
[41] See Folker Siegert, *Zwischen hebräischer Bibel und Altem Testament. Eine Einführung in die Septuaginta*, MJSt 9 (Münster: LIT, 2001), 258; Oepke, "ἔκστασις," 457.
[42] See for lists with instances Spicq, "ἐξίστημι," 25; Moxon, *Nightmare*, 358–9.
[43] Spicq, "ἐξίστημι," 26.
[44] See also Moxon, *Nightmare*, 359.

blindness and lack of cognition clearly stands out. Here, the vision (ὅρασις) of the seer Daniel is contrasted with the inability of his companions to see it and the reason for this inability is that "a great ecstasy fell on them (καὶ ἔκστασις μεγάλη ἐπέπεσεν ἐπ᾽ αὐτούς) and they fled with fear." The punishment for false prophets can be that God "waters them with a spirit of numbness (πνεύματι κατανύξεως)," thus making them out of their minds (ἔκστητε) (Isa 29:9). To fall into ἔκστασις here means that the prophets lose their ability to predict hidden things (Isa 29:10). Also, in wisdom literature God is the one who "has confused" (ἐξέστησεν) those who oppose him (Job 5:13; 12:17).

In accordance with this, the word group around ἔκστασις is hardly ever used in relation to prophetic visions or auditions. To describe these events the biblical text uses expressions like "the hand of the Lord was on him"[45] (Ezek 1:3) or "the spirit of the Lord came on him" (Judg 3:10). The only exception is the account of Abraham's audition he receives shortly before God makes a covenant with him. Here, the Greek translator decided to render the exceptional state that falls on Abraham as ἔκστασις. This is how he translates the Hebrew term תַּרְדֵּמָה ("deep sleep"). But also here, Abraham's ἔκστασις does not *only* seem to be a state of sound mind and clear consciousness. Although he clearly hears God's message, the narrator reports that "fear" and "great darkness" (Gen 15:12) fell on him.

4 ἔκστασις / ἐξίστασθαι in the Synoptic Tradition (Mark and Matthew)

In the synoptic tradition, we find ἔκστασις / ἐξίστημι / ἐξιστάνω[46] in the context of three miracle stories. The term is part of the acclamation of those who witness the miracle and designates surprise, amazement and/ or joy (Mark 2:12: healing of a paralyzed man; Mark 5:42: healing of Jairus's daughter), but also confusion or fear (Mark 6:51: Jesus walking on the sea and calming the storm). While Matthew adopts the three miracle stories, he leaves out the expressions ἔκστασις / ἐξίστασθαι / ἐξιστάνω as descriptions for the states of mind of the people or the disciples. Instead,

---

[45] Translation from New International Version.
[46] See Kurt Aland and Barbara Aland, "ἐξίστημι," *Griechisch-deutsches Wörterbuch zu den Schriften des Neuen Testaments und der frühchristlichen Literatur* (Berlin: de Gruyter, ⁶1988), 559.

he puts emphasis on the faith of those who are the beneficiaries of the miracle. It seems as though in Matthew's view "being out of his mind" does not fit very well with the faith of Jairus whose daughter is already dead when he trusts Jesus to bring her back to life (Matt 9:18[47]). Neither does it fit very well with the faith of the disciples who confess Jesus as the Son of God after the calming of the storm (Matt 14:33). In the Markan version (Mark 6:45–52), ἐξίστασθαι occurs (v. 51) and designates a lack of understanding—a topic that is typical for Mark. In Mark 16:8, the original ending of the gospel, the women are depicted as fleeing from the empty grave, "because trembling (τρόμος) and ἔκστασις had seized them." In sum, Mark uses ἐξίστασθαι more as an expression of fear that does not designate understanding but rather a confused state of mind. Additionally, he once uses the expression in the sense of "being insane" (Mark 3:21). Jesus's family assess his words and deeds as deviant and abnormal and accuse him of being "mad": "He is out of his mind / he is insane (ὅτι ἐξέστη)." Both Matthew and Luke omit this accusation perhaps because they considered it indecent. Overall, Matthew and Mark do not go beyond the LXX in their usage of ἐξίστασθαι.

5 The Use of ἔκστασις / ἐξίστασθαι / ἐξιστάνω in Luke-Acts

It is in Luke's two-volume work where we find the majority of New Testament references to the word-group around ἔκστασις. Compared to Mark (six references) and Matthew (one reference) Luke has sixteen references. Only in 2 Cor 5:13 do we find a reference of the word-group in the context of the Pauline epistles.[48]

First, Luke takes over two of the three Markan pericopes with ἔκστασις references (Jairus's daughter: Luke 8:40–56; the paralyzed man: Luke

---

[47] Contrast Mark 5:23: the daughter is still alive.

[48] Whether Paul here speaks of an ecstatic state or not is debated but due to space it cannot be discussed here; see Clair E. Mesick., "Driven by Grief, Inspired by Christ: Paul 'Beside Himself' in 2 Cor 5:13," *NT* 61 (2019):137–55; Andrew C. Ballard, "Tongue-tied and taunted: Paul, poor rhetoric and paltry leadership in 2 Corinthians 5.13," *JSNT* 37.1 (2014): 50–70.

5:17–26)⁴⁹. As in the LXX tradition and Mark he uses the word to describe a state of great astonishment or fear when people are confronted with God's mighty deeds. In Luke ἔκστασις / ἐξίστασθαι / ἐξιστάνω can also refer to a confused state of lack of understanding (Luke 24:22: the disciples of Emmaus; Acts 2:7.12: Pentecost, people wondering at the disciples talking in different languages). Beyond that he seems to put more emphasis on ἐξίστασθαι as a state of fervent joy among those who are already believers: In Acts 10:45 the circumcised believers "are out of themselves," when they see that the holy spirit is also poured out on the Gentiles. Simon Magus who initially astonished others with his magic (Acts 8:9: ἐξιστάνων; Acts 8:11: ἐξεστακέναι αὐτούς), "is out of himself" after having been baptized and now seeing the mighty miracles of God (Acts 8:13: ἐξίστατο).

5.1 Acts 10:9: Peter's ἔκστασις on the Rooftop in Joppa
Luke adds some new color to the picture of ἔκστασις that is not predominant in the biblical tradition or in Mark or Matthew. In the pericope of the conversion of Cornelius the apostle Peter comes into a state of ἔκστασις (Acts 10:10: ἐγένετο ἐπ' αὐτὸν ἔκστασις) that is related to a vision and an audition: he sees a huge sheet coming down from heaven filled with different animals, reptiles and birds, and he hears a voice: "Rise, Peter, kill and eat!" In Acts 22:17 Luke uses the noun ἔκστασις again: Paul tells the Jews of Jerusalem who want to kill him how God gave him the message to leave Jerusalem and to bring the gospel to the Gentiles shortly after his conversion. Paul speaks of an ecstasy that happened to him (Acts 22:17: γενέσθαι με ἐν ἐκστάσει) while praying in the temple. In both cases, Peter and Paul are not simply touched by a strong affect but the ecstasy describes a state of direct contact with God and receiving a message that is of great importance for the further development of events.

In his study, Moxon points to the striking difference between Peter's ἔκστασις and the preceding vision of Cornelius (Acts 10:1–8). While Cornelius's vision, which is called a ὅραμα (v. 3), is painted in conventional

---

⁴⁹ Luke omits Jesus walking on the water and the calming of the storm (cf. the so-called "great Lucan gap": Mark 6:45–8:26), maybe to avoid duplications (cf. another storm calming story in Mark 4:35–41; Luke 8:22–25).

biblical colors[50], Peter's vision, which in contrast is referred to as an ἔκστασις, contains more unconventional, unexpected elements.[51] In the following I will outline these elements and add some more observations. First of all, Cornelius is visited by a heavenly messenger, the ἄγγελος τοῦ θεοῦ, a figure that appears in the LXX from Genesis to Daniel (e.g., Gen 16:7-11; Judg 13:3-21; Zech 1:11-12; 3:1-6; Dan 3:95). In the case of Peter, there is only a voice: ἐγένετο φωνὴ πρὸς αὐτόν (v. 13) and the identity of the voice is not clarified.[52] Secondly, Luke says that Cornelius sees the angel "clearly" (v. 3: φανερῶς). Cornelius has no difficulty in understanding the angel's message as can be seen from his immediate reaction: Cornelius immediately does what the angel has told him to do (v. 7). Furthermore, the element that Cornelius is at first afraid (v. 4: ἔμφοβος γενόμενος) is a conventional part of angelophany stories in biblical texts (Gen 21:17; Judg 13:6; Esth 5:2; 3 Macc 6:18-19; 4 Macc 4:10). In contrast, Peter does not understand what the vision with the sheet and the animals means—he "is at a loss" (v. 17: διηπόρει) and he also refuses to carry out the order: "kill and eat!" (v. 13).[53] Thirdly, the temporal setting of Cornelius's ὅραμα is significant. It takes place "about the ninth hour of the day" (v. 3: περὶ ὥραν ἐνάτην τῆς ἡμέρας), the daily time for afternoon offering at the temple in Jerusalem and normal Jewish prayer time (three o'clock).[54] This prayer in the afternoon is the second of two obligatory prayers of Jewish believers, the first taking place in the early morning (see 1 Chr 23:30).[55] The Jewish prayer times are related to the daily sacrifices in the temple, as Josephus tells us in Jewish Antiquities: "twice a day, in the morning and at the ninth hour (περὶ ἐνάτην ὥραν), they performed the sacred ceremonies at the altar" (Josephus, A.J. 14, § 65). But it is the daily sacrifice or rather prayer

---

[50] For the form-typical elements of Cornelius's vision see also Josef Zmijewski, *Die Apostelgeschichte*, RNT (Regensburg: Pustet, 1994), 418; for typical elements of angelophanies and references see Michael Wolter, *Das Lukasevangelium*, HNT 5 (Tübingen: Mohr Siebeck, 2008), 77.

[51] See Moxon, *Nigthmare*, 323-24.326-27.

[52] See Moxon, *Nigthmare*, 324.

[53] See Moxon, *Nigthmare*, 326-37.

[54] See James D.G. Dunn, The Acts of the Apostles (Eerdmans: Grand Rapids, MI, 2016), 136; Darrell L. Bock, Acts, BECNT (Baker Academic: Grand Rapids, MI, ³2009), 387.

[55] See Charlesworth, James H., "Prayer in Early Judaism," ABD 5:449-50, 449.

time (ἐν ὥρᾳ θυσίας) where according to Dan 9:21 the prophet Daniel received a divine revelation from the angel Gabriel. It is highly likely that Luke is thinking of this encounter of Daniel with the angel when he gives his account of Zechariah's vision while carrying out the daily sacrifice in the temple (Luke 1:11–17).[56] The close relation of sacrifice and prayer is also emphasized in Luke 1, where the people are praying outside, while Zechariah carries out the sacrifice in the sanctuary (Luke 1:9–11). In sum, it is not surprising, that Cornelius receives a vision during the ordinary Jewish prayer time. When Cornelius four days later tells Peter and the Jews who have come with him from Joppa about his vision, he points to its special timing: "Four days ago, I was praying in my house until this hour, the ninth (μέχρι ταύτης τῆς ὥρας ἤμην τὴν ἐνάτην προσευχόμενος), and behold, a man stood before me..."[57] (Acts 10:30). This repetition of Cornelius's experience is of particular importance if one considers that Cornelius refers to it in the context of his speech not only in front of his family and close friends (v. 24), God-fearing Gentiles like himself, but also in front of *Jewish* Christ-followers who have come with Peter (v. 23.45: οἱ ἐκ περιτομῆς πιστοί). By telling these Jews that his vision took place at the ordinary Jewish prayer time and that the vision he saw was the direct consequence of his piety according to the Jewish law, i.e. his regular prayer and alms giving (v. 31), Cornelius can prove in front of a Jewish audience that his experience was in accordance with the scriptures and the will of God. In using conventional biblical colors to create the account of Cornelius's vision, Luke can depict the experience of the Gentile outsider Cornelius as completely "normal" within a Jewish frame of reference and thus as legitimate, which means that it is in accordance with God's will and purpose.[58]

But what about the conventional Jewish elements surrounding Peter's ἔκστασις? We left the track of comparison between Cornelius's ὅραμα and

---

[56] See Joseph A. Fitzmyer, The Gospel according to Luke I–IX, AB 28.1 (New Haven: Yale, 1986), 324; Raymond E. Brown, *An Introduction to the New Testament* (New York: Doubleday, 1997), 270–1.

[57] English Standard Version.

[58] For the purpose or plan of God as an important theme in Luke-Acts see Brian Schmisek, "Luke as the Master Architect of 'God's Plan': An Analysis of a Distinctive Lucan Concept," *BTB* 50.4 (2020): 227–35.

Peter's ἔκστασις on pointing to the special time setting of Cornelius's vision. Concerning the timing of Peter's praying on the rooftop, about the sixth hour (v. 9: περὶ ὥραν ἕκτην), the case is less clear. We have no Jewish testimony about *noon* being a regular prayer time.[59] Nevertheless, we find evidence that praying *three times* a day was part of Jewish piety, but there is no exact time given (Ps 55:18; Dan 6:11).[60] What may also be of importance here is the idea that noon is the time where supernatural encounters happen. Henry J. Cadbury points to the reception of Ps 91:6 in the LXX and the Latin tradition, where "the destruction that wastes at noonday"[61] was personalized as a demon, i.e., understood as δαιμονίος μεσημβρινοῦ (Ps 90:6 LXX) and later as a *meridianus daemon.*[62] In the light of this tradition the reference to noon appears as a somewhat disturbing setting and could point to Peter's ἔκστασις as an unsettling experience. But Luke has the vision of Paul also occur in the middle of the day (Acts 22:6: περὶ μεσημβρίαν; Acts 26:13: ἡμέρας μέσης) and Abraham's encounter with the Lord or the three men in Mamre takes place "in the heat of the day"[63] in the LXX rendered as μεσημβρία (Gen 18:1).[64] Thus noon is not only a time for unsettling experiences or demonic influences but also a time when God's beneficial action can take place in the form of visions or divine encounters. However, we can note that the time of Peter's prayer remains more enigmatic than the setting of Cornelius's prayer.

Furthermore, the note that Peter was hungry before the ἔκστασις took place (v. 10) needs further consideration. While Peter is praying or at least

---

[59] See Barrett, Acts, 504; Fitzmyer, Acts, 454; contrast the older study of Otto Holtzmann, "Die täglichen Gebetsstunden im Judentum und Urchristentum," *ZNW* 12.2-3 (1911): 90–107, 104, who points to a remark of Josephus, *C. Ap.* 2.105, that the priests enter the temple in the morning and again at noon, which seems to imply that they have rested after the morning sacrifice. Holtzmann concludes that this restarting of the temple service each day at noon was also accompanied by prayers from the Jewish congregation.

[60] See Israel Abrahams, "Prayer," *EncJud* 13: 977–81, 980; Str-B II:696–99 provides evidence for a morning, an afternoon and an evening prayer, but no prayer at noon.

[61] English Standard Version.

[62] See also Gerrit C. Vreugdenhil, *Psalm 91 and Demonic Menace*, OTS 77 (Leiden: Brill, 2020), 290–304.

[63] English Standard Version.

[64] See Henry J. Cadbury, "Some Lucan Expressions of Time," *JBL* 82.3 (1963): 272–78, 275.

has the intention to do so (v. 9: προσεύξασθαι)[65] he eventually becomes hungry (πρόσπεινος). To abstain from food, i.e., to be in a state of fastening can be related to ecstatic experiences in ancient Jewish and in Greek literature.[66] Consequently, commentators of Acts interpret Peter's longing to eat (v. 10) as a sign of fasting.[67] The connection between fasting and ecstatic experiences is well attested in Greco-Roman and Jewish contexts. The Greek philosopher Iamblichus tells us about the prophet of the oracle of Klaros and also the priestess of the oracle of Didyma who both kept a three-day ἀσιτία before exercising their mantic practice (Iamblichus, *de myst.* 3,11). We have similar accounts for example of Apollonios of Tyana[68] (Philostratus, *Vit. Apoll.* 1,8; 2,37; 8,5.7) and Pythagoras (Cicero, *Div.* II 58,119; Iamblichus, *vita Pyth.* 106f), who perform different types of fasting to prepare for revelation.[69] In the Jewish context we also find a connection of fasting to prophecy. The seer Daniel is fasting (ἐν νηστείαις) and turns to God (Dan 9:3) with a lengthy penitential prayer (Dan 9:4–19), before the "man" (ὁ ἀνήρ) Gabriel "approaches" (προσήγγισέ) (see also Dan 10:3). In apocalyptic literature the connection between fasting, prayer and dreams or visions is intensified. The apocalyptic seer fasts or follows special dietary rules and prays before the *angelus interpres* approaches or a voice from heaven reveals cosmic secrets (e.g., 4 Ezra 5:13.19–20; 6:31.35 etc.; 2 Bar. 9:2; 12:5 etc.; Apoc. Ab. 9:7).[70] If we turn our attention again to the account of Peter's ἔκστασις (Acts 10:10), we do not find the conventional terminology for fasting there: νῆστις, νηστεύειν or νηστεία.[71] It is also not

---

[65] See Moxon, *Nightmare*, 177 on the option that the infinitive προσεύξασθαι is an infinitive of intent here (with further literature).

[66] See Pfister, "Ekstase," 969.

[67] See Pervo, *Acts*, 269; Pesch, *Die Apostelgeschichte*, 338, n. 36.

[68] On Apollonius of Tyana see Erkki Koskenniemi, "Apollonius of Tyana, the Greek Miracle Workers in the Time of Jesus and the New Testament," in *Hermeneutik der frühchristlichen Wundererzählungen: Geschichtliche, literarische und rezeptionsorientierte Perspektiven.* Edited by Bernd Kollmann and Ruben Zimmermann, WUNT 339 (Tübingen: Mohr Siebeck, 2014), 165–81, esp. 165–173.

[69] See for these texts and traditions Rudolphus Arbesmann, *Das Fasten bei den Griechen und Römern*, RVV 21/1 (Gießen: Töpelmann, 1929. Repr. Berlin: de Gruyter, 1966, Repr. Berlin: de Gruyter, 2018), 99–100.

[70] See for further textual evidence Rudolphus Arbesmann, "Fasten," *RAC* 7:447–93, 452.

[71] For the terminology see Arbesmann, "Fasten," 447–49.

said that Peter abstains willingly from food as does Daniel: "I ate no delicacies, no meat or wine entered my mouth, nor did I anoint myself at all, for the full three weeks." (Dan 10:3)[72]. Instead, Luke says that Peter "became hungry" (ἐγένετο ... πρόσπεινος) and "wanted to eat" (ἤθελεν γεύσασθαι[73]), using expressions that he does not use anywhere else where he is talking about fasting in a religious sense. With the word πρόσπεινος he uses a rare term that is attested only once in a medical context.[74] Moxon, who is also critical about the interpretation that Acts 10:10 implies fasting, additionally points to textual evidence of the cultural context that "extremes of hunger ... could cause bizarre dreams."[75] Thus, the contextualization of Peter's ἔκστασις within regular religious fasting is at least questionable.

A third element contributes to a more abnormal or at least unusual characteristic of Peter's vision. Peter's ἔκστασις is clearly marked as a vision because he "sees" (θεωρεῖ). But in contrast to the epiphany of an angelic messenger Peter "sees the heaven opened" (v. 11: θεωρεῖ τὸν οὐρανὸν ἀνεῳγμένον). That the heaven opens so that the prophet can see is a motif that in the Hebrew Bible only occurs once (Ezek 1:1) but is common in apocalyptic literature (2 Bar. 22:1; 1 En. 34:2; 35; 36:1–2; Rev 4:1; see also T. Levi 2:6).[76] Here, God sends a human being not only one clearly distinct message as e.g., in the case of Manoah and his wife (Judg 13), but he reveals to the seer knowledge about the whole cosmos and the end of history.[77]

In sum, in Peter's ἔκστασις the unexpected and thus unusual or "abnormal" within a biblical framework is highlighted especially in comparison with the vision of Cornelius. Here, the question arises as to why Luke

---

[72] Translation from English Standard Version.

[73] Also, the use of γεύομαι in an absolute sense is very rare and only attested quite late. Normally it means "to taste"; see *LSJ* 346.

[74] Kurt Aland and Barbara Aland, "πρόσπεινος," *Griechisch-deutsches Wörterbuch*, 1438, with reference to Demosthenes Opthalmicus cited by Aetius of Amida.

[75] Moxon, *Nightmare*, 168.178.

[76] See Fritzleo Lentzen-Dies, "Das Motiv der 'Himmelsöffnung' in verschiedenen Gattungen der Umweltliteratur des Neuen Testaments," *Biblica* 50 (1969):301–27, 309.

[77] Luke uses this motif also in his account ot Stephen's vision shortly before he dies (Acts 7:56).

depicts Peter's supernatural experience on the rooftop as an incident that appears unconventional and shows traces of abnormality. This question is crucial because Peter in Luke-Acts is a respectable and important person (e.g., Luke 6:14; Acts 1:13.15; 2:14; 15:7). Falling into an ecstasy that connotes confusion and madness could appear indecent. An answer as to why Luke nevertheless depicts Peter's vision in the way outlined, lies in the significance the events of Acts 10 have for the whole of Luke-Acts. As commentators emphasize Peter's vision in Joppa is decisive for the inauguration of the Gentile mission.[78] Cornelius is not the first non-Jew who becomes a Christ-follower in the context of Luke-Acts but his conversion "marks the final critical stage in the extension of the Gospel and the expansion of the Church."[79] It is his conversion that explicitly challenges the Jewish Christians of Jerusalem to take a stand in the question of communion between Jews and non-Jews as can be seen from Acts 11:1-18, where Peter tells them about his and Cornelius's visions. Although initially cynical (11:2), in the end they recognize that "to the Gentiles also God has granted repentance unto life"[80] (11:18). The importance of Peter's vision for the inauguration of a mission among Gentiles is emphasized by various repetitions:[81] First recounted in 10:9-15 Luke alludes to it in 10:28, recounts it in more detail in 11:5-10 and refers to it again in 15:7-9. The latter is Luke's representation of the Jerusalem council (cf. Gal 2:1-10) where the acceptance of Gentiles in the Christ congregation is formally recognized.[82] Thus, Peter's vision in Acts 10 has to be seen as a groundbreaking event that prepares the way for the final acceptance of Gentiles in the Church.[83] The ambivalent and extraordinary character of Peter's ἔκστασις points to the issue that is negotiated here: It is nothing less than table fellowship between Jews and non-Jews in the Christian congregation and thus the overcoming of deep- rooted ritual and cultural reservations about outsiders on the Jewish side. To associate

---

[78] Fitzmyer, *Acts*, 453–54; Barrett, *Acts*, 491.

[79] Barrett, *Acts*, 491.

[80] Translation by Barrett, *Acts*, 491.

[81] See Haacker, *Apostelgeschichte*, 184.

[82] See Fitzmyer, *Acts*, 453–54.

[83] For the refusal of table fellowship with Gentiles by circumcised Christ-followers, see Acts 11:2-3.

with Gentiles and to have table fellowship with them could have provoked fears about "apostasy in relation to their ancestral faith."[84] But by undergoing an extraordinary and deviant ecstatic experience Peter, and with him the hearers and readers, learn to transcend the conventions of their cultural context and to imagine a new form of communion as God's will for his people. In Luke's account of Peter's ἔκστασις the critical, creative, and innovative potential of deviant religious experience is visible and at work.

Having explained why Luke depicts Peter's ecstatic experience in more extraordinary colors, the question remains as to how he presents the unexpected, abnormal, or religiously deviant in the wider context of his double-volume work. In my opinion Luke does not stop in contrasting the experiences of Cornelius and Peter, highlighting the abnormality of the latter. He also applies signals to the account that *integrates* Peter's ἔκστασις into the setting of a prophetic revelation well known to a Jewish audience.

ἔκστασις and Prayer

As noted above Luke does not relate Peter's vision to a particular prayer-time but nevertheless does not refrain from situating it within a context of prayer (v. 9: προσεύξασθαι). The element of prayer links Cornelius's and Peter's visions to one another and highlights their character of a closely related revelatory event, a double vision.[85] The embedding of the extra-ordinary state of ἔκστασις in Jewish piety and its explicit connection especially with prayer must be seen in relation to the great importance Luke gives the theme of prayer in his two volumes. At the beginning of his narrative Luke depicts Israel as a congregation of praying people who gather at the hour of the daily sacrifice outside the temple (Luke 1:10: πᾶν τὸ πλῆθος ἦν τοῦ λαοῦ προσευχόμενον). Zechariah, the priest, is also portrayed as a someone whose supplication is heard by God (Luke 1:13). With the prophetess Hannah Luke also presents a Jewish woman who

---

[84] Moxon, *Nightmare*, 325.

[85] Double visions are also used at other important points of Luke's narrative: see the double vision of Zachariah and Mary (Luke 1:8–22.26–38) and Saul/Paul and Ananias (Acts 9:3–6.10–16).

Eva-Maria Kreitschmann

"serves God with fastings and prayers (νηστείαις καὶ δεήσεσιν λατρεύουσα) night and day" (2:37). Thus: "Earnest and tenacious prayer is portrayed as an essential characteristic of the godly in Israel at the outset of Luke's story."[86] Jesus himself is portrayed as model of prayer and admonishes and teaches his disciples to pray constantly (Luke 11:1–13; 18:1–8; 21:36; 22:40.46 etc.).[87] In the ongoing course of Luke-Acts, praying is presented as an important characteristic of the Jesus community.[88] This can be seen especially from the summaries in Luke 24:53, Acts 1:14 and Acts 2:42–47, where prayer (προσευχή) appears as an important feature of Christian life alongside teaching (διδαχή), community (κοινωνία), the Lord's supper (ἡ κλάσις τοῦ ἄρτου) and joint property (εἶχον ἅπαντα κοινά). Thus Luke depicts communal praying as an important identity-marker of the young Christian congregation. For Luke prayer is the means to unify all Jesus followers in the shared worship of God.[89]

An integral aspect of the Lucan depiction of prayer as an identity-marker of the emerging church is the evidence that Luke clearly roots Christian prayers in the prayers of pious Israel. Contrary to Matthew and the Didache where there is a clear construction of the Jewish "other" in establishing a Christian practice of prayer,[90] Luke is not interested in drawing a sharp line between Jewish and Christian prayers.[91] On the contrary, he shows the first Christians as participants in the daily prayer hours and the temple service (Luke 24:52–53; Acts 2:46; 3:1; 5:42; 10:3.30). The parallels between the vision of Zechariah during the daily offering and prayer and the vision of Cornelius[92] also show that in Luke's view there is a clear accordance between praying Jews and other praying

---

[86] Holmås, "Prayer," 102.
[87] For a comprehensive list of all relevant passages, see Holmås, "Prayer," 102.
[88] For a comprehensive list of all relevant passages, see Holmås, "Prayer," 102, n. 44.
[89] See Niclas Förster, *Das gemeinschaftliche Gebet in der Sicht des Lukas*, BToSt 4 (Leuven: Peters, 2007), 427–28.
[90] For a deeper analysis of these texts in comparison with Luke see Förster, *Gebet*, 242–44.
[91] Nevertheless, Luke also has the idea that Jesus established a special practice of prayer among his disciples: Luke 11:1–4.
[92] In both scenes prayer and the time of the daily sacrifice are directly connected with the appearance of an angel and the revelation of an important heavenly message.

members of the community. Luke's aim is to emphasize the continuity between pious Israel and the Christian congregation.[93] Geir O. Holmås sees the function of this continuity in the "apologetic effort"[94] of Luke to emphasize the continuity of Israel and the emerging church to "legitimate the young Christian 'sect'"[95]. Förster in his comprehensive study of prayer in Luke presents in detail that in Greek philosophy prayer was also characteristic of the ideal religious community.[96] Having its roots in the Aristotelian ideal of the θεωρητικὸς βίος, the contemplative way of life was highly appreciated, and regular prayer was seen as an important element of it. Prayer plays an important role in ancient descriptions of religious communities such as the Pythagoreans,[97] the Therapists (Philo, *Contempl.* 27-28. 89) or the Essenes (Josephus, *B.J.* 2.128). Consequently, Luke with his emphasis on communal prayer (Acts 1:14; 2:42) intends to show the Christian congregation as a community who leads the ideal θεωρητικὸς βίος of those religious und philosophical elites which were highly valued among educated Greeks.[98]

By showing that Peter's ἔκστασις is embedded in prayer customs that are highly esteemed both in Jewish and in Greek culture, Luke shows that Peter's extraordinary ecstatic experience is linked to a "normal" and venerable practice of piety.

ἔκστασις and Abraham

The *Novum Testamentum Graece* in its 28th edition provides in Acts 10:10 a reference in the margin to Gen 15:12, the account of Abraham's ἔκστασις. This leads to the question as to whether Luke was here engaging in intentional intertextual reference to Gen 15. To form Peter's ἔκστασις based on the model of Israel's honored ancestor would be an important

---

[93] See Förster, *Gebet*, 436.

[94] Holmås, "Prayer," 102.

[95] Geir O. Holmås, "'My House shall be a House of prayer': Regarding the Temple as a Place of Prayer in Acts within the Context of Luke's Apologetical Objective," *JSNT* 27.4 (2005): 393–416, 416.

[96] See Förster, *Gebet*, 340–66.

[97] Testimonies about the Pythagorean community are many and widespread; see for references Förster, *Gebet*, 352–59.

[98] See Förster, *Gebet*, 367–68.

Eva-Maria Kreitschmann

signal of relating Peter's strange supernatural experience to an important biblical text and thus adjusting it to a widely known and greatly appreciated narrative. An argument to support this assumption is first and foremost that the noun ἔκστασις is not a conventional and usual term for inspired states in the Jewish religious literature of the time. The LXX uses the noun twenty-eight times, but only in Gen 15:12 does it signify the state of a person while receiving a divine revelation. Thus, it is not unlikely, that for Jews familiar with the LXX the connection between ἔκστασις and vision in Acts 10:10 pointed directly to the special experience of their ancestor shortly before the covenant was made. It is now recognized more and more that Luke is not only the evangelist of the Gentiles but at the same time is deeply rooted in Jewish piety and very familiar with the LXX, using themes and motifs from Exodus and Isaiah (for example)[99] and also Jewish exegetical techniques such as Rewritten Bible.[100] Today there is much support for the idea that Luke belonged to the circles of the so called *God-Fearers* rather than having been a Gentile without any relations to Judaism before becoming a Christ-follower.[101] Luke knows Gen 15 well as is clear from Acts 7, where he refers to this text explicitly (see Acts 7:6)[102], especially to Gen 15:13–14, the promise Abram receives after the ἔκστασις has fallen on him. But what complicates the case with regard to Acts 10 is the observation that besides the buzzword ἔκστασις there are no further allusions in Peter's vision to Gen 15 on the level of words or motifs. Even

---

[99] See Kerstin Schiffner, *Lukas liest Exodus: Eine Untersuchung zur Aufnahme ersttestamentlicher Befreiungsgeschichte im lukanischen Werk als Schrift-Lektüre*, BWANT 172 (Stuttgart: Kohlhammer, 2008); Frederik Poulsen, "A light to the Gentiles: The Reception of Isaiah in Luke-Acts," in *Rewriting and Reception in and of the Bible: Festschrift für Mogens Müller*, ed. Jesper Høgenhaven et al., WUNT 396 (Tübingen: Mohr Siebeck, 2018), 163–80.

[100] See Craig A. Evans and James A. Sanders, *Luke and the Scripture. The Function of Sacred Tradition in Luke-Acts* (Minneapolis: Fortress, 1993), 3.

[101] See for example Brown, *Introduction*, 268; François Bovon, *Lk 1,1–9,50*, vol. 1 of *Das Lukasevangelium*, EKK 3.1 (Zürich: Benziger, 1989), 22; Christoph Schaefer, *Die Zukunft Israels bei Lukas: Biblisch-frühjüdische Zukunftsvorstellungen im lukanischen Doppelwerk im Vergleich zu Röm 9–11*, BZNW 190 (Berlin: de Gruyter, 2012), 379.

[102] For the reception of the land promise to Abraham in Gen 15 in Acts 7 see J. Cornelis De Vos, *Heiliges Land und Nähe Gottes. Wandlungen alttestamentlicher Landvorstellungen in frühjüdischen und neutestamentlichen Schriften*, FRLANT 244 (Göttingen: Vandenhoeck & Ruprecht, 2012), 162–63.

247

the exact wording of Gen 15:12 is probably not reproduced by Luke. Gen 15:12 reads: περὶ δὲ ἡλίου δυσμὰς ἔκστασις ἐπέπεσεν τῷ Αβραμ. Regarding Luke's text there are several manuscripts that read ἐπέπεσεν ἐπ' αὐτὸν ἔκστασις, taking over the formulation of Gen 15:12. The listed manuscripts all stem from later centuries (6th–12th centuries) but include the majority text as well as the Syriac und Latin traditions. On the other hand, old manuscripts with high textual quality support ἐγένετο and it is more natural to explain an original ἐγένετο being aligned with the well-known text of Genesis by later copyists than an original allusion to Gen 15:12 having been removed. Consequently, the assumption that Luke wrote ἐγένετο ἐπ' αὐτὸν ἔκστασις is highly probable. So, in the phrase where Luke could have highlighted the connection of his account to Abraham's experience, he does not do so. It is only later copyists who feel the need to include a parallel to Abraham's ἔκστασις.

However, even though there is no connection between the two texts on the level of vocabulary, the specific form of Peter's ἔκστασις can invoke Gen 15 LXX as a pretext. There, Abraham's ἔκστασις, although depicted as a state of confusion and fear (15:12), is secondarily combined with a speech of God (13–16).[103] God reveals to Abraham the future course of Israel's history. As already noted, this is the only passage in the LXX where ἔκστασις indicates a state of mind where the physiological boundaries of the senses are transcended, and the person affected receives special knowledge. Later, apocalyptic authors are particularly interested in Abraham's ecstatic experience in Gen 15. In 4 Ezra, 2 Baruch and the Apocalypse of Abraham[104] the authors take over only some very basic elements of Gen 15, e.g., the "night" (4 Ezra 3:14) or "the night of the animal sacrifice" (2 Bar. 4:5) and use them as a starting point for visions or heavenly journeys which have hardly anything to do with the preview of

---

[103] See Lukas Bormann, "Vom Tiefschlaf zur Ekstase: Das Außergewöhnliche in der Bibel und ihrer Rezeptionsgeschichte," in *Wahnsinn und Ekstase. Literarische Konfigurationen zwischen Antike und Mittelalter*, ed. Cora Dietl, Nadine Metzger and Christoph Schanze, Imagines Medii Aevi 49 (Wiesbaden: Reichert, 2020), 1–14, 9–10.
[104] For the Apocalypse of Abraham, see Anke Mühling, *Blickt auf Abraham, euren Vater. Abraham als Identifikationsfigur des Judentums in der Zeit des zweiten Tempels*, FRLANT 236 (Göttingen: Vandenhoeck & Ruprecht, 2011), 308–16.

exodus and conquest which we find in Gen 15:13–16.[105] Abraham, the exemplary just man, is here depicted as an apocalyptic seer who sees the course of history, the new age and creation and the heavenly Jerusalem (4 Ezra 3:14–15; 2 Bar. 4:1–7; Apoc. Ab. 9–31). The apocalypses show that Jewish authors of the Second Temple period feel very free in adapting Gen 15, sometimes just picking up a buzzword or a motif to use it as a spring-board for their own story. It is not implausible that with the use of the term ἔκστασις and its special connection with a divine speech, Luke points to Gen 15:12, Abraham's extraordinary experience at an important point of Israel's history, namely the establishment of the covenant.

Another argument for the presence of Abraham's experience in Acts 10 is the occurrence of the expression δίκαιος καὶ φοβούμενος τὸν θεόν (Acts 10:22) that adds some Abrahamic color to Luke's account. Philo, in his treatise *On Abraham*, regroups the whole material about Abraham as he finds it in Gen 11–25 under the keywords of εὐσέβεια (60–207) und δικαιοσύνη (208–276). As Martina Böhm convincingly argues, Philo in this work addresses non-Jews who are interested in the philosophy of Moses. Therefore Philo depicts Abraham as a prototype of proselytes and God-fearers,[106] referring to the ethical categories of worshipping God (εὐσέβεια) and doing justice (δικαιοσύνη), values that were highly esteemed and commonly accepted in the Hellenistic world.[107] That Luke is especially interested in this concept of Abraham as an ancestor who perfectly

---

[105] The motif of a heavenly journey occurs in the Testament of Abraham (T. Ab. 10–14), but it is not linked to Gen 15.

[106] See Martina Böhm, *Rezeption und Funktion der Vätererzählungen bei Philo von Alexandria. Zum Zusammenhang von Kontext, Exegese und Hermeneutik im frühen Judentum*, BZNW 128 (Berlin: de Gruyter, 2005), 168–77.

[107] See Klaus Berger, *Markus und Parallelen*, vol. 1 of *Die Gesetzesauslegung Jesu: Ihr historischer Hintergrund im Judentum und im Alten Testament*, WUNT 40 (Neukirchen-Vluyn: Neukirchener, 1972), 143–51; Dieter Sänger, "Tora für die Völker—Weisungen der Liebe: Zur Rezeption des Dekalogs im frühen Judentum und Neuen Testament," in *Weisheit, Ethos und Gebot: Weisheits- und Dekalogtraditionen in der Bibel und im frühen Judentum*, ed. Henning Graf Reventlow, BthSt 43 (Neukirchen-Vluyn: Neukirchener, 2001), 97–146, 113; see also J. Cornelis de Vos, "Summarizing the Jewish Law in Antiquity: Examples from Aristeas, Philo, and the New Testament," in *The Challenge of the Mosaic Torah in Judaism, Christianity, and Islam*, ed. Antti Laato, Studies on the Children of Abraham 7 (Leiden, Boston, MA: Brill, 2021), 191–204.

performed εὐσέβεια and δικαοισύνη can be seen from the *Benedictus* at the beginning in Luke's narrative, where the fulfillment of the Abrahamic covenant is seen in the formation of a community living ἐν ὁσιότητι καὶ δικαιοσύνῃ (Luke 1:73–75). The pious couple Zechariah and Elizabeth are already depicted in this way as δίκαιοι ... ἐναντίον τοῦ θεοῦ (Luke 1:6). The Abrahamic touch of this statement is supported by the observation, that in the depiction of this couple further elements of the Abraham-and-Sarah-story emerge.[108] However, if we return to Peter's ἔκστασις in Acts 10, it is not Peter but rather Cornelius who appears as εὐσεβής and δίκαιος. This characterization is reported three times and is thus strongly emphasized (Acts 10:2.22.35). It is this Abrahamic conduct which is the reason that Cornelius, the god-fearing Gentile or proselyte, is integrated into the community of God (Acts 10:34–35). To sum up, the whole of Gen 15:1–21 including Abraham's ἔκστασις is not clearly used as a pretext for Peter's ἔκστασις in Acts 10. Yet the connection of Peter's ἔκστασις with a speech from heaven that is only found in Gen 15:12 LXX in a similar way can point to a relation between the two texts. The reception of Gen 15:12 in later apocalyptic literature shows that it was especially the divine revelation to Abraham that piqued the interest of Jewish authors. Additionally, a connection to Abraham could be the aforementioned noon setting, which occurs also in the account of the three visitors at Mamre (Gen 18:1), but admittedly this is a very loose connection. Nevertheless, Luke does not strengthen these references but seems more interested in integrating Cornelius into the Abrahamic community as he understands it. Again, we see that in the case of Peter's ἔκστασις the extraordinary and ambiguous takes the upper hand while in Cornelius's case integration into the Jewish culture is emphasized.

5.2 Acts 22:17: Paul's ἔκστασις in the Jerusalem Temple

In Acts 22:17, as in Acts 10:3.9, Luke presents the ἔκστασις of his protagonist in close connection to prayer. But while Peter's prayer was performed outside Jerusalem, in the peripheral city of Joppa, Paul tells the

---

[108] See Joel B. Green, "The Problem of a Beginning: Israel's Scriptures in Luke 1–2," *BBR* 4 (1994): 61–86; Stephen J. Lampe, *Abraham in Luke-Acts. An Appropriation of Lucan Theology through Old Testament Figures* (PhD diss., Pontificia Universitas Gregoriana, 1993), 86–100.

Eva-Maria Kreitschmann

audience about his prayer at the center of Jewish religiosity, the Jerusalem temple. The account of Paul's temple vision in Acts 22:17 is part of his longer speech to a hostile Jewish audience (Acts 22:1–21) shortly after his visit to the Jerusalem temple and a potential riot. The Jews accuse Paul of having taught "everyone everywhere against the people and the law and this place" (Acts 21:28) and moreover of having defiled the temple by bringing Gentiles (Ἕλληνας) into this holy place (v. 28). The Roman authorities are alerted and to suppress any form of turmoil they arrest Paul (Acts 21:31–33). Before being brought into the Antonia Fortress[109] Paul asks for permission to speak to the Jewish crowd. Why he wants to do this is clear from his first sentence. He wants to give a defense speech, an ἀπολογία (Acts 22:1). In what follows he tells the audience his story from being a persecutor of the Christian community to becoming a proclaimer of the good news to all humanity (μάρτυς ... πρὸς πάντας ἀνθρώπους, v. 15). The account of Paul's temple ἔκστασις forms the end and climax[110] of Paul's speech. Paul here recounts that he received a vision and an audition (v. 18) during his stay in Jerusalem, where he had moved after his experience in Damascus: while praying in the temple and falling into ἔκστασις he "sees him" (ἰδεῖν αὐτόν) and hears him talking (λέγοντά μοι), whereby it is not totally clear whether "him" refers to Jesus or God.[111] Although, the divine message in the temple contains hints that a christophany is implied—the voice speaks of the "testimony about me" (v. 18) that Paul will give—, there are no sharp lines drawn between "the God of the fathers" (v. 14) and Jesus. Jesus is called ὁ δίκαιος (v. 14)[112]—an acceptable Jewish descriptor—and is depicted as acting in accordance with the θέλημα of God (v. 14). From here, the Jewish audience in Jerusalem can easily infer that

---

[109] See Fitzmyer, Acts, 699; εἰς τὴν παρεμβολήν (Acts 21:34) signifies the Roman military camp in Jerusalem, i.e., the Antonia Fortress, which was situated at the northwestern part of the temple (Josephus, B.J. 5.238–47).

[110] See Beverly Roberts Gaventa, The Acts of the Apostles, ANTC (Nashville, TN: Abingdon, 2003), 309.

[111] See Jervell, Apostelgeschichte, 17–18, who argues for God; Bock, Acts, 662, who points to the narrative context, where Jesus as the exalted Lord is directing Paul.

[112] See Pervo, Acts, 565: The title "Just One" avoids the inflammatory terms "Messiah" and "Son of God".

251

the person Paul hears and sees in the ἔκστασις appears to him because of the will of the God of Israel.

Thus, for a Jewish audience it is the highest authority[113] who reveals his will to Paul in his prayer-induced, ecstatic state. This is an important point if we take the apologetic context of Paul's speech into account. The apologetic context can also help to explain on the narrative level[114] why Paul's temple ἔκστασις in the religious center of Jerusalem is only recounted here, and not in the two other accounts of Paul's conversion and subsequent visit to Jerusalem (Acts 9:1-31; 26:4-20). The message Paul receives in the Jerusalem temple via revelation is that he shall go to the Gentiles (Acts 22:21). This special mission of Paul was already recounted in Acts 9:15, but only as a divine revelation to Ananias. In Acts 22:21 it is transferred into "a dialogue between Paul and the heavenly Christ"[115] and to no lesser place than the Jerusalem temple itself. This location of the theophany or christophany is especially important in the context of a speech to a Jewish audience because in Jewish thinking the sanctuary is the place where theophanies and angelophanies usually happen (1 Sam 3:3-10; 1 Kgs 3:4-5; Dan 9:20-27[116]; Josephus, *A.J.* 11.326-328; 13.282-83; b. Yoma 39b).[117] That the commission to go to the Gentiles is given to Paul during an ecstatic experience while praying in the temple is thus an important piece of information that has the potential to convince the Jewish audience of the divine legitimacy of Paul's actions. By pointing to his ἔκστασις in the temple which appears to be a vision (with audition) like those the biblical prophets normally experience (see the programmatic Num 12:6-8[118]), Paul can counter the accusation of his Jewish opponents

---

[113] See Jervell, *Apostelgeschichte*, 544-45.

[114] Classically, the problem of the differing accounts of Paul's conversion and subsequent stay in Jerusalem (Acts 9:1-31; 22:1-22; 26:4-20) is solved source-critically by attributing them to different sources; see Jervell, *Apostelgeschichte*, 545 with literature in footnote 77; Hans Conzelmann, *Die Apostelgeschichte*, HNT 7, 2nd ed. (Tübingen: Mohr Siebeck, 1972), 135-36.

[115] Pervo, *Acts*, 565.

[116] Daniel's vision takes place "in the hour of the evening sacrifice" (Dan 9:21), so the cultic context is also given here.

[117] See Pervo, *Acts*, 566; see Robert K. Gnuse, "The temple Theophanies of Jaddus, Hyrcanus, and Zechariah," *Biblica* 79.4 (1998): 457-72.

[118] See for this text Nicolaas F. Schmidt and Philip J. Nel, "Theophany as type-scene in the Hebrew Bible," *JSem* 11.2 (2002): 256-81, 258-59.

Eva-Maria Kreitschmann

that he taught "against the people and the law"[119] and against the temple (Acts 21:28). He stands firmly on the ground of biblical Israel which is directed by divine dreams and visions. This rhetorical aim of Paul to find common ground with the angry group of his compatriots can be seen throughout his speech, especially at the beginning: Paul addresses his audience using the intimate title "brothers and fathers" (Ἄνδρες ἀδελφοὶ καὶ πατέρες, 22:1). He talks to them in Hebrew or Aramaic (τῇ Ἑβραΐδι διαλέκτῳ, 22:1) and gives further "empathic assertions"[120] of his Jewish identity by pointing to his ethnic affiliation (ἐγώ εἰμι ἀνὴρ Ἰουδαῖος; v. 3) and his Jewish education παρὰ τοὺς πόδας Γαμαλιήλ (v. 3), which took place "according to the strict manner of the law of our fathers" (κατὰ ἀκρίβειαν τοῦ πατρῴου νόμου, v. 3). Consequently, he talks of himself "being" or rather "having been zealous" (ζηλωτὴς ὑπάρχων, v. 3) for God as his compatriots are now (καθὼς πάντες ὑμεῖς ἐστε [v. 3]). In sum, Luke depicts Paul and his commission not as something entirely new but as the continuation of God's beneficial action for his people Israel, whom he has always protected and guided throughout history. Even more than in Acts 10 where hints of an ambivalent or even confusing religious experience remain, in Acts 22:17 Luke portrays the ecstatic experience as an ordinary event and thus uses it as a means of legitimizing Paul's mission to the Gentiles for the Jerusalem Jews.[121] Nevertheless, the specific content of Paul's ἔκστασις, namely, to leave Jerusalem and to continue his mission among the Gentiles, transcends the norms of the Jerusalem Jews who want to keep the veneration of God in the sanctuary free from Gentiles (21:28). The transgression of the social and religious norm that Gentiles cannot be part of God's people is highlighted by the representation of Paul's expe-

[119] English Standard Version.
[120] Gaventa, Acts, 305.
[121] That prophetic experiences were not only valued by Jews but also by their pagan environment is shown by the example of Josephus. He can present himself as a prophet in front of Vespasian (B.J. 3,400–402), a pagan military leader who was "concerned to find ways to legitimize [his] status in the absence of good birth and lineage" (Idan Breier, "'If You Are Not the King You Will Be Eventually...': Eastern and Western Prophecies Concerning the Rise of Emperors," Religions 11.4 (2020): 1–18, doi:10.3390/rel11010004., 6). It is not unlikely that one among several reasons why Josephus was not executed by Vespasian and Titus was his prophecy (see Breier, "Prophecies," 5) and thus his high estimation as an oriental or rather a Jewish prophet.

253

rience by the unusual term of ἔκστασις that underlines the extraordinary and innovative character of Paul's vision. The term ἔκστασις also relates Paul's experience to Peter's, underlying the parallelism of both events.

6 Conclusion

Luke is particularly interested in extraordinary religious and ecstatic phenomena such as dreams, visions and inspired prophetic speeches. Regarding these events under the perspective of normality and abnormality, it is important to note the basic sociological insight that the definition of what is "normal" or "deviant" always depends on underlying cultural norms.[122] Luke, who is part of the ancient Jewish and Greek frame of reference, can draw on dreams and visions as a "conventional plot mechanism"[123] widely known in Jewish and Greek religious (and non-religious) literature. But a closer look at his work shows that things are more complex. Luke says that the emerging Christian community had to face the accusation of behaving abnormally or even being mad. The inspired prophetic speech of the Christ-followers at Pentecost is seen by outsiders as drunkenness (Acts 2:12–13.15). The Roman prefect Festus states that Paul is mad after having heard the account of Paul's christophany at Damascus and of the resurrection of Jesus: "Paul, you are mad (μαίνῃ, Παῦλε). Your great learning is driving you insane (εἰς μανίαν περιτρέπει)." (Acts 26:24). Here we encounter accusations of religious deviance that Christ-followers may have had to cope from the very beginning. While Judaism in the Greco-Roman world was sometimes seen as an honored and ancient *ethnos* which could attract outsiders, the young Christian congregation faced problems of self-definition when they were excluded from Jewish communities.[124] Luke's reception of and interest in

---

[122] See Siegfried Lamnek, *Theorien abweichenden Verhaltens: 1. Klassische Ansätze*, vol. 1 of *Theorien abweichenden Verhaltens: eine Einführung für Soziologen, Psychologen, Juristen, Journalisten und Sozialarbeiter*, ed. idem (Paderborn: Wilhelm Fink, 2018), 34–39.

[123] Harris, "Hallucinations," 290.

[124] See Steve Mason, "Jews, Judaeans, Judaizing, Judaism: Problems of Categorization in Ancient History," *JSJ* 38 (2007): 457–512, see 512; Mason, Jews, 497.499, points to remarks of Celsus and Julian, who blame Christians especially of having abandoned the Jewish way of life, i.e., the ancestral customs of the Jewish ethnos (Orig., Cels. 2.1, 3; 5.35; Julian, C. Gal.

Eva-Maria Kreitschmann

Jewish-biblical themes and his positive attitude towards Jewish piety (e.g., temple service, prayer) points to an apologetic purpose in his work, namely to show that the Christian group does not practice sinful deviance from the ancestral laws but fulfills God's will and purpose. Thus Luke is interested in depicting the unusual and supernatural experiences of important leaders of the community, as in accordance with the established Jewish system of beliefs. He *reintegrates* the abnormality of ecstatic experiences into an accepted and institutionalized religion.[125] This can be seen from Cornelius's and Peter's visions in Acts 10:1–16, where Cornelius is depicted as a pious God-Fearer in the manner of Abraham. At the same time, Peter's strange ecstatic experience (ἔκστασις) is related to the theme of prayer, the normal and accepted place of divine encounters or revelations in Jewish thinking. Paul's ἔκστασις is also contextualized by the generally accepted place (temple) and practice (prayer).

Nevertheless, Luke leaves space for the abnormal and the deviant in his account and he uses it artfully to position his message of Gentile inclusion as a transgression of socio-religious boundaries. This can be seen especially in his unusual use of the noun ἔκστασις for the revelations to Peter and Paul: a lexical investigation of ἔκστασις and cognate verbs in the non-biblical and biblical environment has shown that the primary meaning is not "receiving higher knowledge," but that aspects of confusion, of losing one's sound state of mind, and even illness and madness are paramount. The use in Plato and Philo show that there was discussion about the character of divine madness and an effort to relate it to more honored forms of supernatural experience and piety. Especially in Acts 10:9–16, Luke does not remove these ambiguous connotations. Instead, he

---

343c–d, 346e–347c; Ep. 20.453; 41.436c–d). While Mason's perspective on ancient Judaism not as "religion" in the modern sense, but as cultural embedded "religion," as ethnos, sheds light on the processes of identity formation in early Christianity, his attempt has also been criticized as an oversimplification. Seth Schwartz convincingly argues that perceptions of Judaism as an ethnos and as a religion, i.e., a system of practices and beliefs people could attend via conversion, coexisted in antiquity (see Seth Schwartz, "How many Judaisms Were There? A Critique of Neusner and Smith on Definition and Mason and Boyarin on Categorization," JAJ 2 (2011): 208–238).
[125] For the integration of ecstatic experiences into institutionalized religions see Gladigow, "Ekstase," 39–40.

shapes the narrative context of Peter's ἔκστασις in contrast to the clear and conventional angelophany of Cornelius. In my opinion, he does this to emphasize that the recognition of the young Jewish-Christian congregation that Gentiles are to be fully admitted was something crucial and extraordinary. Luke shows in his work that this recognition was initiated and accompanied by extraordinary and unusual ecstatic experiences that even transcended the experiences that the pious of Israel had made throughout history. Especially Peter's ἔκστασις marks the beginning of the important religious innovation that Jews and non-Jews can be united in table fellowship. The critical and creative potential of deviant ecstatic experiences by which alternative forms of reality are imagined can be seen in Peter's vision and also in Paul's.

Theories on deviant behavior state that it can have an innovative character because it destabilizes former contexts of meaning and can lead to reconstitutions of communities or societies.[126] Luke shows how the extraordinary experiences of Peter and Paul led to a fundamental change in the idea of who belongs to the people of God. But at the same time, he balances it with his aim to (re-)integrate the ecstatic experiences of the Christ followers into the recognized Jewish religion by showing that the inclusion of Gentiles happened in accordance with the will of Israel's God.

---

[126] Nina Oelkers, Abweichendes Verhalten. socialnet Lexikon (Bonn: socialnet, 2019), *https://www.socialnet.de/lexikon/Abweichendes-Verhalten.*

Part III: Patristics

Who Really is a Fool and Who is Not? Wisdom of Solomon 5:4 in Early Christian Interpretation

Anni Maria Laato

1 Introduction

The concepts of madness and folly are found both in the Scriptures (e.g. 1 Cor 1–2) and in its early Christian interpretations, and are ambiguous terms in both; they can denote negative and positive behavior, sometimes at the same time.[1] In early Christian literature, these concepts were often used to explore and explain behavior that was seen as abnormal or deviant in the eyes of the outsiders, whoever they were. Precisely the ambiguity of these concepts made it possible for the early Christian theologians to negotiate who, in the end, was mad or a fool and, conversely, who was wise.

In this paper, I explore the early Christian interpretation of just one verse mentioning madness or folly, namely Wisdom of Solomon 5:4. In this verse, the outsiders see that they—instead of the suffering righteous whom they had regarded as fools—have been the fools, and say in remorse:

> These are persons whom we once held in derision and made a byword of reproach—fools that we were! We thought that their lives were madness and that their end was without honor. (NRSV)

---

[1] For madness and folly in Antiquity and Early Christian literature, see Laura Nasrallah, *An Ecstasy of Folly. Prophecy and Authority in Early Christianity* (Cambridge, MA: Harvard University Press, 2003); and Anni Maria Laato, "Adam's Ecstasy and Prophecy in Tertullian," in *Adam and Eve Story in Jewish, Christian and Islamic Perspectives.* eds. Antti Laato and Lotta Valve, Studies in the Reception History of the Bible 8 (Winona Lake, IN: Eisenbrauns, 2017), 71–83.

Wisdom of Salomon 5:4 in Early Christian Interpretation

οὗτος ἦν ὃν ἔσχομέν ποτε εἰς γέλωτα καὶ εἰς παραβολὴν ὀνειδισμοῦ οἱ ἄφρονες· τὸν βίον αὐτοῦ ἐλογισάμεθα μανίαν καὶ τὴν τελευτὴν αὐτοῦ ἄτιμον. (LXX)
Hi sunt quos habuimus aliquando in risu et in similitudine inproperii. nos insensati vitam illorum aestimabamus insaniam et finem illorum sine honore. (Vetus Latina)

I focus on two different kinds of cases in which this particular verse was used by early Christian authors to discuss contemporary situations where the behavior of certain Christians provoked criticism amongst the 'outsiders.'[2] First, Cyprian used this verse to describe the martyrs in Carthage in the third century; and second, Jerome used it to characterize female ascetics in his circle in the fourth century. In both cases, a Christian interpreter of the Bible claimed that the behavior of some particular Christians was explicitly called "madness" (amentia, insania) by others. In neither case was the madness a question of being out of one's senses or a prophecy, ecstasy or something similar in the more usual meaning of these Latin words. Instead, in these particular instances it was a behavior that was incomprehensible in the eyes of the majority, and thus deviant from what was usually expected in their culture. In Cyprian's context, the martyrs were willing to die rather than making a simple offering to the Roman gods; and in Jerome's context, some Roman aristocratic women gave up their life of luxury, choosing poverty instead—something that was considered madness by two different groups of people, namely pagan Romans and many moderate, less-ascetic-minded Christians in Rome. By using the biblical figure of a suffering righteous one whom others labelled as mad, the situation of these two groups of contemporary Christians was, thus, explained and new forms of normal and abnormal behavior were constructed and promoted.

In this paper I analyse more closely passages from Cyprian and Jerome where they interpret Wis 5:4; first, in order to see what both mean by madness and other kinds of abnormal behavior in their interpretations of

---

[2] I have found the passages in Cyprian with the help of Biblia patristica (Biblia patristica. Index des citations et allusions bibliques dans la littérature patristique. 5 vols. [Paris: Éditions du Centre national de la recherche scientifique, 1975-]), and in Jerome while working with a book on early Christian women (Anni Maria Laato, Matres Ecclesiae [Helsinki: Perussanoma, 2011]).

this biblical passage and, second, to determine what they want to say about that in their own contexts. In both cases the Christian authors emphasize that what is regarded as abnormal or deviant behavior depends on who is defining it; and in both cases, the Christian authors not only want to argue against those in positions of power but also promote new ways of living.

2 The Original Context and Meaning of Wis 5:4

The Wisdom of Solomon (*Sapientia Salomonis*) was written in Alexandria during the first century BCE. Its chapters 2–5 form a single literary unit that deals with the problem of the suffering of the righteous at the hands of their enemies.[3] The question posed in the text is: why do enemies prosper, while the righteous one, who trusts in God and serves him, has to suffer? In the eyes of the wicked, the righteous one looks like a fool, like a mad man; the author, however, problematizes this view and asks rhetorically who, in the end, is foolish and who is wise and demonstrates understanding (Wis 3:2; 5:4). In answer, the author claims that the present sufferings and successes are only temporary and eventually, in the afterlife, the roles will be reversed: The righteous will be rewarded, but the wicked ones will realize what they have done, see that they themselves were the foolish ones and will be punished (Wis 4:20; 5:5). In the end, it is the righteous ones who are wise and the wicked ones are those who do not understand the secrets of God (Wis 2:22).

It is worth noting that the author of this text has quoted and interpreted Isa 53 in a way that does not contain the idea of a vicarious atoning suffering;[4] instead the focus is on encouraging those who do suffer, giving them hope of a future reward. Wis 5:4 summarises three important questions that are present in chapters 2–5: the identities of both "the others" and "the righteous"; what is meant by the insanity; and finally, how the situation of the two groups should be evaluated.

---

[3] David Winston, *The Wisdom of Solomon*, AB 43 (Garden City: Doubleday, 1979), 59–63; Antti Laato, *Who is the Servant of the Lord? Jewish and Christian Interpretations on Isaiah 53 from Antiquity to the Middle Ages* (Winona Lake, IN: Eisenbrauns 2012), esp. 88.
[4] See Antti Laato, "Ancient, Medieval, and Modern Jewish Traditions" in *The Oxford Handbook of Isaiah*. ed. Lena-Sofia Tiemeyer (Oxford: Oxford University Press, 2020), 507–30, esp. 519.

In the patristic period, this verse was quoted or alluded to, among others, by Cyprian and Jerome, who can be seen as representing two different kinds of ways of using this verse, and more broadly, the whole passage Wis 2–5. Neither of them explained what the text meant in its original context, but instead directly applied it to their own times.

3 Christian Martyrs in Carthage

In the midst of the persecutions, Christians found the Wisdom of Solomon 2–5 very useful.[5] In the eyes of the pagan Romans, the stubbornness of the Christians must have seemed insane indeed, as can be seen in many of the martyr-stories.[6] Cyprian, writing in the middle of the third century, quoted Wis 5:4 three times, always to explain the fate of the martyrs, and to encourage suffering Christians with the promise of rewards in the afterlife. In his interpretation, "the others" who regard the life of the martyrs as madness, were those who were responsible for the persecution of the Christians.

In his letter to Fortunatus (*Epistola ad Fortunatum de exhortatione martyrii*),[7] possibly a fellow-bishop in North Africa, Cyprian encourages Christians in the midst of persecutions. This letter is in fact a collection of Scriptural passages, organized by Cyprian under different themes dealing with questions concerning the martyrs.[8] He quotes biblical passages without explaining them in his own words—doing this in order to let "the

---

[5] In pre-Constantinian texts, parts of it are often quoted; see Biblia Patristica.

[6] See e.g. in the Passion of the Scillitan Martyrs from 180 AD, the proconsul Saturninus cries to the imprisoned Christians, "Do not participate in this folly (*dementia*) of his," in *Greek and Latin Narratives about the Ancient Martyrs*, ed. Éric Rebillard (Oxford: Oxford University Press 2017), 356–57. For the attitudes of the Roman officials towards the Christian martyrs, see Glen W. Bowersock, Martyrdom and Rome (Cambridge: Cambridge University Press, 2010) and Jan Willem van Henten, "The Martyrs as Heroes of the Christian People. Some Remarks on the Continuity between Jewish and Christian Martyrology, with Pagan Analogies," in: Mathijs Lamberigts and Peter van Deun (eds), *Martyrium in Multidisciplinary Perspective*, BETL 107, Leuven: Leuven University Press/Uitgeverij Peeters, 1995, 303–22.

[7] *Epistola ad Fortunatum* (CCSL 3:181–216).

[8] Johan Leemans and Anthony Dupont, "Scripture and Martyrdom," in *The Oxford Handbook of Early Christian Biblical Interpretation*, eds. Paul M. Blowers and Peter W. Martens (Oxford: Oxford University Press, 2019), 417–38, esp. 20–22) present Cyprian's rubrics in this work as a good overview of his martyr theology.

Lord speak" as he states in the preface.[9] Near the end of the text, in chapter 12, he deals with the rewards the martyrs will receive after the sufferings in this world and also the punishment that their enemies will face. Among several other passages[10] he also quotes Wis 5:4. He does not explain explicitly what insanity means in this verse, but it is clear that refusing to offer sacrifices to Roman gods in the midst of severe persecutions certainly looked foolish to the eyes of non-Christians.

Cyprian's *Testimonia* collection is constructed in a similar way. He has collected Scriptural quotes under thematic titles. In 3.16, under the title *Of the benefits of martyrdom*, he quotes Wis 5:1-9 among sixteen other quotations. He writes,

> In the Proverbs of Solomon: "The faithful martyr delivers his soul from evils." Also in the same place: "Then shall the righteous stand in great boldness against them who have afflicted them, and who took away their labours. When they see them, they shall be disturbed with a horrible fear; and they shall wonder at the suddenness of their unhoped-for salvation, saying among themselves, repenting and groaning with distress of spirit, These are they whom some time we had in derision, and in the likeness of a proverb; we fools counted their life madness, and their end without honour. How are they reckoned among the children of God, and their lot among the saints! Therefore we have wandered from the way of truth, and the light of righteousness has not shined upon us, and the sun has not risen upon us. We have been wearied in the way of iniquity and of perdition, and we have walked through difficult solitudes; but we have not known the way of the Lord. What has pride profited us? Or what has the boasting of riches brought to us? All these things have passed away as a shadow." (Wis 5:1–9)[11]

The third quotation is found in Cyprian's letter to Demetrianus, a proconsul of Africa; the letter is an apology for Christians, or rather a counter-attack against a Roman magistrate. Foolishness is a recurring

[9] *Epistola ad Fortunatum*, Preface 3 (CCSL 3:184).
[10] Wis 3.1;3.4; Ps 135:3,8; Ps 143; Matt 5:10; Luke 6:22; 9:24; 18:29; Rev 20:4.
[11] CSEL 3.1, 128–29. English translation by Robert Ernest Wallis. *Ante-Nicene Fathers*, Vol. 5. Edited by Alexander Roberts, James Donaldson, and A. Cleveland Coxe (Buffalo, NY: Christian Literature, 1886). Revised and edited for New Advent by Kevin Knight.

theme in this letter. Cyprian quotes several biblical passages to show that the true fools are those who persecute and not the persecuted Christians. In fact, he claims it is actually quite useless to write to Demetrius who is a true fool, and quotes two proverbs, "Speak not in the ears of a fool, lest when he hear you he should despise the wisdom of your words" (Prov 23:9) and "Answer not a fool according to his folly, lest you also be like him" (Prov 24:9).

Even if he thinks that it might be useless to write to "a madman" (i.e. the proconsul, Demetrianus), nonetheless, he decides to do so.

> For when you used often to come to me with the desire of contradicting rather than with the wish to learn, and preferred impudently to insist on your own views, which you shouted with noisy words, to patiently listening to mine, it seethed to me foolish to contend with you; since it would be an easier and slighter thing to restrain the angry waves of a turbulent sea with shouts, than to check your madness by arguments. Assuredly it would be both a vain and ineffectual labour to offer light to a blind man, discourse to a deaf one, or wisdom to a brute; since neither can a brute apprehend, nor can a blind man admit the light, nor can a deaf man hear.[12]

In chapter 24, Cyprian quotes Wis 5:1–9 to express both the reward that the Christians are going to receive and the punishment their persecutors will meet. He first refers to the prophecy of the Day of Judgement in Isa 66:24, and continues with Wis 5:1–9:

> And again: "Then shall the righteous men stand in great constancy before the face of those who have afflicted them, and have taken away their labours. When they see it, they shall be troubled with horrible fear, and shall be amazed at the suddenness of their unexpected salvation; and they, repenting and groaning for anguish of spirit, shall say within themselves, These are they whom we had some time in derision, and a proverb of reproach; we fools counted their life madness, and their end to be without honour. How are they numbered among the children of God, and their lot is among the saints! Therefore have we erred from the way of truth, and the light of righteousness has not shined upon us, and the sun rose not on us. We wearied ourselves in the way of wickedness and destruction; we have

---

[12] Cyprian, *Demetr.* 1 [2.1] (CCSL 3A: 35).

Anni Maria Laato

gone through deserts where there lay no way; but we have not known the way of the Lord. What has pride profited us, or what good has the boasting of riches done us? All those things are passed away like a shadow. (Wis 5:1–9)[13]

The Christians, however, did not interpret Wis 2–5 only as referring to the fate of the Christian martyrs; it was also seen as a prophecy of the suffering and the death of Christ. The passage 2:12–22, in particular, was seen as prefiguring Christ on the cross.[14] People mocked the suffering righteous, Christ, but eventually they will be seen as having been blind.[15]

In martyrological literature, martyrdom was commonly seen as *imitatio Christi*. It is a frequently recurring idea that just as Christ had borne witness in front of a Roman magistrate, so did the martyrs; just as he had suffered and died, so did the martyrs who followed him; and just as he rose from the death, so will they (1 Tim 6:13; 1 Pet 2:21; Rom 6:3).[16] A good example of these ideas is *The Martyrs of Lyon and Vienne* (1.10; 2.2 and 1.30 which makes an explicit mention of 1 Tim 6:13).[17] The martyrs became *exempla* for perseverance in suffering, an example for other Christians to follow. In some texts, their suffering and death seems to have had some kind of salvific (expiatory) meaning, but in most cases their death is not presented as being beneficial to others but rather as the means for the martyr him/herself to come to God in the afterlife.[18] An important idea in Cyprian's martyr theology is that martyrdom should not be sought voluntarily, but rather accepted when it comes at the appointed time.[19] Both the Martyrdom of Polycarp (19) and The Martyrs of Lyon and Vienna use Isa 53 to interpret the fate of the martyrs.[20]

---

13 CCSL 3A:49–50.
14 E. g. Cyprian, *Test.* 2.14 (CSEL 3.1:79).
15 Cf. Augustine, *Faust.* 12.44 (CSEL 25/1:373).
16 Leemans and Dupont, "Scripture and Martyrdom," 418–19.
17 Lugd. 1.10, 30; 2.2 (TU 172:54, 60, 74).
18 See e.g. Ign. *Rom.* 2.2; 4.2; Ign. *Eph.* 21.1; Ign. *Smyrn.* 10.2. See Leemans and Dupont, "Scripture and Martyrdom," 419.
19 For this so called kairological martyrdom, see Leemans and Dupont, "Scripture and Martyrdom," 429–31.
20 *Lugd.* 1.23 (TU 172:58). For Isa 53 in Christian Martyr-texts, see Laato, *Who is the Servant of the Lord*, 229.

265

In sum, in times of persecution, the image of the suffering righteous whom all others considered a fool, was applied both to Christ and to the suffering Christians. It was thought that in the same way as the righteous in Wisdom of Solomon, the Christian martyrs would eventually have their reward; moreover their persecutors will be revealed to be the real fools and receive their due punishment. Cyprian does not explain precisely what he means by foolishness or the madness of the righteous but, similar to the author of Wisdom of Solomon, he contrasts those in this world who are regarded as mad by others with those who will eventually be proven to be mad. Thus he argues against those who were currently in power, such as the proconsul, Demetrius.

4 "Her Life was Accounted as Madness": Lea, Asella, Paula and Jerome

In the second half of the fourth century, the persecutions of the Christians had ceased, and being a Christian was no longer seen as abnormal; it had become normalized in Roman society. In this situation, a new way of interpreting Wis 5:4 emerged. Jerome, a skilled rhetor, used this passage to promote an ascetic life-style and to console those who were criticized for their ascetic choices.

On the same day that Lea, a leader of a women's ascetic community in Ostia or in Rome, suddenly died, Jerome wrote a letter of consolation to their mutual friend, Marcella.[21] This letter, letter 23, was written in Rome in December 384 or in January 385, shortly before Jerome left the city and settled in Bethlehem. In it, Jerome recalls the life of Lea, and states that her life was regarded by others as madness, *amentia*.[22] He quite clearly alludes to Wis 5:4.

Jerome recounts that Lea had originally been a rich aristocrat and mistress of a large household, but had subsequently chosen an ascetic life

---

[21] Lea belonged to the network of aristocratic women who had chosen ascetic life. Jerome calls her *monasterii princeps, mater virginum* (*Ep.* 23.2.2 [CSEL 54:212]). Marcella, too, was an aristocratic woman who had chosen an ascetic life long before Jerome came to Rome, and led a community of female ascetics on the Aventine hill. For more on both, see Silvia Letsch-Brunner, *Marcella—Discipula et Magistra. Auf die Spuren einer römischen Christin des 4. Jahrhunderts*, BZNW 91 (Berlin; New York: de Gruyter, 1998), especially pp. 146–55.
[22] Jerome, *Ep.* 23.3.3 (CSEL 54:213).

and given up her status and wealth. Having first described Lea's life of humility and poverty, Jerome then compares her life with that of a consul-elect, Vettius Agorius Praetextatus, who died about the same time as Lea. Whereas Lea had lived in poverty, the consul had spent his days in richness; Lea had worn simple clothing while the consul was clothed in purple; Lea was shut up in her cell whereas the consul had celebrated triumph publicly. Jerome concludes that with the death of both individuals, things changed: "*O quanta rerum mutatio!*" Lea, whose life was regarded as madness by others, is now enjoying everlasting felicity, but the consul is in Tartaros.[23] Jerome ends the comparison of Lea to Praetextatus with an allusion to Wis 5:4 stating, "Now she follows Christ" (*Christum sequitur*).[24] Thinking of Wis 5:4, where outsiders look at the life of the suffering righteous, Jerome, too, regards Lea's life from the point of view of the outsiders *cuius vita putabatur amentia*, "whose life was accounted as madness."[25]

Who though are "the others" in Jerome's letter? Are they the non-Christian Roman aristocracy, such as Praetextatus, in the eyes of whom Lea's choice must have looked insane, or are they perhaps more likely to be those Roman Christians who were less than enthusiastic about excessive asceticism and criticized it? From the point of view of both these groups, Lea's abnormal behavior, her madness, consisted of her voluntarily giving up her position and wealth and choosing a life of poverty, serving others instead.

In order to be able to answer this question, we first look at Jerome's letter and then at Jerome's views on asceticism more broadly.[26] In the letter about Lea, Jerome uses the life of the consul-elect Praetextatus, an "arch-pagan" as Curran calls him,[27] as a mirror: he is an epitome of a successful Roman life. The two are compared with the rich man and Lazarus (Luke

---

[23] Jerome, *Ep.* 23.2.1 (CSEL 54:212). In this era Tartaros simply means "hell" or "underworld"; this word is used in *Vetus Latina* e.g. in 2 Pet 2:4–5.

[24] Jerome, *Ep.* 23.3.3 (CSEL 54:213).

[25] Jerome, *Ep.* 23.3.3 (CSEL 54:213).

[26] For the different attitudes towards asceticism in Rome at this time, see John Curran, *Pagan City and Christian Capital. Rome in the Fourth Century* (Oxford: Oxford University Press, 2000), especially pages 260–320.

[27] Curran, *Pagan City and Christian Capital,* 266.

16:19–24).[28] Jerome claims that their positions are reversed in the afterlife: in a similar way to how the pauper in the bosom of Abraham sees the rich man in torment, Lea sees the consul in mourning and asking for a drop of water. Praetextatus is now a prisoner in darkness, but Lea is enjoying everlasting happiness. Jerome compares both the outer and inner life of the two deceased. He concludes that the comparison teaches us that worldly power and its associated richness must be rejected, and eternal things are to be chosen instead. Jerome, an ardent proponent of the ascetic life, asks, in "tears and trepidation," his readers to choose 'either-or': either life in the world or life in Christ. One cannot have both Christ and the world.

Even though Jerome wrote this letter of consolation to Marcella and not primarily to the larger Christian community in Rome, he most probably had a larger audience in mind. Nevertheless, on the basis of this letter alone, we cannot conclude who "the others" in Jerome's interpretation actually are. The comparison to Praetextatus hints towards the non-Christian aristocracy, as Jerome painted a clear contrast between this-worldly success, personified in Praetextatus, and its counterpart, madness and abnormal behavior, personified in Lea. However, we do know from elsewhere that not many other Roman Christians shared Jerome's and his friends' excessive asceticism.[29] In fact, it may be that his main target was not the pagans at all, but rather other, more moderate, Christians in Rome.[30]

By describing Lea's ascetic life in detail and praising it, Jerome clearly wanted to promote a new Christian ascetic life-style. He emphasized the new ideals compared to pagan ones, but also criticized the, at least in his mind, too-worldly Christians. The end-goal for him, however, was not specific life-styles in this world but rather life everlasting. The final outcome is what really counts, as is the case in Wis 5:4. Jerome claims that what was regarded as madness by "others," would eventually lead to

---

[28] Jerome, *Ep.* 23.3.1 (CSEL 54:213).

[29] Stefan Rebenich, *Jerome* (London; New York: Routledge 2002), 34–36; Jer. *Ep.* 22.16.2–3; *Ep.* 66.13.

[30] For the conflict between moderate Christians and extreme ascetics in Rome, see Curran, *Pagan City and Christian Capital*, 269, 280.

happiness. Eventually there will be a complete role reversal: those who regarded the righteous as insane will perish. This is quite in line with the original meaning of the verse.

In a letter to Asella (*Ep.* 45), another woman ascetic in the same circle, Jerome contrasts the way of life of the ascetics and that of more moderate Christians even more sharply.[31] Written at the harbor prior to leaving Rome because of accusations made against him, Jerome again extolls the life of poverty, simplicity, grief and fasting, and criticizes a life spent in luxury.[32] Each of these two kinds of people sees the other group as insane (*invicem nobis videmur insani*).[33] Even here, the insanity Jerome speaks about is one of giving up a life of luxury and choosing to live a life of poverty and fasting. In the historical context of this letter, where other Christians heavily criticized Jerome and forced him to leave Rome, it seems more likely that "the others" are actually those who regarded Jerome and his friend as insane, i.e., they were not primarily non-Christians but rather other Roman Christians.

A third example of Jerome's extolling "insane" ascetic women is that of Paula, who together with her daughter, Julia Eustochium, followed Jerome to Bethlehem and founded a monastery there.[34] In Jerome's epitaph to Paula, letter 108, he describes her life at great length. Born in the senatorial class in Rome, a descendant of one of the oldest families and mother to several children, Paula renounced everything and chose to live as an ascetic. She donated all her wealth—piece by piece—to the poor and to the church, and on so doing quoted the Gospel: "What does it benefit a man if he gains the whole world but loses his life?" (Matt 16:26) and "Do not love this world nor the things of this world, for everything that is in this world is desire of the flesh, and desire of the eyes, and pride in this life

---

[31] For Asella, see Letsch-Brunner, *Marcella*, 155–60.

[32] After the death of pope Damasus, Jerome soon ended up in conflict with moderate Christians in Rome. See Rebenich, *Jerome*, 39.

[33] Jerome, *Ep.* 45.5.2 (CSEL 54:327).

[34] For Paula, see Anni Maria Laato, "What Makes the Holy Land Holy? A Debate between Paula, Eustochium, and Marcella (Jer.ep.46)," in *Holy Places and Cult*, eds. J. Cornelis de Vos and Erkki Koskenniemi, Studies in the Reception History of the Bible 5 (Winona Lake, IN: Eisenbrauns, 2014), 169–99.

which do not come from the Father but are of this world. And the world and its desire will pass away" (1 John 2:15–17).[35]

Jerome writes about how the others saw Paula:

> I am aware that some telltale (the worst kind of person) had told her (pretending to do so out of kindness) that some people thought her insane because what they considered her excessive zeal for virtue; they thought she needed counselling. To these she replied: 'We have been made a spectacle to the world, to angels and to mortals; we are fools for Christ's sake but the foolishness of God is wiser than men (1 Cor 4:9–10, 1:25).[36]

Like Lea, Paula is reported to have followed Christ. Jerome recounts that Paula referred to how Jesus's relatives thought he was mad (Mark 3:21), and highlighted several other biblical passages that express the difference between Christ and Christians on the one hand, and the world on the other. Much of what Christ did looked like insanity in the eyes of the world. Jerome concludes: "She used these and other similar passages from the Scripture to arm herself with the armour of Christ."[37] A little later on, Jerome states that Paula "followed the Lamb everywhere he went and she who was hungry is now filled."[38] As in the case of Lea, Jerome calls this a fortunate exchange: Paula wept, was hungry, was poor and so on, but everything changed with her death. Jerome quotes Isa 65:13–14, where the final fate of the servants of the Lord and "the others" is contrasted: "Behold my servants will eat but you will be hungry, my servants will drink but you will be thirsty, me servants will rejoice but you will be put to shame."[39]

In this letter, Jerome does not quote Wis 5:4, but he does, nonetheless, present the same ideas about folly. Ascetics, who have renounced their wealth in this world, look insane and mad in the eyes of the people of this

---

[35] Jerome, *Ep.* 108.19.3 (CSEL 55:332–33).
[36] Jerome, *Ep.* 108.19.5 (CSEL 55:333). English translation by William H. Fremantle, George Lewis and William G. Martley. Nicene and Post-Nicene Fathers, Second Series, Vol. 6. Edited by Philip Schaff and Henry Wace (Buffalo, NY: Christian Literature, 1893). Revised and edited for New Advent by Kevin Knight.
[37] Jerome, *Ep.* 108.19.8 (CSEL 55:334).
[38] Jerome, *Ep.* 108.22.1 (CSEL 55:338).
[39] Jerome, *Ep.* 108.22.2 (CSEL 55:339).

world, but that will change. In the end, those who accused them will be shown to be insane. As earlier, even this context, "the others" include both pagan Romans and the more moderate Christians.

However, it was not only these women who were accused of insanity; in a letter to Laeta, Jerome states that Paula's son Toxotius and Toxotius's father-in-law, Albinus, thought that Jerome himself was insane and drunk (*insanus et ebrius*). Despite this clash, he expressed the hope that Albinus might convert to Christianity: "For though he may spit upon my letter and laugh at it, and though he may call me a fool or a madman, his son-in-law did the same before he came to believe. Christians are not born but made."[40] In this letter, the madness in the eyes of non-Christians is simply being a Christian.

All these examples show that Jerome used the concepts of madness and being insane (*amentia, insanus esse*) rhetorically in order to create a contrast between ascetic Christians on the one hand and both non-Christian aristocracy as well as those moderate Christian groups who were less keen on ascetic life-styles on the other. Only in the first example does he actually allude to Wis 5:4, but the idea of folly is, nonetheless, present in all the examples. His examples of insanity are quite simple and under-standable; that a rich person chooses to leave his or her life of wealth to live in poverty certainly looked foolish in the eyes of aristocratic Romans and in the eyes of many Christians in Rome, too. In Jerome's interpretation, the inability of the others to understand the life of the righteous is explained by their blindness (cf. Wis 2:21 "their wickedness blinded them").

Jerome quite clearly connects the insanity of the ascetics to their following of Christ. He explicitly reminds his readers that Christ was regarded as mad, too, and his followers should not expect any other kind of fate.

5 Conclusions

The Wisdom of Solomon 2–5, and in particular verse 5:4, contrasts the successful life of people in this world with the sufferings of the righteous.

---

[40] Jerome, *Ep.* 107.1.4 (CSEL 55:291).

The life of the righteous looks insane in the eyes of the wicked, but eventually the wicked will notice that they themselves had erred. The righteous will be rewarded while the wicked will receive their just punishment. The early Christians interpreted this passage both Christologically and as referring to the fate of the martyrs and the extreme ascetics. The step from Christological interpretation to applying it to Christians is a natural one; the idea that Christians who follow Christ share his fate is already present in the New Testament.[41] Both Wisdom of Solomon 2–5 and 1 Pet 2:22 use Isa 53 and apply it to the suffering righteous, and thus belong to the reception history of this chapter. Isa 53, for its part, was interpreted both Christologically and as referring to the martyrs in the early church (e.g. Mart. Polyc.).

Cyprian applied Wis 5:4 to Christian martyrs who were labelled mad by others, and to their persecutors, who, according to him, were the truly mad. It was not a random choice that caused Jerome to apply the same verse, Wis 5:4, used earlier in martyr-theology, to ascetics. At the end of letter 108, Paula's epitaph, he actually calls Paula's asceticism "a long martyrdom,"[42] and says, "It is not only the shedding of blood that is considered a confession: the service performed by a devout mind is also a daily martyrdom. Both are rewarded with a crown."[43] Even if the simplicistic claim that ascetic renunciation took the place of martyrdom long after the latter had ceased no longer holds true, there is, nevertheless, some truth in it. The ascetics of the fourth century did sometimes see themselves as following the path of the martyrs, as shown above.

In the cases presented above, the madness does not imply prophecy or ecstasy but rather the following of Christ that took forms that deviated from the choices of the majority. The stubbornness of the martyrs in their refusal to offer sacrifice to the Roman gods was, of course, a deviation of normal behavior in the eyes of Roman officials, as was the excessive asceticism in the eyes of both the Romans and more moderate Christians. The abnormality in these texts was thus both real—the behavior of the martyrs and the ascetics deviated from the standard (even if Jerome did

---

[41] E.g. 1 Tim 6:13; 1 Pet 2:21–22; Rom 6:3.
[42] Jerome, *Ep.* 108.31.1 (CSEL 55:349).
[43] Jerome, *Ep.* 108.31.1 (CSEL 55:349).

exaggerate things a bit)—but it was also constructed, both by the majority who labelled them as mad, and by Cyprian and Jerome who accepted the label rhetorically but then turned it into something positive, so that the opposite meaning was posited: i.e., the ones who looked insane were the truly wise. Cyprian and Jerome used Wis 5:4 and other similar passages to explain the situation of the accused and to encourage them. At the same time, new forms of normal and abnormal behavior were constructed and promoted.

Abnormalities of Old Testament Figures in Patristic Exegesis

Martin Meiser

Sub specie aeternitatis, "Abnormalities in the behavior of Biblical persons" in the sense of "abnormal thoughts, emotions, behavior, and relationships to others" (WHO definition of abnormality) is an issue shaped by modern interests. Abnormalities in the behavior of Biblical figures are not always of interest *per se* within ancient anti-Christian critiques[1] or within patristic "Questions-and-Answers"-literature or Patristic commentaries.[2] Discussing abnormalities is focused within divergent contexts in divergent ways—and this is mirrored in the order of this study. There are concepts of ἔκστασις in non-prophetic and prophetic contexts which are presented in a neutral way. 1 Kgs 9:9 raises questions concerning the notion of prophetic "seeing." Abnormalities in context of signs are mostly easily explained by the message which is the main point of a biblical passage, whereas 1 Kgs 19:24–25 raises questions of imperfect people being prophets. The next context of abnormality focuses on the abnormal behavior of the wise, righteous, or holy. The examples of Noah, David, and Jesus are important. The topic "Abnormality as Punishment" will be exemplified by the King of Babylon; the topic "abnormality within a prophetic argument" will be illustrated by the exegesis of Ezek 16; 23.

---

[1] Cf. in general John Granger Cook, *The Interpretation of the Old Testament in Greco-Roman Paganism*, STAC 23 (Tübingen: Mohr Siebeck, 2004).

[2] In this contribution, I use the following abbreviations for the edition-series: CCSG = Corpus Christianorum, Series Graeca, CCSL = Corpus Christianorum, Series Latina (Turnhout: Brepols), CSEL = Corpus Scriptorum Ecclesiasticorum Latinorum (Prague/Vienna/Leipzig: Hoelder/Pichler/Tempsky), GCS = Die griechischen christlichen Schriftsteller der ersten Jahrhunderte (Leipzig; Hinrichs / Berlin: Akademie); GNO = Gregorini Nyssensis Opera (Leiden: Brill), PG = Migne, Patrologia Graeca (Paris: Migne), PL = Migne, Patrologia Latina (Paris: Migne), SC = Sources Chrétiennes (Paris: Cerf).

1 Prophecy and Abnormalities

1.1 Concepts of ἔκστασις

The term ἔκστασις is characterized by a semantic openness.[3] According to Gen 2:21ᴸˣˣ, God gave Adam an ἔκστασις when creating Eve while Adam slept. Christian exegesis includes both explaining and justifying this ἔκστασις, sometimes in its relation to Adam's sleep,[4] sometimes in relation to the following context in Gen 2:23–24.

From the beginning, concepts of ἔκστασις as sleep and as prophecy stand side-by-side. Concepts of ἔκστασις as sleep invite the reader to infer anthropological assumptions.

Within a treatise on dreams, Tertullian[5] distinguishes between the resting of the body and the moving of the soul which he, following Stoic thought, conceptualizes as an immortal but corporeal being.[6] That the soul moves while the body sleeps was a common idea in ancient dream theory. Due to the ἔκστασις, the soul is no longer able to understand rational proposals but is able to grasp truths which are not accessible to the mind.[7]

John Chrysostom seeks to justify why God gave an ἔκστασις to Adam when creating Eve:

> "It wasn't simply drowsiness that came upon him nor normal sleep; in-
> stead, the wise and skillful creator of our nature was about to remove one
> of Adam's ribs. Lest the experience cause Adam afterward to be badly dis-

---

[3] The distinguishing of different kinds of ἔκστασις is a pre-Christian phenomenon, cf. Philo, *Her.* 249–62, and Lukas Bormann in this volume.

[4] In *Cels.* 4:38 (GCS 2:308–9), Origen refutes the anti-Christian mockery which presupposes a literal reading of the story. It is, however, uncertain whether the anti-Christian mockery refers to the motif of ecstasy. More likely is the reference to the notion of God in this tale.

[5] On Tertullian's reception of Gen 2:21 cf. Anni Maria Laato, "Adam's Ecstasy and Prophecy in Tertullian," in *Adam and Eve Story in Jewish, Christian and Islamic Perspectives*, eds. Antti Laato and Lotta Valve, SRB 8 (Turku: Åbo Akademi/Winona Lake, IN: Eisenbrauns, 2017), 71–83.

[6] Petr Kitzler, "Tertullian's Concept of the Soul and His Corporealistic Ontology," in *Tertullianus Afer. Tertullien et la littérature chrétienne d'Afrique*, eds. Jérôme Lagouanere and Sabine Fialon, Instrumenta Patristica et Mediaevalia 70 (Turnhout: Brepols, 2015), 43–62 (45–46, referring to Tertullian, *De anima* 22.2 [CCSL 2:814]).

[7] Burkhard Freiherr von Dörnberg, *Traum und Traumdeutung in der Alten Kirche. Die westliche Tradition bis Augustin* (Leipzig: Evangelische Verlagsanstalt, 2008), 47.

Martin Meiser

posed toward the creature formed from his rib and through memory of the pain bear a grudge against this being at its formation, God induced in him this kind of sleep."[8] This slumber deprived Adam of the use of his senses. It was so that when he woke up Adam would not notice what had happened. For he was to be informed of it later, although at the very moment he had no knowledge of it.[9]

Epiphanius gives divergent reasons for ecstasy, exorbitant wondering, losing one's normal state in madness, and sleep where the ecstasy κατὰ τὴν φυσικὴν ἐνέργειαν in my view is to be interpreted as the moving of the soul.[10] Methodius of Olympus regards Adam's ecstasy as a prefiguration of Christ's ecstasy at the cross. Adam's sleep is understood as precondition before the coming of a new reality. Eve stands symbolically for the church.[11] Beneath of this notion of Adam's ἔκστασις as ἔκστασις of sleep stands the other of Adam's ἔκστασις as prophecy, due to Gen 2:23-24 and Eph 5:31-32. According to Tertullian, God gave Adam amentiam ... spiritalem vim, qua constat prophetia.[12] Adam spoke Gen 2:23-24 as a prophecy

---

[8] English Translation: Andrew Louth and Marco Conti (eds.), Genesis 1–11, ACCS 1 (Downers Grove: Intervarsity Press, 2001), 67.

[9] John Chrysostom, Hom. Gen. 15.2 (PG 53:119-20); similarly, Theodore of Mopsuestia, according to La Chaîne sur la Genèse, Frgm. 299 (TEG 1:205-6). I did not find any influence of the readings καταφορά (Aquila) or κάρον (Symmachus) in the exegetical debate on Gen 2:21 (La Chaîne sur la Genèse, Frgm. 295 [TEG 1:202]). The same is true for the readings κόρος (Aquila) and κάρος (Symmachus) in Gen 15:12 (La Chaîne sur la Genèse, Frgm. 960 [TEG 3:56]).

[10] Epiphanius, Pan. 48.4.6 (GCS 31:226): ἔκστασις δὲ κατὰ διαφορὰς πολλὰς ἔχει τὸν τρόπον. ἔκστασις δι᾽ ὑπερβολὴν θαύματος λέγεται καὶ ἔκστασις λέγεται ἡ μανία διὰ τὸ ἐκστῆναι τοῦ προκειμένου. ⁷ἐκείνη δὲ ἡ τοῦ ὕπνου ἔκστασις κατ ἄλλον τρόπον ἐρρέθη, κατὰ τὴν φυσικὴν ἐνέργειαν, μάλιστα διὰ τὸ βαθυτάτως αὐτὴν ἐπινηνέχθαι τῷ ἁγίῳ Ἀδὰμ καὶ ἐν χειρὶ θεοῦ πεπλασμένῳ. Theodoret, Qu. Gen. 30 (PG 80:128bc) asks why Eve is taken from Adam's rib, but does not deal with the problem of ἔκστασις. He also does not deal with the phenomenon of ἔκστασις in Gen 15:12. Gennadius does not offer anything.

[11] Methodius of Olympus, Symp. 3.8 (SC 95:106).

[12] Tertullian, Anim. 21.3 (CCSL 2:813). According to Anni Maria Laato, "Ecstasy," 74, Tertullian chose the negatively connoted term amentia because his adversaries rebuked the Montanistic prophecy as amentia. He picked up the polemic and turned it into ironic self-definition, based on the claim that really the Holy Spirit was at work in the Montanistic

277

about Christ and the church.[13] Augustine interprets Adam's *sopor* "as a secret vision, not seen by bodily eyes but inner understanding"; during this ecstasy, Adam participated in the meeting of the angels.[14]

Procopius of Gaza combines the divergent interpretations of Adam's ἔκστασις. First, he refers to the concept of ἔκστασις in Philo of Alexandria (*Qu. Gen.* 1:24), that the dissociation of natural perception is given by God for reasons of salvation history. Due to the ἔκστασις given by God, Abraham was able to receive divine revelation. Procopius continues with Theodore of Mopsuestia's reasoning that whether God took the rib from Adam when he was awake without his sensation and Adam thought it was his imagination or whether he perceived it at all—Adam did not have to endure pain. So it is natural that Adam, stepping out of the habitual state through divine revelation, received the knowledge of what had happened as though in a dream. Procopius concludes his commentary by quoting another author unknown to us: according to some, the fact that Adam slept does not mean that he slept only briefly while God created woman, but rather indicates the outward form of ecstasy. The revelations of the prophets also occurred in this way, often while they were awake by divine influence, but as in a dream, they received the vision of the things he wanted to reveal to them.[15]

In Gen 15:12, we find another biblical reference to ἔκστασις which is not necessarily to be interpreted in terms of prophecy. Given that Abraham's ἔκστασις was an ἔκστασις of fear,[16] Augustine feels the necessity to justify[17] Gen 15:12 (*pavor ... timor*) against the possible objection that a wise man cannot be so fearful. He quotes Aulus Gellius, *Noctes Atticae* 19.1 where a philosopher refers to the Stoic doctrine that emotions of fear can

---

movement. Adam's prophesying is a transitory phenomenon; the soul is not by nature spiritual (Anni Maria Laato, "Ecstasy," 73).

[13] Tertullian, *Anim.* 21.3 (CCSL 2:813). For other references in Tertullian's work on this issue cf. Anni Maria Laato, "Ecstasy," 80–81.

[14] Anni Maria Laato, "Ecstasy," 77, with reference to Augustine, *De Genesi adversus Manichaeos* 2:12/16 (CSEL 91:137–38) and to Augustine, *De Genesi ad litteram* 9:19/36 (CSEL 28/1:294).

[15] Procopius of Gaza, *Cat. Gen.* (GCS NF 22:114).

[16] So also Epiphanius, *Pan.* 48.7.7 (GCS 31:229).

[17] In contrast, Didymus, in Procopius of Gaza, *Cat. Gen.* (GCS NF 22:251), states: Ὁ δὲ Ἀβραὰμ ... ἐφοβήθη φόβῳ τελείῳ προσήκοντα.

fall upon a wise man but not dominate him. The state of perturbation presupposes that the mind recedes; but if the mind is able to resist, there is no perturbation.[18]

Didymus of Alexandria combines different interpretations of Gen 15:12. First, he separates ecstasy from madness. Abraham's ecstasy is the amazement and the change from the visible to the invisible. Didymus also justifies also the reference to fear in Gen 15:12. Fear is not that which participates in darkness but in wisdom, and it is not easily recognized, and since this fear is great, it falls upon important men. According to 2 Sam 22:12 ("He makes the dark his hiding place"), the examination of the oversized teachings and their understanding also causes even great men to feel dizzy.[19]

Other statements on ecstasy are explicitly understood as referring to prophetic ecstasy, though the translators of the Septuagint never characterize the prophetic charisma by the term ἔκστασις.[20] At least in later literature, Ps 115:2[21] or 2 Cor 5:13 (εἴτε γὰρ ἐξέστημεν, θεῷ, εἴτε σωφρονοῦμεν, ὑμῖν) and Acts 10:10; 11:5 the ἔκστασις of Peter); 22:17 (the ἔκστασις of Paul) were influential though these passages are rarely quoted explicitly. Furthermore, not every reference to ἔκστασις in connection to David must be prophetic ἔκστασις. Athanasius interprets the title of Psalm 30 (Εἰς τὸ τέλος· ψαλμὸς τῷ Δαυιδ· ἐκστάσεως) as follows: τὸν ψαλμὸν εἴρηκεν ὁ Δαβὶδ εἰς τοὺς τελείως ἐκστάντας ἀπὸ τῆς ἁμαρτίας, καὶ ἐπιστρέψαντας ἐπὶ τὸν Κύριον.[22] Psalm 30:23 (ἐγὼ εἶπα ἐν τῇ ἐκστάσει μου) is interpreted by Theodoret, due to the context, as follows: Ἔκστασιν δὲ εἰκότως τὴν ἁμαρτίαν ἐκάλεσε.[23] Of course, I cannot give an exhaustive study here; but some remarks should suffice.

---

[18] Augustine, *Qu. Gen.* 30 (CCSL 33:12–13). He also feels the need to justify Jesus's sorrow in this context, cf. Augustine, *Io. ev. tr.* 60,3 (CCSL 36:479). On this Stoic concept of freedom from any perturbation by fear cf. DiogL 7:120, 127.

[19] Didymus, in Procopius of Gaza, *Cat. Gen.* (GCS NF 22:251).

[20] Friedrich Pfister, "Art. Ekstase," *RAC* 4 (1959): 944–87 (948).

[21] Eusebius of Caesarea, *Comm. Ps.* (PG 23:1360d) refers the ἔκστασις to the adherence to God's words.

[22] Athanasius, *Tit. Ps.* (PG 27:756b). He refers Ps 115:2 (ἐγὼ εἶπα ἐν τῇ ἐκστάσει μου) to distance from the world (ἀπετιθήμην τὰ τοῦ κόσμου πάντα), perhaps envisaging the precondition of true prophecy (Athanasius, *Tit. Ps.* [PG 27:756b]).

[23] Theodoret, *Comm. Ps.* (PG 80:1085b).

Justin distinguishes between seeing with the eyes (αὐτοψίᾳ, ἐν κατάστάσει ὤν) and seeing through revelation.[24] Athenagoras offers an elaborated concept of prophetic ἔκστασις. When the Divine Spirit moved the prophets, they "spoke out what they were in travail with, their own reasoning falling into abeyance and the Spirit making use of them as a flautist might play upon his flute."[25] The comparison with a musician has its analogies in Philo;[26] and the term ἔνθεον πνεῦμα is also found in Philo,[27] "but the image of the flute seems to be independent of Philo. Original is the idea of God working with (as well as through) the prophet, an idea suggested by Athenagoras's terms συγχρησαμένου and ἃ ἐνηργοῦντο (cf. 1 Cor 12:6)."[28]

According to Gregory of Nyssa, the possession of real goodness is the seeing of the true and intellectual light which surpasses all earthly light. Gregory of Nyssa exemplifies this vision of David's: "He has been lifted by the power of the Spirit out of himself and saw the boundless and incomprehensible Beauty (i.e., concerning the First Good) in a blessed state of ecstasy. He saw in that way that is possible for a human being to see who quitted the corporeal envelopments and entered by the mere power of thought, upon the contemplation of the incorporeal and intellectual

---

[24] Justin, *Dial.* 115.3 (ed. Bobichon, 1:492).
[25] Athenagoras, *Leg.* 9.1 (SC 379:98): οἱ κατ' ἔκστασιν τῶν ἐν αὐτοῖς λογισμῶν, κινήσαντος αὐτοὺς τοῦ θειοῦ πνεύματος, ἃ ἐνηργοῦντο ἐξεφώνησαν, συγχρησαμένου τοῦ πνεύματος ὡς εἰ καὶ αὐλητὴς αὐλὸν ἐμπνεῦσαι. English Translation: *Athenagoras. Embassy for the Christians. The Resurrection of the Dead, Translated and Annotated* by Joseph Hugh Crehan (New York: Newman Press, 1955), 39.
[26] Philo, *Immut.* 24, "compares the soul to a lyre whose strings God attunes, so that the owner of it can lead a virtuous life." (Crehan, *Athenagoras*, 132 Note 53). For parallels in Plato (Ion 534c), Plutarch and Philo cf. Christoph Riedweg, *Ps.-Justin (Markell von Ankyra), Ad Graecos de vera religione. Einleitung und Kommentar, Teil II: Kommentar*, SBA 25/2 (Basel: Reinhardt, 1994), 277–79. Plato, *Ion*, 533c contrasts: Πάντες ... οἱ ... ποιηταὶ οἱ ἀγαθοὶ οὐκ ἐκ τέχνης ἀλλ' ἔνθεοι ὄντες, id. Ion, 534c contrasts τέχνη and θείη δύναμις. God removes their νοῦς and uses them as ὑπερηταί (Ion, 534c).
[27] Philo, *Decal.* 175. Philo, *Spec. Leg.* 1:49 differentiates between seeing with the eyes and seeing by the διάνοια which is necessary for an adequate perception of the divine powers.
[28] Crehan, *Athenagoras*, 132 Note 53. Theophilos, *Autol.* 2:9.1 (PTS 44:52); Clement of Alexandria, *Str.* 6:168 (GCS 52:518) and Ps.-Justin, *Cohort.* 8.4 (ed. Riedweg, 277–78), follow this idea of Athenagoras; in their concept, the prophet is an ὄργανον of the divine voice.

world."[29] Therefore, David's comment that "every human being is a liar" (Ps 115:2) is true, not because of any hatred but because of the weakness of human explanation.

First Samuel 9:9 (ὅτι τὸν προφήτην ἐκάλει ὁ λαὸς ἔμπροσθεν Ὁ βλέπων) gives cause to reflect on the nature of the prophets' vision. The temporal difference and the role of the λαός are not discussed. In the context of the debate about true and false prophecy (Ezek 13:3), Origen explains that false prophets prophesy from their hearts, true prophets prophesy on the basis of divine revelation. "Seeing" is not seeing with the eyes of the flesh, but a spiritual sight given by God as a gift of grace.[30] To be a trustworthy prophet requires a pure heart.[31] What seems to be a simple moral requisite in the ancient Church is to be understood as combination of 1 Kgs 9:9 and Matt 5:8.

It is perhaps Theodore of Mopsuestia who in his comment on Gen 15:12 explains ἔκστασις as follows: Τουτέστι τὸ ἔξω τῆς τῶν παρόντων αἰσθήσεως γεγονὸς κατέστη (i.e.: Abraham) τὴν διάνοιαν εἰς τὸ τὴν τῶν ἀποκαλυπτομένων δέξασθαι θεωρίαν.[32] Regardless, it is Theodore of Mopsuestia who declares: By ecstasy, the prophets "received the knowledge of things beyond description, since it was possible for them in their minds to

---

[29] Gregory of Nyssa, *Virg.* 10 (GNO 8/1:290): ὃς ἐπειδὴ πότε τῇ δυνάμει τοῦ πνεύματος ὑψωθεὶς τὴν διάνοιαν καὶ οἷον ἐκβὰς αὐτὸς ἑαυτὸν εἶδεν τὸ ἀμήχανον καὶ ἀπερινόητον κάλλος (i.e., περὶ τὸ πρῶτον ἀγαθόν) ἐν τῇ μακαρίᾳ ἐκείνῃ ἐκστάσει. εἶδε δὲ πάντως ὡς ἀνθρώπῳ γε δυνατὸν ἰδεῖν ἔξω τῶν τῆς σαρκὸς προκαλυμμάτων γενόμενος καὶ εἰσελθὼν διὰ μόνης τῆς διανοίας εἰς τὴν τῶν ἀσωμάτων καὶ νοητῶν θεωρίαν. The English translation is based on William Moore and Henry Austin Wilson, *Select Writings and Letters of Gregory, Bishop of Nyssa, Translated, with Prolegomena, Notes, and Indices*, NPFN 5 (Edinburgh: T&T Clark, 1892), 355. Wilhelm Blum, *Gregor von Nyssa. Über das Wesen des christlichen Bekenntnisses. Über die Vollkommenheit. Über die Jungfräulichkeit. Eingeleitet, übersetzt und mit Anmerkungen versehen*, BGL 7 (Stuttgart: Hiersemann, 1977), 149 n. 17 refers to the Platonic background of Gregory's thought (e.g. Symp. 210c; Rep. 516b). Ekkehard Mühlenberg, *Die Unendlichkeit Gottes bei Gregor von Nyssa. Gregors Kritik am Gottesbegriff der klassischen Metaphysik*, FKDG 16 (Göttingen: Vandenhoeck & Ruprecht, 1966), 144 emphasizes also the difference between Plato and Gregory: according to Gregory, we will not reach this in our earthly life.

[30] Origen, *Hom. Ez.* 2.3.4 (GCS 33:344–45).

[31] Origen, *Hom. Gen.* 4.4 (GCS 29:53).

[32] *La Chaîne sur la Genèse*, Frgm. 964 (TEG 3:58).

be quite removed from their normal condition and thus capable of devoting themselves exclusively to contemplation of what was revealed."[33]

The nature of "seeing" is sometimes disputed by other authors. According to Ambrose, the prophets are called "videntes" *quia per revelationem ea, quae errant abscondita, mente cernebant.*[34] Gregory of Nyssa gives a physiognomic and allegorical interpretation of "seeing": just as the eyes are arranged at the top of the body and serve to guide the whole body, those who guide to the truth are called ὁ βλέπων or ὁ ὁρῶν or σκοπός by scripture.[35] Augustine states that the prophet understands what he foretells; rational thinking is not overridden but enlightened in the Holy Spirit.[36]

In his comment on 1 Sam 9:9, The Venerable Bede follows the ancient concept of prophecy insofar as he underlines that the examiner and teller of hidden things is rightly called a prophet "and not unfittingly is named a seer, because with the purified eyes of his heart he examines the secrets which those who are less perfect cannot."[37] By referring to 1 Cor 14:32, The Venerable Bede refutes a "cataphrygian" (i.e. Montanist) concept of ecstasy where the prophet does not know what he is actually saying.[38]

1.2 Signs of Prophets

1.2.1 Isaiah's Nakedness (Isaiah 20:2)

The motif is an issue only for some commentators;[39] in Questions-and-Answers-literature, I have not yet found any reference.

---

[33] Theodore of Mopsuestia, in Nahum 1:1 (PG 66:401c). English Translation: *Theodore of Mopsuestia, Commentary on the Twelve Prophets*, Translated by Robert C. Hill, FaCh 108 (Washington, DC: The Catholic University of America Press, 2004), 249.

[34] Ambrose, *In Psalm 118*, 11.8 (CSEL 62:238).

[35] Gregory of Nyssa, *Hom. Cant.* 13 (GNO 6:394).

[36] Augustine, *Trin.* 4.22 (CCSL 50:189). On Augustine's concept of prophecy cf. Marco Frenschkowski, Art. Prophet, *RAC* 28 (2018): 274–339 (328–29).

[37] English Translation: *Bede, On First Samuel. Translated with Introduction and Commentary* by Scott DeGregorio and Rosalind Love, Translated Texts for Historians 70 (Liverpool: Liverpool University Press, 2019), 224.

[38] The Venerable Bede, *In 1 Sam* (CCSL 119:80).

[39] For patristic commentaries on Isaiah see Origen, *In Is.* (GCS 33:242–89); Eusebius of Caesarea, *Comm. Is.* (GCS 57); Ps.-Basil, *Comm. Is.* (PG 30:117d–668c, Covering Isa 1–16); John Chrysostom, *Comm. Is.* (SC 304; covering Isa 1–8); Cyril of Alexandria, *Comm. Is.* (PG 70:9a–

Martin Meiser

Origen characterizes the nakedness and the naked feet of Isaiah as severity against himself.[40] According to Eusebius of Caesarea, the prophet's behavior is a sign of his obedience to God and a sign of devaluing human ideas of honor.[41] Theodoret of Cyrus does not comment this motif; the commentary of Ps.-Basil covers only Isa 1–16. The overview of the chapters of Isaiah in Hesychius of Jerusalem does not mention the prophet's nakedness. Jerome and Cyril of Alexandria interpret the nakedness as a symbol of the captivity of the Egyptians under the Assyrian king;[42] Jerome compares this command to Isaiah with the command given to Ezekiel to enclose himself in his house (Ezek 3:24).[43] Following a line of interpretation that can also be found in Jerome, Ambrose emphasizes the disturbing nature of Isaiah's behavior especially in view of the presence of women. Isaiah's nakedness was meant to announce the exile in a shocking way, more than preaching alone could ever have achieved.[44]

According to Gregory the Great, it is *caritas* which prevents the prophet's blushing; *subducto carnali velamine, mysteria superna penetravit*.[45]

I conclude this paragraph with a reference to Filastrius who, generally not very trustworthy, reports of a sect where all must go barefoot. He despises it as *humana ac vanae superstitionis*[46]. In Filastrius's report, founders or other teachings of this group are not mentioned.

1450c); Theodoret of Cyrus, *In. Is.* (SC 276; 295; 315); Jerome, *In Is.* (CCSL 73); Procopius of Gaza, *In Is.* (PG 87/2:1817a–2718b).

[40] Origen, *Cels.* 7:7 (GCS 3:159). Origen's *Homiliae in Isaiam* do not cover Isa 20.

[41] Eusebius of Caesarea, *Comm. Is.* (GCS 58:137–38).

[42] Jerome, *in Is.* 5:20.1–6 (CCSL 73:201); Cyril of Alexandria, *In Is.* (PG 70:480c). Cyril's explanation is repeated in the catena of Procopius of Gaza, *In Is.* (PG 87/2:2157c).

[43] Jerome, *In Ez.*1:3.23b–24 (CCSL 75:40–41).

[44] Ambrose, *Epist.* 27[58].10 (CSEL 82:184).

[45] Gregory the Great, *Mor.* 10.6/9 (CCSL 143:542).

[46] Filastrius, *Haer.* 81 (CCSL 9 A:252); cf. also Ps.-Augustinus, *Haer.* 78 (CCSL 46:330–31), where also we do not find any reliable information. A work called *De haeresibus* is not found in Augustine's *Retractationes*, therefore the work quoted here is probably pseudonymous.

1.2.2 Ezekiel's Muteness (Ezekiel 3:26)

According to Jerome, Ezekiel's muteness underlines that the people are not worthy to hear his message to be corrected.[47] Gregory the Great quotes Ezek 3:26 in order to prove that due to the wickedness of the hearer sometimes also a righteous teacher is not able to speak.[48] Sometimes, however, the reader should ask whether the wickedness of the hearers or the wickedness of the preacher is responsible for the preachers' muteness.[49] Perhaps we have to note a non-literal witness of the reception of this motif in PGM 4.3039–3041 where Solomon's seal is placed "on Jeremiah's tongue with the result that the prophet spoke."[50]

1.2.3 Ezekiel's Lying on the Left Side and on the Right Side (Ezek 4:4, 6)

This motif is also the subject of discussion only in technical exegesis. Jerome interprets the "sleeping"[51] on one side without turning to the other as reference to the captivity.[52] In the following, Jerome is interested in the periods of 390 (MT[53]) and 40 years, but not in the external form of this prophecy.[54] At the end of his long explanation, he refers to the divergent readings in the Hebrew text and the Septuagint, but also in "the Three." He wants to avoid any appearance of arrogance, but he claims to be the first who has put forward a solution to this difficult problem.[55] Theodoret is not interested in the "lying" as such but reconstructs the history of Israel after

---

[47] Jerome, *In Ez.* 1:3.25–26 (CCSL 75:41). Origen and Gregory the Great wrote homilies, Jerome and Theodoret commentaries on Ezekiel. Origen and Gregory do not comment Ezek 3:26ff.
[48] Gregory the Great, *Mor.* 30.27/82 (CCSL 143 B:1547).
[49] Gregory the Great, *Hom.* 12.152 (CCSL 142:191).
[50] Cook, *Interpretation*, 44, who suggests that Jeremiah was confused for Ezekiel.
[51] Jerome, *In Os.* 1:1.8–9 (CCSL 76:14), states that this command should be understood in a figurative way—in a literal way it is impossible.
[52] Similarly, Petrus Chrysologus, *Serm.* 166.6 (CCSL 24 B:1022).
[53] In the Septuagint, Ezek 4:5 does not mention 390, but 190 days, perhaps (Hermut Löhr, Ezek. 1–19, in Almut Hammerstaedt-Löhr et al., "Jezekiel / Ezechiel / Hesekiel," in: *Septuaginta Deutsch. Erläuterungen und Kommentare zum griechischen Alten Testament*, eds. Martin Karrer and Wolfgang Kraus (Stuttgart: Deutsche Bibelgesellschaft, 2011), 2849–3007 [2867]) as combination of 150 + 40 due to Gen 7:17 (40 days) and Gen 7:24 (150 days).
[54] Jerome, *In Ez.* 1:4.4–6 (CCSL 75:44).
[55] Jerome, *In Ez.* 1:4.4–6 (CCSL 75:47).

Martin Meiser

Solomon's death.⁵⁶ He counterbalances the forty years of Ezek 4:6 and the seventy years of Jer 25:11–12; 36[29]:10 by reference to the beginning of Ezekiel's prophetic ministry in the thirty years of Israel's exile.⁵⁷

1.2.4 Ezekiel's Eating Human Dung (Ezekiel 4:15)

Jerome discusses a seeming biblical discrepancy: why is the uncleanness of human dung avoided by Ezekiel while Hosea is coupled with a harlot? The solution to this riddle is not found at the level of literal but of symbolic exegesis. Both issues have a symbolizing effect.⁵⁸ He ends with hate-filled anti-Jewish polemics. The Jews do not eat their bread in human dung—i.e., they do not commit idolatry—but they eat their bread in the dung of cattle —i.e. they do all things for earthly gain—whereas Christians eat the bread of life which is an angelic nourishment (Ps 77:25) and comes from heaven.⁵⁹

According to Theodoret, Ezechiel was forced to use human dung (ἀναγκασθείς).⁶⁰ Theodoret interprets the human dung as proof of the coming uncleanness when the addressees are dispersed among the nations; φάγονται in Ezek 4:13 is understood in a future sense.⁶¹ That was an ἀνάγκη for the Israelites to institute their life not according to God's command but to the laws of the surrounding nations.⁶²

1.2.5 The Sharp Sword (Ezekiel 5:1)

The sword as sharp as a barber's razor was not of significant interest for ancient Christian commentators. Jerome debates the difference between the threefold (Hebrew) and the fourfold (Septuagint) division in Ezek 5:1; he concludes that the Hebrew text is preferable due to Ezek 5:12.⁶³ Theodoret of Cyrus is not interested in the abnormality but explains the historical background of Israel's punishment.⁶⁴ The threefold division

---

⁵⁶ Theodoret of Cyrus, *In Ez.* (PG 81:856b).
⁵⁷ Theodoret of Cyrus, *In Ez.* (PG 81:856d).
⁵⁸ Jerome, *In Ez.* 1:4.13–15 (CCSL 75:51).
⁵⁹ Jerome, *In Ez.* 1:4.13–15 (CCSL 75:52).
⁶⁰ Theodoret of Cyrus, *In Ez.* (PG 81:861a).
⁶¹ Theodoret of Cyrus, *In Ez.* (PG 81:860c); cf. also NETS, 950 ("shall eat").
⁶² Theodoret of Cyrus, *In Ez.* (PG 81:860d).
⁶³ Jerome, *In Ez.* 2:5.1–4 (CCSL 75:54).
⁶⁴ Theodoret of Cyrus, *In Ez.* (PG 81:861b–d).

means fire, hunger, and death. Gregory the Great interprets this passage as a detraction of the sacramenta of the Jewish priesthood.[65] According to Isidore of Seville, Ezek 5:1 is the biblical basis for the requirement of tonsure for the clergy.[66]

1.2.6 The Death of the Prophet's Wife and His Behavior (Ezekiel 24:15-17)

Jerome states that the abandonment of mourning was *contra morem omnium*.[67] According to Theodoret, the prophet shall not mourn for it was against God's will to punish Israel. For God, φιλανθρωπία and ἀγαθότης are characteristic. He does not wish for the death of the wicked one, rather his repentance (Ezek 18:23). His punishment is forged (βιαζόμενος) by the exorbitance of wickedness.[68] The prophet himself became a sign (τέρας ... καὶ σημεῖον) for Israel.[69]

1.3 Imperfect Prophets

1.3.1 Saul (1 Kgs 19:24-25)

The starting point of the reception of 1 Sam 19:24-25 is that Saul, as a king rejected by God, cannot be a prophet like Isaiah or Jeremiah. I did not find his characterization as a false prophet, but the evaluations of Saul are inconsistent.

According to Origen, Saul's prophecy is the result of contingency (περίστασις), as is the case with Caiaphas or Balaam.[70] According to Grego-

---

[65] Gregory the Great, *Mor.* 2:35 (CCSL 143:94-5), repeated in Paterius of Brescia, *Exp. V.N.T.* 2:5.12 (PL 79:986d).

[66] Isidore of Seville, *eccl.* 2:4.2 (PL 83:779c); cf. Sergej Vorontsov, "*Ipsius domini et apostolorum habemus exemplum et praecepta*: Functions of the Biblical Text in De eclesiasticis officiis of Isidore of Seville," in *Christian Discourse in Late Antiquity. Hermeneutical, Institutional and Textual Perspectives*, eds. Anna Usacheva and Anders Christian Jacobsen (Paderborn: Ferdinand Schöningh, 2020), 175-94, 186.

[67] Jerome, *In Ez.* 7.24.15-27 (CCSL 75:330).

[68] Theodoret of Cyrus, *In Ez.* (PG 81:1057b).

[69] Theodoret of Cyrus, *In Ez.* (PG 81:1060a).

[70] Origen, *Comm. Ioh.* 28:175-77 (SC 385:146), on John 11:49-51. Origen discusses at length Caiaphas's prophecy but also other prophesying figures whose prophecy is debatable, such as the Python in Acts 16 (*Comm. Ioh.* 28:121-77 [SC 385:122-46]).

Martin Meiser

ry of Nazianzus, the fate of the prophets depends on their self-dedication to the Holy Spirit. Saul is an example of imperfection.[71]

Gregory of Nyssa uses 1 Sam 19:24–25 in order to refute Eunomius's notion that the similarity of terms include in the substantial similarity of things. Eunomius concluded from the term "son," attributed to Jesus, the subordination of Jesus and rejected Jesus's co-eternality.[72] Gregory of Nyssa answers: the term "son" of Jesus Christ does not characterize his οὐσία as γεννηθεῖσα;[73] similarly, when Saul was in anger against the prophets, the prophetic spirit intended to educate him by having him driven by God himself; τὸ παράλογον τῆς συντυχίας παροιμία τῷ μετὰ ταῦτα γέγονε βίῳ. The parabolic question: "Is Saul among the prophets?" (1 Kgs 10:11) denotes this irregularity.[74] The term "prophet" does not correspond to Saul's real identity.

Ambrosiaster uses 1 Sam 19:24–25 in order to explain 1 Cor 13:2. Similarly to Balaam or Caiaphas, the latter of whom prophesied not due to his merits but due to his rank of high priest, Saul prophesied due to God who wished to save David, and even though at the time he was filled with an evil spirit due to his disobedience. These biblical examples demonstrate the truth of 1 Cor 13:2 that prophecy without love is futile.[75] In a somewhat milder tone, Augustine integrates 1 Sam 19 into his concept of prophecy. There is also a *prophetia transitoria*, for which Saul is an example.[76] The bishop of Hippo Rhegius can also use 1 Sam 19 for an argument concerning discipline within the church: Saul's example refutes the thesis of some heretics who claim that nothing can be given by the Holy Spirit to those who do not belong to the class of the holy. These people may have received baptism, which, when they come to the Catholic Church, should not be disputed or given to them as if they were unbaptized. However, baptism is no guarantee of salvation. One must enter into the communion of unity with the bond of love, without which, whatever

---

[71] Gregory of Nazianzus, *Or.* 9.2 (SC 405:302–6).
[72] εἰ ἡ κατὰ φύσιν σχέσις παρεισάγει τῶν ὀνομάτων τούτων τὴν χρῆσιν (Gregory of Nyssa, *C. Eun.* 3:87 [GNO 2:33]).
[73] Gregory of Nyssa, *C. Eun.* 3:88 (GNO 2:34).
[74] Gregory of Nyssa, *C. Eun.* 3:90 (GNO 2:34).
[75] Ambrosiaster, *In 1Cor* (CSEL 81/2:145).
[76] Augustine, *Qu. Simpl.* 2:1.2 (CCSL 44:60).

they may have and whatever is worthy of veneration, they are still nothing.[77] The Venerable Bede explains Saul's prophesying in madness as divine concession, similarly to the concession given to Balaam and Caiaphas; in this way, the innocent David had the possibility to escape.[78]

1.3.2 Imperfect Prophets as Example (Hosea 9:7b, 8)

Cyril of Alexandria characterizes the prophet mentioned in Hos 9:7 as ψευδοπροφητής and circumscribes the term παρεξεστηκώς with ἐνθοὺς (fanatic) καὶ μαινόμενος, καὶ ἀπολωλεκὼς τὰς φρενάς.[79] Cyril emphasizes the difference between the legitimate prophet and the false prophet[80]—both kinds of prophets can be named σκοποί as the comparison between Hos 9:8 and Ezek 3:17 makes clear. The false prophet mentioned here is false prophet of false gods.[81] Theodore of Mopsuestia interprets the term παρεξεστηκώς as ἔκστασιν πολλὴν ἐκ τῆς τοῦ πονηροῦ πνεύματος ἐνεργείας καταστάντος, καὶ οὐδὲ τῶν παρόντων αἴσθησιν ἔχοντος—the influence of an evil spirit and denial of reality are typical.[82]

In the interpretation of Theodoret of Cyrus, the prophet compares Israel with a false prophet who failed completely; instead of "watching" Israel (Ezek 3:17) and leading the neighboring nations to the knowledge of God, he leads Israel to the worship of idols.[83] The ἔκστασις of this prophet, explained as fickleness, is a result of his sinfulness.[84] Jerome reads this text—which rebukes Israel who called the true prophet *stultum et insanum*—as a rebuke against heretics who tell lies against God by characterizing Jesus as created.[85]

---

[77] Augustine, *Qu. Simpl.* 2:1.10 (CCSL 44:73).
[78] The Venerable Bede, *In 1 Sam* (CCSL 119:180-81).
[79] Cyril of Alexandria, *Comm. Os.* (PG 71:221a). Similarly, Julian of Aeclanum, *Comm. Os.* 2 (CCSL 88:187): *rationis ... imparticeps flagra et stimulus exegisti.*
[80] According to Jerome, *Comm. Os.* (CCSL 76:96), the translator of the Septuagint wrote ψευδοπροφήτης in v. 7, but we have no evidence from manuscripts.
[81] Theodore of Mopsuestia, *Comm. Os.* (PG 66:180a).
[82] Cyril of Alexandria, *Comm. Os.* (PG 71:221d-224b).
[83] Theodoret, *Comm. Os.* (PG 81:1600d-1601a).
[84] Theodoret, *Comm. Os.* (PG 81:1600d).
[85] Jerome, *Comm. Os.* (CCSL 76:96).

1.4 Moral Abnormalities as Metaphor within Prophetical Messages: The Imagery of Sexuality and Prostitution (Ezekiel 16; 23)

Origen is not offended by sexual imagery but takes it as an indication of the necessity of allegorical interpretation because the literal description of a girl's bodily development does not make sense when describing a city.[86] Nor does the imagery of Ezek 16; 23 offend Theodoret of Cyrus. Jerome explains fornication as a symbol of idolatry; therefore, he is not offended either.[87] At one point Augustine shows a little bit of sensitivity[88] but of course does not criticize the biblical wording. Within his treatise on Judges, Quodvultdeus compares Samson's marriages to the sisters Oholah and Oholibah (Ezek 23), Samaria and Jerusalem: Samaria deserted her first husband and dedicated herself to heretics; Jerusalem is compared with Delilah who put Samson to death and completed the mystery of the passion of Jesus Christ.[89]

2 Wise Men and Unwise Behavior

2.1 Noah's Drunkenness and Prophecy (Gen 9:20–27)

Sometimes the events described in Gen 9:20–27 serve as a supporting argument within discussions concerning the notion of God.[90] Origen seeks to justify the passage "and do not lead us into temptation" in the Lord's Prayer which must be explained with regard to the apparent contradiction in Gal 5:17 and Job 7:1. God leads people into temptation by abandoning them to their evil inclinations. We should not pray that God will not tempt us at all, but we should pray that we will not succumb to temptation. The thought does not contradict the axiom that God is good and—Origen polemicizes against Marcion—does not justify imagining another God besides the good God. In temptation, evil inclinations which lay in human

---

[86] Origen, *Hom. Ez.* 6.8 (SC 352:234). Elsewhere, he can introduce Ezek 23 only by the phrase Ἰερουσαλήμ, ἣν Ὀλίβαν λέγει (Origen, *Frgm. Lament.* 40 [GCS 6:253]).

[87] Jerome, *In Ez.* 7.23.1–10 (CCSL 75:305).

[88] Augustine, *De serm. Dom.* 1.12/36 (CCSL 35:39): *Cum enim tam assidue idolatriam scriptura fornicationem dicat.*

[89] Quodvultdeus, *Lib. prom.* 2:22 (CCSL 60:112).

[90] Concerning Noah's drunkenness cf. Peri Verbuyken, "Art. Noe. Christlich, I–III," *RAC* 25 (2013): 954–60, 957–58.

beings before the event of temptation become visible. If Noah had not drunk, the insolence of Ham and the reverence of his brothers towards their father would not have been revealed.[91]

Other authors use Gen 9 as a supporting argument in terms of behavior. According to Epiphanius, the encratites argued with Gen 9:20–27 and Gen 19:30–38 and Prov 23:29–30 in order to foster their position: drinking wine initiates sexual desire.[92]

The esteem in which Noah is held as ἄνθρωπος δίκαιος, τέλειος ὤν ἐν τῇ γενεᾷ αὐτοῦ ("a righteous human being, perfect in his generation," Gen 6:9[93]) makes one wonder how the incident described in Gen 9 could have come about. According to Basil of Caesarea, Noah was drunk not by custom but by a lack of experience whereas the saints should imitate the life in paradise where no one drinks wine.[94] John Chrysostom gives the biblical rationale for this missing experience by referring to Gen 9:20: ἤρξατο Νῶε ἀνὴρ γεωργός. He did not know the ratio in which one had to mix water and wine.[95] Elsewhere, John Chrysostom claims that Noah drank out of grief at the sight of the barren earth and used the wine as a medicine.[96] He also deals with the question as to why wine came into

---

[91] Origen, *Or.* 29.18 (GCS 3:392). In another passage, he diminishes Noah's behavior: Noah was in his house, not in public (*La Chaîne sur la Genèse*, Frgm. 787 [TEG 2:177]).

[92] Epiphanius, *Pan.* 47:2.3 (GCS 31:217). Jewish tradition also uses Gen 9:20–21 as a warning against excess in drinking wine, cf. GenR 36.4.1, 4 and Pirke Aboth 8 (Sayings of the Fathers. Edited with Translations and Commentaries by Isaac Unterman [New York: Twayne, 1964], 119–20): Satan formed a partnership with Noah concerning this vineyard, "brought a sheep and slew it under the vine; then he brought in turn a lion, a pig, and a monkey, slew each of them and let their blood dip into the vineyard and drench the soil. He hinted thereby that before a man drinks wine he is simple like a sheep and quite like a lamb in front of its shearers. When he has drunk in moderation, he is strong like a lion and declares there is none to equal him in the world. When he has drunk more than enough, he becomes like a pig wallowing in filth. When he is intoxicated, he becomes like a monkey, dancing about, uttering obscenities before all, and ignorant of what he is doing."

[93] In rabbinic tradition, Gen 6:9 is sometimes read as restriction: Noah was righteous in his generation, but not in other generations (bSanh 108a). On Jewish reception of Noah cf. Gabrielle Oberhänssli-Widmer, *Biblische Figuren in der rabbinischen Literatur. Gleichnisse und Bilder zu Adam, Noah und Abraham im Midrasch Bereschit Rabba*, Judaica et Christiana 17 (Bern: Peter Lang, 1998), 204–58.

[94] Basil of Caesarea, *Ieiun.* 1:5 (PG 31:169b).

[95] John Chrysostom, in Procopius of Gaza, *Cat. Gen.* (GCS NF 22:220).

[96] John Chrysostom, *De Laz. conc.* 6.7 (PG 48:1037–1039).

Martin Meiser

human life at all. In his answer he combines arguments from experience and arguments from the Bible. Not the wine itself is bad, but human use in excess; sin was in the world before wine was present.[97]

Ambrose contrasts Noah's drunkenness with his former glory: *per vinum patuit deformitati, qui per diluvim excrevit ad gloriam*.[98] Wine, enjoyed in moderation, promotes health and the ability to think, but enjoyed in excess it tempts to sin. God reserved the decision on how much to drink, the *liberum arbitrium*.[99] But the bishop of Milan also plays down Noah's failure. Noah "drank from the wine"—it is said—but not "drank wine"; the glutton drinks all the wine, the continent man regards an adequate measure of drinking, in accordance with 1 Tim 5:23.[100]

These interpretations discussed the incident at a literal level. In an allegorical interpretation, Noah's nakedness symbolizes the mortality of Jesus's human flesh, a scandal for the Jews, foolishness for the gentiles, a saving power for those called, both Jews and Gentiles.[101] An unidentifiable author within Procopius's *catena*, however, gains an allegorical and typological interpretation related to Jesus Christ. Noah was the first to drink wine; Christ took suffering upon himself and became an example; Noah became drunk on wine; Christ was perfected in suffering. Noah was stripped bare, Christ was crucified by the Jews.[102] Leander of Seville, however, declares that even if this event was a prediction of the mystery of

---

[97] John Chrysostom, *Hom. Gen.* 29.3 (PG 53:265).
[98] The contrast between Gen 6:8-9 and Gen 9:20-24 is noted also in Jewish tradition (Oberhänssli-Widmer, *Biblische Figuren*, 234). Cf. also the later Jewish legend of Noah's castration in bSanh 70a (Oberhänssli-Widmer, *Biblische Figuren*, 231-34; Husam Aly, *Die Noahgeschichte in rabbinischer Literatur und bei Koraninterpreten*, Diss. Duisburg-Essen 2007, 161).
[99] Ambrose, *Hex.* 3:72 (CSEL 32/1:109).
[100] Ambrose, *Noe* 111 (CSEL 32/1:488).
[101] Augustine, *Faust* 12:23 (CSEL 25/1:351).
[102] Procopius of Gaza, *Cat. Gen.* (GCS NF 22:221); cf. also *La Chaîne sur la Genèse*, Frgm. 788 (TEG 2:177). Similarly, Augustine declares: The wine Noah drinks corresponds to the Passion of Christ, the nakedness of the drunken Noah recalls the crucified Christ (Augustine, *Faust.* 12/23-24 [CCSL 32:350-53]). In contrast, the incident reported in Gen 9:20-27 is understood as a negative typology in Jewish tradition (GenR 36.4.2), as a prefiguration of Israel's exile.

Christ, Noah's behavior was wrong in the literal sense. In a similar way, Lot's drinking wine also was a cause for scandal and blame.[103]

2.2 David

Abnormalities in David's behavior are reported in the two books of Samuel. Theodoret, Cyril of Alexandria, Gregory the Great, Paterius of Brescia (a notary and a compiler of the works of Gregory the Great, who died in 606), and The Venerable Bede wrote "Questions and answers" or commentaries on 1 Samuel[104]; Cyril's commentary, however, is only fragmentary. Theodoret wrote questions on 2 Samuel; Cyril's exegesis of 2 Samuel is transmitted only in fragments which need not necessarily belong to a thoroughgoing commentary. Paterius of Brescia compiled treatises of Gregory the Great on passages from both 1 and 2 Samuel.[105]

2.2.1 David's Madness (1 Kgs 21:11–16)

Some authors feel the need to justify David's behavior.[106] If, according to Ambrose, he had not done so for fear of being recognized, he would never have escaped the reproach of recklessness.[107] Theodoret states that by simulating an epileptic attack, David escaped from the threat of death. The Holy Scripture shows his piety also by asking God.[108] Theodoret does not question David's behavior. Quodvultdeus is not interested in David's behavior but in the reaction of the king (*Quid mihi introduxistis istum fanaticum*) which he compares to the rebuke against Jesus that he is possessed by a demon (John 8:48).[109] The Venerable Bede gives an exposition of the first book of Samuel in terms of Christology and anti-

---

[103] Leander of Seville, *Reg.* 9 (PL 72:885c).

[104] Theodoret, *Qu. 1 Reg.* (PG 80:529d–596d); Cyril of Alexandria, *Frgm. 1 Reg.* (PG 69:679a–682d); Paterius of Brescia, *Exp. V.N.T.* 1:7 (PL 79:789d–798b).

[105] Theodoret, *Qu. 2 Reg.* (PG 80: 597a–668a); Cyril of Alexandria, *Frgm. 1 Reg.* (PG 69:683a–688a); Paterius of Brescia, *Exp. V.N.T.* 1:7–8 (PL 79:793bc–806d).

[106] The fragments of Cyril of Alexandria do not include comments on this passage. The commentary of Gregory the Great ends with 1 Kgs 16:13. Paterius of Brescia does not comment on this passage.

[107] Ambrose, *Off.* 1.43/214 (CCSL 15:79).

[108] Theodoret, *Qu. 1 Reg.* 55 (PG 80:577b); similarly, Cyril of Alexandria, *Comm. Ps.* (PG 69:864d).

[109] Quodvultdeus, *Lib. Prom.* 2:25 (CCSL 60:122).

Jewish typology. Presupposing the reading *immutavit os suum*, the English exegete refers this reading to Jesus's proclamation in parables "lest he entrust that which is holy to dogs or pearls to swine."[110] Even the reaction of the king is compared with negative reactions to Jesus (Mark 3:20–21) and the apostles (Acts 26:24).[111]

The reception history of this story would be incomplete if I did not include the titulus of Ps 33[34]. This titulus offers a problem: the phrasing ἠλλοίωσεν τὸ πρόσωπον refers to 1 Kgs 21:14, but the king who is named in the Psalm is Abimelech mentioned in 1 Kgs 21:1–10, not Achis.[112] Eusebius of Caesarea considers this error to be due to the wish to mention not an foreigner but the high priest.[113] Other exegetes, however, mostly resolve the problem by referring the formula ἠλλοίωσεν τὸ πρόσωπον to David's denying his flight in his claim to be sent by the king with regard to an important matter.[114] In addition, Theodoret states that the story of 1 Kgs 21:11–16 does have anything in common with the content of the Psalm.[115] Basil of Caesarea solved the problem by the thesis that "Abimelech" was not a proper name but a title given to all the kings of Geth;[116] Theodoret

---

[110] The Venerable Bede, *In 1 Sam.* (CCSL 119:201), with allusion to Matt 7:6 (English translation: DeGregorio and Love, *Bede. On First Samuel*, 417).

[111] The Venerable Bede, *In 1 Sam.* (CCSL 119:203).

[112] Also, in the manuscript tradition of this titulus, variations of Αβιμελεχ/Αχιμελεχ thoroughgoing are witnessed in accordance to the manuscript tradition of 1 Kgs 21:2 which offers both αβιμελεχ and αχειμελεχ, witnessed especially in the Antiochene text, witnessed also in Nicephorus Blemmyda, *Comm. Ps.* (PG 142:1444bc) as variants whereas the reading Αγχους or something like that in the titulus of Ps 33[34] is missing.

[113] Eusebius of Caesarea, *Comm. Ps.* (PG 23:289c).

[114] Diodor of Tarsus, *Comm. Ps.* (CCSG 6:193); Ps.-Athanasius, *Comm. Ps.* (PG 27:165d–168a); Cyril of Alexandria, *Comm. Ps.* (PG 69:864). According to Theodore of Mopsuestia, *Comm. Ps.* (CCSL 88 A:148), this psalm is sung *sub persona Ezechiae, qui superato Assyrio semper se benedicturum Dominum promittit*; similarly, Diodor of Tarsus as alternative explanation.

[115] Theodoret, *Comm. Ps.* (PG 80:1101c–1104a). According to Theodoret, some scribes of Septuagint manuscript wrongly transmitted another title referring to Anchous.

[116] Basil of Caesarea, *Comm. Ps.* (PG 29:349c–352a), quoted by Euthymius Zigabenus, *Comm. Ps.* (PG 128:380d–381a); similarly, Nicephorus Blemmyda, *Comm. Ps.* (PG 142:1444b). See also the recent work of David Willgren, "'May YHWH Avenge Me on You; But My Hand Shall Not Be against You' (1 Sam. 24:13): Mapping Land and Resistance in the 'Biographical' Notes of the 'Book' of Psalms," *JSOT* 43/3 (2019): 417–35, 421, with reference to Peter C. Craigie and Marvin E. Tate, *Psalms 1–50*, WBC 19 (Waco, TX: Word Books, 2004), 278.

stated that the kings had two names.[117] On the other hand, Augustine and Cassiodorus suggest that the changing of the name is a conscious act of the author in order to disclose a mystery on the basis of etymological explanation: whereas "Achis" means *quomodo est* and includes ignorance, "Achimelech" means *Patris mei regnum* and makes sense if spoken in the person of Christ.[118]

Most of the interpreters of 1 Kgs 21:9 do not problematize David's claim[119] but Eusebius of Caesarea does not deny that David was lying.[120]

2.2.2 David's Dance (2 Kgs 6:14)

The Christian reception history of David's dance begins with a refutation of false conclusions drawn from David's behavior. If David danced, why should it be forbidden to attend spectacles at the theatre? Novatian states that we should show virtue; 2 Kgs 6:14 is by no means a permission to attend the gentile errors.[121] In Ambrose's treatise on the temperance, the fourth cardinal virtue, Ambrose also mentions David's dancing. According to the bishop of Milan, David is not to be condemned, but Ambrose emphasizes that Samuel deserves praise because he did not dance.[122] In another context, Ambrose contrasts the lustful dances within the theatre with David's holy dance.[123] Gregory of Nazianzus contrasts David's dance with the dancing Herodias who is responsible for the death of John the Baptist.[124] Theodoret does not deal with David's dancing but with Melchol's critique: she did not realize David's divine desire.[125] According to to Maximus of Turin, David foresaw in the Holy Spirit *Mariam ab germinoso Christi thalamo sociandam, unde ait: Et ipse tanquam sponsus procedet e thalamo suo* (Ps 18:6). The believers should dance spiritually

---

[117] Theodoret, *Comm. Ps.* (PG 80:1101c).
[118] Augustine, *Enarrat. Ps.* 33, s. 1.1–8 (CCSL 38:273–79); s. 2.2 (CCSL 38:282); Cassiodorus, *Exp. Ps.* (CCSL 97:293). The details of 1 Kgs 21:12–16 appear uninteresting for ancient Christian exegetes.
[119] Diodor of Tarsus, *Comm. Ps.* (CCSG 6:193), praises David's σύνεσις καὶ ... πανουργία.
[120] Eusebius of Caesarea, *Comm. Ps.* (PG 23:292a).
[121] Novatian, *Spect.* 2:3 (CCSL 4:169).
[122] Ambrose, *Off.* 1.43/214 (CCSL 15:79).
[123] Ambrose, *Paen.* 2.6/42 (CSEL 73:181); similarly, idem, *Epist.* 27[58].6–7 (CSEL 82:182).
[124] Gregory of Nazianzus, *Or.* 5.35 (SC 309:368).
[125] Theodoret, *Qu. 2 Reg.* 20 (PG 80:613a).

Martin Meiser

because of the wedding (cf. John 3:29) between Jesus Christ and the Church.[126] Ambrose relates the comment that the children did not dance (Matt 11:17) to the unbelieving Jews while attributing to the Gentiles that they danced in a spiritual way. David also danced in this spiritual way.[127] Thus he ascended to the heights of Christ's throne, so that he saw and heard "the Lord said to his Lord, sit at my right hand..." (Ps 109[110]:1).[128] According to Gregory the Great and Paterius of Brescia, public dancing is convenient to *mos vulgi* but not for a king; David, however, danced in obedience to God, in humility despite himself, and this is more admirable than his victories.[129] The motif of humility is important for some depictions of the dancing David in the history of art, especially in the Carolingian period where David was regarded as a model for contemporary rulers.[130] The Venerable Bede does not deal with 2 Kgs 6:14.

2.3 Jesus as Glutton and Drunkard (Matt 11:19 parr. Luke 7:34)
There are both literal and figural interpretations of this motif; the literal, however, dominates. According to Origen, an ascetic way of life was necessary for John the Baptist due to his human nature whereas for Jesus it was not, due to his divinity.[131] This literal line of interpretation is taken up when John Chrysostom, in order to console Olympia with regard to quarrels concerning the church of Constantinople after John Chrysostom's exile, refers to the rebuke against Jesus which he suffered patiently.[132] For Jerome, all things which Jesus did and said during his meals were for the salvation of humanity; his critics who rebuked him did not understand this.[133] Augustine and The Venerable Bede explain Jesus's behavior as a

---

[126] Maximus of Turin, *Serm.* 42.5 (CCSL 22:171).
[127] Therefore, his dance was not a denial of Christ (Ambrose, *Epist.* 27[58].4 [CSEL 82:181]).
[128] Ambrose, *Epist.* 27[58].8 (CSEL 82:183).
[129] Gregory the Great, *Mor.* 27.46/77 (CCSL 143 B:1390); Paterius of Brescia, *Exp. V.N.T.* 1:8.5 (PL 79:800b).
[130] Cf. Adam S. Cohen, "King Edgar Leaping and Dancing before the Lord," in *Imagining the Jew in Anglo-Saxon Literature and Culture*, ed. Samantha Zacher (Toronto: University of Toronto Press, 2016), 219–36, 225–28.
[131] Origen, *Comm. Matt.*, Frgm. 235 (GCS 41:111).
[132] John Chrysostom, *Epist. ad Olympiam* 1.3 (PG 52:553–54).
[133] Jerome, *Ep.* 21.2 (*ad Damasum*), on Luke 15:11–32 (CSEL 54:114–15).

295

portrayal of *laetitia regni*, i.e. *regni Dei*.[134] According to John Chrysostom, the contrast between the Baptist and Jesus should prevent the unbelieving Jews from criticizing either of them.[135] Jesus was not ashamed to be called a glutton but lived in this way in order to reach his goal, the conversion of the tax collector.[136] This should be a warning for all those who intend to achieve glory through fasting.[137] For Augustine, this contrast has a practical application: we should not despise another's religious way of life.[138] For Leo, Matt 11:19 has dogmatic relevance: Jesus's eating proves his humanity.[139] In Cassiodorus's view, Matt 12:14 (the rebuke that Jesus is possessed by a demon) and Matt 11:19 are the fulfilment of Ps 68:8 (*propter te supportavi improperium*).[140] Theophylact continues the line of John Chrysostom's exegesis: καὶ γὰρ χαριέστατος ὁ Κύριος, πᾶσι συγκαταβαίνων ἵνα πάντας κερδήσῃ τούτους, καὶ βασιλείαν εὐαγγελιζόμενος.[141] The term συγκατάβασις names Jesus's activity in God's οἰκονομία as well as the preachers' activity in order to lead the masses to a Christian life. Euthymius Zigabenus underlines the similarity of the "work" of the Baptist and of Jesus despite their divergent lifestyles; οἰκονομικῶς Jesus went to the meals with the tax collectors in order to lead them to repentance.[142] Due to the following context, The Venerable Bede emphasizes that neither fasting nor eating guarantees righteousness, and the kingdom of God is not food or drink (Rom 14:17).[143]

---

[134] Augustine, *Qu. Ev.* 2:11 (CCSL 33:54), referring to Phil 4:12–13; 1 Cor 8:8; Rom 14:17; The Venerable Bede, *In Luc.* (CCSL 120:164), referring to Rom 14:17. Ambrose does not comment this motif. The explanation would be expected in Ambrose, *Exp. Luc.* 6.5 (CCSL 14:176).

[135] John Chrysostom, *Hom. Matt.* 14.1 (PG 57:218); Theophylact, *In Luc.* (PG 124:792b); similarly, Jerome, *Comm. Matt.* (SC 242:226). Also, according to Hilarius of Poitiers, *In Matt.* 11.8 (SC 254:260), the people were not willing to accept any teaching.

[136] In this regard, already Origen, *Comm. Matt.*, Frgm. 233 (GCS 41:110).

[137] John Chrysostom, *Hom. Matt.* 30.2 (PG 57:364); similarly, idem, *Hom. Matt.* 37.3 (PG 57:423).

[138] Augustine, *Epist.* 36.26 (CCSL 31:148); similarly, Augustine, *Qu. Ev.* 2.11 (CCSL 44 B:54).

[139] Leo, *Tract.* 66 (CCSL 138 A:404).

[140] Cassiodorus, *Exp. Ps.* (CCSL 97:609).

[141] Theophylact, *In Matt.* (PG 123:253a). ἵνα πάντας κερδήσῃ τούτους is maybe an allusion to 1 Cor 9:24–27.

[142] Euthymius Zigabenus, *In Matt.* (PG 129:792ab).

[143] The Venerable Bede, *In Matt.* (PG 92:58b); similarly, already The Venerable Bede, *In Luc.* (CCSL 120:164).

Martin Meiser

The figural line of interpretation also begins with Origen who, in his interpretation on Cant 1:2, refers the "wine" to Jesus's teaching according to Matt 5:21–22, 27–28.[144] Not all commentators of Canticles, however, repeat this exegesis.[145]

3 Abnormality as Punishment: The King of Babylon (Daniel 4:30) as Example

The Christian reception history of this passage of Daniel begins before thoroughgoing commentaries are written[146] and, at first, includes comparisons with other biblical kings. Tertullian contrasts the penitent king of Babylon to the king of Egypt who is not willing to repent.[147] Ephraem implicitly compares Julian the Apostate (361–363) with the king of Babylon.[148] In a more text-immanent way, Hippolytus declares why the king is punished: τοῦτο γὰρ πρὸς παιδείαν ἐγένετο τῷ βασιλεῖ, ἵνα μηκέτι ὑψηλοφρονῶν δυνηθῇ λοιπὸν λέγειν καὶ πάντας τοὺς πορευομένους ἐν ὑπερηφανίᾳ δύναται ταπεινῶσαι.[149] In this way, the king abandoned his ὑπερηφανία.[150] All this was written πρὸς νουθεσίαν καὶ ὑπομνήμην πάντων τῶν ἀνθρώπων.[151] Concerning the motif of νουθεσία, we have to consider another statement of Hippolytus: οὐδὲν γὰρ ἀργὸν κηρύττουσιν ἡμῖν αἱ θεῖαι γραφαί, ἀλλὰ πρὸς μὲν τὴν ἡμῶν αὐτῶν νουθεσίαν, τῶν δὲ προφητῶν τούτων μακαρισμὸν καὶ πάντων τῶν ὑπ᾽ αὐτῶν λελαλημένων ἀπόδειξιν.[152] The Holy Scripture confirms the trustworthiness of the prophets. According to Theodoret, the king's behavior is to be characterized by μανία[153] and to be

---

[144] Origen, Comm. Cant. 1 (GCS 33:95).
[145] Such a link is missing e.g., in Apponius, Comm. Cant.; Gregory the Great, Comm. Cant.
[146] Hippolytus, In Dan. (GCS NF 7); Cyril of Alexandria, Frgm. Dan. (PG 70:1461a–1462b); Theodoret, In Dan. (PG 81:1255b–1546a).
[147] Tertullian, Paen. 12,7–8 (CCSL.1:339–40).
[148] Ephraem, Canticum in Julianum Apostatem 1.4.
[149] Hippolytus, In Dan. 3.10.4 (GCS NF 7:156).
[150] Hippolytus, In Dan. 3.11.5 (GCS NF 7:158).
[151] Hippolytus, In Dan. 3.12.1 (GCS NF 7:158).
[152] Hippolytus, In Dan. 1.7.2 (GCS NF 7:14).
[153] Theodoret, In Dan. (PG 81:1369b). Paterius of Brescia, Exp. V.N.T. 6:3 (PL 79:998a), names it tumor mentis.

297

compared with being vexed by demons.[154] The king was neglected by the divine providence, but also by the charity of his family.[155] He did not understand (οὐ συνῆκεν) that the God of Israel is the highest; therefore the divine punishment is justified (εἰκότως καὶ μάλα δικαίως ... κατεδικάσθη). But the human-loving Lord freed him from his punishment (φιλάνθρωπος ... λῦσας τιμωρίαν), which shows that he who is the Lord of all restored him and trusted him with his continued reign.[156]

Other forms of reception include issues of Christian moral life. Cyprian and Ps.-Athanasius were not offended by the king's fate but state that he could have escaped it if he had been willing to show charity.[157] According to Origen, his conversion is an example of fruitful conversion.[158]

4 Conclusion

We can conclude this short contribution with some observations:

1. Ancient Christian exegesis sometimes registers the abnormality but is not really interested in solving the associated problems. More important is the message which is included in such passages of abnormality especially with regard to signs of prophets.

2. Sometimes this meager reception history is part of the meager reception history of these biblical books (or parts of them) in general, as witnessed by the uneven references within critical indices.

3. Comments on abnormalities follow the common intention of biblical exegesis to help support a Christian life in faith and morality and to counterbalance apparent contradictions. Obviously, ambiguous biblical figures more often are criticized than positive ones but the behavior of both has to be justified.

---

[154] Theodoret, *In Dan.* (PG 81:1369c): It is a characteristic of the mindless, not only to say mindless and disordered things but also to eat all things which are disponible for them. You can observe this also by the people who are vexed by demons in our time. They do the same as they suffer.

[155] Theodoret, *In Dan.* (PG 81:1369d).

[156] Theodoret, *In Dan.* (PG 81:1372a).

[157] Cyprian, *Op. el.* 5 (CCSL 3 A: 58); Ps-Athanasius, *Qu. Ant.* 88 (PG 28:652c).

[158] Origen, *Comm. Matt.* 4.4 (GCS 41:267, *on Matt.* 7:19). The king of Babylon is called "tree" in Dan 4:11.

Martin Meiser

4. Ancient exegetes do not presume in any case the modern way of reading statements of negative figures as to be neglected in theological terms—even the characterization of Jesus as a glutton and drunkard must be explained in a positive way.

5. We can ask not only who determines what is abnormal but also why aberrant behavior is so often rebuked in ancient Christian literature. The answer to the first question is simple: it is theologians and bishops in pastoral care for their congregation and in contradistinction to Greco-Romans, Jews, and deviant Christians. For the second question we have to note that those who live in an abnormal way also justified their behavior with reference to biblical texts and concepts. Theodoret mentions men who justified their sexual debauchery by referring to Abraham.[159] Augustine mentions male monks with long hair in defiance of 1 Cor 11:7; they justified their long hair by referring to the idea of mutilation for the kingdom of God (Matt 19:12): because they vowed to live in sexual abstinence, they are no longer more male.[160]

6. Our own perception of normality and abnormality influences our interpretation of texts which have a different code of values. Our perception can be a heuristic tool but may not prejudice the results of our reading. Sometimes more scepticism like that of Pyyrhon of Elis is useful.

---

[159] Theodoret, *Qu. Gen.* 67 (PG 80:175a–c).
[160] Augustine, *Op. mon.* 32/48 (CSEL 41:591–92).

299

Vicious Murderers, Suicidal Maniacs and Shameful Fornicators: Interpretations of Violent Old Testament Figures (Moses, Phinehas, Razis) in Augustine

Timo Nisula   .

1 Introduction

Sometimes the devil lies in the details. The three brief cases of biblical violence and spontaneous aggression considered in this article are not of major importance for Augustine's own exegesis and theology. I present Augustine's views on three sudden outbursts of violence in the Old Testament: Moses suddenly killing the Egyptian abusing a Hebrew slave (Exod 2:11–14); Phinehas killing two lovers on the spur of the moment (Num 25:1–13), thus showing "zeal for the Lord"; and finally Razis committing suicide (or a series of suicide attempts the last of which is successful), thus preferring death over renouncing the Jewish faith at the hands of his persecutors (2 Macc 14:37–46). All three cases appear in Augustine's monumental corpus only a very few times and he does not invest any particular interest in developing his views on these cases. On the contrary, as two of the three cases (Moses and Razis) presented here had a directly polemical exegetical context, in which Augustine's biblical interpretation is aimed at a known theological adversary, it seems the episodes were more or less brought to his attention by others, meaning he had to offer a competing exegesis. Only one of the cases presented here (Phinehas) does not have an immediate polemical context. Finally, the texts discussing the episodes were composed in diverse times and varying contexts, and thus had no circumstantial connection with Augustine's career. However, the three stories analysed in this article do have one important feature in common: each of these cases arises from the contents of the stories at hand and the biblical narratives present a spontaneous and emotional act of violence committed by a person who is viewed in a positive light in the original story. What kind of moral or theological conclusions does Augustine draw from these narratives? What kind of motives does he consider crucial behind the actions? How is violence explained in the stories? How should the stories be applied to the present Christian situation? The importance of these three marginal episodes in Augustine's biblical exegesis lies precisely in their unimportance: by studying crumbs from the table of the bishop of Hippo we may be able to perceive more clearly the very basic DNA, as it were, of his biblical exegesis.

2 Moses Slays the Egyptian: "Tamen amore peccavit"

Contra Faustum is Augustine's most extensive work against the Manichaeans.[1] It was written at the turn of the 5th century against a prominent Manichaean, who is also mentioned elsewhere in Augustine's oeuvre.[2] Book 22 is the longest book in *Faust.*[3] It is a response to Faustus's critique of the central figures of the Old Testament, including the patriarchs, Moses, David and the prophets (Augustine refers to the book later as *de uita patriarcharum).*[4] Faustus had claimed that the God of the Old

---

[1] The editions consulted on Augustine are those collated by Karl Heinz Chelius in *Augustinus-Lexikon* ("Augustins Werke und Kritische Editionen," *Augustinus-Lexikon 3*, ed. Cornelius Mayer [Basel: Schwabe, 2010]), xi–xxxii.

[2] For Faustus, see François Decret, *Aspects du manichéisme dans l'Afrique romaine. Les controverses de Fortunatus, Faustus et Felix avec saint Augustin* (Paris: Études Augustiniennes, 1970), 51–70. For a discussion of Faustus and his role in Augustine's own conversion, see Jason BeDuhn, *Augustine's Manichaean Dilemma, I: Conversion and Apostasy, 373–388 C.E.* (Philadelphia: University of Philadelphia Press, 2010), 106–34 and Johannes van Oort, "Augustine's Manichaean Dilemma in Context," *VC* 65 (2011): 558–64.

[3] For a recent study on the book, see Anni Maria Laato, "Faustus and Augustine: A Manichaean-Catholic Debate on the Mosaic Torah," in *The Challenge of the Mosaic Torah in Judaism, Christianity, and Islam*, ed. Antti Laato, STCA 7 (Leiden: Brill, 2020), 169–87.

[4] For the character of Moses in Augustine, see Martine Dulaey, "La geste de Moïse dans l'oeuvre d'Augustin (1): De l'Égypte aux combats du désert," *Revue d'études augustiniennes et patristiques* 57 (2011): 1–43, and pp. 4–5 on Moses slaying the Egyptian in particular. See also eadem, "La geste de Moïse dans l'oeuvre d'Augustin (2): La présence de Dieu au désert et la figure de Moïse," *Revue d'études augustiniennes et patristiques* 57 (2011): 189–237.

Testament acted under various immoral emotions such as envy (*inuidus*)[5], fear (*timens*) and anger (*irascens*). Moreover, central Old Testament figures not only suffered from reproachful sexual desires but were also driven by greed, committed serious crimes such as homicide in addition to all other kinds of atrocities. Faustus concludes, in a vein reminiscent of Marcionite Bible criticism, that the Old Testament appears to be a distorted and immoral collection of Jewish texts and should not carry any authority for Christians.[6] Thus, Faustus thinks that Augustine fails to discern between natural laws and "shameful Jewish atrocities."

Augustine's reply in *Faust.* 22 opens with an extensive quotation of Faustus's work (Faust. *Faust.* 22, 1–5), which is then followed by Augustine's massive argumentation against each of Faustus's allegations. Faustus's examples of immoral behaviour of the central figures of the Old Testament included Abraham lying about his wife to foreign kings, Lot having sexual intercourse with his two daughters, the immoral family relations of both Isaac and Jacob living with several spouses (*inter quattuor scorta certamen, quaenam eum uenientem de agro prior ad concubitum raperet*), the story of Judas and Tamar; the adulterous and murderous affair of king David; the insatiable sexual relations of king Solomon, the prophet Hosea living with a prostitute and finally, the murder (*Moyses homicidium fecerit*) and plundering committed by Moses during the exodus.[7]

The story of Moses slaying the Egyptian does not often appear in Augustine's works (only in *Faust.* 22, *Civ.* 16, and *qu.* 2). Indeed, the apologetic discussion in *Faust.* 22 is the most extensive in his entire oeuvre.[8] While Faustus's critique seems to have mentioned Moses's action

---

[5] For God's envy in the Genesis narratives see Thomas Raveaux, *Augustinus, contra adversarium legis et prophetarum. Analyse des Inhalts und Untersuchung des geistesgeschichtlichen Hintergrunds* (Würzburg: Augustinus, 1987), 64–65.

[6] For the Manichaean criticism and its Marcionite roots, see Samuel Lieu, *Manichaeism in the Later Roman Empire and medieval China* (Tübingen: Mohr Siebeck, 1992), 51–53, 154–58.

[7] Already Origen had had to defend Moses from the Gnostic charge of homicide. See Dulaey, "La geste de Moïse (1)," 4.

[8] A brief mention in *Civ.* 16, 43 *cum Israelitam defenderet, Aegyptium occiderat et territus fuerat*. For other interpretations preceding Augustine, see e.g. Ps.-Cypr. *Mont.* 9 and Ambr. *Cain* 2, 4, 14. Ambrose represents a moral interpretation, as Dulaey ("La geste de Moïse," 5)

only in passing, Augustine dedicates a rather longish defence to Moses in *Faust.* 22. Whereas the plundering of Egypt was a crime that could be justified by the divine commandment (*Faust.* 22, 71), Moses's murder of the Egyptian attacking a Hebrew slave seems not to have happened on God's order. How, then, should a faithful reader make sense of this episode, if one wishes to maintain that Moses truly was a "servant of the Lord, whom we owe our love and admiration, and whom we are to imitate as much as our abilities allow" (*Faust.* 22, 69)?

Here Augustine does not resort to the easiest solution, that is, argue that Moses's action was a divinely ordered prefiguration of future events in the history of salvation. Instead, he reads the episode in a plain historical sense.[9] He admits that Moses was not permitted to kill another human being, even with a justified reason.[10] What, then, is the sense of this episode? In brief, it displays Moses and his character before God started to "cultivate" its potential into something powerful and virtuous. In other words, Moses's aggressive reaction and violent impulses reflected a promising prospect for God to call him into His service and mould him into a great leader of the nation.

> [I]n minds where great virtue is to come, there is often an early crop of vic-
> es, in which we may still discern a disposition for some particular virtue,
> which will come when the mind is duly cultivated. For as farmers, when
> they see land bringing forth huge crops, though of weeds, pronounce it
> good for grain ... so the disposition of mind which led Moses to take the law
> into his own hands, to prevent the wrong done to his brother, living among
> strangers, by a wicked citizen of the country from being unrequited, was

---

has pointed out. For the apologetic arguments in the Jewish tradition, see Pekka Lindqvist, "Early Jewish Struggle with The Violent Moses in Exodus 2," in this volume.

[9] However, a bit later, Augustine cannot resist the typological exegesis for the episode, and compares Moses to Christ, who killed the devil in our defense. *Faust.* 22:90 (CSEL 25/1:697) *fratrem defendens occidit Aegyptium, cuiuis facillime occurrit iniuriosum nobis in hac peregrinatione diabolum a domino Christo nobis defensis occidi.*

[10] *Faust.* 22:70 (CSEL 25/1:666) *ut interim omittam, quod cum percussisset Aegyptium, quamquam illi deus non praeceperit, in persona tamen prophetica ad hoc diuinitus fieri permissum est, ut futurum aliquid praesignaret, unde nunc non ago, sed omnino tamquam nihil significauerint facta illa discutio [...]*

not unfit for the production of virtue, but from want of culture gave signs of its productiveness in an unjustifiable manner.[11]

In fact, as Augustine points out, the same pattern can be observed in the apostles as well, as both Peter and Paul had violent and fierce characters before they were called to minister as leaders of God's people. Thus, for Augustine, the violent actions, aggressive personality and intemperate behaviour here are what a rich soil, fertile with weeds, is to the eye of the farmer: a rich and promising prospect.[12]

Finally, Augustine concludes by appealing to the correct motives of Moses, Peter, and Paul in their violent actions before they were called to lead.

> In both cases the trespass originated not in inveterate cruelty, but in a hasty zeal which admitted of correction. In both cases there was resentment against injury, accompanied in one case *by love for a brother*, and in the other *by love*, though still carnal, *of the Lord* (italics mine). Here was evil to be subdued or rooted out; but the heart with such capacities needed only, like good soil, to be cultivated to make it fruitful in virtue.[13]

Thus, the psychological motive of revenging a perceived injustice, or, as Augustine calls it, love (*amor*), offers an excuse for a concerned reader of the episode. It was love, albeit in an uncultivated and inordinate form, that prompted Moses to cast the fatal blow against another human being. Thus, an episode that seems violent and offensive, at least in its historical and

---

[11] *Faust.* 22:70 (CSEL 25/1:666–67, trans. Richard Stothert, NPNF I/4, 299) *uerumtamen animae uirtutis capaces ac fertiles praemittunt saepe uitia, quibus hoc ipsum indicent, cui uirtuti sint potissimum adcommodatae, si fuerint praeceptis excultae. sicut enim et agricolae quam terram uiderint quamuis inutiles, tamen ingentes herbas progignere, frumentis aptam esse pronuntiant [...] sic ille animi motus, quo Moyses peregrinum fratrem a ciue inprobo iniuriam perpetientem non obseruato ordine potestatis inultum esse non pertulit, non uirtutum fructibus inutilis erat, sed adhuc incultus uitiosa quidem, sed magnae fertilitatis signa fundebat.*
[12] *Faust.* 22:70.
[13] *Faust.* 22:70 (CSEL 25/1:668, trans. Richard Stothert, NPNF I/4, 299) *uterque enim non detestabili inmanitate, sed emendabili animositate iustitiae regulam excessit, uterque odio inprobitatis alienae, sed ille fraterno, iste dominico, licet adhuc carnali, tamen amore peccauit. resecandum hoc uitium uel eradicandum, sed tamen tam magnum cor tamquam terra frugibus, ita ferendis uirtutibus excolendum.*

literal sense, can be interpreted in a correct way with the rule of love, as formulated in *doctr. Chr.*[14] Notably here, Augustine does not recourse to a figurative reading, even though he acknowledges the violent and illicit nature of Moses's behaviour. Nonetheless, the act is given an ethical justification based on Moses's divinely perceived potential as a leader and on his fundamental motivation of love. Briefly mentioning the episode in his *Questions on the Heptateuch* some twenty years later, Augustine refers to *Faust.* 22 as a definitive discussion of the verses, albeit subsequently wondering whether Moses had been acting on a divine commandment, after all.[15]

3 Phinehas's Spear: "Dilectione fecisset"

Our second episode of a sudden, spontaneous burst of deadly violence in a character who is depicted in a positive light in the Old Testament, comes from Num 25:1–13. Phinehas (lat. *Phinees, Finees*), of the house of Aaron, kills an Israelite called Zimri, together with his Midianite lover, Cozbi, with a single blow of a spear, impaling the couple together through their bellies. The action is not only praised but it also works as atonement for the idolatrous offences of all the Israelite leaders (Num 25:10–13). The Bible

---

[14] For rules of literal and figurative interpretation in reading narratives on possibly offending episodes in the Bible, see *Doctr. chr.* 3, 18 (Simonetti 194) *quae autem quasi flagitiosa imperitis uidentur, siue tantum dicta siue etiam facta sunt uel ex dei persona uel ex hominum quorum nobis sanctitas commendatur, tota figurata sunt, quorum ad caritatis pastum enucleanda secreta sunt;* 3, 23 (Simonetti 200) *seruabitur ergo in locutionibus figuratis regula huiusmodi, ut tam diu uersetur diligenti consideratione quod legitur, donec ad regnum caritatis interpretatio perducatur. si autem hoc iam proprie sonat, nulla putetur figurata locutio.* See here Karla Pollmann, *Doctrina Christiana: Untersuchungen zu den Anfängen der christlichen Hermeneutik unter besonderer Berücksichtigung von Augustinus, De doctrina christiana* (Freiburg: Universitätsverlag, 1996), esp. p. 139.

[15] *Quaest Hept.* 2.2 (CCL 33:70–71) *de facto Moyse, cum occidit Aegyptium ad defendendos fratres suos, satis disputauimus in illo opere, quod de uita patriarcharum aduersus Faustum scripsimus: utrum indoles in eo laudabilis fuerit, qua hoc peccatum admiserit, sicut solet uber terrae etiam ante utilia semina quadam herbarum quamuis inutilium feracitate laudari, an omnino ipsum factum iustificandum sit. quod ideo non uidetur, quia nullam adhuc legitimam potestatem gerebat nec acceptam diuinitus nec humana societate ordinatam. tamen, sicut Stephanus dicit in actibus apostolorum, putabat intellegere fratres suos, quod per eum deus daret illis salutem, ut per hoc testimonium uideatur Moyses iam diuinitus admonitus—quod scriptura eo loco tacet—hoc audere potuisse.*

text names Phinehas's zeal for the Lord as the correct motivation for his action. The character of Phinehas and his zealous act also appears in Ps 106:28-30 (quoted once by Augustine) and in 1 Macc 2:26, 54 and Sir 45:23-26 (not quoted).

Phinehas's act of violence has several applications in Augustine's theology. These are not directly polemical (except in *Leg.* 1, 29) but rather appear in exegetical commentaries on a somewhat challenging story. Such is the case in Augustine's musings in *Quaest. Hept.* 4, 52 (written in 419), in which Augustine concludes that Phinehas's action served as a satisfactory fulfilment of God's commandment to "impale all the chiefs of the people in the sun before the Lord" (Num 25:4). The commandment was never implemented because Phinehas stands up and kills the Israelite-Midianite couple in some kind of prefiguration of the crucifixion and atonement.[16] In any case, Phinehas's action demonstrates to all Christian believers how serious a crime adultery and idolatry are.

Phinehas is recalled in Ps 106:28-30 (*Enarrat. Ps.* 105.26, written after 418) and Augustine mentions him as acting by a justified motivation, love (*dilectio*), thus providing atonement for all who had sacrificed to the idols among the people of Israel.[17] As Phinehas's zeal arises from love, his violence is, according to Augustine, also imputed as righteousness (*reputaretur ad iustitiam*). Augustine's interpretation of Phinehas's action is, however, filtered through his own understanding of what the new

---

[16] *Quaest. Hept.* 4.52 (CCL 33:268) *cur ex eo, quod Phinees filius Eleazar transfixit adulteros, placatum fuisse dominum scriptura testatur plagamque cessasse? quasi crucifixis ducibus, sicut praeceperat dominus, adhuc indignatio perseuerans alio modo placanda uideretur, cum procul dubio falsum esse non posset, quod praenuntiauerat et promiserat dominus dicens: accipe duces populi et ostenta eos domino contra solem; et auertetur ira animationis domini ab Israhel [Nm 25,4]. si ergo factum erat, quis dubitet iram domini auersam fuisse ab Israhel? quid itaque opus erat, ut adhuc Phinees ad placandum deum sic in adulteros uindicaret eique testimonium scriptura perhiberet, quod eo modo placauerit dominum? nisi forte intellegamus, cum illud de ducibus populi Moyses, quod praeceperat, inplere disponeret, eum uoluisse etiam secundum legem talia punire flagitia et sacrilegam audaciam, ut iuberet quemque interficere proximum suum diis alienis nefarie consecratum atque interea etiam illud Phinees faceret ac sic ira domini iam placata non opus fuisse duces populi crucifigi. haec sane seueritas illi tempori congrua quantum malum sit fornicationis et idolatriae prudentium fidei satis euidenter ostendit.*

[17] *Enarrat. Ps.* 105.26 (CCL 40:1563) *quod si odio eorum, non dilectione fecisset, dum eum comederet zelus domus dei, non ei reputaretur ad iustitiam.*

covenant in Christ means for the church discipline in his own time: Phinehas's actions were more severe than what Christ would allow, but consequences in the times of the new covenant, in turn, are more serious than in the Old Testament era:

> Admittedly Christ our Lord has willed that discipline should be gentler, now that the New Covenant has been revealed. Yet the threat of hell is much more horrifying, and we do not read that God included hell in his menaces under the dispensation in force at that time.[18]

Apart from the exegetical contexts of *Quaest. Hept.* and *Enarrat. Ps.*, Phinehas's action is interpreted as an early example of church discipline in *de fide et operibus* (written in 413) too, where Augustine admits that it is not always possible to discern between good and bad members of the Church. However, this should not be taken as a licence to allow practically anything in the congregation. Enter Moses and his leadership of the people of Israel: the act of Phinehas who impaled two adulterers, can be read

---

[18] *Enarrat. Ps.* 105, 26 (CCL 40:1563, trans. Maria Boulding, WSA III/19: 215) *leniorem quidem reuelato testamento nouo dominus Christus esse uoluit disciplinam; sed atrocior est comminatio gehennae, quam tunc in illis comminationibus dei pro temporum dispensatione non legimus.* The comparison of crime and punishment in the Old and New Testament is also made in a rather peculiar and colourful manner in *Leg.* 1, 29, (written in 419–420) where Augustine opposes a presumably Manichaean writer on the question of the unity of Old and New Testament. Augustine's argument is construed on the coherently severe nature of God in both testaments. Indeed, Phinehas's act pales in comparison with the threats made in the New Testament on the fate of those who are to be condemned in the eternal damnation. *Leg.* 1, 29 (CCL 49:57) *quis autem utriuslibet sexus homo non mallet gladio trucidari, etiam illo modo, quo trucidauit sacerdos Phinees fornicarios, in ipso complexu nefariae uoluptatis, terribile constituens aduersus exsecrandas libidines ultionis exemplum, propter quod maxime deo placuit: quis, inquam, non mallet tali genere mortis interfici, quis non postremo igne consumi uel ferinis morsibus per ipsa pudenda laniari, quam mitti in gehennam ignis aeterni? cur igitur deus christianorum peccantes talibus mortibus puniat, ut post corporis interitum transitorium sequatur in gehenna sine fine supplicium, nisi quia testamenti utriusque unus est deus? nam possent Iudaei dicere aduersus huius impietatem, quantumlibet exaggeret bella, caedes, uulnera, funera, sanguinem, longe incomparabiliter deo nostro deum se habere mitiorem, longe scilicet mitius punientem transitoriis mortibus corporum quam flammis perpetuis gehennarum.* While these considerations do not add any particularly new perspectives to Augustine's insights on the character of Phinehas, they testify for his interest on the figure during 419–420.

figuratively in present times to mean ecclesiastic discipline in the form of defrocking and excommunications, "as the visible sword has been abandoned in the discipline of the church."[19] Indeed, in this way, Phinehas' violence prefigures the apostle Paul, who handed over to Satan the man who was living with his father's wife (1 Cor 5:1-5).

Even though Augustine's readings of Phinehas appear in rather casual contexts and show no particular interest or deeper theological investment in Phinehas's character, they nonetheless demonstrate Augustine's tendency to qualify and modify the violent nature of the story, especially as he is prone to read it as a picture of the disciplinary conventions for the church to come. Thus, he explicitly does not take the stance of his Catholic predecessor Optatus, who seems to have read the story as a straightforward and cold-hearted justification of violence against spiritual adulterers, that is, the Donatists. Here Augustine moves more along the lines of Parmenian who thought that the applications of the Phinehas story needed to be filtered through the non-violent example of Christ.[20] For Augustine the gist of interpreting Phinehas's violent behaviour lies in his reading the episode as a manifestation of tough love. The lethal and even gory violence

---

[19] *Fid. op.* 3 (CSEL 41:37) *quibus respondens hoc primum dico, ne quis ea testimonia scripturarum, quae conmixtionem bonorum et malorum in ecclesia uel praesentem indicant uel futuram praenuntiant, sic accipiat, ut disciplinae seueritatem siue diligentiam soluendam omnino atque omittendam non illis edoctus litteris, sed sua opinatione deceptus existimet. neque enim, quia illam primi populi permixtionem Moyses dei famulus patientissime perferebat, ideo non in multos etiam gladio uindicauit; et Phinees sacerdos adulteros simul inuentos ferro ultore confixit. quod utique degradationibus et excommunicationibus significatum est esse faciendum hoc tempore, cum in ecclesiae disciplina uisibilis fuerat gladius cessaturus. nec quia beatus apostolus inter falsos fratres tolerantissime congemescit et quosdam etiam diabolicis inuidentiae stimulis agitatos Christum tamen praedicare permittit, ideo parcendum censet illi, qui uxorem patris sui habuit—quem praecipit congregata ecclesia tradendum satanae in interitum carnis.*

[20] See Optatus, *C. Parm.* 3.5-7 (CSEL 26:85-89) and Brent Shaw, *Sacred Violence: African Christians and Sectarian Hatred in the Age of Augustine* (Cambridge: Cambridge University Press, 2011), 329, 495, for Optatus's straightforward literal reading. Ambrose had also praised Phinehas' zeal as a virtue fitting for Christian priests in fighting the heretics, but in a non-violent, spiritual way (Ambr. *In psalm.* 118, 18, 11[CSEL 62:402-3]). For the episode as a model for spiritual battle against the heretics, see also Quodvultdeus, *Adv. quinque haer.* (*Sermo* 10.)4.13 (CCSL 60:270): *magna res, cum uolo Iudaeum ferire, sicut Finees, fortissimus uir hastam uerbi sui uibrauit et misit ut per Iudaeum ad Sabellianum transiret Arrianumque percuteret.*

of the source text either demonstrates Phinehas's redemptive love (*dilectio*) by which God's wrath was placated, or, in its applied sense, refers to the Christian ecclesial discipline aimed at curing erring souls. Unlike in the case of Moses, Augustine shows no qualms or hesitation in relaying Phinehas's action, no doubt due to the positive interpretation it already has in Num 25 and Ps 106. Again, Phinehas's inner motivation, that is, his love for his people, justifies the vicious act of impalement.

4 Razis's Pious Suicide: "Narrata, non laudata"

At a quick glance, the action of Razis (lat. *Razias*, or *Raxius*) in 2 Macc 14:37–46 is similar to that of Moses and Phinehas except that Razis's violent and lethal outburst is directed against himself rather than others. Razis, a pious Jew, is persecuted by Nicanor, a Greek gentile, and his five hundred soldiers. Nicanor attempts to capture Razis alive to "exhibit the enmity that he had for the Jews" (2 Macc 14:39). Being a zealous believer, Razis, however, prefers to die rather than giving himself over to the pagans.

> Being surrounded, Razis fell upon his own sword, preferring to die nobly rather than to fall into the hands of sinners and suffer outrages unworthy of his noble birth. But in the heat of the struggle he did not hit exactly, and the crowd was now rushing in through the doors. He courageously ran up on the wall, and bravely threw himself down into the crowd. ... [H]e tore out his entrails, took them in both hands and hurled them at the crowd, calling upon the Lord of life and spirit to give them back to him again. This was the manner of his death (2 Macc 14:41–46, NRSV).

Augustine's discussion of this particular episode in 2 Macc is restricted to an openly polemical context. While he uses 2 Macc more often than, for example, 1 Macc, the story of Razis appears only in connection with the violent events in Timgad in ca. 420, when the Donatist bishop of the city, Gaudentius, opposed imperial legislation and actions against the Donatist church.[21] The imperial tribune of the time, Dulcitius, sought Augustine's

---

[21] For a more thorough report of the events, circumstances, and characters involved in this case, see Shaw, *Sacred Violence*, 732–46. The merit in Shaw's discussion from our point of

advice in the case, as Gaudentius had threatened to burn himself, his congregation and his church, if Dulcitius and his troops entered the Donatist church in Timgad in order to enforce the imperial sanctions against the dissidents.

The story of Razis is, in fact, initially part of Gaudentius's biblical argumentation, and Augustine seems somewhat surprised by its use in the Donatist justification of extreme actions under the threat of imperial violence: "I recall—I must admit—that I have never as yet replied to them [sc. arguments for suicide as a form of martyr death] with regard to the elderly Razis."[22] In answering Dulcitius's letter on the matter (*ep.* 204), Augustine firmly states that "whosoever kills another person without lawful authority, is a murderer; and whosoever kills himself, he will not be a murderer only if he is not a person."[23] From this statement Augustine proceeds to criticize the Donatist biblical interpretation of reading the stories of Jewish characters as moral examples in too straightforward a manner.

---

view lies in his emphasis of suicide being conceived as something special and very different from other kinds of violent and lethal actions only after Augustine—that is, the difference between the killings of Moses, Phinehas and Razis was not that clear in this respect for Christians in 5th century. For more neutral and concise accounts, see Serge Lancel, "Gaudentium Donatistarum episcopum (Contra-)," in *Augustinus-Lexikon* 3, ed. Cornelius Mayer (Basel: Schwabe 2004), 90–95; and, idem, "Gaudentius," in *Augustinus-Lexikon* 3, ed. Cornelius Mayer (Basel: Schwabe 2004), 95–96.

[22] *Ep.* 204.6 (CSEL 57:320-21, trans. Roland Teske, WSA II/3: 374) *uerum tamen, quod fatendum est, de isto Raxio seniore [...] adhuc eis numquam respondisse me recolo.* See the discussion of Shaw, *Sacred Violence*, 742. While the Maccabean martyrs were well-known in the Latin West, the figure of Razis seems to have been referred to less often.

[23] *Ep.* 204.5. For Augustine, suicide is thus a form of murder (*homicidium*), see *Civ.* 1:17–19; 1: 21; 1:25 (CSEL 40/1:31-37, 39, 44–45); *Ench.* 45 (CCSL 46:74); *Ep.* 155. 3 (CSEL 44:432–34); *Tract. Ev. Io.* 51, 10 (CCSL 36:443). Bels, Jacques. "La mort volontaire dans l'oeuvre de saint Augustin." *Revue de l'histoire des religions* 187 (1975): 147–80. Detlef Liebs, "Homicida, homicidium," in *Augustinus-Lexikon* 3, ed. Cornelius Mayer (Basel: Schwabe, 2004), 379–81. See also Shaw, *Sacred Violence*, 727–30, who emphasizes Augustine's crucial influence on Western attitudes about suicide. A not too far-fetched analogy for Razis's action would be the final moments of Samson, to which Augustine refers in *Gaud.* 1, 39, with the rather flimsy observation that Samson was told by the Spirit of the God to kill both himself and a great number of his enemies. Samson's suicide is elsewhere mentioned only in *Civ.* 1, 21, together with the same excuse as in *Gaud.*

If they are ready to apply to the life of the Christian people as examples all the actions from the Jewish people and those writings, let them apply this as well. In them there are many actions of those persons who are praised by the truth of those writings, but they are not suitable to the present time or were not correctly done even at that time. Such is the act that this Razis committed upon himself.[24]

Unlike the previous cases, where Moses's actions were praised as showing a promising future in cultivating virtues and Phinehas was commended for his loving zeal, Razis is now censored because of his pride (*elatio superba*). Razis' solution, therefore, is not an example of faith or morals but rather a symptom of his vice. Furthermore, Augustine rather incorrectly claims that the narrative in 2 Macc does not recommend or praise Razis's actions, but merely recounts them—an obviously false interpretation to everyone familiar with the verses.[25]

In his subsequent response to Gaudentius's text (*Gaud.* 1, 32–40), Augustine first reports Gaudentius's own rather brief mention of Razis (*Gaud.* 1, 32), and then presents his own polemical interpretation of the episode. Augustine concedes that 2 Macc presents authoritative cases of how to act under persecution but argues that the story of Razis is not one of them. A Christian should follow the example of the Jewish mother and her seven sons (2 Macc 7) rather than the haughty model of Razis, whose behaviour highlights Jewish confidence in their own righteousness and inheritance, later called excrement (*stercora*) by Paul.[26] Augustine thus admits that Razis's actions are indeed praised in the story, but in a way that is ambivalent, underlining virtues that Christians should no longer

---

[24] *Ep.* 204.6 (CSEL 57:321, trans. Roland Teske, WSA II/3: 375) *si ad uitam christianorum de Iudaea gente atque illis litteris parati sunt omnium factorum exempla transferre, tunc et hoc transferant. si autem sunt illic plurima eorum quoque hominum, qui litterarum illarum ueritate laudati sunt, uel huic iam tempori non conuenientia uel etiam illo tempore non recte facta, tale etiam hoc est, quod in se ipsum Raxius iste commisit.*

[25] *Ep.* 204.7 (CSEL 57:321) *in his autem Machabaeorum libris quamuis homo fuerit ipse laudatus, factum tamen eius narratum est, non laudatum, et iudicandum potius quam imitandum ante oculos constitutum, non sane nostro iudicio iudicandum, quod nos quoque ut homines habere possumus, sed iudicio doctrinae sobriae, quae in ipsis quoque libris ueteribus clara est.*

[26] *Gaud.* 1:37–38 (CSEL 53:236–38).

cultivate. For him, Razis's actions can be called "noble" (*nobilis*), "manly" (*uiriliter praecipitauit*), and even "great" (*magna*), but they do not show signs of the true Christian virtue, humility.[27] Finally, Augustine quibbles with the most theological content of Razis's suicide (2 Macc 14:46, "he tore out his entrails, took them in both hands and hurled them at the crowd, calling upon the Lord of life and spirit to give them back to him again") and claims that even such a steadfast conviction of resurrection does not mean that Christians should be impressed by Razis's behaviour.[28] All in all, as Augustine claimed to Dulcitius in *Ep.* 204, the entire story of Razis is a history of past events, not a moral example to be followed.[29] Here Augustine rephrases his own usual counterargument against Manichaean Bible criticism of morally dubious narratives in the Old Testament (*narrata sunt ista, non laudata*), presented several times in *Faust.* 22.[30]

As if unsure of his argumentation, Augustine appeals to the different status of the books of Maccabees compared to the law, prophets and writings, which are authoritative *for Jews*.[31] Moreover, Augustine repeats his criticism of Razis's conduct and its erroneous inner motivation (fear of humility, impatience), which had earlier been central in judging the moral quality of the previous cases of Moses and Phinehas.

Finally, Augustine starts to sound oddly familiar when listing the immoral behaviour of several Old Testament characters. As in Faustus's argumentation two decades prior to Gaudentius, these include the adulterous and murderous affair of king David; the insatiable sexual relations of king Solomon; the story of Judah and Tamar—but also some other figures, such as the drunken and naked Noah and suicidal Samson. In other words, with this deft move, Augustine turns elements of Manichaean Old Testament criticism against his Donatist opponent. These examples of Old Testament

---

[27] This insight is close to Augustine's discussion of suicide in *Civ.* 1, see *Civ.* 1:17-27 (CSEL 40:31–49).

[28] *Gaud.* 1:37 (CSEL 53:236–37).

[29] *Gaud.* 1:37 (CSEL 53:237) *istam uero eius mortem mirabiliorem quam prudentiorem narrauit quemadmodum facta est, non tamquam facienda esset scriptura laudauit.*

[30] See e. g., *Faust.* 22:45 (CSEL 25/1:637: *de opere filiarum Loth narrata ista sunt, non laudata*); 22:62; 22:95 (CSEL 25/1:658, 701-2).

[31] *Gaud.* 1:38 (CSEL 53:237) *hanc quidem scripturam, quae appellatur Macchabaeorum, non habent Iudaei sicut legem et prophetas et Psalmos.*

figures are presented to alert readers of the Bible to assess morally complex narratives with sound judgment. For Augustine, this means that he is
able to discern elements in the story of Razis that praise the protagonist
(*laudata*) from elements that are only reported in the story (*narrata*), but
even the elements of praise in the source text are assessed with his
general hermeneutical tool kit of inner motivation, that is: were the
actions committed under the virtue of love or the vice of pride?

Augustine's argumentation here truly has an air of what Brent Shaw
describes as "innovating under pressure," and his polemical interpretation
of the spontaneous violence of Razis against himself has an urgency unlike
his more academic dispute against Faustus's Manichaean criticism of the
Old Testament, as his reading is ultimately aimed at undermining
Gaudentius's justifications of violent resistance against an imperial
official.[32]

5 Conclusions

The three aberrant cases of sudden outbursts of lethally violent behaviour
in the Old Testament did not receive voluminous treatment from
Augustine. Indeed, if it had not been for the case of the Donatist bishop,
Gaudentius, the figure of Razis would probably never have appeared in
Augustine's works at all. Likewise, Moses's violent manslaughter of the
Egyptian and the zealous murder by Phinehas are mentioned in Augustine's extant oeuvre only a very few times. However, as such, these minor
blinks in the vast constellation of Augustine's Biblical exegesis display—in
an interesting way—how the major principles of his Biblical interpretation
are reflected even in the more minute details of marginal episodes of
ambivalent and even outright problematic episodes of Biblical narrative.

Taking Augustine's reading of Moses slaying the Egyptian, for example;
the episode appears only once in Augustine's corpus, but this does not
mean he treats the story disambiguously. On the contrary, even in an

---

[32] Shaw, *Sacred Violence*, 744. I am not equally convinced of Shaw's (p. 745–6) conclusion that
the story of Razis "had long been regarded as an exemplary one in the dissident church." See
the pertinent remark by Alan Dearn, "Donatist Martyrs, Stories, and Attitudes," in *The
Donatist Schism: Controversy and Context*, ed. Richard Miles (Liverpool: Liverpool University
Press, 2018), 98–99.

apologetical and polemical context Augustine reads the episode carefully, literally and in an innovative way, albeit the idea of Moses's reproachable behaviour as showing potential for later virtuous leadership seems rather far-fetched to the modern eye. For some reason, the easy way of figurative reading does not appeal to Augustine in this instance, and he even admits that Moses, the lawgiver and divinely chosen leader of the Hebrew people, committed a sin (*peccauit*) in spontaneously killing the Egyptian for his unjust behaviour.

Furthermore, in all three cases presented above Augustine is interested in the psychological and ethical inner motivation of the characters. Admittedly, Moses committed a sin, but he did so because of "love" (*tamen amore peccauit*) and Phinehas's action was fierce and thus could not be taken as a model for Church discipline but, nonetheless, he did what he did because of "love" (*dilectione fecisset*). Finally, the one case in which Augustine is, for obviously polemical reasons, critical of the main character, Razis, demonstrates once again Augustine's interest in analysing the inner motivations of Biblical characters as the Jewish martyr chooses a voluntary death because of his pride (*elatio superba*) and not out of a humble love for his people. Thus, even in such aberrant and minor cases in difficult stories, Augustine's basic hermeneutical principle of referring the teachings and narratives of the Bible to *caritas* is discernible.

Finally, all readings of the three episodes of the Old Testament figures involved in a form of direct aggression also show Augustine hesitating—qualifying (Moses), criticising (Razis), and distancing (Phinehas) the raw and literal violent element in the stories—and this may be one of the most important features in Augustine's way of reading sudden outbursts of zealous and pious violence: slaying fornicators and heretics literally, based on the examples of Moses and Phinehas, was not a viable option for Augustine.

"Beyond Nature": The *Akedah* as Paradigm for Human Agency in John Chrysostom's Homilies

Michaela Durst

1 The Topic of this Paper: Human Agency in Genesis 22

At one place in his homilies, John Chrysostom (c. 349–407) describes Abraham's behaviour in sacrificing his son as "beyond nature."[1] This is not to evaluate Abraham as being inhuman in a negative sense. By contrast, the unnatural act of a father murdering his son classifies Gen 22 as a narrative reflecting on 'human agency' in general. John does this not within a theoretical treatise, but in the context of a preaching practice that could be placed in the broad field of psychagogy.

2 Mental Disorders: Psychagogy and Exegesis

In late antiquity, the Christian preacher, willingly or unwillingly, took on the role of a speaker who had to compete with other rhetors and philosophers.[2] John Chrysostom did not have to shy away from this competition. The praise of the rhetor Libanios about his student John,

---

1 Cf. *In Genesim homilia* 47.4, see the analysis below. I would like to thank Eva Holder for improving the English text.

2 Cf. John's dialogue *De sacerdotio*, esp. book V; see also e.g. Silke-Petra Bergjan, "'Das hier ist kein Theater, und ihr sitzt nicht da, um Schauspieler zu betrachten und zu klatschen'— Theaterpolemik und Theatermetaphern bei Johannes Chrysostomos," *ZAC* 8,3 (2005): 567–92; Frauke Krautheim, *Das öffentliche Auftreten des Christentums im spätantiken Antiochia: Eine Studie unter besonderer Berücksichtigung der Agonmetaphorik in ausgewählten Märtyrerpredigten des Johannes Chrysostomos*, STAC 109 (Tübingen: Mohr Siebeck, 2018), chapter 4.

although probably legendary, may refer to his rhetorical brilliance,[3] as well as his later byname 'Chrysostom.' Connected with the rhetorical demand is the preacher and priest's self-image as a 'soul leader' who shapes the soul of his audience.[4] Research in recent years has rediscovered the homilies of John Chrysostom as psychagogical texts.[5] The late antique preacher sees himself as a 'therapist,'[6] as a

> [P]sychagogue in the classical sense, a teacher of his own (albeit Christian) philosophical school.... Like philosophers in the psychagogic stream, his goal is the health of his students' souls....[7]

---

[3] Cf. Sozomenus, *Historia ecclesiastica* VIII 2, GCS NF 4:349,23–350,5.

[4] Cf. e.g. John Chrysostom, *De sacerdotio* VI.6, SC 272:324,17–36.

[5] For the classical definition of psychagogy, cf. Platon, *Phaidros* 261a; in general, Hermann Stauffer, "Psychagogie," *HWRh* 7 (2005): 406–14. For late antiquity, see esp. Wendy Mayer, "The Persistence in Late Antiquity of Medico-Philosophical Psychic Therapy," *Journal of Late Antiquity* 8,2 (2015): 337–51; eadem, "Shaping the Sick Soul: Reshaping the Identity of John Chrysostom," in *Christians Shaping Identity from the Roman Empire to Byzantium: Studies Inspired by Pauline Allen*, ed. by Geoffrey D. Dunn and Wendy Mayer, SVigChr 132 (Leiden: Brill, 2015), 140–64; Christopher Gill, "Philosophical Therapy as Preventive Psychological Medicine," in *Mental Disorders in the Classical World*, ed. by William V. Harris, CSCT 38 (Leiden: Brill, 2013), 339–60; Nadine Metzger, "'Not a *Daimōn*, but a Severe Illness': Oribasius, Posidonius and Later Ancient Perspectives on Superhuman Agents Causing Disease," in *Mental Illness in Ancient Medicine: From Celsus to Paul of Aegina*, ed. by Chiara Thumiger and Peter Singer, Studies in Ancient Medicine 50 (Leiden: Brill, 2018), 79–106; Jessica Wright, "Between Despondency and the Demon: Diagnosing and Treating Spiritual Disorders in John Chrysostom's *Letter to Stageirios*," *Journal of Late Antiquity* 8,2 (2015): 352–67; for the Western tradition and Augustine, see Charlotte Köckert, "Therapie der Affekte: Augustins *Confessiones* als Dokument christlich-philosophischer Seelsorge," *ZKG* 127,3 (2016): 293–314.

[6] Cf. λόγος as φάρμακον (Mayer, "Persistence," 341). Cf. in general Susanna Elm, *Sons of Hellenism, Fathers of the Church: Emperor Julian, Gregory of Nazianzus, and the Vision of Rome*, Transformation of the Classical Heritage 49 (Berkeley: University of California Press, 2012) (chapter 9: "A Bloodless Sacrifice of Words to the Word") for Gregory of Nazianz; Jutta Tloka, "Der Λόγος und die λόγοι: Die Bedeutung der Rhetorik für die Konstituierung der christlichen Elite in der Spätantike," in *Logos der Vernunft—Logos des Glaubens*, ed. by Horacio E. Lona and Ferdinand Rupert Prostmeier, Millennium-Studien 31 (Berlin: de Gruyter, 2010), 301–21.

[7] Mayer, "Shaping the Sick Soul," 145.

John therefore stands in the spirit of "ancient philosophical essays," which are concerned with

> [W]hat we might call emotional resilience, that is, the ability to cope with— what are usually seen as—personal disasters or problems without loss of emotional stability or inner calm.[8]

John's letters to Stageirios and Olympias have been viewed in this way.[9] Two homilies on Gen 22, which I will examine in this paper[10]—the forty-seventh homily of John's *Genesis homilies*, as well as the third homily of the *homilies on 2 Corinthians*[11]—, can also be perceived in this way,[12] though dealing with biblical texts, accompanied by verse-by-verse commentary. They address an abnormal and unexpected demand that exceeds human understanding, contradicts human reason and nature, and torments Abraham's soul. The 'obedience' of Abraham is thus combined from the beginning with an anthropology which champions a maximally self-effective conception of man. A 'blank space' in the Abrahamic narrative

---

[8] Gill, "Philosophical Therapy," 341. For the role of biblical texts, see also Robert G. T. Edwards, "Healing Despondency with Biblical Narrative in John Chrysostom's *Letters to Olympias*," *JECS* 28,2 (2020): 203–31.

[9] Cf. Wright, "Between Despondency" (letter to Stageirios), and Mayer, "Persistence" (letter to Olympias).

[10] For the exegesis on Gen 22 in antiquity in general, see e.g. David Lerch, *Isaaks Opferung christlich gedeutet: Eine auslegungsgeschichtliche Untersuchung*, BHTh 12 (Tübingen: Mohr Siebeck, 1950); Martin Meiser, "Gen 12,1f. und Gen 22 in antiker jüdischer und christlicher Rezeption," in *Tempel, Lehrhaus, Synagoge—Orte jüdischen Lernens und Lebens*, FS Wolfgang Kraus, ed. by Christian Eberhart et al. (Paderborn: Schöningh, 2020), 399–419.

[11] Citation follows the *Patrologia Graeca* (for *In Genesim homilia 47*: PG 54:428,11–434,25) and the edition of Frederick Field (for *In epistulam II ad Corinthios 3: Sancti patris nostri Joannis Chrysostomi archiepiscopo Constantinopolitani interpretatio omnium epistularum Paulinarum per homilias facta 3: Epistolam ad Corinthios posteriorem homiliae XXX*, BPEC [Oxford, 1845], 32–50 = PG 61:405,2–418,16); both end of the 4th century; for discussion of chronology cf. Wendy Mayer, *The Homilies of St John Chrysostom: Provenance, Reshaping the Foundations*, OCA 273 (Rome: Pontificio Istituto Orientale, 2005); Max Von Bonsdorff, *Zur Predigttätigkeit des Johannes Chrysostomos: Biographisch-chronologische Studien über seine Homilienserien zu neutestamentlichen Büchern* (Diss. Helsinki, 1922) (foundational, but outdated); John references Gen 22 very often through his œuvre, cf. below note 17.

[12] Cf. as "moral philosophy [...] medico-philosophical psychic therapy" (Mayer, "Shaping the Sick Soul," 145). Mayer criticises the former verdict of John as a moraliser.

thus becomes the central topic: the inner life, the emotions and affects of Abraham, and their relationship to the 'outward,' his actions (i.e. his soul bound to φύσις).[13] Abraham is presented here as an example of virtue, as he is known in the Jewish-Hellenistic tradition of Philon of Alexandria, as well as in the Christian tradition.[14] Thus, it is less about what Abraham *does* exactly and more about what Abraham's behaviour *is based upon.*

---

[13] Cf. *In Genesim homilia* 47.1-2 and 47.3 (PG 54:429,7-11; trans. Robert J. Hill, *John Chrysostom: Homilies on Genesis 46-67,* FOTC 87 [Washington: The Catholic University of America Press, 2010], 15): "It was not as if in ignorance that he put him to the test but that the people of the time and those from that time until now might be instructed in the same love (πόθος) as the patriarch's and in showing obedience (ὑπακοή) to the Lord's commands (πρόσταγματα)." Cf. 47.18 (deeds are better than just listening to the sermon). At the beginning of his homily on Gen 22, John determines a *skopos* and reveals to his audience what he will present to them: a model of virtuous (ἀρετή) behaviour, obedience (ὑπακοή), and love (πόθος)—but also the divine φιλανθρωπία. Cf. Frances M. Young, chapter 32: "Traditions of Exegesis," in *The New Cambridge History of the Bible,* ed. by James Carleton Paget and Joachim Schaper (Cambridge: Cambridge University Press, 2013), (734-51) 740 for the Antiochene exegetical tradition and its focus on "morals and ethical advice for his congregation," and 744: "Antiochene *theoria* (insight) looked for the resemblances in person or event, finding images of dogmatic truth or moral teaching in the *skopos* (overall intent) or narrative sequence [...]."

[14] Cf. on Abraham as virtuous and for a very similar focus on Abraham's emotions and love for God, Philo of Alexandria, *De Abrahamo* 170. For this Maren R. Niehoff, *Philo of Alexandria: An Intellectual Biography* (New Haven, CT: Yale University Press, 2018), 127. For a Christian example, cf. Gregory of Nyssa, *De deitate filii et spiritus sancti et in Abraham,* cf. Theodor Mahlmann, "Gregor von Nyssa: Isaaks Opferung (Gen 22)," in *Isaaks Opferung (Gen 22) in den Konfessionen und Medien der Frühen Neuzeit,* ed. by Johann Anselm Steiger and Ulrich Heinen, AKG 101 (Berlin: de Gruyter, 2006), 773-80 and Barbara Mahlmann-Bauer, "Abraham, der leidende Vater: Nachwirkungen Gregors von Nyssa in Exegese und Dramatik (im 16. und 18. Jahrhundert)," in *Isaaks Opferung (Gen 22),* 309-98. On Abraham as an example of virtue in John, cf. Demetrios E. Tonias, "The Iconic Abraham as John Chrysostom's High Priest of Philanthropy," in *Revisioning John Chrysostom: New Approaches, New Perspectives,* ed. by Chris de Wet and Wendy Mayer, Critical Approaches to Early Christianity 1 (Leiden: Brill, 2019), (563-85), 564-66 ("A Model of Virtue") (though some assumptions in this text should be modified, e.g. the critique on Brown's theses is missing). For the role of ethics and ἀρετή, see Pak-Wah Lai, *John Chrysostom and the Hermeneutics of Exemplar Portraits,* Doctoral Thesis (Durham University, 2010) (URL: http://etheses.dur.ac.uk/425/, 19.09.2020).

Significant for this is the exegetical technique of 'soul-portraits,'[15] in which the guidance of the soul relies on powerful soul-pictures recommended for *mimesis*.[16] The same applies to the Gen 22 interpretation, which turns out to be what may seem implausible at first glance: The scene's tendency to go beyond all humanity is normalised into a paradigm for Christian behaviour in general. To put to rest a misunderstanding: What is to be imitated? Obviously not an obedience that goes as far as murder. In contrast, the *tentatio* of Abraham shows how Abraham can still behave virtuously, even if the crisis reveals the utmost intensity of human bonding to φύσις and πάθη. This human 'obedient' agency during 'mental disorders,' i.e. when confronted with the abnormal and contradictory, qualifies Abraham as virtuous. In one reference to Gen 22, which is not discussed here, John gives this a clearly theological framework: He gives the example of Abraham in a text about divine providence, and thus the scene points to the incomprehensibility of God's wisdom.[17] Admittedly, this exegesis can only work if the Abrahamic narrative is inverted into psychological imagery. Though at the end of the *Genesis homily* the sacrifice is also interpreted as a type for the cross, the focus is mainly on the psychological challenge during the sacrificial narrative, as well as on the sacrificial act(ion) itself as the point of human and divine interplay.

3 The Paradigmatic Abraham: 'Beyond Nature and Affect' (in the Forty-Seventh Genesis Homily)

3.1 "[A] Task Beyond the Powers of Human Nature!"
In the forty-seventh *homily on Genesis* we encounter Abraham, a person who is confronted with a maximum-crisis situation, namely with the divine command to sacrifice his beloved son: "What a terrible burden in

---

[15] For this exegetical practice of 'portrait exegesis,' cf. the study of Margaret M. Mitchell, *The Heavenly Trumpet: John Chrysostom and the Art of Pauline Interpretation*, HUTh 40 (Tübingen: Mohr Siebeck, 2000) (esp. chapter 2: "The Archetypal Image [ἡ ἀρχέτυπος εἰκών]" and chapter 5: "'The Meadow of Virtues' [λειμὼν ἀρετῶν]: Portraits of Paul's Soul").

[16] Cf. Mitchell, *Heavenly Trumpet* (as above), as well as Andreas Heiser, *Die Paulusinszenierung des Johannes Chrysostomos: Epitheta und ihre Vorgeschichte*, STAC 70 (Tübingen: Mohr Siebeck, 2012), 8.

[17] Cf. *Ad eos qui scandalizati sunt* 10 (CPG 4401); cf. the edition of Anne-Marie Malingrey, *Jean Chrysostome: Sur la providence de dieu*, SC 79 (Paris: Cerf, 1961).

the command, a task beyond the powers of human nature (ὑπερβαῖνον ἀνθρωπίνην φύσιν)!"[18] This divine command is explicitly marked by John as transgressing 'human nature,' as something unnatural or superhuman. To be more precise: Every word in the divine command—focused on the beloved son (τὸν ἀγαπητόν; also περιπόθητον) in whom offspring is promised—would be capable, through the triggered affect of fatherly love (φιλοστοργία[19]), of 'moving' the 'soul' of Abraham (καθικέσθαι τῆς τοῦ δικαίου ψυχῆς).[20] Neither Abraham's λογισμός nor his διάνοια, however, is confused:

> His thinking (τὸν λογισμόν) was not deranged, his mind (τὴν διάνοιαν) not confused; he was not at a loss to cope with the strangeness of the command; he sought neither rhyme nor reason (οὐκ ἐνενόησεν, οὐκ ἐλογίσατο) within himself.[21]

The Abrahamic 'obedience' is thus evaluated by John with a look into the interior of Abraham and the decision-making processes taking place there. First of all, he states that Abraham's λογισμός and διάνοια, i.e. the centre of his thinking, do not seek reason within himself (πρὸς ἑαυτόν) for the strangeness (ξένος) of the divine order. That God's promise could still be fulfilled under the condition of the death of the son eludes human logic.[22] Here a further significant pair of terms meet: human ἀκολουθία und God's will (βουληθέντος).[23] Abraham's thinking resists the contradiction arising from human reasoning. The divine command breaks through the cause-effect connection of inner-worldly possibility and necessity:

> This good man, however, entertained none of these thoughts (ἐλογίσατο); instead, like a dutiful servant (εὐγνώμων οἰκέτης) he set aside every human

---

[18] *In Genesim homilia* 47.4 (PG 54:429,24–25; trans. Hill, 16).
[19] On the concept of φιλοστοργία and its relevance in antiquity, see e.g. Geert Roskam, "Plutarch against Epicurus on Affection for Offspring: A Reading of *De amore prolis*," in *Virtues for the People: Aspects of Plutarchan Ethics,* ed. by Geert Roskam and Luc van der Stockt, Plutarchea Hypomnemata (Leuven: Peeters, 2011), 175–202, 178–88.
[20] *In Genesim homilia* 47.4 (PG 54:429,31).
[21] *In Genesim homilia* 47.5 (PG 54:429,45–48; trans. Hill, 16).
[22] For acolythia and logic, cf. Ernst G. Schmidt, "Akoluthie," *HWPh online* (1.07.2021).
[23] Cf. *In Genesim homilia* 47.5 (PG 54:429,59–61).

Michaela Durst

consideration (λογισμὸν ἀνθρώπινον) and had one single concern, to put into effect the command; as though transcending human nature (ὥσπερ ἐκτὸς γεγονὼς τῆς ἀνθρωπείας φύσεως) and putting all compassion (συμπάθειαν) and fatherly affection (πατρικὴν φιλοστοργίαν) second to God's commands, he hastened to their discharge.[24]

Abraham ignores the human λογισμός and is thus able to act as if he were not under the conditions of human nature (ὥσπερ ἐκτός): Compassion (συμπάθεια) and fatherly affection (φιλοστοργία) defer to God's instructions as the guideline for his actions. John calls this a εὐγνώμων servant.

3.2 Some Terminological Considerations: φύσις, λογισμός, εὐγνώμων
Three background assumptions emerged in the previous section that are worth a closer look: the question of the human φύσις and transcending of it, the ambivalence of λογισμοί ('reasoning'), and Abraham's 'obedience' expressed by the term εὐγνώμων.

John speaks again and again of the fact that φύσις is 'transcended' (ὑπερβαίνω). In terms of philosophical therapy, this might mean that he can cope with the disturbing situation, despite a very strong natural feeling of fatherly care. At the level of theology, one could add that assumptions about humanity are relevant in the broadest sense. Contrary to Manichaean[25] and certain philosophical assumptions, John does not consider human flesh to be fundamentally evil, but assumes that humans can control their προαίρεσις and γνώμη[26] independently of the conditions of φύσις: Human essence is thus not determined by the φύσις, but vice versa: "The moral choice (προαίρεσις) determines one rather than the

---

[24] *In Genesim homilia* 47,6 (PG 54:429,62–430,2; trans. Hill, 17).
[25] On Manichaeism cf. Chris L. de Wet, "John Chrysostom on Manichaeism," *HTS* 75,1 (2019): a5515 (URL: https://doi.org/10.4102/hts.v75i1.5515, 18.09.2020) (John insists upon freedom of choice, in contrast to Manichaeism).
[26] On the term προαίρεσις and γνώμη, cf. e.g. Maximilian Forschner, "Epiktets Theorie der Freiheit im Verhältnis zur klassischen stoischen Lehre (*Diss.* IV 1)," in *Epiktet: Was ist wahre Freiheit: Diatribe IV 1*, ed. by Samuel Vollenweider et al., SAPERE 22 (Tübingen: Mohr Siebeck, 2013), 97–118, 106–9; Jan Stenger, *Johannes Chrysostomos und die Christianisierung der Polis*, STAC 115 (Tübingen: Mohr Siebeck, 2019), 64–69. See also note 36.

The Akedah *as Paradigm for Human Agency in John Chrysostom's Homilies*

substance (οὐσία), and it is more 'man' than the other is."²⁷ If the φύσις can be transcended and is not ineluctable, 'judgement' steps into the centre. Extensive treatment is therefore given to Abraham's fight preceding his decision. He battles—John speaks of ἀγών and the unconquerable (ἀκαταγώνιστος)—with the challenging command (ἐπίταγμα). His strength (ἀνδρεία) proves itself in that he does not lose himself in many thoughts (πολυπράγμων),²⁸ but follows God's direction (νεῦμα)²⁹ with loving desire (πόθος). In this regard, however, John is likewise part of a rich monastic tradition of dealing with λογισμοί (cf., for example, Evagrius Ponticus).³⁰ Addressing such 'false beliefs' is also part of philosophical therapy.³¹ Even if the terminology of λογισμοί does not apply directly here, Abraham is confronted with not following the flood of thoughts and human rationality, but instead 'love' for God.³² Thus, Abraham proves by the strength of his soul to be εὐγνώμων. The term γνώμη in John has rightly received some

---

²⁷ Johannes Chrysostomos, *In epistulam ad Colossenses homilia* 8 (5, 255 Field = PG 62:352,54–55). Cf. note 33.

²⁸ Above all, we can also think of the debates with the Anomoeans, in which this term plays an important role, as a polemical insult against those who seek to comprehend God's activity by means of human reason. Cf. John's text *De incomprehensibili dei natura* against the Anomoeans (CPG 4318); Ferdinand Cavallera and Jean Daniélou, "Introduction," in *Jean Chrysostome: Sur L'incompréhensibilité de Dieu*, ed. by idem and Robert Flacelière, SC 28 (Paris: Cerf, 1951), 7–70, 7–15; Raymond J. Laird, "John Chrysostom and the Anomoeans: Shaping an Antiochene Perspective on Christology," in *Religious Conflict from Early Christianity to the Rise of Islam*, ed. by Wendy Mayer and Bronwen Neil, AKG 121 (Berlin: de Gruyter, 2013), 129–49.

²⁹ Cf. *In Genesim homilia* 47,6 (PG 54:430,15–22). Very similarly in 47,7 (where Abraham's justice as well as his προθυμία and πόθος are praised).

³⁰ Cf. Evagrius Ponticus, *De octo spiritibus malitiae tractatus*.

³¹ On Stoic therapy, see Martha C. Nussbaum, *The Therapy of Desire: Theory and Practice in Hellenistic Ethics*, Martin Classical Lectures 2 (Princeton [NJ]: Princeton University Press, 1994), esp. chapter 9–10. Gill, "Philosophical Therapy," 341 states: "The underlying assumption [...] is that all or much human distress is produced by the beliefs held by the people concerned, and that changing these beliefs will help to pre-empt this distress." On John and 'despondency' as a confusion of λογισμοί, cf. Wright, "Between Despondency and the Demon," 353: *Athumia* can be removed "by means of reason, the fundamental therapeutic technique." Cf. note 8.

³² Cf. e.g. Jan R. Stenger, "Where to Find Christian Philosophy?: Spatiality in John Chrysostom's Counter to Greek Paideia," *JECS* 24,2 (2016): 173–98 (where philosophical reasoning is opposed to the monks and to faith).

Michaela Durst

attention in the last years. Laird, by means of Noah, shows in his study on γνώμη in John that εὐγνωμοσύνη (and ἀγνωμοσύνη as the opposite) belong to the characteristic attributes of the biblical paradigm and can be rendered as 'rightmindedness.'[33] Laird's translation with 'mindset' underscores why the γνώμη is so important, because it determines the 'choice' (προαίρεσις)[34] and functions as "the critical faculty of the soul in divine-human relationships."[35] Also in this passage, the emphasis is not so much on Abraham's decision in this concrete 'test' from God, but rather on a kind of habitus that prepares and thus empowers him to deal with conflicting thoughts, even in such an exceptional situation.[36]

3.3 The εὐγνώμων Servant and the Power of his πόθος

That being stated, Abraham's judgement is 'abnormal' but has a trustworthy point of departure. Abraham does not consult with others, but hides from his servants his decision to sacrifice his child, knowing how unusual, how new and paradoxical, his action is. Both terms, καινός and παράδοξος, point to a contradictory but not senseless realm that is not graspable with normal thinking. If God, contradicting nature (φύσις), made Abraham a

---

[33] Laird assumes that John partially anticipates the central position of γνώμη in Maximus the Confessor. Cf. Raymond J. Laird, *Mindset, Moral Choice and Sin in the Anthropology of John Chrysostom*, Early Christian Studies 15 (Strathfield: St. Paul's Publications, 2012); idem, "Mindset (γνώμη) in John Chrysostom," in *The Oxford Handbook of Maximus the Confessor*, ed. by Pauline Allen and Bronwen Neil (Oxford: Oxford University Press, 2015), 194–211. On Noah and εὐγνωμοσύνη, see Laird, *Mindset*, 58–61; on προαίρεσις and judgment Edward Nowak, *Le chrétien devant la souffrance: étude sur la pensée de Jean Chrysostome*, Théologie historique 19 (Paris: Beauchesne, 1972), chapter II.2.

[34] Cf. Laird, *Mindset*, 65.

[35] Laird, "Mindset," 194.

[36] In the *Akedah* scene, John conveys his image of man, which takes its foundation from the late antique Christian reflections on the human will, cf. e.g. Joachim Söder, "Die Selbstmächtigkeit des Menschen: Nemesios von Emesa über das freie Entscheidungsvermögen," in *Wille und Handlung in der Philosophie der Kaiserzeit und Spätantike*, ed. by Jörn Müller and Roberto Hofmeister Pich, BzA 287 (Berlin: de Gruyter, 2010), 259–76; Theo Kobusch, "Der Begriff des Willens in der christlichen Philosophie vor Augustinus," in *Wille und Handlung in der Philosophie*, 277–300; Albrecht Dihle, *Die Vorstellung vom Willen in der Antike* (Göttingen: Vandenhoeck & Ruprecht, 1985).

father the first time,[37] he will now also let that which exceeds, indeed opposes, reason (λογισμός) find a convincing end[38]:

> Whereas his hand carried a visible fire, the fire within scorched his mind (τὴν διάνοιαν), and wasted his thoughts (τὸν λογισμόν), persuading him that he would overcome by his love of God (τῷ πρὸς τὸν Θεὸν πόθῳ) and leading him to reason (παρασκευάζον λογίζεσθαι) that the one who had already caused him to become a father despite human nature (ὑπὲρ φύσιν ἀνθρωπίνην) would now also succeed in achieving what exceeded the bounds of human reason (τὰ ὑπερβαίνοντα τὸν ἀνθρώπινον λογισμόν).[39]

Abraham's soul is tortured by his son's questions about the animal to be sacrificed, yet he remains master of his emotions. Later even his 'white lie' that God would choose the sacrificial sheep becomes a prophecy.[40] Ψυχή, γνώμη, and πόθος follow from premises that exceed human nature (φύσις),[41] but nevertheless determine concrete human action. This becomes most apparent in the sacrificial scene itself. As Abraham raises the sword, John comments:

> Let us not idly pass by these words, dearly beloved, but wonder how his soul (ἡ ψυχή) did not part company with his body, how he managed to bind him with his own hands and place on the faggots his beloved, graceful, his only begotten son. "Abraham put out his hand," the text says, "to take the sword to sacrifice his son (σφάξαι τὸν υἱὸν αὐτοῦ)." What a godly spirit (Ὦ φιλοθέου ψυχῆς)! What a valorous attitude (ὦ γνώμης ἀνδρείας)! What extreme love (ὦ πόθου ἐπιτεταμένου)! What purpose overcoming human nature (ὦ λογισμοῦ νικῶντος ἀνθρωπίνην φύσιν)![42]

---

[37] Cf. also homily 37 on Gen 15, esp. 37,4–8 (on 'faith' and God's 'signs,' as well as on the limits of human nature).

[38] Cf. above on the incomprehensibility of God, note 28.

[39] *In Genesim homilia* 47.8 (PG 54:430,48–54; trans. Hill, 18).

[40] Cf. *In Genesim homilia* 47.9.

[41] On the obedience of Isaac as well as Abraham's φρόνημα, cf. *In Genesim homilia* 47.10.

[42] *In Genesim homilia* 47.10 (PG 54:431,23–31; trans. Hill, 19).

3.4 Obedience and Reward ("On My Account You Did Not Spare Your Beloved Son")

Since Abraham's γνώμη leaves nothing to be desired, God shows that he does not want the sacrifice of the child, but instead lets Abraham's virtue become visible:

> [B]ut that the good man's virtue (τὴν ἀρετήν) be revealed; so he commended the good man for his mindset (ἀπὸ τῆς γνώμης) and his choice (ἀπὸ τῆς προαιρέσεως), and by taking the sacrifice as completed he then gave evidence of his characteristic love (τὴν οἰκείαν ... φιλανθρωπίαν).[43]

The faculty of γνώμη and the choice (προαίρεσις) reveal the virtuous, obedient[44] man (ἀρετή) Abraham. This is true regardless of whether the command is completed or not.[45] Therefore, by means of the voice, God prevents Abraham's impulse (ὁρμή) to complete the sacrifice, for his purpose is the 'instruction' of later generations, not the sacrifice of a murdered child. This part of the homily ends with God's response, i.e. returning the son, providing a lamb for sacrifice, and giving the 'crown of obedience' as 'reward.'

Thus, the structure of the scene is that of psychologically grasped 'obedience,' focused on Abraham's love, his 'mindset' that gave him his agency, and the love of God that rewards Abraham for his 'intention' with the promise of descendants:

> You see, as far as intention (εἰς προαίρεσιν) is concerned, the patriarch stained his right hand in blood, plunging his sword into the child's throat and consummating the sacrifice; hence, the Lord also offers his commendation of the good man for a sacrificial rite brought to consummation in saying, "On my account you did not spare your beloved son." For your part, you did not spare him on my account, and I, for mine, spared him on account of

---

[43] In Genesim homilia 47.11 (PG 54:431,40–44; trans. based on Hill, 20).

[44] Cf. In Genesim homilia 47.11–12.

[45] Cf. Laird, Mindset, 67 in the comparison he draws to Noah: "He proposes that provided works are motivated by a healthy γνώμη, the crown is gained even if those works are unfinished."

your obedience. So, to reward you for such obedience, "I will bless you and truly make you numerous."[46]

The sacrifice of the beloved son for God (cf. Gen 2:22)—which is used as a type for the cross (cf. Rom 8:32)—and God's reward are emphasised by the reciprocal acting for 'my / your sake' (διὰ ἐμέ / σέ). Nevertheless, while it is the orientation towards God and not the 'outcome' (of descendants) which informs Abraham's sacrificial action, it is his γνώμη that enables him to be obedient.[47] Or in other words, his action is not motivated by reward for fulfilling the command, but by his agency based on his 'mindset.'[48]

3.5 Summary

Abraham's crisis represents a timeless conflict of how to remain steadfast in situations surpassing nature and comprehension. His advice does not follow the Stoic focus on reasoning, but brings the divine into play: as the cause of the crisis, insofar as it exceeds human reason(ing), and as the goal of desire that ultimately enables human agency. Without doubt, John holds that every test from God should be welcomed; nevertheless, the punchline is that the care for human γνώμη ('mindset') paves the way for the sharing of human πόθος and divine φιλανθρωπία, i.e. obedience and reward. This is why the *Akedah* is not only a narrative about emotional crises, but stands for a sacrificial narrative that encourages Christian agency, which depends solely on a steadfast orientation towards God and is neither hindered by nature nor by human reasoning. Although contradictory and paradoxical at first glance, such a 'sacrificial will' claims its own 'rationality.'

---

[46] *In Genesim homilia* 47.17 (PG 54:433,48–59; trans. Hill, 23–24).

[47] Cf. also *In Genesim homilia* 47.17, where his audience should study the 'attitude' and not the 'outcome.'

[48] For the discussion under the labels of 'works' and 'grace,' cf. Rudolf Brändle, "'Gott wird nicht allein durch richtige Dogmen, sondern auch durch einen guten Lebenswandel verherrlicht': Zur Verhältnisbestimmung von Glaube und Werken bei Johannes Chryso-stomos," *ThZ* 55 (1999): 121–36, as well as idem, "Synergismus als Phänomen der Frömmig-keitsgeschichte, dargestellt an den Predigten des Johannes Chrysostomos," in *Gnadenwahl und Entscheidungsfreiheit in der Theologie der alten Kirche*, ed. by Ekkehard Mühlenberg, Oik. 9 (Erlangen: Lehrstuhl für Geschichte u. Theologie d. Christl. Ostens, 1980), 69–89, 113–21.

Michaela Durst

A very similar interpretation of Gen 22, found in the *2 Corinthian homilies*, is even more astonishing in this regard. This time, the interpretation is not only interested in what 'mindset' enabled Abraham to sacrifice. Rather, the *Akedah* is used as an illustration of the Christian way of life as baptized person and the sacrifice itself is a μυστήριον that shows the interplay with the divine.

4 The *triplex munus* of the Baptized and the Sacrifice as μυστήριον (in the *Homilies on 2 Corinthians*)

After commenting on Paul's seemingly fickle behaviour towards his congregation, which is explained by the leading of the Spirit and is thus reliable,[49] John refers to 2 Cor 1:21 ("who anointed and sealed us") to show how God strengthens believers through anointing. All the baptized assume the three Old Testament offices. In his explanation of what the *triplex munus* stands for, John also refers to Abraham and the *Akedah*.

4.1 The triplex munus *of the Baptized*
John interprets the *triplex munus* as follows[50]: Kingship refers to the (eschatologically) expected reign and to dominion over the λογισμοί, priesthood to the devotion as sacrifice (cf. Rom 12:1), and prophecy to a knowledge hidden from human perception (cf. 1 Cor 2:9). At the end of his homily, John once again emphasises in pointed terms that they, the believers, are granted these three positions like soldiers marked with the Holy Spirit.[51] John addresses these three functions in more detail in the course of the homily: Kingship is shown most extensively, followed at the end by brief remarks on priest- and prophethood.

---

[49] Cf. *In epistulam II ad Corinthios homilia* 3.3.
[50] On the offices of priest and king in other patristic authors, see also Andreas Merkt, *1 Petrus: Teilband 1*, NTP 21,1 (Göttingen: Vandenhoeck & Ruprecht, 2015), 169–194 (on priest and sacrifice), as well as 194–97 (on kingship, e.g. on moral interpretation in Origen).
[51] Cf. *In epistulam II ad Corinthios homilia* 3.8 (3, 49 Field = PG 61:418,5–7). In contrast to the Jewish rite of circumcision.

4.2 Kingdom: Abraham's Victory over Nature and a 'Marvellous Sword'
The internal λογισμοί are represented this time as troops that have to obey the command of the ideal king. The patriarch Abraham surpasses every such expectation of royal reign:

> For when he was commanded to sacrifice (σφαγιάσαι) his son, consider how many thoughts (λογισμοί) then rose up against him. Nevertheless, he brought all under submission....[52]

Abraham resists one of the sharpest and most cruel attacks, namely through fatherly συμπάθεια, by commanding and calming the λογισμοί (cf. εὐτάκτως, κοσμέω, ἡσυχία).[53] When Abraham draws the sword, his victory outshines every August and Caesar:

> For that righteous man erected a trophy at that moment over the most arbitrary of tyrannies. For nothing is so tyrannical as nature (φύσεως); and find ten thousand tyrannicides, one like this shalt thou never show us. For it was the triumph in that moment of an angel, not a man.[54]

Abraham wins over nature (φύσις) because his conduct is heavenly (ἐν οὐρανοῖς ἐπολιτεύετο). Therefore the victory is announced in heaven, by God himself—ἐν θεάτρῳ τῷ τῆς οἰκουμένης—before the angels, not so much because Abraham did not spare his son, but rather because he did it 'for God's sake' ('for my sake' / ὅτι δι' αὐτόν).

As in the *Genesis homilies*, it is λογισμοί, which springs from fatherly love—here called συμπάθεια and φιλοστοργία—, that Abraham can keep under control. God's honour is the result of Abraham's acting 'for the sake' of God. What is different here is that Abraham's behaviour is placed in a heavenly dimension (angelic lifestyle). Even more thrilling, the following enigmatic interpretation of the sword brings the sacrificial moment all the more into the realm of the extraordinary.

---

[52] *In epistulam II ad Corinthios homilia* 3.5 (3, 42 Field = PG 61:412,24–25; trans. Talbot W. Chambers, *The Homilies of Saint Chrysostom: On the Epistles of Paul to the Corinthians*. The Oxford Translation, rev. with additional notes, NPNF 12 [New York, 1889], 290).
[53] Cf. *In epistulam II ad Corinthios homilia* 3.5, as well as 3.6.
[54] *In epistulam II ad Corinthios homilia* 3.5 (3, 43 Field = PG 61:412,43–45; trans. Chambers, 291).

The sword used for sacrifice is, according to John's interpretation, at the same time dipped in blood and not wetted—thus it is itself astonishing and marvellous (ὦ μαχαίρας θαυμαστῆς):

> It touched not the neck of the child, nor passed through the throat of that holy one: nor was crimsoned with the blood (οὐδὲ ἐφοινίχθη αἵματι) of the righteous; rather it both touched, and passed through, and was crimsoned (ἐφοινίχθη), and was bathed (ἐβαπτίσθη) in it, yet was not bathed.[55]

John admits that his audience must think he is 'beside himself' in the face of so much contradiction (ἐναντιολογῶν) (ἐξίστημι, 'mental confusion'). But the whole scene was wonderful and not contradictory: Abraham's right hand did indeed thrust the sword into the throat of the boy, while the hand of God prevented it from being stained with blood:

> For it was not Abraham alone that held it back but God also; and he by his purpose (διὰ τῆς γνώμης) gave the stroke, God by His voice (διὰ τῆς φωνῆς) restrained it. For the same voice (φωνή) both armed and disarmed that right hand, which, marshalled under God, as if under a leader, performed all things at His beck (τῷ ἐκείνου νεύματι), and all were ministered at His voice (τῇ ἐκείνου φωνῇ). For observe; He said, "Slay (σφάξον)," and straightway it was armed: He said "Slay not (μὴ σφάξῃς)," and straightway it was disarmed....[56]

The action, though inherently contradictory, follows completely the divine νεῦμα and the divine φωνή, i.e. it is entirely according to the divine instruction. More than in the interpretation in the *Genesis homilies*, divine assistance and conformity of human will to the divine 'appeal' are stressed as a paradoxical event. In the *Genesis homily*, it was the divine 'voice' that prevented the impulse (ὁρμή) to carry out a sacrifice that was supposed to show an 'intention' not based on human logic and nature. Now the interpretation focuses entirely on the voice, which can no longer be

---

[55] *In epistulam II ad Corinthios homilia* 3.6 (3, 45 Field = PG 61:414,41–45; trans. Chambers, 292).

[56] *In epistulam II ad Corinthios homilia* 3.6 (3, 46 Field = PG 61:414,50–415,4 with the textcritical variant in the main text: καὶ ὥπλισε τὴν δεξιὰν καὶ κατέστειλε; trans. Chambers, 292).

assigned clearly to God or to Abraham—it is this voice that fully directs Abraham's action. Fittingly, John uses the description of the sword as part of a shocking mystery (φρικτόν and μυστήριον).[57] Depicting the action of sacrifice as an analogy for the human will, the sacrifice is enacted, the sword is reddened, although the narrative itself interrupts the sacrificial act; what is at stake with the sword being simultaneously reddened and not reddened is the mystery of God's guidance and conformity to his will. Thus the child—as John notes—does not accuse his father of 'madness' (μανία), though this would be understandable. (Instead, the child's behaviour displays honourable strength of soul.)

The kingship of the Spirit-led baptised means that all their deeds are not dominated by sin, i.e. ill-mindedness,[58] but are characterised by a heavenly lifestyle in total accord with God's will. A small side note from John is important yet: He rejects the suspicion that God actually wanted the death of the son. God would never have accepted blood, John finally clarifies; a murder was not permitted, since blood is a meal (τράπεζα) only for demons. (It is necessary to emphasise that Abraham nevertheless could not foresee the outcome.)

4.3 Abraham as Priest and Prophet
John concludes his homily with a brief reference to Abraham as priest and prophet. Abraham, who stands before the altar with fire and sword, is the priest:

> For he offered (προσήνεγκε) a son, he offered also a ram (προσήνεγκε καὶ πρόβατον), yea, more and above all, his own will (τὴν ἑαυτοῦ γνώμην). And with the blood of the lamb he consecrated his right hand, with the sacrifice (τῇ δὲ σφαγῇ) of his son, his soul (τὴν ψυχὴν ἡγίασεν).[59]

---

[57] *In epistulam II ad Corinthios homilia* 3.6 (3, 45 Field = PG 61:414,40–41). For the notion of φρίκη in the context of John's text *De incomprehensibile dei natura* (see note 28), see Cavallera and Daniélou, "Introduction" (part III: "La terreur sacrée"), 33–45.
[58] For the relation of mindset and sin, see Laird, *Mindset*, chapter 10.
[59] *In epistulam II ad Corinthios homilia* 3.7 (3, 49 Field = PG 61:417,5–9; trans. Chambers, 293).

As in Old Testament practice, the priest is sanctified by the blood, i.e. the blood of sacrificial animals dedicated to God. John frames this anew as Abraham being consecrated as a priest and gaining holiness because of the sanctifying of his soul (ψυχή) and, again, it is the γνώμη which allows his priesthood.[60] Finally, John 8:56 proves that Abraham is a prophet. Although the passage remains in many regards open-ended, it is obvious that what we now are presented with in the *2 Corinthian homily* is the process of the Christian's perfection that John identifies as the underlying structure of the *Akedah* that becomes accessible for all the baptized who are led by the Spirit.

5 Human Agency between Psychagogy and Mystery

To sum up: John's approach to Abraham's behaviour is clearly a psycha-gogical one. In other words, it is about human agency that depends on a healthy ψυχή. That the virtuous Abraham is not really mad, but instead can show something important about Christian behaviour, seems to be clear from the outset. In this regard John presents his audience with a psychagogic lesson as preparation for coping with challenging situations (e.g. the death of a child[61]). As the crisis for Abraham is caused by a divine command, Abraham's behaviour is not the symptom of abnormal madness—what is would have been, seen from the viewpoint of human logic and natural affects—but the sign of a mindset guided by πόθος and the divine 'voice.'

About the divine, two things are implicitly stated: Like in the promise in Gen 15 of descendants exceeding nature, divine agency does not follow human reasoning—as some philosophical and Anomoean positions assume, we might add. Further, divine 'reward' and divine voice 'conform' to human γνώμη, which represents the realm of human freedom; this freedom requires psychagogical effort in order to realise the agency it has been granted.

It is Abraham's action that is totally abnormal and needs explanation. Two angles of response are conceivable: One addresses the ethical

---

[60] Cf. *In epistulam II ad Corinthios homilia* 3.7 (3, 49 Field = PG 61:417,9–10).
[61] See the beginning of the homilies *In epistulam II ad Corinthios homilia* 1.5.

dilemma, whether God really could want the sacrifice of a child and whether man really prefers this as a trustworthy guideline. John mitigates this perspective by hinting that God does not accept such blood, that the sacrifice 'for the sake of God' counts and not the act of sacrifice itself or, insofar as the homily has a psychagogic purpose, that the focus is on something occurring outside one's own control.

The other angle is the one John mainly pursues, i.e. from whence does Abraham get his ability to act, if nature and reason are not the sources? John does not advocate side-stepping rationality or reason as such or even justifying deviant and irrational behaviour as God-willed—his framework is undoubtedly virtuous human agency. His point is about being virtuous even when knowledge and reason reach their limits. What is at stake, theologically speaking, is divine providence[62] and, as the other side of the coin, the fact that humans are free to judge and evaluate the surrounding world, even if they cannot change it or make sense of it by their own efforts. 'Nature' is nevertheless not the determining factor. What distinguishes the virtuous man is his 'mindset'; someone like Abraham is motivated by love for God, and through the act of sacrifice he showcases the interplay of the human and the divine. In so doing, John moves a truly troubling story into the field of virtuous behaviour. He does this by allowing the paradoxical and puzzling narrative to unfold as an exploration of how the mind functions, in which mental faculties are presented in a new light by the biblical viewpoint.

---

[62] See above note 17.

Normal and Abnormal in Noah's Drunken Behaviour (Genesis 9:20–27) and its Reception in Syriac Exegesis

Catalin-Stefan Popa

This paper offers a reading of narratives that justify Noah's drunken behaviour as innocent and, respectively, highlights several patristic interpretations interwoven with metaphors that transcend the boundaries of the biblical episode. Additionally, it brings into discussion representations of wine and of the state of inebriation across Syriac texts, evaluating the extent to which Noah is associated with these concepts in moral ascetic writings.

For those who are not familiar with Syriac Christianity, I would like to first briefly map the broader field to which the article's theme belongs. The Syriac Churches adhere to a Christian tradition that developed along and across the Byzantine Empire's borders and, importantly, lived under Muslim rule from the 7th century onwards. Many Syriac scholars produced an important patristic and spiritual heritage, notable among them being Ephrem the Syrian, Narsai, Jacob of Sarug, Isaac of Nineveh, Ishodad of Merv, Dionysius Bar Salibi, Gregorius Barhebraeus and many others.

To return to the core topic of this paper and to the figure of Noah, it is common knowledge that Noah is one of the most defining representatives of the Old Testament. He is the successor of the human race after the Great Flood. After coming out from the Ark, Noah established a covenant with God, enshrined through the appearance of a rainbow, a sign that gave hope for the continuity of the human race. Besides a series of positive episodes, we must also acknowledge an abnormal biblical episode in which Noah is the protagonist that is somehow different from previous ones: Noah's drunkenness (Gen 9:20–27).

1 The Vineyard, and Noah's Drunken Behaviour in Syriac Exegetical Tradition

The figure of Noah is discussed in various patristic texts, but the approach of Syriac exegesis seems to be particular, owed in no small part to its richness in using a multitude of exegetic tools such as metaphors and analogies in portraying Noah as righteous and innocent in his behaviour. In the first part of this paper, I will offer a reading of Syriac narratives that justify Noah's drunken behaviour as innocent. A natural question here arises, in the context of Noah's drunken behaviour: is Noah himself to be blamed for his drunken behaviour, or not?

Let us first look at this episode of Noah's drunkenness by dividing it into three sections: (1) Noah before inebriation (here we include the planting of the vineyard and the production of wine); (2) Noah during his inebriation (discussing Noah's deeds while he got drunk and laid uncovered inside his tent, how Ham saw his father naked and how he told his brothers about this and how they covered him); and (3) Noah after having been drunk (when he awoke, found out what his youngest son had done to him and afterwards cursed Canaan).

(1) For the first section, we will begin with some Syriac ideas regarding the planting of the vineyard. When did this event occur? Reading the work of the greatest Syriac poet and exegete, Ephrem the Syrian, in his *Commentary on Genesis*, the author dismisses the idea that Noah's drunkenness [ܡܒܘܬܐ ܕܚܡܪܐ] is owed to an excess intake of alcohol from the very outset. Ephrem points out that during the flood Noah did not have the opportunity to drink any wine, since this practice was prohibited to him:

> Noah's drunkenness was not from an excess of wine, but because it had been a long time since he had drunk [any wine]. In the ark he had drunk no wine; although all flesh was going to perish, Noah was not permitted to bring any wine onto the Ark.[1]

---

[1] "[Scripture] recorded about Noah, that he planted a vineyard and drank of its wine, got drunk, fell asleep, and lay uncovered in his tent. Ham saw the nakedness of his father and told his two brothers outside" (Raymond-M. Tonneau (ed.), *Sancti Ephraem Syri in Genesim et in*

Further on, Ephrem also believes that Noah did not plant the vineyard as soon as the flood ceased. He argues that at the end of the flood it was already towards the end of spring at Noah's descent from the ark (twenty-seventh of Iyyar [May])—"not the time for planting a vineyard." In addition, Ephrem also considers that 3 to 4 or 6 years would have needed to pass before the vineyard reached its maturity. Concerning the question how Noah came to plant the vineyard, Ephrem states that he "planted the vineyard from the grape stones that he brought with him on the Ark," which shows that vineyards already existed before the flood and that, consequently, Noah had known the taste of wine before the calamity; his drunkenness, therefore, is due to the fact that he was no longer accustomed to wine[2].

Interestingly, Ephrem invokes several further arguments to absolve Noah of guilt. Based on the biblical phrase "Ham went out into the street and told his brothers," the author points out that the construction of a city with streets would have taken years, thereby indicating that such a long period must have passed before Noah again experienced the taste of wine:

> Therefore, the building of the village and the laying out of its streets also bear witness that it had been years, as we said, since the old man had drunk any wine, and for that reason it made him drunk.[3]

With regard to the timing of Noah's cultivation of the vineyard, a further West Syriac author, Philoxenos of Mabbug (d. 523) asserts that "Noah planted the vineyard in the first year after the Flood, and in the third year

---

Exodum Commentarii, CSCO 152-53 / Syr 71-72 [Louvain: Imprimerie Orientaliste Durbecq, 1955], 63 [Syr.], 50 [Lat.]).

[2] "Because, therefore, Noah did not drink [any wine] in the year of the Flood, and in the year that he left [the Ark], he did not plant a vineyard, for he came out of the ark on the twenty-seventh of Iyyar [May]—not the time of [fruit] maturing and not the time for planting a vineyard—and so, because in the third year he planted the vineyard from the grape stones that he brought with him on the ark, until there was a [productive] vineyard in three or even four years, there were six years of interval during which the just one had not tasted any wine" (Tonneau [ed.], *Sancti Ephraem Syri in Genesim et in Exodum Commentarii*, 63-64 [Syr.], 50-51 [Lat.]).

[3] Tonneau (ed.), *Sancti Ephraem Syri in Genesim et in Exodum Commentarii*, 64 (Syr.), 51 (Lat.).

after the flood he drank the wine and got drunk."[4] Ephrem and Philoxenos agree that Noah planted the vineyard in the first year after the Flood. But, where Ephrem presents a wider range of possibilities, Philoxenos categorically affirms that Noah's inebriation happened in the third year after the cultivation.

A further detail comes from the *Cave of Treasures*, an apocryphal work most likely written in the 5th century, which presents the planting of the vineyard as not an individual but rather a collective act: the passage uses plural verbal forms for the sowing, planting, and pressing of the vineyard; in this view, Noah was apparently not alone in his agricultural endeavour.[5]

In his *Commentary on Genesis*,[6] Ishodad of Merv (9th century) is adamant that no one cultivated vineyards before the time of Noah.[7] He considers the episode of his inebriation his first experience with wine. Moreover, Ishodad believes that Noah's involvement in preparing the wine was assisted by God, such that he acted in accordance with divine providence, which if nothing else is an interesting way to justify Noah's later drunken behaviour:

> Having therefore eaten grapes and noticed that there was a juice (duke) in it, he pressed their water, according to whether God also assisted him, so that this (new) species started with him.[8]

---

[4] See Paul de Lagarde (ed.), *Materialien zur Kritik und Geschichte des Pentateuchs*, vol. 2 (Leipzig: Teubner, 1867), 86, ll. 25–29; Harold Sidney Davidson, *De Lagarde's Ausgabe der arabischen Übersetzung der Genesis (Cod. Leid. Arab. 230) nachgeprüft* (Leipzig: Drugulin, 1908), 16; Adam C. McCollum, "An Arabic Scholion to Genesis 9:18–21 (Noah's Drunkenness) attributed to Philoxenos of Mabbug," *Hugoye: Journal of Syriac Studies*, Vol. 13.2 (2010): 125–48, esp. 132–33.

[5] Carl Bezold (ed.), *Die Schatzhöhle*, vol. 2 (Leipzig: Hinrichs, 1888), 104–5.

[6] Jacques-Marie Voste and Ceslas Van den Eynde (ed.), *Commentaire d'Isodad de Merv sur L'Ancien Testament, I. Genèse*, CSCO 126, Syr 67 (Louvain: Imprimerie Orientaliste L. Durbecq, 1950), 127–30. French translation by Ceslas Van den Eynde, CSCO 156 / Syr 75 (Louvain: Imprimerie Orientaliste L. Durbecq, 1955), 137–39.

[7] "So, when Noah saw that the previous state (of the world) had changed into an excellent state, he began to cultivate the ground, [...] and he planted a vineyard" (*Commentaire d'Isodad de Merv sur L'Ancien Testament, I. Genèse*, 127 [Syr.], 137 [Fr.]).

[8] *Commentaire d'Isodad de Merv sur L'Ancien Testament, I. Genèse*, 127 (Syr.), 137 (Fr.).

(2) With regard to the episode's second section, namely Noah' inebriation, Barhebraeus's (d. 1286) *Scholia on the Old Testament* recounts the event in the same spirit of innocence that we saw in Ephrem. According to Barhebraeus, Noah got drunk "because he was not accustomed to drinking wine and he regarded it as water"[9]. As for the effects of his inebriation, Ishodad of Merv's commentary tells that after getting drunk Noah was entirely convinced that he was alone in the tent while the others were at work, and for that reason he undressed himself and then fell into sleep. Ham came home in search of an axe. Ishodad proposes the hypothesis that Ham was very likely unaware of Noah's drunkenness; Ham laughed at him, considering him "a lazy man that disliked work."[10] According to Ishodad, we know that Ham told his brothers about his find, and that they came and covered Noah up.[11]

Ephrem does not view the gesture of Noah's sons as a simple gesture of covering the father's shame; rather, he makes a profound Christological link in his *Hymns on Nativity*: "Two brothers covered up Noah: they had seen the Only-Begotten of God who would come to cover up the nakedness of Adam who had become drunk with pride."[12]

(3) In what follows, let us tackle the third section of this episode, namely Noah's awakening and his acts when realizing what happened during his sleep.

---

[9] Martin Sprengling and William Creighton Graham (ed.), *Barhebraeus' Scholia on the Old Testament, Part I: Genesis–II Samuel* (Chicago: The University of Chicago Press, 1931), 40 (Syr.), 41 (Engl.)

[10] "He drank it, got drunk and undressed himself in the middle of his tent, thinking that there was no one in the tent except him, the men and women having gone to work. But it seems that Ham came to the house looking for an ax or something other, and, seeing his father naked, he did not cover him, but he laughed at him like a lazy man disliking to work, and therefore plunged into sleep. It is likely that Ham, too, was unaware that (Noah) was drunk. And he went to report the matter to his brothers" (*Commentaire d'Isodad de Merv sur L'Ancien Testament, I. Genèse*, 127 [Syr.], 137–38 [Fr.]).

[11] *Commentaire d'Isodad de Merv sur L'Ancien Testament, I. Genèse*, 127 (Syr.), 137–38 (Fr.).

[12] Ephrem the Syrian, *Hymne de Nativitate* I.23, see Sebastian P. Brock, "Sobria Ebrietas According to some Syriac Texts," *ARAM periodical* 17 (2005): 185–91, esp. 186, n. 6. See also Kathleen E. McVey, trans., *Ephrem the Syrian: Hymns* (New York: Paulist, 1989), 66: "The two brothers who hid Noah looked for the Only-Begotten of God to come and hide the nakedness of man, intoxicated with pride."

An interesting question is how Noah found out that Ham saw him naked in the tent. On this matter, Ishodad claims a divine revelation, placing God once again in Noah's proximal space and thereby placing Noah on the same level with his forefather, Adam:

> But by a divine revelation which was communicated to him in a dream, Noah knew everything that (Ham) had done to him, in the same way as Adam (became aware of) the formation of Eve, etc.[13]

Another author, Gregory Barhebraeus, points out that "Noah awoke and saw what his youngest son had done to him".[14]

If we take a closer look at the following section, we can see that, in the end, Noah perhaps surprisingly did not curse Ham but rather Canaan, who was Ham's son and Noah's nephew. The question is: why did Noah do so? The Syriac authors are almost unanimous in their consideration of this matter. For example, Ishodad writes that: "It was Canaan who looked first, and revealed this to Ham. Likewise, because (Ham) had received the blessing from his brothers."[15]

In addition, Barhebraeus offers an explanation that "Ham was not the 'youngest son' of Noah, but rather the middle (intermediary) [ܡܨܥ ܒ]." From the expression "little son" it results that the first to see Noah naked was his grandson (Canaan).[16] Morever, Ishodad believes that even though

---

[13] *Commentaire d'Isodad de Merv sur L'Ancien Testament, I. Genèse*, 128 (Syr.), 138 (Fr.).

[14] *Barhebraeus' Scholia*, 40 (Syr.), 41 (Engl.)

[15] *Commentaire d'Isodad de Merv sur L'Ancien Testament, I. Genèse*, 128 (Syr.), 138 (Fr.).

[16] *Barhebraeus' Scholia*, 40 (Syr.), 41 (Engl.). If we look at the text of Ishodad, we observe that the author offers an elaborate perspective: "Noah blamed Ham for three faults: first, because he looked at his father's nudity; second, because he did not cover it up; third, because he went to reveal it to his brothers" (*Commentaire d'Isodad de Merv sur L'Ancien Testament, I. Genèse*, 127–28 [Syr.], 138 [Fr.]). Ishodad does not remain limited to this interpretation, but also offers other anonymous patristic vantage points according to which: "Canaan (was cursed) because he had first looked upon his grandfather's nudity and revealed it to his father, and his father in turn ran to reveal it to his brothers." Concerning the effect of the curse, Ishodad considers that the curse had immediate repercussions on Canaan, turning his skin black: "And instantly, by the force of the curse (uttered) by the righteous, his face and his whole body became black. It is this black color that persists in his descendants and (which therefore does not come from) the heat of the sun, as others have believed." (*Commentaire d'Isodad de Merv sur L'Ancien Testament, I. Genèse*, 128 [Syr.], 139 [Fr.]). Moreover, Ishodad

Canaan is the one directly cursed by Noah, Ham is nevertheless also indirectly touched by the curse for being his father: "as Noah suffered from what Ham sinned, he would suffer from the curse of his son too".[17] Additionally, Ishodad mentions two reasons why Noah does not curse Ham directly: firstly, because he had been rescued with him in the ark, and thereby had once received God's blessing.[18] The second reason assumes that, similar to "Adam who has transgressed the command, and was not cursed by God, but the earth was cursed because of him, so too Noah, imitating God, did not curse his son but his grandson."[19]

2 Noah's Inebriation in Moral Ascetic Writings

The second part of this paper discusses some representations and depictions of wine and of the state of inebriation, evaluating how Noah is associated with these concepts in Syriac moral ascetic writings. In it, I will try to demonstrate what the purpose of these associations with Noah was.

In addition to the Syriac exegetical interpretations on the biblical story of Noah's inebriation presented above, I will now discuss a moral perspective of Syriac literature when it comes to wine and în particular its association with the episode of Noah. In Syriac exegesis and monastic literature, the topic of wine and its representations are sometimes intertwined with several allusions to Noah's drunkenness. Even if wine is associated with the joy of the heart, there are cases when it makes those who consume it intoxicated with confusion, violating ordinary moral and social rules. Syriac literature occasionally urges the need for moderation in

---

states that not all authors hold the same opinion, such that: "according to others, the white color comes from Adam, as we know from the relationship between (him), the father, and Seth, whom he engendered at his resemblance; the black color comes from Ham, who had conjugal relationships in the ark, despite the defense of his father." (*Commentaire d'Isodad de Merv sur L'Ancien Testament, I. Genèse*, 129 [Syr.], 139 [Fr.]). Barhebraeus follows Ishodad in believing that Canaan, son of Ham, saw Noah first, and then showed this to his father who, then, further showed his two brothers. This is the reason why, according to Barhebraeus, "Canaan was accursed and not Ham, and by the very curse he became black, and the blackness was transmitted to his descendants" (*Barhebraeus' Scholia*, 40 [Syr.], 41 [engl.])

[17] *Commentaire d'Isodad de Merv sur L'Ancien Testament, I. Genèse*, 128 (Syr.), 138 (Fr.).
[18] *Commentaire d'Isodad de Merv sur L'Ancien Testament, I. Genèse*, 128 (Syr.), 138 (Fr.).
[19] *Commentaire d'Isodad de Merv sur L'Ancien Testament, I. Genèse*, 128 (Syr.), 139 (Fr.).

the consumption of wine, and Noah's example is sometimes associated with this parallel even though Noah remains a well-received figure in Syriac literature.

For example, in *Hymns on Virginity* we see how Ephrem urges nuns to consume wine in moderation, by making allusions to Noah:

> Fear wine that laid Noah bare:
> it made drunk the righteous who conquered;
> A little wine conquered the one
> who had been able to conquer the floodwaters.
> The one the Flood did not prevail over on the outside,
> Wine prevailed over on the inside.
> Since wine laid bare and cast down Noah,
> The head of families,
> Then how much more will it conquer you, solitary woman![20]

Although Ephrem defends Noah's righteous and innocent profile, he nevertheless does not hesitate to advise his readers to maintain the balance in relation to wine and its negative effects.[21] A similar motif appears in *Carmina Nisibena*, in a dramatic confrontation between Satan and Death. Satan mocks Noah's weakness in having succumbed to wine and thus humiliated by Ham, yet Death responds: "It was not Noah that was damaged, but your instrument (Ham) / He clothed himself in curses, as you clothed yourself in him, and he became a servant."[22]

---

[20] Edmund Beck (ed. and trans.), *Des heiligen Ephraem der Syrers Hymnen de Virginitate*, CSCO 223–24 / Syr 94–95 (Louvain: Secrétariat du CorpusSCO, 1962), 3 (Syr.), 3 (germ.); Kathleen E. McVey, trans., *Ephrem the Syrian: Hymns*, 264; Adam C. McCollum, "An Arabic Scholion to Genesis 9:18–21," 142.

[21] In his poems *Carmina Nisibena*, Ephrem depicts Noah as one "who conquered the flood like death," but also the one "whom wine conquered" (Edmund Beck [ed. and trans.], *Des heiligen Ephraem des Syrers Carmina Nisibena*, CSCO 240–41 / Syr 102–3 [Louvain: Secrétariat du CorpusSCO, 1963]), 85 [Syr.], 74 [Germ.]).

[22] Edmund Beck (ed.), *Des heiligen Ephraem des Syrers Carmina Nisibena*, 85 (Syr.), 74 (Germ.); Laura Lieber, "Portraits of Righteousness: Noah in Early Christian and Jewish Hymnography," *Zeitschrift für Religions- und Geistesgeschichte* 61.4 (2009): 332–55, esp. 340.

Another Syriac poet who emphasizes the need to consume wine in moderation and associates it with the episode of the vineyard planting and Noah's inebriation is Narsai of Nisibis (d. 502), who, in his *Homily on the Flood,* views Noah's incident as an act of divine economy by which God instructed humans:

> He (God) instructed the simple
> With the new laws which He wrote
> And conferred upon them the understanding
> To cultivate the barren earth.
> Noah commenced work
> and planted a vineyard and it yielded fruits
> and he drank of its wine and became drunk
> and he erred through it in the newness of its force.
> He hadn't (yet) experienced
> that drinking it leads the mind astray
> and he did not know how
> its drinkers use it.[23]

Narsai's thesis is similar to Ephrem's approach in considering Noah's lack of experience with wine to be the cause of his drunken behaviour. Even though Narsai recognizes Noah's righteous virtues, he does not hesitate to expose the negative consequences that drunkenness can have for those who consume wine:

> Noah drank and forgot himself
> and wine debased the honourable one
> and the impudence of will
> Of licentious (trivial) Ham mocked him.[24]

---

[23] Judith Frishman (ed.), *The Ways and Means of the Divine Economy, An Edition, Translation and Study of Six Biblical Hormilies by Narsai* (unpublished PhD Thesis, Leiden, 1992), 48–49 (Syr.), v. 821-32.
[24] Frishman (ed.), *The Ways and Means of the Divine Economy*, 49 (Syr.), v. 833-36.

According to Narsai the biblical account of Noah's drunk behaviour has the role of teaching people to maintain the ethics of moderation:

> The Creator noted the story
> Of Noah the honorable one who was exposed
> In order to instruct the knowing through him
> That they not pride themselves on wine.
> Along with the purity of his members
> He noted the error which he erred through wine [ܟܪܝܗܘ]
> In order to highly warn that in moderation [ܒܩܠܝܠ]
> Its drinkers use it.[25]

The theme of inebriation is also treated in isolation from the case of Noah, in a strict context of spiritual progress. Sebastian P. Brock shows how some ascetical authors perceive the topic of inebriation in a spiritual way. Abraham of Nathpar urges the monks that the drunkenness caused by wine at night to be replaced with the stage of being drunk with the love of God.[26] Additionally, Jacob of Sarug also extends the meaning of inebriation conferring it a mystical connotation: he relates Abraham with the wine from Golgotha.[27] Brock points out that the concept of "being drunk with love" is a motif adopted in many texts, for example in the *Book of Grace* attributed to Shem'on the Graceful, in which one finds the experience of being inebriated with divine love in various stages of spiritual growth;[28] or in the writings of Isaac the Syrian dealing with the inebriation as a stage of the love of the martyrs for God.[29] Beyond these mystical pictures, a direct

---

[25] Frishman (ed.), *The Ways and Means of the Divine Economy*, 49–50 (Syr.), v. 853–60.

[26] See Brock, "Sobria Ebrietas," 188; Sebastian P. Brock "A monastic anthology from twelfth-century Edessa," in *Symposium Syriacum* VII, ed. René Lavenant, OCA 256 (Rome: Pontificium Institutum Studiorum Orientalium, 1998), 227.

[27] Paul Bedjan (ed.), *Mar-Jacobi Sarugensis Homiliae Selectae*, IV (Paris/Leipzig: Harrassowitz, 1908), 79: 19 (Syr.); See Brock, "Sobria Ebrietas," 188.

[28] Alphonse Mingana (ed.), *Early Christian Mystics*, Woodbrooke Studies VII (Cambridge: Cambridge University Press, 1934), 54 (f.310b); 51, f.309a); Brock, "Sobria Ebrietas," 189.

[29] Arent Jan Wensinck (ed.), *Mystic Treatises by Isaac of Nineveh* (Amsterdam: Koninklijke Akademie van Wetenschappen, 1923; repr. Wiesbaden: Sändig, 1969), 149; Brock, "Sobria Ebrietas," 188, n. 17.

reference to Noah from the perspective we are interested in, is obvious in a text of Sahdona, an East Syriac author from the early 7th century, contemporary of Isaac the Syrian, who defends Noah in claiming that he was not aware of the nature of wine and proceeds to recommend caution in its consumption.

> Wine has handed over a righteous person to mockery, and it was the cause of Canaan's curse (Gen. 9:25). For Noah was not to be blamed (for his drunkenness) since he had not learnt about wine from experience, whereas we, who have learnt about its savage nature, should be wary of ourselves.[30]

3 Conclusion

In becoming more familiar with Syriac exegetical texts, one can acknowledge that this form of Eastern Christianity has established itself in the universal theological heritage as a source of extraordinary symbolism that renders theology better understood through images, metaphors and gestures, which sometimes transcend the boundaries of the biblical framework. True to form, the biblical story of Noah's inebriation is adopted almost unitarily into Syriac literature, with the focus of the story adamantly maintained on exegetic attempts to defend Noah and his righteousness. The abnormal drunken behaviour of Noah is vindicated by the Syriac authors, whereby these exegetes portray him as innocent owing to his lack of experience with wine.

The narrative surrounding Noah's drunkenness is especially used in monastic and theological literature in order to urge caution and moderation in wine consumption. In addition, the theme of drunkenness is assumed by ascetic literature as a profound allegory for being exhilarated with God's love. Consequently, we can conclude our foray with the interesting realisation that, without blaming Noah, the Syriac exegetes dutifully warn about the sensitivity of the issue at hand, and attempt to show Syriac monks that it is a virtue to moderate one's consumption of wine, or even run away from it.

---

[30] *Sahdona, Book of Perfection* II.7.18, ed. André de Halleux, *Martyrius (Sahdona). Oeuvres spirituelles*, II, *Le livre de la perfection* (Leuven: Peeters, 1961), 79; Brock, "Sobria Ebrietas," 185.

Index of Selected Passages

Hebrew Bible

Deuterocanonical Works

Index of Selected Passages

Index of Biblical Figures

List of Contributors

Guido Baltes, Adjunct Professor of New Testament, University of Marburg

Lukas Bormann, Professor of New Testament, University of Marburg

Michaela Durst, University Assistant (post doc), Institute of Church History, Christian Archaeology and Ecclesiastical Art, University of Vienna

Aliyah El Mansy, Adjunct Professor of New Testament, University of Marburg

Kirsi Huoponen, PhD, ThD, Åbo Akademi University

Bart J. Koet, Em. Professor of New Testament and Early Christian Literature, Tilburg University

Eva-Maria Kreitschmann, PhD student (New Testament), University of Marburg

Anni Maria Laato, Senior Lecturer in Systematic Theology, Åbo Akademi University

Antti Laato, Professor in Old Testament and Judaic Studies, Åbo Akademi University

Pekka Lindqvist, University lecturer in Exegetics and Jewish studies, Åbo Akademi University

Martin Meiser, apl. Professor, Saarland University, retired.

Timo Nisula, Docent in Dogmatics, Åbo Akademi University

Mikael Nouro, PhD student, Åbo Akademi University

Catalin-Stefan Popa, Research Professor in Church History, Romanian Academy

Topias K. E. Tanskanen, Postdoctoral Researcher in Old Testament Exegetics, Åbo Akademi University

Lotta Valve, University Lecturer of Biblical Studies, University of Eastern Finland, Joensuu

www.ingramcontent.com/pod-product-compliance
Lightning Source LLC
Chambersburg PA
CBHW020430130626
46549CB00001B/70